Foundations of Jini™ 2 Programming

Jan Newmarch

Apress®

Foundations of Jini™ 2 Programming

Copyright © 2006 by Jan Newmarch

ISBN-13: 978-1-4302-1183-9

ISBN-13 : 978-1-4302-0328-5 (eBook)

Lead Editor: Steve Anglin
Editorial Board: Steve Anglin, Ewan Buckingham, Gary Cornell, Jason Gilmore, Jonathan Gennick, Jonathan Hassell, James Huddleston, Chris Mills, Matthew Moodie, Dominic Shakeshaft, Jim Sumser, Keir Thomas, Matt Wade
Production Director and Project Manager: Grace Wong
Copy Edit Manager and Copy Editor: Nicole LeClerc
Assistant Production Director and Production Editor: Kari Brooks-Copony
Compositor: Ellie Fountain
Proofreader: Elizabeth Berry
Indexer: Ed Rush
Cover Designer: Kurt Krames
Manufacturing Director: Tom Debolski

For information on translations, please contact Apress directly at 2855 Telegraph Avenue, Suite 600, Berkeley, CA 94705. Phone 510-549-5930, fax 510-549-5939, e-mail info@apress.com, or visit http://www.apress.com.

The source code for this book is available to readers at http://www.apress.com in the Source Code/ Download section. You will need to answer questions pertaining to this book in order to successfully download the code.

Contents at a Glance

Contents

About the Author

JAN NEWMARCH is Associate Professor in the Information Technology faculty at Monash University, Australia. He teaches and does research in the field of distributed computing and currently specializes in pervasive systems. His interests are broad and include user interfaces, security, and web-based technologies. He has published over 80 papers, and this is his fourth book. It is based on his online tutorial (http://jan.netcomp. monash.edu.au/java/jini/tutorial/Jini.xml), which has introduced Jini to thousands of programmers.

Acknowledgments

I would like to acknowledge the hard work and visionary thinking of the Jini team for making this technology possible. I have received comments and encouragement from the team in developing this book from an initial short tutorial. I would also like to thank the many Jini programmers who have used this book in its online form, and who have often given helpful comments and made corrections. Thanks go to Bill Venners, who tech reviewed the first edition.

Parts of this book were completed while I was on a sabbatical program at the Beijing University of Post and Telecommunications and the University of California, Berkeley. I would like to thank Dr. Xiaosheng Tang and Professor Jan Rabaey for their hospitality.

Finally, my thanks to the many students over the past eight years who have attended my courses and done further development with Jini.

Introduction

The business and academic worlds have long accepted the use of networking technologies, allowing users to share files and applications and to exchange information using network services such as e-mail. The continuing explosive growth of the Internet and the Web has made everyone conscious of the importance of networked applications, and this importance is increasing with the emergence of home, mobile, and sensor networks.

For the programmer, building distributed applications can be a complex business. There are issues related to network stability and accessibility involved, in addition to partitioning applications into portions that can run separately but still be linked into larger functional units. A variety of frameworks—both experimental and commercial—have been devised to make it easier to build and deploy distributed applications.

Service-oriented architectures (SOAs) have come to the fore recently as a means of structuring and linking components into distributed applications. There is much reinvention going on in this area, but people are beginning to realize that as long ago as 1998, Jini addressed and solved many of the issues that arise in building SOA systems. This has led to a resurgence of interest in what is all of a philosophy of building applications, an API, and an implementation.

Who This Book Is For

This book is aimed at the professional programmer who wants to build robust and reliable distributed applications. It assumes you have a background in Java programming and network programming. It also assumes that you are familiar with network concepts such as remote procedure calls, are familiar with Java syntax, and have a working knowledge of the Java core classes.

What This Book Covers

This is a hands-on, study-the-code book. My intention is to introduce you to code that can be readily understood and that can be copied and adapted for your own programs. The book covers the full range of Jini concepts, from the basics through to advanced topics, such as security, transactions, user interfaces, and linking Jini and Web Services.

This book originated from an online tutorial that began at ten pages in 1999 and has grown steadily since. In 2001, the tutorial was published as *A Programmer's Guide to Jini Technology* (Apress) and dealt with Jini version 1.1. Jini has continued to develop, and the tutorial has continued to evolve, so it's now appropriate to release this new edition covering Jini 2.1.

> **Note** Jini 2.1 requires at least JDK 1.4, but it will also work with JDK 1.5.

The first nine chapters of this book deal with the basics of Jini programming, leading to a complete, but simple, application. The subsequent chapters discuss more advanced material. Most aspects of the Jini technology are covered, but of course there are always complexities that will take you beyond the bounds of this book. There is an active Jini mailing list, http:// archives.java.sun.com/archives/jini-users.html, with many helping hands, if you find yourself in need of further assistance.

■ ■ ■

CHAPTER 1

Overview of Jini

Jini grew from early work in Java to make distributed computing easier. It intends to make network devices and network services into standard components of everyone's computing environment. The computing world is currently abuzz about service-oriented systems, and Jini has been a major platform for service-oriented computing since its inception, long before the term became popular.

Jini supports both software and hardware services. When you buy a new piece of office computing equipment such as a desk lamp, or a new home computer appliance such as an alarm clock, it will not only carry out its "traditional" functions, but will also join a network of other computer devices and services. The desk lamp will turn itself off when you leave your desk, informed of your departure by sensors in your chair; the alarm clock will tell your coffee-maker to switch on a few minutes before it wakes you up. These hardware services will interact with software services such as calendar and diary services, and possibly with external services such as weather and stock exchange services (to wake you up early if the weather is cold or if there is sudden movement on the market). Jini doesn't care what is behind services; it just makes the services available to applications.

Homes, offices, and factories are becoming increasingly networked. Current twisted-pair wiring will remain, but it will be augmented by wireless networks and networks built on phone lines and power cables. On top of this will be an infrastructure to allow services to communicate. TCP/IP will be a part of this, but it will not be enough. There will need to be mechanisms for service discovery, for negotiation of properties, and for event signaling (e.g., "My alarm has gone off—does anyone want to know?").

Jini supplies this higher level of interaction. This chapter provides a brief overview of Jini, and the components of a Jini system and the relationships between them.

■Note The licensing model for Jini has now changed to an open source Apache license from a proprietary license. This change, plus the continued quality of the middleware, has sparked renewed interest in Jini.

Jini

Jini is the name for a distributed computing environment that can offer *network plug and play*, meaning that a device or a software service can be connected to a network and announce its presence, and clients that wish to use such a service can then locate it and call it to perform tasks. Jini can be used for mobile computing tasks where a service may be connected to a network for only a short time, but it can more generally be used in any network where there is some degree of change. Jini is useful in a large number of scenarios, including the following:

- A new printer can be connected to the network and announce its presence and capabilities. A client can then use this printer without having to be specially configured to do so.

- A digital camera can be connected to the network and present a user interface that will not only allow pictures to be taken, but also be aware of any printers so that the pictures can be printed.

- A configuration file that is copied and modified on individual machines can be made into a network service from a single machine, reducing maintenance costs.

- New capabilities extending existing ones can be added to a running system without disrupting existing services, or without any need to reconfigure clients.

- Services can announce changes of state, such as when a printer runs out of paper. Listeners, typically of an administrative nature, can watch for these changes and flag them for attention.

Jini is not an acronym for anything, and it does not have a particular meaning (although it gained the post-hoc interpretation of "Jini Is Not Initials"). A Jini system or *federation* is a collection of clients and services all communicating by the Jini protocols. Often this federation will consist of applications written in Java, communicating using the Java Remote Method Invocation (RMI) mechanism. Although Jini is written in pure Java, neither clients nor services are constrained to be in pure Java. They may include native code methods, act as wrappers around non-Java objects, or even be written in some other language altogether. Jini supplies a *middleware* layer to link services and clients from a variety of sources.

When you download a copy of Jini, you actually get a mixture of things. First, Jini is a specification of a set of middleware components, including an application programming interface (API) so that you as a programmer can write services and components that make use of this middleware. Second, it includes an implementation (in pure Java) of the middleware, as a set of Java packages. By including these packages in the classpath of your client or service, you can invoke the Jini middleware protocols to join in whatever Jini services and clients are currently running. (This collection of clients and services is sometimes called a *djinn*.) You also get source code to these packages as a bonus. Finally, Jini requires a number of "standard" services, and Sun gives basic implementations of each. These implementations are not an official part of Jini, but are included to get you going, and in practice, most users find these implementations sufficient to do substantial work with Jini.

Jini was not born in a vacuum. It was based on long experience within Sun Microsystems of building networking applications and frameworks. Many of the most important lessons from this were summarized in the Eight Fallacies of Distributed Computing. For the last few years Jini has not been highly visible. There are various non-technical reasons for this, but also technology that works and works well is often not reported. Nevertheless, to show that Jini came from somewhere and has been used in substantial projects, in the subsections that follow, I discuss the Eight Fallacies of Distributed Computing and how they relate to Jini, and I also describe some Jini success stories.

Eight Fallacies of Distributed Computing

Since the early days, computers have been linked in networks. For over 20 years, the mantra from Sun Microsystems has been "The Network Is the Computer," and this idea has been a cornerstone of much work in distributed computing. Based on the experience of Sun engineers over many years, Peter Deutsch took a critical look at the state of distributed computing in 1999 and concluded that early optimism was in many ways misplaced. Networks and applications that run on them are prone to all sorts of problems that do not occur with stand-alone applications, and ignoring these problems can lead to unreliable and unstable applications. Deutsch identified the following fallacies of networking (extended by James Gosling):

- The network is reliable.

- Bandwidth is infinite.

- The network is secure.

- Topology doesn't change.

- There is one administrator.

- Transport cost is zero.

- The network is homogeneous.

- Latency is zero.

Typical ways of "hiding" the network such as remote procedure calls (RPCs) assume these fallacies are all true. For example, Sun's RPC was one of the earliest widespread RPC frameworks. This *does* assume that the network is reliable, and it *does* assume that bandwidth is infinite, so applications assume that remote calls will always succeeed and that there is no overhead in making remote calls. Network calls are several orders of magnitude slower than local function calls and do sometimes fail, but there is no recognition of this in the RPC programming model—that was its purpose: to hide the network! These assumptions have been continued into many later middleware systems such as CORBA, and even into quite recent (and popular) frameworks.

Jini recognizes these fallacies and attempts to deal with them. For example, specifications of services have to be marked as "potentially remote" and all method calls have to handle possible network failures.

Jini Success Stories

Jini has been around since 1999, and while it has achieved some notable successes, it does not have the visibility of many other middleware systems. In part, this is because Jini simply *works* and has been a stable but evolving platform over these years. The Sun web site lists many successful projects using Jini. This section covers a couple of them plus some other systems. For more stories, visit http://www.sun.com/software/jini/news/success.xml.

Note You should be aware that Jini is only one competitor in a growing market. What conditions the success or failure of Jini is partly the politics of the market, but also (hopefully) the technical capabilities of Jini. This book deals with some of these technical issues involved in using Jini.

Note that the systems described in the sections that follow often have to deal directly with the issues raised by the Eight Fallacies described in the previous section. For example, they need to work in changing topologies, on unreliable networks, and with limited bandwidth. Jini is middleware designed to manage such issues, but it is not perfect. Nevertheless, it recognises the Fallacies and provides mechanisms adequate for many systems, with the possibility of sophisticated configuration for more demanding situations.

Rubean, A.G.

Frank Sommers reports on a banking system developed by Rubean, A.G., in an article at http://www.artima.com/lejava/articles/banking_on_jiniP.html. A group of German and Swiss banks with 35,000 customers run a centralized Java 2 Platform, Enterprise Edition (J2EE) system. However, this system needs to interact with ATM machines, cash-dispensing machines, and other devices linked to PCs typically through an RS232 cable. These devices have differing capabilities, their PCs are not always on, and they have IP addresses assigned by the Dynamic Host Configuration Protocol (DHCP), so they are continually changing. This dynamic environment could be a maintenance nightmare to a centralized system. The solution by Rubean uses Jini services running on each PC, talking to the devices using the Java Comms API. Each service advertises itself to Jini lookup services, which can handle the dynamic nature of the services without needing configuration. The J2EE system just sees collections of services and is unaware of configuration details.

Magneti Marelli

Magneti Marelli Motorsport builds monitoring equipment for Formula One racing cars, and its hardware and software is used by most racing teams. However, its software used to run on proprietary platforms and lacked the flexibility and robustness required. In the cars, sensors collect a great deal of information, which is relayed by radio links to teams in the pits. The environment in the pits is often hot and noisy, and real-time responses are needed to deal both with the data itself and with a changing environment (computers die, network cables are tripped over, etc.). New software was developed using not only the discovery mechanisms of Jini, but also its ability to self-heal the service environment. Being able to run in multiple operating system environments was also a help. The project is described at http://wiki.javapolis.com/confluence/display/JP05/Formula+One+Telemetry+with+Java.

Nedap N.V.

Nedap N.V. is a security management company used by over 6 million people every day. Some years ago, the company saw the need for a next generation of security systems and began to design one from the ground up. The heart of the system is a 64MB controller with an Ethernet connection to the network and CAN connection to devices. Each controller exposes itself to the network as a Jini service. Examples of use include the security system controlling elevators within the Eiffel Tower in Paris. Every time an elevator comes within wireless range of a Jini lookup service, it is discovered. This allows security access of an elevator to any floor to be controlled, with Jini dynamic service management handling access to services. This system is described at `http://www.jini.org/meetings/eighth/J8abstracts.html#Wegman`.

Orbitz

The previous examples seem to suggest that Jini is just for linking hardware systems into software systems. Jini is certainly good at doing this, since it makes the devices appear as services, making them first-class citizens in a service-oriented system. But that is not all that Jini is good for: it *is* a framework for service-oriented middleware, and it excels in purely software-based systems too. An example of such a system is Orbitz, a multibillion dollar online travel company based in the United States. Orbitz uses over 1,000 Linux servers, and it has both a changing set of machines and evolving applications running on them. For example, if a supplier is having a sale, Orbitz will allocate more services to that company. Obviously, reconfiguring applications to use new services could be an ongoing horrific task, but Jini dynamic discovery allows it to be done transparently. In addition, services can be upgraded in place and the new versions become automatically available. The Orbitz system is described here: `http://www.sun.com/software/jini/news/Jini_Orbitz_Profile_Final.pdf`.

Orange

Orange is a major mobile communications company, with over 44 million customers worldwide. It offers a range of services, many of them supplied by external organizations. Again, this is a dynamic service environment, with new services begin deployed and existing services being revised, all in a high-volume environment, and Jini manages many aspects of this dynamism automatically. For more information, see `http://www.sun.com/products-n-solutions/telecom/docs/orangesp_1.pdf`.

Jini Licensing and Apache

Jini for may years has been licensed under a Sun Community License. While generous in many respects (for example, Jini source code has always been available) it is, nevertheless, a proprietary license. Recently the Jini group has decided that this has possibly limited the uptake of Jini, and so early in 2006 the license was changed to the open source Apache license.

However, grander changes are underway. At the time of writing, negotiations are under way to turn Jini into an Apache "incubator project," and later perhaps into a top-level Apache project. This will turn Jini into a true open source project and hopefully will bring in a new set of users and developers, in addition to being built on, and contributing to, other Apache projects. Among the issues still to be resolved is the name of the project—since Jini is a concept for middleware, a specification and API, and an implementation, the name might change in moving to Apache. One possible name that has been suggested is Babylon. Associative thinking leads to "Rivers of Babylon," then to "disco," and from there to "discovery"—which is one of the principal features of Jini :-)

Until recently, the primary site for Jini was `http://www.jini.org`. A new site has been added at `https://jini.dev.java.net/` and most of the projects have been moved to there. In the future, it is hoped that Jini will be on the Incubator's page on the Apache site at http://incubator.apache.org/ and later on perhaps will have its own top-level page on the main Apache site.

Jini in One Hour

Our homes are becoming full of more and more complex pieces of electronic equipment—TVs, microwaves, stereo systems, and so forth—and many of these items have clocks. It's pretty common to find one or more of these clocks flashing; particularly the one on the VCR. Whenever there is a power failure, all the clocks on these pieces of equipment start up again with an incorrect time and signal this by flashing until they are manually corrected. Many offices synchronize the clocks in a building to a central time server, but this is a luxury most homes do not have. But wouldn't it be nice if every clock in the house could find a correct, central clock and set itself? In this section, we'll walk through the steps of setting up a Jini system that will do this for some "software" clocks. No real clocks currently support Jini, but it would be nice if they did!

The first step is to get the Jini classes, which you can download from http://www.jini.org by following the "Getting Started" link to the Jini Downloads page. This page has several options; you only need the Jini Technology Starter Kit for now, but you may like to download other projects as well.

The Starter Kit installation process for platforms such as Windows and Linux will check your network settings and Java installation, and start up a key component of Jini called a *registrar*. Once you see a window called Service Browser with the message "1 registrar, not selected," you'll know this key component is running and you can start up some services and clients. You should see something similar to Figure 1-1.

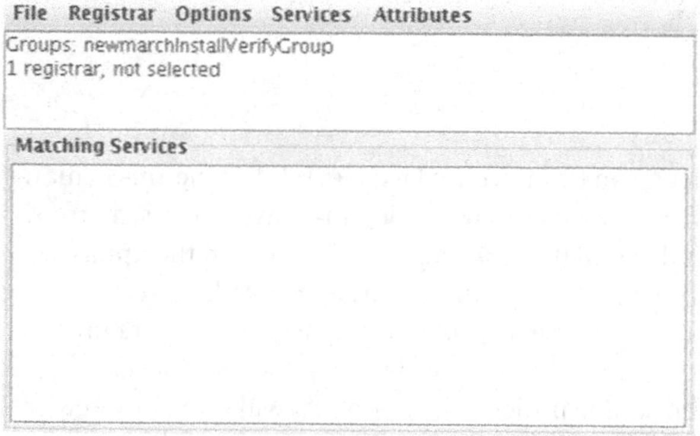

Figure 1-1. *Service Browser window showing the registrar running*

At later times, you can get to this page by just running the command LaunchAll from the installverify directory.

At this stage, you will use three files in the Jini directories:

- jsk-lib.jar, in the lib directory, contains many of the Jini classes.

- jsk-platform.jar, in the lib directory, contains more Jini classes.

- jsk-all.policy, in the installverify/support directory, controls Jini security, and here just turns it off. (This is OK for the purposes of this demonstration, but not for real systems!)

As you already know, this book is all about how programmers can build Jini services and clients. The flashing clocks problem has all the source code explained in Chapter 18. For now, you can download .jar files containing all the compiled classes from http://jan.netcomp. monash.edu.au/java/jini/tutorial/programs.zip. Unzip the files into any directory you want. Three .jar files are of interest, under the dist directory:

- clock.clock.ticker.jar: This file contains the class files for a standard "dumb" clock that starts off with a random time and just ticks away. However, it is smart enough to look around the network to see if there are any other clocks it can synchronize with.

- clock.clock.computer.jar: This file is a "smarter" clock that gets its time from the built-in computer clock, which we assume has the correct time. This clock also looks around the network to see of there are clocks that should synchronize with it.

- clock.clock-dl.jar: This file contains special classes that can be downloaded across the network. Systems like CORBA and web services rely on getting references to remote services and making calls using specific protocols by these references. Jini, on the other hand, relies on downloading Java classes representing a service: once a client has these classes, then it just makes local calls and doesn't care how the downloaded classes talk to the service.

When clients find services, they download a proxy for the service. Support code for this proxy is usually in a .jar file on an HTTP server. So the file clock.clock-dl.jar has to be on an HTTP server somewhere. You can copy this file to an HTTP server you have access to, or you can just use the file on the HTTP server that I run at jan.netcomp.monash.edu.au. (If you have a firewall between my server and your computers, then it may be easier to put the file on a local server than to get Java to talk through the firewall. You *can* get away with not using these classes in this example; the clocks will work fine, but the service browser won't see the services properly.)

That's all you need to get this demonstration working. You can start up a flashing clock by running Java from, say, a command box under Windows or a terminal window under Unix. You will need to set your classpath so that it contains the Jini files jsk-platform.jar and jsk-lib.jar, and also the clock file clock.clock.ticker.jar. For example, under Unix you could run

```
JINI_HOME=...
CLOCK_DIR=...
CLASSPATH=$JINI_HOME/lib/jsk-lib.jar:$JINI_HOME/lib/jsk-platform.jar: \
$CLOCK_DIR/clock.clock.ticker.jar
export CLASSPATH
```

and under Windows, you could run

```
set JINI_HOME = ...
set CLASSPATH = %JINI_HOME%/lib/jsk-lib.jar;%JINI_HOME%/lib/jsk-platform.jar; \
%CLOCK_DIR%/clock.clock.ticker.jar
```

After setting the classpath, run a dumb ticking clock:

```
java \
    -Djava.rmi.server.codebase= \
http://jan.netcomp.monash.edu.au/classes/clock.clock-dl.jar \
    -Djava.security.policy=JINI_HOME/installverify/support/jsk-all.policy \
    clock.clock.TickerClock \
    "Ticking Clock"
```

where JINI_HOME is replaced by the directory name where you installed Jini. The first parameter (codebase) lets the service tell clients where the downloadable files are; the second parameter (security) sets the policy for what remote code is allowed to do to this service. The third parameter is the main class file, and the last parameter is just a string to be displayed as the title in the window frame.

You should see a clock like the one shown in Figure 1-2, flashing every second.

Figure 1-2. *Jini service browser*

You can run this command as often as you want, on the same or different machines. Each one should start up a new flashing clock. These clocks will all discover one another, but since none of them shows a valid time, there is nothing they can do to each other.

Now start up a "smart" clock that is showing the right time. The classpath needs to be set to the Jini files jsk-platform.jar and jsk-lib.jar again, but this time it should include clock.clock.computer.jar instead of clock.clock.ticker.jar. Then you run the good clock as follows:

```
java \
    -Djava.rmi.server.codebase= \
http://jan.netcomp.monash.edu.au/classes/clock.clock-dl.jar \
    -Djava.security.policy=JINI_HOME/installverify/support/jsk-all.policy \
    clock.clock.ComputerClock \
    "Computer Clock"
```

As this one starts up, it will discover the other clocks and they will discover it. The wrong clocks will ask the right clocks for the correct time; the right clocks will tell the wrong clocks to reset their time. This is a peer-to-peer system, and I don't know whether right tells wrong the correct time or wrong gets the correct time from right—it doesn't matter. All that matters is that the correct time will soon show on all clocks. Later, the clocks will "drift," but after reading Chapter 18 you will easily be able to add code to resynchronize on a regular basis.

If you now start up another possible flashing clock, it will quickly discover the other correct clocks and may not even flash at all.

So, what is going on with these clocks that is valuable to a distributed application's programmer?

- The clocks demonstrate discovery. New clocks start and both discover and are discovered by existing clocks. This is a general property of Jini: clients discover services they are interested in.

- A clock can make a call on another clock to get or set the time. The clocks are making remote method calls, but as you will discover later, the *protocol* isn't specified by Jini: all each clock knows is that it has a local proxy representing the remote service and is making local calls on that proxy. How the proxy talks to its service is of no interest to the client. Of course, it *is* of interest to the service programmer, and Jini allows the service programmer full control of how this is done, while giving default mechanisms good enough for many cases.

- Some clocks can crash and the others will carry on. Well, OK, there isn't much interaction going on. But a clock can crash *after* but *before* being called. Jini will throw exceptions to signal failed calls so that the client programmer can handle failure.

- While method calls are synchronous, Jini also allows events to be generated and delivered asynchronously to listeners. When a clock changes state, it can inform any interested listener. So Jini can handle both synchronous and asynchronous method calls.

Finally in this section, let's look at pseudocode for the clocks:

```
main:
    allow remote code to be downloaded and run within this VM
    start a thread to asynchronously discover proxies for clock services,
        calling us as listener
service discovered:
    if we are invalid and the remote clock is valid
        set our time from the remote clock
        set state to valid
    else if we are valid and the remote clock is invalid
        set the time on the remote clock
```

That's it! The rest of the clocks' code (less than 700 lines total) is the service specification, user interface classes, and code to keeping the clocks ticking.

Components

When running a Jini system, you are dealing with three main players: a service, a client, and a lookup service. The *service* could be something such as a printer, a toaster, a marriage agency, and so forth. The *client* would like to make use of this service, and the *lookup service* acts as a broker/trader/locator between the service and client. (The generic term for the lookup service seems to be settling on *service cache manager*.) An additional component is a *network* connecting all three main players, and this network will generally be running TCP/IP. (The Jini *specification* is fairly independent of network protocol, but the only current *implementation* is on TCP/IP.)

Code is moved around between these three pieces by *marshaling* the objects. Marshaling involves serializing the objects in such a way that they can be moved around the network, stored in a "freeze-dried" form and later reconstituted by using included information about the class files as well as instance data. This process is performed using Java's socket support to send and receive objects.

In addition, objects in one Java Virtual Machine (JVM) may need to invoke methods on an object in another JVM. Often this will be done using RMI, although the Jini specification does not require this, and there are many other possibilities.

Figure 1-3 shows the components of a Jini system discussed in this section.

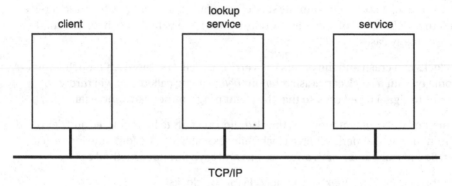

Figure 1-3. *Components of a Jini system*

Service Registration

As mentioned previously, a *service* is a logical concept such as a blender, a chat service, or a disk. It will usually turn out to be defined by a Java interface, and often the service itself will be identified by this interface. Each service can be implemented in many ways, by many different vendors. For example, there may be Joe's dating service, Mary's dating service, and any number of others. What makes them the "same" service is that they implement the same interface; what distinguishes one from another is that each different implementation uses a different set of objects (or maybe just one object) belonging to different classes.

A service is created by a *service provider*. A service provider plays a number of roles:

- It creates the objects that implement the service.

- It registers one of these objects, the *service object*, with lookup services. The service object is the publicly visible part of the service, and it will be downloaded to clients.

- It stays alive in a server role, performing various tasks such as keeping the service "alive."

In order for the service provider to register the service object with a lookup service, the server must first find the lookup service. This can be done in two ways. If the location of the lookup service is known, then the service provider can use unicast TCP to connect directly to it. If the location is not known, the service provider will make UDP multicast requests, and lookup services may respond to these requests. Lookup services will be listening on port 4160 for both the unicast and multicast requests. (Port 4160 is the decimal representation of hexadecimal (CAFEBABE). Oh well, these numbers have to come from somewhere.) When the lookup service gets a request on this port, it sends an object back to the server. This object, known as a *registrar*, acts as a proxy to the lookup service and runs in the service's JVM. Any requests that the service provider needs to make of the lookup service are made through this proxy registrar. Any suitable protocol may be used to do this, but in practice the implementations that you get of the lookup service (such as those from Sun) will probably use RMI.

What the service provider does with the registrar is *register* the service with the lookup service. This involves taking a copy of the service object and storing it on the lookup service as shown in Figures 1-4, 1-5, and 1-6.

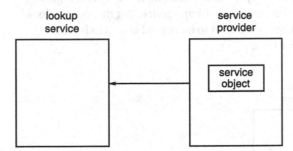

Figure 1-4. *Querying for a service locator*

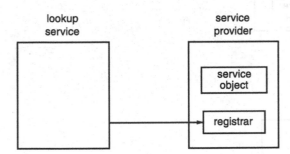

Figure 1-5. *Registrar returned*

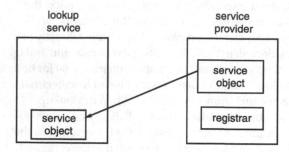

Figure 1-6. *Service uploaded*

Client Lookup

The client, on the other hand, is trying to get a copy of the service into its own JVM. It goes through the same mechanism to get a registrar from the lookup service. But this time it does something different, which is to request the service object to be copied across to it. This process is shown in Figures 1-7, 1-8, 1-9, and 1-10.

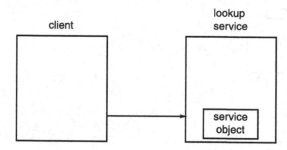

Figure 1-7. *Querying for a service locator*

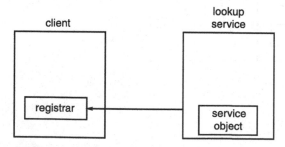

Figure 1-8. *Registrar returned*

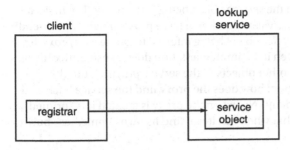

Figure 1-9. *Asking for a service*

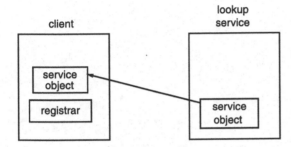

Figure 1-10. *Service returned*

At this point, the original service object is running on its host, there is a copy of the service object stored in the lookup service, and there is a copy of the service object running in the client's JVM. The client can make requests of the service object running in its own JVM.

Proxies

Some services can be implemented by a single object, the service object. How does this work if the service is actually a toaster, a printer, or is controlling some piece of hardware? By the time the service object runs in the client's JVM, it may be a long way away from its hardware. It cannot control this remote piece of hardware all by itself. In this situation, the implementation of the service must be made up of at least two objects: one running in the client and another distinct one running in the service provider.

The service object is really a *proxy*, which will communicate back to other objects in the service provider, probably using RMI. The proxy is the part of the service that is visible to clients, but its function will be to pass method calls back to the rest of the objects that form the total implementation of the service. There isn't a standard nomenclature for these server-side implementation objects. I will refer to them in this book as the *service back-end* objects.

The motivation for discussing proxies is when a service object needs to control a remote piece of hardware that is not directly accessible to the service object. However, it need not be hardware: there could be files accessible to the service provider that are not available to objects running in clients. There could be applications local to the service provider that are useful in implementing the service. Or it could simply be easier to program the service in ways that involve objects on the service provider, with the service object being just a proxy. The majority of service implementations end up with the service object being just a proxy to service back-end objects, and it is quite common to see the service object being referred to as a *service proxy*. It is sometimes referred to a the service proxy even if the implementation doesn't use a proxy at all!

The proxy needs to communicate with other objects in the service provider, but this begins to look like a chicken-and-egg situation: how does the proxy find the service back-end objects in its service provider? Use a Jini lookup? No, when the proxy is created it is "primed" with its own service provider's location so that when run it can find its own "home," as shown in Figure 1-11.

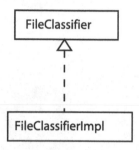

Figure 1-11. *A proxy service*

How is the proxy primed? This isn't specified by Jini, and it can be done in many ways. For example, an RMI naming service can be used, such as rmiregistry, where the proxy is given the name of the service. This isn't very common, as RMI proxies can be passed more directly as returned objects from method calls, and these can refer to ordinary RMI server objects or to RMI activateable objects. Another option is that the proxy can be implemented without any direct use of RMI and can then use an RMI-exported service or some other protocol altogether, such as FTP, HTTP, or a home-grown protocol. These various possibilities are all illustrated in later chapters.

Client Structure

Internally a client will look as shown in Table 1-1.

Table 1-1. *Client Pseudocode*

Pseudocommand	Where Discussed
prepare for discovery	Chapter 4, "Discovering a Lookup Service"
discover a lookup service	Chapter 4, "Discovering a Lookup Service"
prepare a template for lookup search	Chapter 5, "Entry Objects" and "Client Search"
look up a service	Chapter 7, "Client Search"
call the service	

The following code is a simplified version of a real case, with various checks on exceptions and other conditions omitted. It attempts to find a FileClassifier service, and then calls the method getMIMEType() on this service. The full version of the code is given in a later chapter. I don't provide detailed code explanations right now, as this example is just intended to show how the preceding schema translates into actual code.

```
package nonworking;
public class TestUnicastFileClassifier {
    public static void main(String argv[]) {
        new TestUnicastFileClassifier();
    }
    public TestUnicastFileClassifier() {
        LookupLocator lookup = null;
        ServiceRegistrar registrar = null;
        FileClassifier classifier = null;
        // Prepare for discovery
        lookup = new LookupLocator("jini://www.all_about_files.com");
        // Discover a lookup service
        // This uses the synchronous unicast protocol
        registrar = lookup.getRegistrar();
        // Prepare a template for lookup search
        Class[] classes = new Class[] {FileClassifier.class};
        ServiceTemplate template = new ServiceTemplate(null, classes, null);
        // Lookup a service
        classifier = (FileClassifier) registrar.lookup(template);
        // Call the service
        MIMEType type;
        type = classifier.getMIMEType("file1.txt");
        System.out.println("Type is " + type.toString());
    }
} // TestUnicastFileClassifier
```

Server Structure

A server application will internally look as shown in Table 1-2.

Table 1-2. *Server Pseudocode*

Pseudocode	Where Discussed
prepare for discovery	Chapter 4, "Discovering a Lookup Service"
discover a lookup service	Chapter 4, "Discovering a Lookup Service"
create information about a service	Chapter 5, "Entry Objects" and "Client Search"
export a service	Chapter 6, "Service Registration"
renew leasing periodically	Chapter 8, "Leasing"

Again, the following code is simplified, with various checks on exceptions and other conditions omitted. It exports an implementation of a file classifier service as a FileClassifierImpl object. The full version of the code is given in a later chapter. I don't provide detailed code explanations right now, as this example is just intended to show how the preceding schema translates into actual code.

```
package nonworking;
public class FileClassifierServer implements DiscoveryListener {

    protected LeaseRenewalManager leaseManager = new LeaseRenewalManager();
    public static void main(String argv[]) {
        new FileClassifierServer();
        // keep server running (almost) forever to
        // - allow time for locator discovery and
        // - keep reregistering the lease
        Thread.currentThread().sleep(Lease.FOREVER);
    }
    public FileClassifierServer() {
        LookupDiscovery discover = null;
        // Prepare for discovery - empty here
        // Discover a lookup service
        // This uses the asynchronous multicast protocol,
        // which calls back into the discovered() method
        discover = new LookupDiscovery(LookupDiscovery.ALL_GROUPS);
        discover.addDiscoveryListener(this);
    }

    public void discovered(DiscoveryEvent evt) {
        ServiceRegistrar registrar = evt.getRegistrars()[0];
        // At this point we have discovered a lookup service
        // Create information about a service
        ServiceItem item = new ServiceItem(null,
                                           new FileClassifierImpl(),
                                           null);
        // Export a service
        ServiceRegistration reg = registrar.register(item, Lease.FOREVER);
        // Renew leasing
        leaseManager.renewUntil(reg.getLease(), Lease.FOREVER, this);
    }
} // FileClassifierServer
```

Partitioning an Application

Jini uses a *service* view of applications, in contrast to the simple object-oriented view of an application. Of course, a Jini "application" is made up of objects, but these will be distributed out into individual services, which will communicate via their proxy objects. The Jini specification claims that in many monolithic applications, there are one or more services waiting to be released, and making them into services increases their possible uses.

To see this, let's look at a smart file viewer. This application will be given a file name, and the structure of the name will determine what type of file it is (.rtf is Rich Text Format file, .gif is a Graphics Interchange Format file, etc.). Using this classification, the application will then call up an appropriate viewer for a given type of file, such as an image viewer or document viewer. A UML class diagram for this application might look like Figure 1-12.

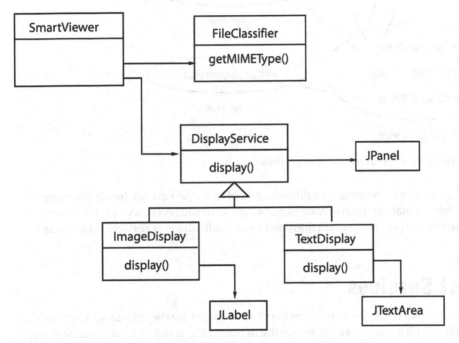

Figure 1-12. *A UML diagram for a smart file viewer application*

If we take a service-oriented view of the smart file viewer, then we can see a number of possible services in this application. Classifying a file into types is one possible service (which will be used heavily in the sequel, because it is simple). A file classification service can be used in many different situations, in addition to determining the file type for viewing contents of files. Each of the different viewer classes is another possible candidate for a service: an image display service, a text display service, and so on. This is not to say that every class should become a service; that would be overkill. What makes these qualify as services is that they

- Have a simple interface

- Are useful in more than one situation

- Can be replaced or varied

They are *reusable*, and this is makes them good candidates for services. They do not require high-bandwidth communication and are not completely trivial.

If the application is reorganized as a collection of services, it might look like Figure 1-13.

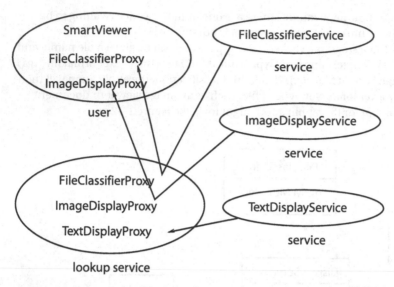

Figure 1-13. *An application as a collection of services*

Each service may be running on a different machine on the network (or on the same machine; it doesn't matter). Each service exports a proxy to whatever service locators are running. The SmartViewer application finds and downloads whatever services it needs, as it needs them.

Support Services

As previously discussed, the three components of a Jini system are clients, services, and service locators, each of which can run anywhere on the network. These will be implemented using Java code running in JVMs. The implementation may be in pure Java, but it could make use of native code by Java Native Interface (JNI) or make external calls to other applications. Often, each application will run in its own JVM on its own computer, although they could run on the same machine or even share the same JVM. When they run, they will need access to Java class files, just like any other Java application. Each component will use the CLASSPATH environment variable or use the classpath option to the runtime to locate the classes it needs to run.

Jini also relies heavily on the ability to move objects across the network, from one JVM to another. In order to do this, particular implementations must make use of support services such as an HTTP server. The particular support services required depend on implementation details, and so may vary from one Jini component to another.

The End of Protocols

Client/server systems built from scratch typically require the design of a communications protocol. For example, before the Web could became as important as it is today, the Hypertext Transfer Protocol, or HTTP, had to be designed so that clients and servers could communicate.

This protocol has been through several public versions: 0.9, 1.0, and 1.1. Clients and servers have had to be rebuilt on each version change of even this simple protocol.

RPC systems such as Sun's ONC, CORBA, COM+, and more recently SOAP also rely on a fixed protocol. In these cases, though, there are usually tools available that will generate code to manage the protocol messaging. However, these tools need to generate *two* sets of code: one for the *client* side and one for the *server* side. Any change to the protocol means that both client and server need to have this code regenerated.

This dependence on protocol is tightly bound to how clients address services, which depends on how they *find* these services. For example, to address a web service, you often need a Web Services Description Language (WSDL) document that contains the URL of the service's server and method names of the service. Coupled with knowledge that the service is addressed using SOAP, a client can then talk to it. With CORBA, you could obtain an object reference in a variety of ways (through a name server, using "stringified" references, or through a trader). Given this reference and the knowledge that CORBA uses the IIOP protocol, a client could then talk to a server.

Changes to a protocol are a nightmare once the protocol has become popular. It took years for all clients and servers to upgrade to HTTP 1.1, and the situation was similar for CORBA protocol changes. The protocol used by sendmail hasn't been touched for years because of the chaos to e-mail that would almost certainly result from any changes, even though many people think it is well past its use-by date.

When you discover a Jini service, you don't get an address to be dealt with by a particular protocol. Instead, you get a Java proxy object with known methods. This alters the playing field in a significant way: the client doesn't need to know the communications protocol *at all*. It just makes local method calls on the proxy.

The proxy comes from the server, and this is key to *client ignorance*. The client doesn't know the protocol used between proxy and service since it never has to know. The communications protocol is private to the proxy and the service. That means that the proxy and the service can use any protocol they wish, and it has no effect on the client at all. The proxy and service can change the protocol, and the client never knows.

There is often an assumption that Jini systems must be "all Java." This isn't quite true. Certainly, the client has to be a Java client, although even here there are caveats: strictly speaking, the client must be able to invoke a Java object through a JVM, and there are many languages that can now do this. The proxy needs to be JVM bytecode. Most likely, this bytecode is generated from Java source code, but not necessarily. But on the service side, who knows? The proxy can talk to any service it wants to, using any protocol it has chosen. For example, many people (including myself) have built proxies that will talk SOAP to UPnP devices or web services. The client is ignorant of the service language and has no need to care.

It isn't quite the end of protocols, unfortunately. Jini leads to the end of client knowledge of *invocation* protocols, but the client still has to *discover* the Jini proxy; a discovery protocol is still involved. However, the Jini discovery protocol is fairly lightweight and is customized to just this task rather than being a general-purpose protocol. Jini discovery involves a simple protocol to discover a lookup service and then a mechanism for downloading bytecode. In the last section, I pointed out the use of an HTTP server to deliver the proxy bytecode, but this is not a prescribed mechanism for Jini. It would be possible to use other mechanisms such as e-mail or FTP, although I don't think anyone has yet seriously considered doing this, since HTTP seems to be good enough so far.

Summary

In this chapter, you learned that a Jini system is made up of three parts:

- Service

- Client

- Service locator

Code is moved between these applications. A registrar acts as a proxy to the lookup locator and runs on both the client and service.

A service and a client both possess a certain structure, which is detailed in the following chapters. Services may require support from other non-Jini servers, such as an HTTP server.

■ ■ ■

CHAPTER 2

Troubleshooting Jini

Jini is advertised as being "network plug and play," which carries with it the idea of *zero administration*, where you buy a device or install a software service, switch it on, and *voila!*—it is there and available. Well, this may happen in the future, but right now there are a number of backroom games that you have to succeed at. Once you have won these games, "network plug and play" *does* work, but if you lose at any stage, you have an uphill battle to fight.

The difficult parts are getting the right files in the right places with the right permissions. About 50 percent of the messages in the Jini mailing list relate to these configuration problems, which shouldn't occur.

This chapter looks at some of the problems that can arise in a Jini system, most of which are configuration issues of some kind. Each of the early sections contains step-by-step instructions on what to do to get the example programs working. Because this is only the second chapter in this book, and right now you shouldn't have managed to fail at anything, feel free to skip to the next chapters, but do come back here when things go wrong.

Java Packages

The following is a typical Java package-related error:

```
Exception in thread "main" java.lang.NoClassDefFoundError:
basic/InvalidLookupLocator
```

Most of the code in this tutorial is organized into packages. To run the book's examples, the classes must be accessible from your classpath. For example, one of the programs in the basic directory is InvalidLookupLocator.java. This defines the class InvalidLookupLocator in the package basic. The program must be run using the fully qualified path name, as follows:

```
java basic.InvalidLookupLocator
```

(Note the use of ".", not "/".)

To find this class, the classpath must be set correctly for the Java runtime. If you have copied the file classes.zip, then you can find the class files for this tutorial there. You only need to reference this:

```
CLASSPATH=classes.zip:...
```

If you have downloaded the source files, then you can find the class files in subdirectories such as basic, complex, and so on. After compilation, the class files should also be in these subdirectories, for example, basic/InvalidLookupLocator.class. An alternative to using classes.zip is to set the classpath to include the directory containing those subdirectories. For example, if the full path is /home/jan/classes/basic/InvalidLookupLocator.class, then set classpath to

```
CLASSPATH=/home/jan/classes:...
```

An alternative to setting the CLASSPATH environment variable is to use the -classpath option to the Java runtime engine:

```
java -classpath /home/jan/classes basic.InvalidLookupLocator
```

Jini and Java Versions

There are five versions of Jini: 1.0, 1.1, 1.2, 2.0, and now 2.1. The core classes are the same in each version. In this book, we'll deal only with the new version, 2.1. Jini 2.1 requires Java Development Kit (JDK) 1.4 or later, not earlier versions of Java. It will work with JDK 1.5 but does not require it.

The changes for 2.1 are listed in the document jini2_1/doc/release-notes/new.html. The main classes that have changed for 2.0 are as follows:

- LookupDiscovery (now has an additional constructor)

- LeaseRenewalManager

- ServiceIDListener

The main new classes are as follows:

- LookupLocatorDiscovery

- LookupDiscoveryManager

- ClientLookupManager

If you get syntax errors or runtime errors relating to these classes, it is possible that you are using Jini 1 instead of Jini 2. If you get "deprecated" warnings, it is likely that you are using the Jini 1 classes in a Jini 2 environment. The old classes are supported for now, but are not approved.

Jini Packages

The following is a typical Jini package-related error:

```
Exception in thread "main" java.lang.NoClassDefFoundError:
net/jini/discovery/DiscoveryListener
```

The Jini class files are all in .jar files. The Jini distribution has them in a subdirectory, lib. The files were repackaged in Jini 2.0: formerly you would use jini-core.jar, jini-ext.jar and sometimes sun-util.jar. Now you should use jsk-platform.jar and jsk-lib.jar.

A compile or run of a Jini application will typically have an environment set something like this:

```
JINI_HOME=wherever_Jini_home_is
CLASSPATH=.:$JINI_HOME/lib/jsk-platform.jar:$JINI_HOME/lib/jsk-lib.jar
```

HTTP Server

Jini requires a server to deliver class files to a client. Usually this is done using an HTTP server. One of the common errors related to this is as follows:

```
java.rmi.ServerException: RemoteException in server thread; nested exception is:
java.rmi.UnmarshalException: unmarshalling method/arguments; nested exception is:
java.lang.ClassNotFoundException: could not obtain preferred value for: ...
```

The most likely cause of this exception is that you aren't running an HTTP server on the machine that java.rmi.server.codebase is pointing to. Note that using localhost is a common error, since it may refer to a different machine from the one intended.

Network Configuration

A long-term aim in pervasive computing is to have *zero configuration*, whereby you can plug devices into a network and things "just work." Jini goes a long way toward making this possible at the *service* level, but the current implementation relies heavily on a functioning network layer: misconfiguration of the network can cause a great deal of problems in Jini.

The following is a typical network configuration error:

```
java.rmi.ConnectException: connection refused or timed out to
BasicObjectEndpoint[88133900-39f9-466a-880b-de8ce6653a63,
TcpEndpoint[0.0.0.0:1831]]; nested exception is: java.net.ConnectException:
Connection refused
```

This error can occur by using the new configuration mechanism, where a service is exported by Jeri as follows:

```
exporter = new BasicJeriExporter(TcpServerEndpoint.getInstance(0),
                                 new BasicILFactory());
```

"Exporting a service" means finding the localhost, getting its hostname and IP address, and listening on any available port. I lost several days' work over this, as the hostname on one machine was incorrectly set, and the Java network layer (by InetAddress.getLocalHost()) was unable to determine the IP address of localhost and returned "0.0.0.0"—and nothing could connect to that address!

The solution was to correctly set the hostname on that machine; then services could be found and run on that machine. Alternatively, TcpServerEndpoint.getInstance(0) could be replaced by TcpServerEndpoint.getInstance("my_ip_address", 0) (for a suitable "my_ip_address", of course!) in the configuration files for the services in that machine.

Could Not Obtain Preferred Value

When you receive a "Could not obtain preferred value for . . ." message, it means that Jini can't find a class file—something is wrong with the classpath or the codebase. This can occur if the codebase points to a directory, and the value is not terminated with a forward slash (/).

Lookup Service

The following is a typical lookup service-related error:

```
java.rmi.activation.ActivationException: ActivationSystem not running; nested excep-
tion is: java.rmi.NotBoundException: java.rmi.activation.ActivationSystem
java.rmi.NotBoundException: java.rmi.activation.ActivationSystem
```

The command rmid starts the activation system running. If the activation system cannot start properly or dies just after starting, you will get this message. Usually it is caused by incorrect file permissions.

RMI Stubs

This is a typical RMI stubs-related error:

```
java.rmi.StubNotFoundException: Stub class not found: rmi.FileClassifierImpl_Stub;
nested exception is: java.lang.ClassNotFoundException: rmi.FileClassifierImpl_Stub
```

This error does not occur as frequently as it used to. From Jini 2.0 onward, proxies should be generated using Jeri instead of RMI, and this error will only occur when using RMI. If it does occur, then the best thing to do is change the application to use Jeri. See Chapter 10 for more details.

Garbage Collection

The following is a typical garbage collection-related error:

```
java.rmi.ConnectException: connection refused or timed out
to BasicObjectEndpoint[afeb7958-8cff-41cb-8042-ec884a52e9a6,
TcpEndpoint[192.168.2.1:3558]]; nested exception is: java.net.ConnectException:
Connection refused
```

If the service has been garbage collected, then there will be no server listening for connections to it, so any connection request will be refused. This error is more likely to happen with Jini 2.0, where objects may be garbage collected if there are no active references.

The solution is to ensure that an active reference is kept to the service. The main() method should contain a reference to the server (not just create it, but also keep a variable pointing to it). The server should also keep a reference to the service implementation. An alternative is to keep a static reference to the service implementation. Similarly, if you are using a JoinManager to keep services leased, then there should be an active reference to it or it may be garbage collected and cause any leases to expire.

Debugging

Debugging a Jini application is difficult because there are so many bits to it, and these bits are all running separately: the server for a service, the client, lookup services, possibly remote activation daemons, and HTTP servers. There are a few (not many) errors within the Jini objects themselves, but more important, many of these objects are implemented using multiple threads, and the flow of execution is not always clear. There are no magic debug flags that can be turned on to show what is happening.

On either the client or service side, a debugger such as jdb can be used to step through or trace execution of the client or the server. Having lots of print statements helps, too, and you can also turn on the following three flags:

```
java -Djava.security.debug=access \
    -Dnet.jini.discovery.debug=1 \
    -Djava.rmi.server.logCalls=true ...
```

These flags don't give complete information, but they do give some, and can at least tell you if the application parts are still living.

The logging API introduced in Jini 1.4 has been adopted by Jini 2.0. It can also be used for debugging and is discussed in Chapter 20.

Summary

As discussed in this chapter, getting a Jini application to run should be easy, but sometimes it isn't. Issues specific to Jini that you may encounter include the following:

- Using the correct Jini packages

- Running an HTTP server

- Having a properly configured network

- Codebase settings

- Weak references causing services to be garbage collected

CHAPTER 3

∎∎∎

Ant

Ant is becoming increasingly widely used as a build and deploy tool for Java applications. This chapter covers how I am using Ant in this book; the material covered has nothing in particular to do with Jini. Feel free to skip this chapter until you start building and deploying the examples from this book.

Applications consisting of multiple source files benefit from having a build tool to automate compilation, deployment, testing, and so on. Many of these tools are operating system-specific, such as make (although Windows versions now exist). Ant has become an increasingly popular tool for Java applications since it offers cross-platform support and Ant build files can be written in an operating system-independent way.

This book is adapted to use ant instead of make and Unix shell scripts. This chapter covers the use of ant for this book; it is not about Jini at all, so unless you want to see how the applications are currently built, I recommend that you skip this chapter. Individual build files for each project will be given in the relevant chapters.

Top-Level Build File

Two general parameters need to be set for your own environment:

- jini.home: The pathname to the location where Jini has been unpacked. This parameter is used to define the jini.jars variable that contains the standard Jini class files.

- localhost: The IP address or hostname of the current machine. In my testing, I run basic tests from this machine.

These parameters are defined in build.xml in the book's root directory on http://jan.netcomp.monash.edu.au/java/jini/tutorial/.

Similar to many projects, I adopt the following directory structure:

- src: The directory for all source files.

- build: The location where all class files are built.

- dist: The location where distribution files such as .jar files are created.

- resources: The location where things like policy files and configuration files are kept.

- httpd.classes: This is nonstandard, but it is the location where we need to copy files so that an HTTP server can find them.

These directories are all defined in the build.xml file in the book's root directory. The following targets are defined:

- compile: Compile all source files.

- dist: Build the distribution, typically .jar files.

- build: Compile and distribute (redundant).

- deploy: Copy files to their destination, typically some .jar files to an HTTP server.

- clean: Remove all class files, .jar files and source backups.

- run -DrunFile=...: Run a project.

- usage: Print a list of options.

The top-level file build.xml defines these targets. The main function of each target is to run the target again in each of the projects. So compile runs compile in each project and deploy runs deploy in each project, whereas run calls run only in the selected project. The projects are each defined in an Ant file in the antBuildFiles directory. The build.xml file is as follows:

```
<project name="Jini book" default="usage" basedir=".">
    <!-- CONFIGURABLE STUFF HERE -->
    <property name="jini.home" value="/usr/local/jini2_1"/>
    <property name="localhost" value="dhcp-62-145.EECS.Berkeley.edu"/>
    <!-- END CONFIGURABLE STUFF -->
    <!-- Libraries -->
    <property name="jini.jars"
            value="${jini.home}/lib/jsk-platform.jar;${jini.home}/lib/jsk-lib.jar"/>
    <path id="compile.classpath">
        <pathelement path="${jini.jars}" />
        <pathelement path="build" />
    </path>
    <!-- Directories -->
    <property name="src" value="${basedir}\src"/>
    <property name="dist" value="${basedir}\dist"/>
    <property name="build" value="${basedir}\build"/>
    <property name="res" value="${basedir}/resources"/>
    <property name="httpd.classes" value="/home/httpd/html/classes/"/>
    <!-- Show the usage options to the user -->
    <target name="usage" >
        <echo message=" compile"/>
        <echo message=" dist"/>
        <echo message=" build"/>
        <echo message=" deploy"/>
        <echo message=" clean"/>
        <echo message=" run -DrunFile='...' [-Dconfig='...']"/>
        <echo message=" usage"/>
    </target>
    <target name="all" depends="init,compile"/>
    <!-- CLEAN -->
```

```xml
    <target name="clean">
        <!-- Delete our the ${build}, and ${dist} directory trees -->
        <delete dir="${build}"/>
        <delete dir="${dist}"/>
        <!-- delete all ~ backup files -->
        <delete>
            <fileset dir="." defaultexcludes="false" includes="**/*~"/>
        </delete>
        <!-- delete all .bak backup files -->
        <delete>
            <fileset dir="." defaultexcludes="false" includes="**/*.bak"/>
        </delete>
    </target>
    <target name="init">
        <!-- Create the build directory structure used by compile N deploy -->
        <mkdir dir="build"/>
        <mkdir dir="dist"/>
    </target>
    <!-- call "compile" target in all build files in "antBuildFiles" dir -->
    <target name="compile" depends="init">
        <subant target="compile" inheritall="true">
            <fileset dir="antBuildFiles"
                     includes="*.xml"/>
        </subant>
    </target>
    <!-- call "dist" target in all build files in "antBuildFiles" dir -->
    <target name="dist" depends="compile">
        <subant target="dist" inheritall="true">
            <fileset dir="antBuildFiles"
                     includes="*.xml"/>
        </subant>
    </target>
    <!-- call "deploy" target in all build files in "antBuildFiles" dir -->
    <target name="deploy" depends="dist">
        <subant target="deploy" inheritall="true">
            <fileset dir="antBuildFiles"
                     includes="*.xml"
            />
        </subant>
    </target>
    <target name="build" depends="dist,compile"/>
    <!-- call "run" on antfile determined by "runFile" property -->
    <target name="run">
        <ant
            antfile="antBuildFiles/${runFile}.xml"
            target="run"/>
    </target>
</project>
```

Project Files

Each project is defined in an Ant file in the `antBuildFiles` directory. The purpose is to implement the top-level build targets for each project. Each of these project files inherits values from the top-level file, namely the following:

- `jini.home`

- `jini.jars`

- `src`

- `dist`

- `build`

- `httpd.classes`

Each project uses only a small number of the files from the `src` directory; these are defined in the `src.files` variable. For example, for the `complete.FileClassifierServer` project discussed in Chapter 9, the source files are defined as follows:

```
<property name="src.files"
        value="
                common/MIMEType.java,
                common/FileClassifier.java,
                complete/FileClassifierImpl.java,
                complete/FileClassifierServer.java
                "
/>
```

Since Jini is a distributed system, not all class files are required by all components. Typically, a server will require some files, whereas a client will require others. These are defined by two further variables:

```
<!-- Class files to run the server -->
<property name="class.files"
        value="
                common/MIMEType.class,
                common/FileClassifier.class,
                complete/FileClassifierImpl.class,
                complete/FileClassifierServer.class
                "
/>
<!-- Class files for the client to download --->
<property name="class.files.dl"
        value="
                complete/FileClassifierImpl.class
                "
/>
```

The rest of each project file is fairly straightforward. The `compile` target compiles all files in the `src.files` list; the `dist` target builds `.jar` files (usually two of them: one for the server and one for the client); the `deploy` target copies the `.jar` files for the client to an HTTP server; and the `run` target starts a JVM with appropriate parameters. Note that the JVM must be started as a separate VM, as it sets a security policy (discussed later), which cannot be done within an already running Ant JVM.

The complete project file for `complete.FileClassifierServer` is in the file `complete.FileClassifierServer.xml`:

```
<!--
    Project name must be the same as the filename which must
    be the same as the main.class. Builds jar files with the
    same name
  -->

<project name="complete.FileClassifierServer">
    <!-- Inherits properties from ../build.xml:
        jini.home
        jini.jars
        src
        dist
      . build
        httpd.classes
        localhost
     -->
    <!-- files for this project -->
    <!-- Source files for the server -->
    <property name="src.files"
            value="
                    common/MIMEType.java,
                    common/FileClassifier.java,
                    complete/FileClassifierImpl.java,
                    complete/FileClassifierServer.java
                    "/>
    <!-- Class files to run the server -->
    <property name="class.files"
            value="
                    common/MIMEType.class,
                    common/FileClassifier.class,
                    complete/FileClassifierImpl.class,
                    complete/FileClassifierServer.class
                    "/>
    <!-- Class files for the client to download -->
    <property name="class.files.dl"
            value="
                    common/MIMEType.class,
                    common/FileClassifier.class,
                    complete/FileClassifierImpl.class
```

```xml
                        "/>
    <!-- Uncomment if no class files downloaded to the client -->
    <!-- <property name="no-dl" value="true"/> -->
    <!-- derived names - may be changed -->
    <property name="jar.file"
             value="${ant.project.name}.jar"/>
    <property name="jar.file.dl"
             value="${ant.project.name}-dl.jar"/>
    <property name="main.class"
             value="${ant.project.name}"/>
    <property name="codebase"
             value="http://${localhost}/classes/${jar.file.dl}"/>
    <!-- targets -->
    <target name="all" depends="compile"/>
    <target name="compile">
        <javac destdir="${build}" srcdir="${src}"
               classpath="${jini.jars}"
               includes="${src.files}">
        </javac>
    </target>
    <target name="dist" depends="compile"
            description="generate the distribution">
        <jar jarfile="${dist}/${jar.file}"
             basedir="${build}"
             includes="${class.files}"/>
        <antcall target="dist-jar-dl"/>
    </target>
    <target name="dist-jar-dl" unless="no-dl">
        <jar jarfile="${dist}/${jar.file.dl}"
             basedir="${build}"
             includes="${class.files.dl}"/>
    </target>
    <target name="build" depends="dist,compile"/>
    <target name="run" depends="build,deploy">
        <java classname="${main.class}"
              fork="true"
              classpath="${jini.jars}:${dist}/${jar.file}">
            <jvmarg value="-Djava.security.policy=${res}/policy.all"/>
            <jvmarg value="-Djava.rmi.server.codebase=${codebase}"/>
        </java>
    </target>
    <target name="deploy" depends="dist" unless="no-dl">
        <copy file="${dist}/${jar.file.dl}"
              todir="${httpd.classes}"/>
    </target>
</project>
```

Summary

Ant is now used in many Java projects to control the build and distribution process. This book also uses Ant, and this chapter has described how this is done. Please note that the material in this chapter is not essential to understanding how Jini works, though.

■ ■ ■

CHAPTER 4

Discovering a Lookup Service

Jini uses a lookup service in much the same way as other distributed systems use naming services and traders. Services register with lookup services, and clients use them to find services they are interested in. Jini lookup services are designed to be an integral part of the Jini system, and they have their own set of classes and methods. This chapter looks at what is involved in discovering a lookup service/service locator; this is common to both services and clients. The chapter also discusses issues particular to the Sun lookup service reggie.

Running a Lookup Service

A client locates a service by querying a lookup service (service locator). In order to do this, it must first locate a lookup service. Similarly, a service must register itself with the lookup service, and in order to do so it must also first locate a lookup service.

The initial task for both a client and a service is thus discovering a lookup service. Such a service (or set of services) will usually have been started by some independent mechanism. The search for a lookup service can be done either by unicast or by multicast. *Unicast* means that you know the address of the lookup service and can contact it directly. *Multicast* is used when you do not know where a lookup service is and have to broadcast a message across the network so that any lookup service can respond. In fact, the lookup service is just another Jini service, but it is one that is specialized to store services and pass them on to clients looking for them.

reggie

Sun supplies a lookup service called reggie as part of the standard Jini distribution. The specification of a lookup service is public, and in the future we can expect to see other implementations of lookup services.

There may be any number of these lookup services running in a network. A local area network (LAN) may run many lookup services to provide redundancy in case one of them crashes. Similarly, across the Internet, people may run lookup services for a variety of reasons; for example, a public lookup service is sometimes running on http://jan.netcomp.monash.edu.au to aid people trying Jini clients and services so they don't need to also set up a lookup service. Other lookup services may act as coordination centers, such as a repository of locations for all of the atomic clock servers in the world.

Anybody can start a lookup service (depending on access permissions), but it will usually be started by an administrator, or started at boot time. Starting a lookup service used to be the hardest part of getting Jini working for the beginner. It could take hours or even days of playing with configuration files and network settings. It has now been made substantially easier: just run a DOS batch file or Unix shell script. At the top level of the Jini distribution is the directory installverify. Change to this directory and run the program LaunchAll, which will start an HTTP server, the lookup service reggie, and several other useful services.

For the curious, LaunchAll uses the ServiceStarter described in a later chapter, which in turn uses the configuration file startAll.config. Configuration files are described in Chapter 19.

Unicast Discovery

Unicast discovery can be used when you know the machine on which the lookup service resides and can ask for it directly. This approach is expected to be used for a lookup service that is outside of your local network, but that you know the address of anyway (such as your home network while you are at work, or a network identified in a newsgroup or e-mail message, or maybe even one advertised on TV).

Unicast discovery relies on a single class, LookupLocator, which is described in the next section. Basic use of this class is illustrated in the sections on the InvalidLookupLocator program. The InvalidLookupLocator should be treated as an introductory Jini program that you can build and run without having to worry about network issues. Connecting to a lookup service using the network is done with the getRegister method of LookupLocator, and an example program using this is shown in the UnicastRegistrar program in the "getRegistrar" section.

LookupLocator

The LookupLocator class in the net.jini.core.discovery package is used for unicast discovery of a lookup service. There are two constructors:

```
package net.jini.core.discovery;
public class LookupLocator {
    LookupLocator(java.lang.String url) throws
        java.net.MalformedURLException;
    LookupLocator(java.lang.String host,int port);
}
```

For the first constructor, the URL must be of the form jini://host/ or jini://host:port/. If no port is given, it defaults to 4160. The host should be a valid Domain Name System (DNS) name (such as www.jini.monash.edu.au) or an IP address (such as 137.92.11.13). No unicast discovery is performed at this stage, though, so any rubbish could be entered. Only a check for syntactic validity of the URL is performed. This syntactic check is not even done for the second constructor.

InvalidLookupLocator

The following program creates some objects with valid and invalid host/URLs. They are only checked for syntactic validity rather than existence as URLs; that is, no network lookups are performed. This should be treated as a basic example to get you started building and running a simple Jini program.

```
package basic;
import net.jini.core.discovery.LookupLocator;
/**
 * InvalidLookupLocator.java
 */
public class InvalidLookupLocator  {
    static public void main(String argv[]) {
        new InvalidLookupLocator();
    }

public InvalidLookupLocator() {
    LookupLocator lookup;
    // this is valid
    try {
        lookup = new LookupLocator("jini://localhost");
        System.out.println("First lookup creation succeeded");
    } catch(java.net.MalformedURLException e) {
        System.err.println("First lookup failed: " + e.toString());
    }
    // this is probably an invalid URL,
    // but the URL is syntactically okay
    try {
        lookup = new LookupLocator("jini://ABCDEFG.org");
        System.out.println("Second lookup creation succeeded");
    } catch(java.net.MalformedURLException e) {
        System.err.println("Second lookup failed: " + e.toString());
    }
    // this IS a malformed URL, and should throw an exception
    try {
        lookup = new LookupLocator("A:B:C://ABCDEFG.org");
        System.out.println("Third lookup creation succeeded");
    } catch(java.net.MalformedURLException e) {
        System.err.println("Third lookup failed: " + e.toString());
    }
    // this is valid, but no check is made anyway
    lookup = new LookupLocator("localhost", 80);
    System.out.println("Fourth lookup creation succeeded");
    }

} // InvalidLookupLocator
```

Running the InvalidLookupLocator

All programs in this book can be compiled using the JDK 1.4 compiler. The Java 1.5 compiler can be used, although the Jini class libraries do not use any of the 1.5 features.

The following program defines the InvalidLookupLocator class in the basic package. The source code will in the InvalidLookupLocator.java file in the basic subdirectory. From the parent directory, this can be compiled by a command such as this:

```
javac basic/InvalidLookupLocator.java
```

to leave the class file also in the basic subdirectory.

When you compile the code, the CLASSPATH will need to include some Jini .jar files. In versions 2.0 and earlier, the jini-core.jar file was required. This has changed for Jini 2.1; the preferred files are jsk-platform.jar and jsk-lib.jar for compilation of the source code. These files are in the lib subdirectory of the Jini distribution. When a service is run, these Jini files will need to be in its CLASSPATH. Similarly, when a client runs, it will also need these files in its CLASSPATH. The reason for this repetition is that the service and the client are two separate applications, running in two separate JVMs, and quite likely they will be on two separate computers.

The InvalidLookupLocator has no additional requirements. It does not perform any network calls and does not require any additional service to be running. It can be run simply by entering this command:

```
java -Djava.security.policy=policy.all -classpath ... basic.InvalidLookupLocator
```

where the policy file could be the permissive security policy file

```
grant { permission java.security.AllPermission; };
```

An Ant file to build, deploy, and run this class is basic.InvalidLookupLocator.xml:

```xml
<project name="basic.InvalidLookupLocator" default="usage">
    <!-- files for this project -->
    <property name="src.files"   value="basic/InvalidLookupLocator.java"/>
    <property name="class.files" value="basic/InvalidLookupLocator.class"/>

    <!-- derived names - may be changed -->
    <property name="jar.file"
              value="${ant.project.name}.jar"/>
    <property name="jar.file.dl"
              value="${ant.project.name}-dl.jar"/>
    <property name="main.class"
              value="${ant.project.name}"/>
    <property name="no-dl" value="true"/>
    <!-- targets -->
    <target name="all" depends="compile"/>
    <target name="compile">
        <javac destdir="${build}" srcdir="${src}"
               classpath="${jini.jars}"
               includes="${src.files}">
        </javac>
    </target>
    <target name="dist" depends="compile"
            description="generate the distribution">
```

```
            <jar jarfile="${dist}/${jar.file}"
                basedir="${build}"
                includes="${class.files}"/>
            <antcall target="dist-jar-dl"/>
        </target>
        <target name="dist-jar-dl" unless="no-dl">
            <jar jarfile="${dist}/${jar.file.dl}"
                basedir="${build}"
                includes="${class.files.dl}"/>
        </target>
        <target name="build" depends="dist,compile"/>
        <target name="deploy" depends="dist" unless="no-dl">
            <copy file="${dist}/${jar.file.dl}"
                todir="${httpd.classes}"/>
        </target>
        <target name="run">
            <java classname="${main.class}"
                classpath="${jini.jars}:${dist}/${jar.file}"/>
        </target>
</project>
```

Information from the LookupLocator

Two of the methods of LookupLocator are as follows:

```
String getHost();
int getPort();
```

These methods will return information about the hostname that the locator will use, and
the port it will connect on or is already connected on. This is just the information fed into the
constructor or left to default values, though; it doesn't offer anything new for unicasting.
However, this information will be useful in the multicast situation if you need to find out where
the lookup service is.

getRegistrar

Search and lookup is performed by the getRegistrar() method of the LookupLocator, which
returns an object of class ServiceRegistrar.

```
public ServiceRegistrar getRegistrar()
    throws java.io.IOException,
    java.lang.ClassNotFoundException
```

The ServiceRegistrar class is discussed in detail later. This class performs network
lookup on the URL given in the LookupLocator constructor.

UML sequence diagrams are useful for showing the timelines of object existence and the
method calls that are made from one object to another. The timeline reads down, and method
calls and their returns read across. A UML sequence diagram augmented with a jagged arrow
showing the network connection is shown in Figure 4-1. The UnicastRegister object makes a

new() call to create a LookupLocator, and this call returns a lookup object. The getRegistrar() method call is then made on the lookup object, and this causes network activity. As a result, a ServiceRegistrar object is created in some manner by the lookup object, and this object is returned from the method as the registrar.

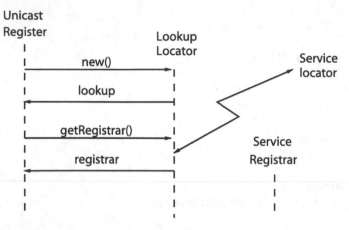

Figure 4-1. *UML sequence diagram for lookup*

By this stage, the UnicastRegister program that implements Figure 4-1 and performs the connection to get a ServiceRegistrar object looks like this:

```
package basic;
import net.jini.core.discovery.LookupLocator;
import net.jini.core.lookup.ServiceRegistrar;
import java.rmi.RMISecurityManager;
/**
 * UnicastRegistrar.java
 */
public class UnicastRegister  {

    static public void main(String argv[]) {
        new UnicastRegister();
    }

    public UnicastRegister() {
        LookupLocator lookup = null;
        ServiceRegistrar registrar = null;
        System.setSecurityManager(new RMISecurityManager());
        try {
            lookup = new LookupLocator("jini://localhost");
        } catch(java.net.MalformedURLException e) {
            System.err.println("Lookup failed: " + e.toString());
            System.exit(1);
```

```
        }
        try {
            registrar = lookup.getRegistrar();
        } catch (java.io.IOException e) {
            System.err.println("Registrar search failed: " + e.toString());
            System.exit(1);
        } catch (java.lang.ClassNotFoundException e) {
            System.err.println("Registrar search failed: " + e.toString());
            System.exit(1);
        }
        System.out.println("Registrar found");
        // the code takes separate routes from here for client or service
    }

} // UnicastRegister
```

The registrar object will be used in different ways for clients and services: the services will use it to register themselves, and the clients will use it to locate services.

Running the UnicastRegister

When the UnicastRegistrar program in the previous section needs to be compiled and run, it has to have jsk-platform.jar and jsk-lib.jar in its CLASSPATH.

```
javac -classpath ... basic/UnicastRegister.java
```

When run, it will attempt to connect to the service locator, so obviously the service locator needs to be running on the machine specified in order for this to happen. Otherwise, the program will throw an exception and terminate. In this case, the host specified is localhost. It could, however, be any machine accessible on the local or remote network (as long as it is running a service locator). For example, to connect to the service locator running on my current workstation, jan.netcomp.monash.edu.au, the parameter to LookupLocator would be jini://jan.netcomp.monash.edu.au.

The UnicastRegister program will receive a ServiceRegistrar from the service locator. However, it does so by a simple readObject() on a socket connected to the service locator, so it does not need any additional support services such as rmiregistry or rmid. The program can be run by this command:

```
java -Djava.security.policy=policy.all -classpath ... basic.UnicastRegister
```

An Ant file to build, deploy, and run this class is basic.UnicastRegister.xml:

```
<project name="basic.UnicastRegister" default="usage">
    <!-- Inherits properties
        jini.home
        jini.jars
        src
        dist
        build
```

```xml
            httpd.classes
     -->
  <!-- files for this project -->
  <property name="src.files"
          value="
                  basic/UnicastRegister.java
                "/>
  <property name="class.files"
          value="
                  basic/UnicastRegister.class
                "/>
  <property name="class.files.dl"
          value="
                "/>
  <property name="no-dl" value="true"/>
  <!-- derived names - may be changed -->
  <property name="jar.file"
          value="${ant.project.name}.jar"/>
  <property name="jar.file.dl"
          value="${ant.project.name}-dl.jar"/>
  <property name="main.class"
          value="${ant.project.name}"/>
  <property name="jini.jars.start"
          value="${jini.jars}:${jini.home}/lib/start.jar"/>
  <!-- targets -->
  <target name="all" depends="compile"/>
  <target name="compile">
      <javac destdir="${build}" srcdir="${src}"
          classpath="${jini.jars.start}"
          includes="${src.files}">
      </javac>
  </target>
  <target name="dist" depends="compile"
        description="generate the distribution">
      <jar jarfile="${dist}/${jar.file}"
          basedir="${build}"
          includes="${class.files}"/>
      <antcall target="dist-jar-dl"/>
  </target>
  <target name="dist-jar-dl" unless="no-dl">
      <jar jarfile="${dist}/${jar.file.dl}"
          basedir="${build}"
          includes="${class.files.dl}"/>
  </target>
  <target name="build" depends="dist,compile"/>
  <target name="run" depends="build">
      <java classname="${main.class}"
```

```
                fork="true"
                classpath="${jini.jars.start}:${dist}/${jar.file}">
                <jvmarg value="-Djava.security.policy=${res}/policy.all"/>
            </java>
        </target>
        <target name="deploy" depends="dist" unless="no-dl">
            <copy file="${dist}/${jar.file.dl}"
                  todir="${httpd.classes}"/>
        </target>
</project>
```

Broadcast Discovery

If the location of a lookup service is unknown, it is necessary to make a broadcast search for one. The User Datagram Protocol (UDP) supports a multicast mechanism that the current implementations of Jini use. Because multicast is expensive in terms of network requirements, most routers block multicast packets. This usually restricts broadcast to a LAN, although this depends on the network configuration and the time to live (TTL) of the multicast packets.

Any number of lookup services can be running on the network accessible to the broadcast search. On a small network, such as a home network, there may be just a single lookup service, but in a large network there may be many—perhaps one or two per department. Each one of these may choose to reply to a broadcast request.

Groups

Some services may be meant for anyone to use, but some may be more restricted in applicability. For example, the engineering department may wish to keep lists of services specific to that department, including a departmental diary service, a departmental inventory, and so forth. The services themselves may be running anywhere in the organization, but the department would like to be able to store information about them and to locate them from their own lookup service. Of course, this lookup service may be running anywhere, too!

So there could be lookup services specifically for a particular group of services, such as the engineering department services, and others for the publicity department services. Some lookup services may cater to more than one group—for example, a company lookup service may want to hold information about all services running for all groups on the network.

When a lookup service is started, it can be given a list of groups to act for as a command-line parameter. A service may include such group information by giving a list of groups that it belongs to. This is an array of strings, such as the following:

```
String [] groups = {"Engineering dept"};
```

LookupDiscovery

The LookupDiscovery class in the net.jini.discovery package is used for broadcast discovery. There are two constructors:

```
LookupDiscovery(java.lang.String[] groups)
LookupDiscovery(java.lang.String[] groups, Configuration config)
```

We will look at only the first one for now. The second one is new to Jini 2.0.

The parameter to the first LookupDiscovery constructor can take three cases:

- null, or LookupDiscovery.ALL_GROUPS, means that the object should attempt to discover all reachable lookup services, no matter which group they belong to. This will be the normal case.

- An empty list of strings, or LookupDiscovery.NO_GROUPS, means that the object is created but no search is performed. In this case, the setGroups() method will need to be called in order to perform a search.

- A nonempty array of strings can be given. This will attempt to discover all lookup services in that set of groups.

DiscoveryListener

A broadcast is a multicast call across the network, and lookup services are expected to reply as they receive the call. Doing so may take time, and there will generally be an unknown number of lookup services that can reply. To be notified of lookup services as they are discovered, the application must register a listener with the LookupDiscovery object, as follows.

```
public void addDiscoveryListener(DiscoveryListener l)
```

The listener must implement the DiscoveryListener interface:

```
package net.jini.discovery;

public abstract interface DiscoveryListener {
    public void discovered(DiscoveryEvent e);
    public void discarded(DiscoveryEvent e);
}
```

The discovered() method is invoked whenever a lookup service has been discovered. The API recommends that this method should return quickly and not make any remote calls. However, the discovered() method is the natural place to register the service, and for a client it is the natural place to ask if there is a service available and to invoke the service. It may be better to perform these lengthy operations in a separate thread.

Other timing issues are involved: when the DiscoveryListener is created, the broadcast is made, and after this, a listener is added to this discovery object. What happens if replies come in very quickly, before the listener is added? The Jini Discovery Utilities Specification guarantees that these replies will be buffered and delivered when a listener is added. Conversely, no replies may come in for a long time—what is the application supposed to do in the meantime? It cannot simply exit, because then there would be no object to reply to! It has to be made persistent enough to last till replies come in. One way of handling this is for the application to have a GUI interface, in which case the application will stay until the user dismisses it. Another possibility is that the application may be prepared to wait for a while before giving up. In that case, the main() method could sleep for, say, ten seconds and then exit. This will depend on what the application should do if no lookup service is discovered.

The discarded() method is invoked whenever the application discards a lookup service by calling discard() on the registrar object.

DiscoveryEvent

The parameter of the discovered()method of the DiscoveryListener interface is a DiscoveryEvent object.

```
package net.jini.discovery;

public Class DiscoveryEvent {
    public net.jini.core.lookup.ServiceRegistrar[] getRegistrars();
}
```

This has one public method, getRegistrars(), which returns an array of ServiceRegistrar objects. Each one of these implements the ServiceRegistrar interface, just like the object returned from a unicast search for a lookup service. More than one ServiceRegistrar object can be returned if a set of replies has come in before the listener was registered—they are collected in an array and returned in a single call to the listener. Figure 4-2 shows a UML sequence diagram augmented with jagged arrows showing the network broadcast and replies.

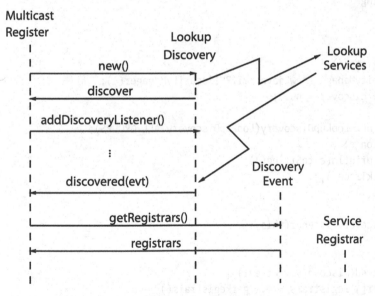

Figure 4-2. *UML sequence diagram for discovery*

In Figure 4-2, the creation of a LookupDiscovery object starts the broadcast search, and it returns the discover object. The MulticastRegister adds itself as a listener to the discover object. The search continues in a separate thread, and when a new lookup service replies, the discover object invokes the discovered() method in the MulticastRegister, passing it a newly created DiscoveryEvent. The MulticastRegister object can then make calls on the DiscoveryEvent, such as getRegistrars(), which will return suitable ServiceRegistrar objects.

By this stage, the program looks like this:

```
package basic;
import net.jini.discovery.LookupDiscovery;
import net.jini.discovery.DiscoveryListener;
import net.jini.discovery.DiscoveryEvent;
import net.jini.core.lookup.ServiceRegistrar;
import net.jini.core.discovery.LookupLocator;
import java.rmi.RemoteException;
/**
 * MulticastRegister.java
 */
public class MulticastRegister implements DiscoveryListener {

    static public void main(String argv[]) {
        new MulticastRegister();
        // stay around long enough to receive replies
        try {
            Thread.currentThread().sleep(10000L);
        } catch(java.lang.InterruptedException e) {
            // do nothing
        }
    }

    public MulticastRegister() {
        System.setSecurityManager(new java.rmi.RMISecurityManager());
        LookupDiscovery discover = null;
        try {
            discover = new LookupDiscovery(LookupDiscovery.ALL_GROUPS);
        } catch(Exception e) {
            System.err.println(e.toString());
            e.printStackTrace();
            System.exit(1);
        }
        discover.addDiscoveryListener(this);
    }

    public void discovered(DiscoveryEvent evt) {
        ServiceRegistrar[] registrars = evt.getRegistrars();
        for (int n = 0; n < registrars.length; n++) {
            ServiceRegistrar registrar = registrars[n];
            // the code takes separate routes from here for client or service
            try {
                System.out.println("found a service locator at " +
                                registrar.getLocator().getHost() +
                                " at port " +
```

```
                                registrar.getLocator().getPort());
            } catch(RemoteException e) {
                e.printStackTrace();
            }
        }
    }
    public void discarded(DiscoveryEvent evt) {
    }
} // MulticastRegister
```

Staying Alive

In the preceding constructor for the MulticastRegister program, we create a LookupDiscovery object, add a DiscoveryListener, and then the constructor terminates. The main() method, having called this constructor, promptly goes to sleep. What is going on here? The constructor for LookupDiscovery actually starts up a number of threads to broadcast the service and to listen for replies. When replies come in, the listener thread will call the discovered() method of the MulticastRegister. However, these threads are daemon threads. Java has two types of threads, daemon threads and user threads, and at least one user thread must be running or the application will terminate. All these other threads are not enough to keep the application alive, so it keeps a user thread running in order to continue to exist.

The sleep() method ensures that a user thread continues to run, even though it apparently does nothing. This will keep the application alive, so that the daemon threads (running in the background) can discover some lookup locators. Ten seconds (10,000 milliseconds) is long enough for that. To stay alive after this ten seconds expires requires either increasing the sleep time or creating another user thread in the discovered() method (for example, by creating an AWT frame) or by some other method.

I have placed the sleep() call in the main() method. It is perfectly reasonable to place it in the application constructor, and some examples do this. However, it looks a bit strange in the constructor, because it looks like the constructor does not terminate (so is the object created or not?), so I prefer this placement. Note that although the constructor for MulticastRegister will have terminated without us assigning its object reference, a live reference has been passed into the discover object as a DiscoveryListener, and it will keep the reference alive in its own daemon threads. This means that the application object will still exist for its discovered() method to be called.

Any other method that results in a user thread continuing to exist will do just as well. For example, a client that has an AWT or Swing user interface will stay alive because there are many user threads created by any of these GUI objects.

For services, which typically will not have a GUI interface running, another simple way to keep them alive is to create an object and then wait for another thread to notify() it. Since nothing will, the thread (and hence the application) stays alive. Essentially, this is an unsatisfied wait that will never terminate—usually an erroneous thing to do, but here it is deliberate.

```
Object keepAlive = new Object();
synchronized(keepAlive) {
    try {
        keepAlive.wait();
```

```
    }
    catch(InterruptedException e) {
        // do nothing
    }
}
```

This will keep the service alive indefinitely, and it will not terminate unless interrupted. This is unlike sleep(), which will terminate eventually.

Running the MulticastRegister

The MulticastRegister program needs to be compiled and run with jsk-platform.jar and jsk-lib.jar in its CLASSPATH.

```
javac -classpath ... basic/MulticastRegister.java
```

When run, the program will attempt to find all service locators that it can. If there are none, it will find none—pretty boring. So one or more service locators should be set running in the near network or on the local machine.

```
java -Djava.security.policy=policy.all -classpath ... basic.MulticastRegister
```

This program will receive ServiceRegistrars from the service locators. However, it does so with a simple readObject() on a socket connected to a service locator, and so does not need any additional support services such as rmiregistry.

An Ant file to build, deploy, and run this class is basic.MulticastRegister.xml:

```
<project name="basic.MulticastRegister" default="usage">
    <!-- Inherits properties
        jini.home
        jini.jars
        src
        dist
        build
        httpd.classes
    -->
    <!-- files for this project -->
    <property name="src.files"
            value="
                    basic/MulticastRegister.java
                "/>
    <property name="class.files"
            value="
                    basic/MulticastRegister.class
                "/>
    <property name="class.files.dl"
            value="
                "/>
    <property name="no-dl" value="true"/>
```

```
<!-- derived names - may be changed -->
<property name="jar.file"
          value="${ant.project.name}.jar"/>
<property name="jar.file.dl"
          value="${ant.project.name}-dl.jar"/>
<property name="main.class"
          value="${ant.project.name}"/>
<!-- targets -->
<target name="all" depends="compile"/>
<target name="compile">
    <javac destdir="${build}" srcdir="${src}"
           classpath="${jini.jars}"
           includes="${src.files}">
    </javac>
</target>
<target name="dist" depends="compile"
        description="generate the distribution">
    <jar jarfile="${dist}/${jar.file}"
         basedir="${build}"
         includes="${class.files}"/>
    <antcall target="dist-jar-dl"/>
</target>
<target name="dist-jar-dl" unless="no-dl">
    <jar jarfile="${dist}/${jar.file.dl}"
         basedir="${build}"
         includes="${class.files.dl}"/>
</target>
<target name="build" depends="dist,compile"/>
<target name="run" depends="build">
    <java classname="${main.class}"
          fork="true"
          classpath="${jini.jars}:${dist}/${jar.file}">
        <jvmarg value="-Djava.security.policy=${res}/policy.all"/>
    </java>
</target>
<target name="deploy" depends="dist" unless="no-dl">
    <copy file="${dist}/${jar.file.dl}"
          todir="${httpd.classes}"/>
</target>
</project>
```

Broadcast Range

Services and clients search for lookup locators using the multicast protocol by sending out packets as UDP datagrams. A LookupDiscovery object makes announcements on UDP 224.0.1.84 on port 4160. How far do these announcements reach? This is controlled by two things:

- The time to live (TTL) field on the packets

- The network administrator settings on routers and gateways

By default, the current implementation of LookupDiscovery sets the TTL to 15. Common network administrative settings restrict such packets to the local network. However, the TTL may be changed by giving the system property net.jini.discovery.ttl a different value. But be careful about setting this, as many people will get irate if you flood the networks with multicast packets.

ServiceRegistrar

The ServiceRegistrar is an abstract class implemented by each lookup service. The actual details of this implementation are not relevant here. The role of a ServiceRegistrar is to act as a proxy for the lookup service. This proxy runs in the application, which may be a service or a client.

This is the first object that is moved from one Java process to another in Jini. It is shipped from the lookup service to the application looking for the lookup service, using a socket connection. From then on, it runs as an object in the application's address space, and the application makes normal method calls to it. When needed, it communicates back to its lookup service. The implementation used by Sun's reggie uses RMI to communicate, but the application does not need to know this, and anyway, it could be done in different ways. This proxy object should not cache any information on the application side, but instead should get "live" information from the lookup service as needed. The implementation of the lookup service supplied by Sun does exactly this.

The ServiceRegistrar object has two major methods. One is used by a service attempting to register:

```
public ServiceRegistration register(ServiceItem item, long leaseDuration)
    throws java.rmi.RemoteException
```

The other method is used by a client trying to locate a particular service:

```
public java.lang.Object lookup(ServiceTemplate tmpl)
    throws java.rmi.RemoteException;
public ServiceMatches lookup(ServiceTemplate tmpl, int maxMatches)
    throws java.rmi.RemoteException;
```

The details of these methods are given in Chapters 6 and 7. For now, an overview will suffice.

A service provider will register a service object (i.e., an instance of a class) and a set of attributes for that object. For example, a printer may specify that it can handle PostScript documents, or a toaster might specify that it can deal with frozen slices of bread. The service provider may register a singleton object that completely implements the service, but more likely it will register a service proxy that will communicate back to other objects in the service provider. Note carefully that *the registered object will be shipped around the network, and when it finally gets to run, it may be a long way away from where it was originally created.* It will have been created in the service's JVM, transferred to the lookup locator by register(), and then to the client's JVM by lookup().

A client is trying to find a service using some properties of the service that it knows about. Whereas the service can export a live object, the client cannot use a service object as a property, because then it would already have the thing, and wouldn't need to try to find one! What it can do is use a class object, and try to find instances of this class lying around in service locators. As discussed later in Chapter 7, it is best if the client asks for an interface class object. In addition to this class specification, the client may specify a set of attribute values that it requires from the service.

The next step is to look at the possible forms of attribute values, and how matching will be performed. This is done using Jini Entry objects. The simplest services, and the least demanding clients, will not require any attributes: the Entry[] array will be null. You may wish to skip ahead to Chapter 6 or Chapter 7 and come back to the discussion of entries in Chapter 5 later.

Information from the ServiceRegistrar

The ServiceRegistrar is returned after a successful discovery has been made. This object has a number of methods that will return useful information about the lookup service. So, in addition to using this object to register a service or to look up a service, you can use it to find out about the lookup locator. The major methods are as follows:

```
String[] getGroups();
LookupLocator getLocator();
ServiceID getServiceID();
```

The first method, getGroups(), will return a list of the groups that the locator is a member of. The second method, getLocator(), is more interesting. This returns exactly the same type of object as is used in the unicast lookup, but now its fields are filled in by the discovery process. You can find out which host the locator is running on and its hostname by using the following statement:

```
registrar.getLocator().getHost();
```

Applications usually do not care where the lookup services are running. However, if you are curious you can use the getLocator() method to find this:

```
public void discovered(DiscoveryEvent evt) {
    ServiceRegistrar[] registrars = evt.getRegistrars();
    for (int n = 0; n < registrars.length; n++) {
        ServiceRegistrar registrar = registrars[n];
        System.out.println("Service locator at " +
            registrar.getLocator().getHost());
    }
}
```

The third method, getServiceID(), is unlikely to be of much use to you. In general, service IDs are used to give a globally unique identifier for the service (different services should not have the same ID), and a service should have the same ID with all service locators. However, this is the service ID of the lookup service, not of any services registered with it.

Summary

Both services and clients need to find lookup services. Discovering a lookup service may be done using unicast or multicast protocols. Unicast discovery is a synchronous mechanism. Multicast discovery is an asynchronous mechanism that requires the use of a listener to respond when a new service locator is discovered.

When a service locator is discovered, it sends a ServiceRegistrar object to run in the client or service. This object acts as a proxy for the locator and may be queried for information, such as the host the service locator is on. The major uses of the ServiceRegistrar object are to register services (covered in Chapter 6) and by clients searching for services (covered in Chapter 7).

CHAPTER 5

■ ■ ■

Entry Objects

A service is exported to lookup services based on its class. Clients search for services using class information, typically using an interface. There is often additional information about a service that is not part of its class information, such as who owns the service, who maintains it, where it is located, and so on. Entries are used to pass additional information about services to a client, and the client can then use that information to determine if a particular service is what it wants.

Entry Class

When a service provider registers a service, it places a copy of the service object (or a service proxy) on the lookup service. This copy is an instance of an object, albeit in serialized form. The server can optionally register sets of attributes along with the service object. Each set is given by an instance of a type or class, so what is stored on each service locator is an instance of a class along with a set of attribute entries.

For example, a set of file editors may be available as services. Each editor is capable of editing different types of files as shown in Figure 5-1.

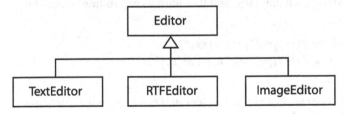

Figure 5-1. *Editor class diagram*

■**Note** The classes in Figure 5-1 would probably be interfaces, rather than instantiable classes.

A client can search for a suitable editor in two ways:

- By asking for an instance of a specific class such as `ImageEditor`

- By asking for an instance of the general class `Editor` with the additional information that it can handle a certain type of file

The type of search performed depends on the problem domain and the amount of information that clients have. Jini can handle either case. It handles the first case by only specifying a class object, such as `ImageEditor.class`. The Jini `Entry` class is designed to help with the second situation by specifying a superclass object such as `Editor.class` and allowing the additional information to be given in the request by adding extra objects.

The `Entry` class allows services to advertise their capabilities in very flexible ways. For example, suppose an editor was capable of handling a number of file types, such as plain text *and* RTF files. It could do so by exporting a service object implementing `Editor` along with an `Entry` object saying that it can handle plain text and another `Entry` object saying that it can handle RTF files. The service implementation can just add more and more information about its capabilities without altering the basic interface.

To manage this way of adding information, we would have a `FileType` class that gives information about the types of files handled:

```
public Class FileType implements Entry {
    public String type; // this is a MIME type
    public FileType(String type) {
        this.type = type;
    }
}
```

For a text editor, the attribute set would be `FileType("plain/text")`. For an RTF editor, the attribute set would be `FileType("application/rtf")`.

For an editor capable of handling both plain text and RTF files, its capabilities would be given by using an array of entries:

```
Entry[] entries = new Entry[] {new FileType("plain/text"),
                               new FileType("application/rtf")
                              };
```

On the other side, suppose a client wishes to find services that can handle the attributes that it requires. The client uses the same `Entry` class to do this. For any particular `Entry`, the client specifies both of the following:

- Which fields must match *exactly* (a non-null value)

- Which fields it does not care about (a `null` value)

For example, to search for a plain text editor, an entry like this could be used:

```
Entry[] entries = new Entry[] {new FileType("plain/text")};
```

If any editor will do, the following entry could be used:

```
Entry[] entries = new Entry[] {new FileType(null)};
```

Attribute Matching Mechanism

The attribute matching mechanism is pretty basic. For example, a printer typically has the capacity to print a certain number of pages per minute, but if it specifies this using an `Entry`, it actually makes it rather hard to find. A client can request a printer service in which it does not care about speed, or it can request a particular speed. It cannot ask for printers with a speed greater than some value. It cannot ask for a printer without a capability, such as anything except a color printer. An attribute must either match exactly or be ignored. Relational operators such as `<` and `!=` are not supported.

If you want to search for a printer with a particular speed, then printer speed capabilities may need to be given simpler descriptive values, such as "fast," "average," or "slow." Then, once you have a "fast" printer service returned to the client, it can perform a query on the service, itself, for its actual speed. This would be done outside of the Jini mechanisms, using whatever interface has been agreed on for the description of printers. A similar problem, that of finding a physically "close" service, is taken up in Chapter 15.

The attribute matching mechanism chosen by the Jini designers, of exact matches with wildcards, is comparatively easy to implement. It is a pity from the programmer's view that a more flexible mechanism was not used. One suggestion often made in the Jini mailing list is that there should be a `boolean matches()` method on the service object. However, that would involve unmarshalling the service on the locator to run the `matches()` method, which would slow down the lookup service and generate a couple of awkward questions:

- What security permissions should the filter run with?

- What happens if the filter modifies its arguments? (Deep copying to avoid this would cause further slowdowns.)

The `ServiceDiscoveryManager`, discussed in Chapter 17, has the ability to do client-side filtering to partly rectify this problem.

Restrictions on Entries

Entries are shipped around in marshalled form. Exported service objects are serialized, moved around, and reconstituted as objects at some remote client. Entries are similarly serialized and moved around. However, when it comes to comparing them, this is usually done on the lookup service, and they are not reconstituted on the lookup service. So when comparing an entry from a service and an entry from a client request, it is the serialized forms that are compared.

An entry cannot have one of the primitive types, such as `int` or `char`, as a field. If one of these fields is required, then it must be wrapped up in a class such as `Integer` or `Character`. This makes it easier to perform "wildcarding" for matching (see Chapter 6 for details). A wildcard for any object can be the "pattern" `null`, which will work for any class, including wrapper classes such as `Boolean`. (But what is the wildcard for `boolean`: `true` or `false`?)

Jini places some further restrictions on the fields of Entry objects. They must be public, nonstatic, nontransient, and nonfinal. In addition, an Entry class must have a no-args constructor.

Convenience Classes

The AbstractEntry class implements the Entry interface and is designed as a convenience class. It implements methods such as equals() and toString(). An application would probably want to subclass this class instead of implementing Entry.

In addition, Sun's implementation of Jini contains a further set of convenience classes, all subclassed out of AbstractEntry. These require the jsk-lib.jar file and are as follows:

- Address: The address of the physical component of a service.

- Comment: A free-form comment about a service.

- Location: The location of the physical component of a service. This is distinct from the Address class in that it can be used alone in a small, local organization.

- Name: The name of a service as used by users. A service may have multiple names.

- ServiceInfo: Generic information about a service, including the name of the manufacturer, the product, and the vendor.

- ServiceType: Human-oriented information about the "type" of a service. This is not related to its data or class types, but is more oriented toward allowing someone to determine what a service (e.g., a printer) does and that it is similar to another, without needing to know anything about data or class types for the Java platform.

- Status: The base class from which other status-related entry classes may be derived.

For example, the Address class contains the following:

```
String country;
String locality;            // City or locality name.
String organization;        // Name of the company or organization that provides this
                            // service.
String organizationalUnit;  // The unit within the organization that provides this
                            // service.
String postalCode;          // Postal code.
String stateOrProvince;     // Full name or standard postal abbreviation of a state
                            // or province.
String street;              // Street address.
```

You may find these classes useful. On the other hand, what services would like to advertise, and what clients would like to match on, is pretty much unknown as of yet. These classes are not part of the formal Jini specification.

Further Uses of Entries

The primary intention of entries is to provide extra information about services so that clients can decide whether or not they are the services the client wants to use. An expectation in this is that the information in an entry is primarily static. However, entries are objects, and they could implement behavior as well as state. Putting code into entry objects should not be used to extend the behavior of a service, since all service behavior should be captured in the service interface specification. There are some occasions, though, when it is worthwhile having code in entries.

A good example of a nonstatic Entry is ServiceType, which is an abstract subclass of AbstractEntry. A ServiceType object contains human-oriented information about a service, and it contains abstract methods such as String getDisplayName(). This method is intended to provide a localized name for the service. Localization (e.g., producing an appropriate French name for the service for French-speaking communities) can only be done on the client side and will require code to be executed in the client to examine the locale and produce a name.

Another use of entries is when defining the user interface for a service. Services do not have or require user interfaces for human users, since they are defined by Java interfaces that can be called by any other Java objects. However, some services may wish to offer a way of interacting with themselves by means of a user interface, and this involves much executable code. Since it is not part of the service itself, the user interface should be left in suitable Entry objects. We examine this topic in detail in Chapter 24.

Summary

As described in this chapter, an entry is additional information about a service, and a service may have any number of entries. Clients request services by class and by entries, using a simple matching system. A number of convenience classes subclass Entry.

CHAPTER 6

■ ■ ■

Service Registration

This chapter looks at how services register themselves with lookup services so that they can later be found by clients. From a lookup service, the service will get a ServiceRegistrar object. The server will prepare a description of the service in a ServiceItem and will then call the ServiceRegistrar's register() method with the ServiceItem as a parameter. The ServiceItem can contain additional information about a service as well as its type, and this information is stored in Entry objects.

ServiceRegistrar

A server for a service finds a service locator using either a unicast lookup with a LookupLocator or a multicast search using LookupDiscovery. In both cases, a ServiceRegistrar object is returned to act as a proxy for the lookup service. The server then registers the service with the service locator using the ServiceRegistrar's register() method:

```
package net.jini.core.lookup;
public Class ServiceRegistrar {
    public ServiceRegistration register(ServiceItem item,
                                 long leaseDuration)
                            throws java.rmi.RemoteException;
}
```

The second parameter here, leaseDuration, is a request for the length of time (in milliseconds) the lookup service will keep the service registered. A request for a time period need not be honored—the lookup service may reject it completely, or only grant a lesser time interval. Leasing is discussed in more detail in Chapter 8.

The first parameter is of the following type:

```
package net.jini.core.lookup;
public Class ServiceItem {
    public ServiceID serviceID;
    public java.lang.Object service;
    public Entry[] attributeSets;
    public ServiceItem(ServiceID serviceID,
```

```
                   java.lang.Object service,
                   Entry[] attrSets);
}
```

ServiceItem

The service provider will create a ServiceItem object by using the constructor and pass it into register(). The serviceID is set to null when the service is registered for the first time. The lookup service will set a non-null value as it registers the service. On subsequent registrations or reregistrations, this non-null value should be used. The serviceID is used as a globally unique identifier (GUID) for the service.

The second parameter, service, is the service object that is being registered. This object will be serialized and sent to the service locator for storage. When a client later requests a service, this is the object it will be given. There are several things to note about the service object:

- The object must be serializable. Some objects, such as Swing's JTextArea, are not serializable at present and so cannot be used.

- The object is created in the service's JVM. However, when it runs, it will do so in the client's JVM, so it may need to be a proxy for the actual service. For example, the object may be able to show a set of toaster controls, but it might have to send messages across the network to the real toaster service, which is connected to the physical toaster.

- If the service object is an RMI proxy, then the object in the ServiceItem is given by the programmer as the UnicastRemoteObject for the proxy stub, not the proxy itself. The Java runtime substitutes the proxy. This subtlety is explored in Chapter 10.

The third parameter is a set of entries giving information about the service in addition to the service object/service proxy itself. If there is no additional information, this can be null.

Registration

The service attempts to register itself by calling register(). This may throw a java.rmi. RemoteException, which must be caught. The second parameter is a request to the service locator for the length of time to store the service. The time requested may or may not be honored. The return value is of type ServiceRegistration.

ServiceRegistration

The ServiceRegistration object is created by the lookup service and is returned to run in the service provider. This object acts as a proxy object that will maintain the state information for the service object exported to the lookup service.

Actually, the ServiceRegistration object can be used to make changes to the entire ServiceItem stored on the lookup service. The ServiceRegistration object maintains a serviceID field, which is used to identify the ServiceItem on the lookup service. The ServiceItem value can be retrieved by getServiceID() for reuse by the server if it needs to do so (which it should, so that it can use the same identifier for the service across all lookup services). These objects are shown in Figure 6-1.

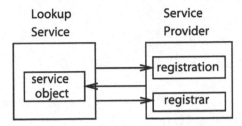

Figure 6-1. *Objects in service registration*

Other methods such as the following can be used to change the entry attributes stored on the lookup service:

```
void addAttributes(Entry[] attrSets);
void modifyAttributes(Entry[] attrSetTemplates, Entry[] attrSets);
void setAttributes(Entry[] attrSets);
```

The final public method for the ServiceRegistration class is getLease(), which returns a Lease object that allows renewal or cancellation of the lease. This is discussed in more detail in Chapter 8.

The major task of the server is then over. It will have successfully exported the service to a number of lookup services. What the server then does depends on how long it needs to keep the service alive or registered. If the exported service can do everything that the service needs to do, and does not need to maintain long-term registration, then the server can simply exit. More commonly, if the exported service object acts as a proxy and needs to communicate back to the service, then the server can sleep so that it maintains the existence of the service. If the service needs to be reregistered before timeout occurs, then the server can also sleep in this situation.

The SimpleService Program

A unicast server that exports its service and does nothing else is shown in the following program:

```
package basic;
import net.jini.core.discovery.LookupLocator;
import net.jini.core.lookup.ServiceRegistrar;
import net.jini.core.lookup.ServiceItem;
import net.jini.core.lookup.ServiceRegistration;
import java.io.Serializable;
import java.rmi.RMISecurityManager;
/**
 * SimpleService.java
```

```java
*/
public class SimpleService implements Serializable {

    static public void main(String argv[]) {
        new SimpleService();
    }

    public SimpleService() {
        LookupLocator lookup = null;
        ServiceRegistrar registrar = null;
        System.setSecurityManager(new RMISecurityManager());
        try {
            lookup = new LookupLocator("jini://localhost");
        } catch(java.net.MalformedURLException e) {
            System.err.println("Lookup failed: " + e.toString());
            System.exit(1);
        }
        try {
            registrar = lookup.getRegistrar();
        } catch (java.io.IOException e) {
            System.err.println("Registrar search failed: " + e.toString());
            System.exit(1);
        } catch (java.lang.ClassNotFoundException e) {
            System.err.println("Registrar search failed: " + e.toString());
            System.exit(1);
        }
        System.out.println("Found a registrar");
        // register ourselves as service, with no serviceID
        // or set of attributes
        ServiceItem item = new ServiceItem(null, this, null);
        ServiceRegistration reg = null;
        try {
            // ask to register for 10,000,000 milliseconds
            reg = registrar.register(item, 10000000L);
        } catch(java.rmi.RemoteException e) {
            System.err.println("Register exception: " + e.toString());
        }
        System.out.println("Service registered with registration id: " +
                            reg.getServiceID());
        // we can exit here if the exported service object can do
        // everything, or we can sleep if it needs to communicate
        // to us or we need to renew a lease later
        //
        // Typically, we will need to renew a lease later
    }

} // SimpleService
```

Running the SimpleService Program

The SimpleService program needs to be compiled and run with jsk-platform.jar and jsk-lib.jar in its CLASSPATH. In order to run the program, a security policy must be specified, as it uses an RMIClassLoader.

When run, the SimpleService program will attempt to connect to the service locator, so obviously one needs to be running on the machine specified in order for this to happen. Otherwise, the program will throw an exception and terminate.

The instance data for the service object is transferred in serialized form across socket connections. The instance data is kept in this serialized form by the lookup services. Later, when a client asks for the service to be reconstituted, it will use this instance data and also will need the class files. At this point, the class files will also need to be transferred, probably by an HTTP server. There is no need for additional RMI support services, such as rmiregistry or rmid, since all registration is done by the register() method.

An Ant file to build and run the SimpleService program is basic.SimpleService.xml:

```
<project name="basic.SimpleService" default="usage">
    <!-- Inherits properties
        jini.home
        jini.jars
        src
        dist
        build
        httpd.classes
    -->
    <!-- files for this project -->
    <property name="src.files"
            value="
                    basic/SimpleService.java
                "/>
    <property name="class.files"
            value="
                    basic/SimpleService.class
                "/>
    <property name="class.files.dl"
            value="
                "/>
    <property name="no-dl" value="true"/>
    <!-- derived names - may be changed -->
    <property name="jar.file"
            value="${ant.project.name}.jar"/>
    <property name="jar.file.dl"
            value="${ant.project.name}-dl.jar"/>
    <property name="main.class"
            value="${ant.project.name}"/>
    <property name="jini.jars.start"
            value="${jini.jars}:${jini.home}/lib/start.jar"/>
    <!-- targets -->
```

```
    <target name="all" depends="compile"/>
    <target name="compile">
        <javac destdir="${build}" srcdir="${src}"
               classpath="${jini.jars.start}"
               includes="${src.files}">
        </javac>
    </target>
    <target name="dist" depends="compile"
            description="generate the distribution">
        <jar jarfile="${dist}/${jar.file}"
             basedir="${build}"
             includes="${class.files}"/>
        <antcall target="dist-jar-dl"/>
    </target>
    <target name="dist-jar-dl" unless="no-dl">
        <jar jarfile="${dist}/${jar.file.dl}"
             basedir="${build}"
             includes="${class.files.dl}"/>
    </target>
    <target name="build" depends="dist,compile"/>
    <target name="run" depends="build">
        <java classname="${main.class}"
              fork="true"
              classpath="${jini.jars.start}:${dist}/${jar.file}">
            <jvmarg value="-Djava.security.policy=${res}/policy.all"/>
        </java>
    </target>
    <target name="deploy" depends="dist" unless="no-dl">
        <copy file="${dist}/${jar.file.dl}"
              todir="${httpd.classes}"/>
    </target>
</project>
```

Information from the ServiceRegistration

The ServiceRegistrar object's register() method is used to register the service, and in doing so returns a ServiceRegistration object. This object can be used to give information about the registration itself. The relevant methods are as follows:

```
ServiceID getServiceID();
Lease getLease();
```

The service ID can be stored by the application if it is going to reregister later. The lease object can be used to control the lease granted by the lookup locator, and will be discussed in more detail in Chapter 8. For now, we can just use the lease object to find out how long the lease has been granted for by using its getExpiration() method:

```
long duration = reg.getLease().getExpiration() -
                System.currentTimeMillis();
```

```
System.out.println("Lease expires at: " +
                   duration +
                   " milliseconds from now");
```

Service ID

A service is unique in the world. It runs on a particular machine and performs certain tasks. However, it will probably register itself with many lookup services; it should have the same "identity" on all of these. In addition, if either the service or one of these locators crashes or restarts, then this identity should be the same as before.

The ServiceID plays the role of unique identifier for a service. It is a 128-bit number generated in a pseudo-random manner, and it should be effectively unique—the chance that a generator might duplicate this number is vanishingly small. There are two ways to get a service ID: ask a lookup service for one or generate it yourself.

If the first argument to ServiceItem is null, this is a request to a lookup service to generate and return a service ID. The returned service ID can then be used as the first parameter to other lookup services. This used to be the preferred method, but if you register with multiple lookup services, it can lead to slightly messy logic.

These days, the preferred method seems to be for a service to generate the service ID itself and give this to all the lookup services it finds, as follows:

```
import net.jini.id.Uuid;
import net.jini.id.Uuidfactory;
Uuid uuid = UuidFactory.generate();
ServiceID serviceID = new ServiceID(uuid.getMostSignificantBits(),
                                    uuid.getLeastSignificantBits());
```

Entries

A service can announce a number of entry attributes when it registers itself with a lookup service. It does so by preparing an array of Entry objects and passing them into the ServiceItem used in the register() method of the registrar. There is no limitation to the amount of information the service can include; in later searches by clients, each entry is treated as though it was OR'ed with the other entries. In other words, the more entries that are given by the service, the greater the chance of matching a client's requirements.

For example, suppose we have a coffee machine on the seventh floor of our building, which is known as both "GP South Building" and "General Purpose South Building." Information such as this, and general information about the coffee machine, can be encapsulated in the convenience classes Location and Comment from the net.jini.lookup.entry package. If this were on our network as a service, it would advertise itself as follows:

```
import net.jini.lookup.entry.Location;
import net.jini.lookup.entry.Comment;
Location loc1 = new Location("7", "728",
                             "GP South Building");
Location loc2 = new Location("7", "728",
                             "General Purpose South Building");
Comment comment = new Comment("DSTC coffee machine");
```

```
Entry[] entries = new Entry[] {loc1, loc2, comment};
ServiceItem item = new ServiceItem(..., ..., entries);
registrar.register(item, ...);
```

Summary

As you learned in this chapter, a service uses the ServiceRegistrar object, which is returned as a proxy from a locator, to register itself with that locator. The service prepares a ServiceItem that contains a service object and a set of entries, and the service object may be a proxy for the real service. It registers this service object and entry information using the register() method of the ServiceRegistrar object. Information about a registration is returned as a ServiceRegistration object, which may be queried for information such as the lease and its duration.

CHAPTER 7

■ ■ ■

Client Search

This chapter looks at what the client has to do once it has found a lookup service and wishes to find a service. From the lookup service, the client will get a ServiceRegistrar object. To find a service from the lookup service, the client needs to prepare a description of the service, which it does using a ServiceTemplate object. The client will then call one of two methods on the ServiceRegistrar to return either a single matching service or a set of matching services.

Searching for Services with the ServiceRegistrar

A client gets a ServiceRegistrar object from the lookup service, and it uses this object to search for a service stored on the lookup service using the lookup() method:

```
public Class ServiceRegistrar {
    public java.lang.Object lookup(ServiceTemplate tmpl)
                            throws java.rmi.RemoteException;
    public ServiceMatches lookup(ServiceTemplate tmpl,
                                  int maxMatches)
                            throws java.rmi.RemoteException;
}
```

The first of these methods just finds a service that matches the request. The second finds a set (up to maxMatches) requested.

The lookup methods use a class of type ServiceTemplate to specify the service looked for:

```
package net.jini.core.lookup;
public Class ServiceTemplate {
    public ServiceID serviceID;
    public java.lang.Class[] serviceTypes;
    public Entry[] attributeSetTemplates;
    ServiceTemplate(ServiceID serviceID,
                    java.lang.Class[] serviceTypes,
                    Entry[] attrSetTemplates);
}
```

Although each service should have been assigned a serviceID by a lookup service, a client might not know the serviceID (e.g., it could be the first time the client has looked for this service). In this case, the serviceID is set to null. If the client does know the serviceID, then it can set the value to find the service. The attributeSetTemplates is a set of Entry elements used to match attributes, as discussed later in this chapter in the "Matching Services" section.

The major parameter of the lookup() method is a list of serviceTypes. We know that services export instances of a class, but how does the client ask so that it gets a suitable instance delivered from the lookup service? Although the lookup services keep instances of objects for the service, the client will only know about a service from its specification (unless it already has a serviceID for the service). The specification will almost certainly be a Java interface, so the client needs to ask using this interface. An interface can have a class object in the same way as ordinary classes, so the list of serviceTypes will typically be a list of class objects for service interfaces.

To be more concrete, suppose a toaster is defined by this interface:

```java
public interface Toaster extends java.io.Serializable {
    public void setDarkness(int dark);
    public void startToasting();
}
```

A Breville "Extra Lift" toaster would implement this interface in one particular way, as would other toasters:

```java
public class BrevilleExtraLiftToaster implements Toaster {
    public void setDarkness(int dark) {
        ...
    }
    public void startToasting() {
        ...
    }
}
```

When the toaster service starts, it exports an object of class BrevilleExtraLiftToaster to the lookup service. However, the client does not know what type of toaster is out there, so it will make a request like this:

```java
System.setSecurityManager(new RMISecurityManager());
// specify the interface object
Class[] toasterClasses = new Class[1];
toasterClasses[0] = Toaster.class;
// prepare a search template of serviceID, classes, and entries
ServiceTemplate template = new ServiceTemplate(null,
                                               toasterClasses,
                                               null);

// now find a toaster
Toaster toaster = null;
try {
    toaster = (Toaster) registrar.lookup(template);
} catch(java.rmi.RemoteException e) {
    System.exit(2);
}
```

Notice that lookup() can throw an exception. This can occur if, for example, the service requested cannot be deserialized.

As a result of calling the lookup() method, an object (an instance of a class implementing the Toaster interface) has been transported across to the client, and the object has been coerced to be of this Toaster type. This object has two methods: setDarkness() and startToasting(). No other information is available about the toaster's capabilities, because the interface does not specify any more, and in this case the set of attribute values was null. So the client can call either of the two methods:

```
toaster.setDarkness(1);
toaster.startToasting();
```

Before leaving this section, you might wonder what the role of System.setSecurityManager (new RMISecurityManager()) is. A serialized object has been transported across the network and is reconstituted and coerced to an object implementing Toaster. We know that here it will, in fact, be an object of class BrevilleExtraLiftToaster, but the client doesn't need to know that. Or does it? Certainly the client will not have a class definition for this class on its side. But when the toaster object begins to run, then it must run using its BrevilleExtraLiftToaster code! Where does it get this code from?

From the server—most likely by an HTTP request on the server. This means that the Toaster object is *loading a class definition* across the network, and this requires security access. So a security manager capable of granting this access must be installed before the load request is made.

Note the difference between loading a serialized instance and loading a class definition: the first does not require access rights; only the second one does. So if the client had the class definitions of all possible toasters, then it would never need to load a class and would not need a security manager that allows classes to be loaded across the network. This is not likely, but may perhaps be needed in a high-security environment.

Receiving the ServiceMatches Object

If a client wishes to search for more than one match to a service request from a particular lookup service, then it specifies the maximum number of matches it would like returned by the maxMatches parameter of the second lookup() method. The client gets back a ServiceMatches object that looks like this:

```
package net.jini.core.lookup;
public Class ServiceMatches {
    public ServiceItem[] items;
    public int totalMatches ;
}
```

The number of elements in items need not be the same as totalMatches. Suppose there are five matching services stored on the lookup service. In that case, totalMatches will be set to 5 after a lookup. However, if you only specified to search for at most two matches, then items will be set to be an array with only two elements.

In addition, not all elements of this array need be non-null! Note that in lookup(tmpl) when asking for only one match, an exception can be returned, such as when the service is not serializable. No exception is thrown here, because although one match might be bad, the others may still be OK. So a value of null as the array element value is used to signify this:

```
ServiceMatches matches = registrar.lookup(template, 10);
// NB: matches.totalMatches may be greater than matches.items.length
for (int n = 0; n < matches.items.length; n++) {
    Toaster toaster = (Toaster) matches.items[n].service;
    if (toaster != null) {
        toaster.setDarkness(1);
        toaster.startToasting();
    }
}
```

This code will start up to ten toasters cooking at once!

Matching Services

As mentioned previously, a client attempts to find one or more services that satisfy its requirements by creating a ServiceTemplate object and using this in a registrar's lookup() call. A ServiceTemplate object has three fields:

```
ServiceID          serviceID;
java.lang.Class[]  serviceTypes;
Entry[]            attributeSetTemplates;
```

If the client is repeating a request, then it may have recorded the serviceID from an earlier request. The serviceID is a universally unique identifier (UUID), so it can be used to identify a service unambiguously. This serviceID can be used by the lookup service as a filter to quickly discard other services.

Alternatively, a client may want to find a service satisfying several interface requirements at once. For example, a client may look for a service that implements both Toaster and FireAlarm (so that it can properly handle burnt toast).

And finally, the client will specify a set of attributes that must be satisfied by each service. Each attribute required by the client is taken in turn and matched against the set offered by the service. For example, in addition to requesting a Toaster with a FireAlarm, a client entry may specify a location in GP South Building. This will be tried against all the variations of location offered by the service. A single match is good enough. An additional client requirement of, say, manufacturer would also have to be matched by the service.

The more formal description from the ServiceTemplate API documentation follows:

- A service item (item) matches a service template (tmpl) if item.serviceID equals tmpl.serviceID (or if tmpl.serviceID is null); and item.service is an instance of every type in tmpl.serviceTypes; and item.attributeSets contains at least one matching entry for each entry template in tmpl.attributeSetTemplates.

- An entry matches an entry template if the class of the template is the same as, or a superclass of, the class of the entry, and every non-null field in the template equals the corresponding field of the entry. Every entry can be used to match more than one template. Note that in a service template, for serviceTypes and attributeSetTemplates, a null field is equivalent to an empty array; both represent a wildcard.

Summary

As described in this chapter, a client prepares a `ServiceTemplate`, which is a list of class objects and a list of entries. For each lookup service that is found, the client can query the lookup service using the `ServiceRegistrar` object's `lookup()` method, to see if the lookup service has a service matching the template. If the match is successful, an object is returned that can be cast into the class required. Service methods can then be invoked on this object.

CHAPTER 8

■■■

Leasing

In distributed applications, there may be partial failures of the network or of components on the network. *Leasing* is a way for components to register that they are alive, but to ensure that they are "timed out" if they fail or are unreachable. Leasing is the mechanism used between applications to give access to resources over a period of time in an agreed-upon manner.

Leases are requested for periods of time, and these requests may be granted, modified, or denied. The most common example of a lease is when a service is registered with lookup services. A lookup service will not want to keep a service forever, because it may disappear. Keeping information about nonexistent services is a waste of resources on the lookup service and also may lead to clients wasting time trying to access services that aren't there. As a result, a lookup service will grant a lease saying that it will only keep information for a certain period of time, and the service can renew the lease later if desired.

Requesting and Receiving Leases

Leases are requested for a period of time. In Jini, a common use of leasing is for a service to request that a copy of the service be kept on a lookup service for a certain length of time, for delivery to clients on request. The service requests a time in the ServiceRegistrar's register() method. Two special values of the time are as follows:

- Lease.ANY: The service lets the lookup service decide on the time.

- Lease.FOREVER: The request is for a lease that never expires.

The lookup service acts as the granter of the lease and decides how long it will actually create the lease for. (The lookup service from Sun typically sets the lease time as only five minutes.) Once it has done that, it will attempt to ensure that the request is honored for that period of time. The lease is returned to the service and is accessible through the getLease() method of the ServiceRegistration object. These objects are shown in Figure 8-1.

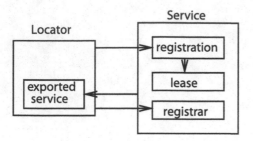

Figure 8-1. *Objects in a leased system*

```
ServiceRegistration reg = registrar.register();
Lease lease = reg.getLease();
```

The principal methods of the Lease object are as follows:

```
package net.jini.core;
public interface Lease {
    void cancel() throws
                UnknownLeaseException,
                java.rmi.RemoteException;
    long getExpiration();
    void renew(long duration) throws
                LeaseDeniedException,
                UnknownLeaseException,
                java.rmi.RemoteException;
}
```

The expiration value from getExpiration() is the time in milliseconds since the beginning of the epoch (the same as in System.currentTimeMillis()). To find the amount of time still remaining from the present, the current time can be subtracted from this, as follows:

```
long duration = lease.getExpiration() - System.currentTimeMillis();
```

Cancellation

A service can cancel its lease by using cancel(). The lease communicates back to the lease management system on the lookup service, which cancels storage of the service.

Expiration

When a lease expires, it does so silently. That is, the lease granter (the lookup service) will not inform the lease holder (the service) that it has expired. While it might seem nice to get warning of a lease expiring so that it can be renewed, this would have to be in advance of the expiration (e.g., "I'm just about to expire; please renew me quickly!"), but this would complicate the leasing system and not be completely reliable anyway (e.g., how far in advance is soon enough?).

Instead, it is up to the service to call renew() before the lease expires if it wishes the lease to continue.

Renewing Leases

Jini supplies a LeaseRenewalManager class that looks after the process of calling renew() at suitable times.

```
package net.jini.lease;
public Class LeaseRenewalManager {
    public LeaseRenewalManager();
    public LeaseRenewalManager(Lease lease,
                               long expiration,
                               LeaseListener listener);
    public void renewFor(Lease lease, long duration,
                         LeaseListener listener);
    public void renewUntil(Lease lease,
                           long expiration,
                           LeaseListener listener);
    // etc
}
```

The LeaseRenewalManager manages a set of leases, which may be set by the constructor or added later by renewFor() or renewUntil(). The time requested in these methods is in milliseconds. The expiration time is measured since the epoch, whereas the duration time is measured from now.

Generally, leases will be renewed and the manager will function quietly. However, the lookup service may decide not to renew a lease and will cause an exception to be thrown. This exception will be caught by the renewal manager and will cause the listener's notify() method to be called with a LeaseRenewalEvent as a parameter, which will allow the application to take corrective action if its lease is denied. If the listener is null, then no notification will take place.

Granting and Handling Leases

The preceding discussion looked at leases from the side of the client that receives a lease and has to manage it. The converse of this is the agent that grants leases and has to manage things from its side. This section contains more advanced material that you can feel free to skip for now; it is not needed until Chapter 16. An example of creating a lease is also presented in Chapter 15.

A lease can be granted for almost any remote service—any one where one object wants to maintain information about another one that is not within the same virtual machine. As with other remote services, there are the added partial failure modes, such as network crash, remote service crash, timeouts, and so on. An object that keeps information on a remote service will hand out a lease to the service and will want the remote service to keep "pinging" it periodically to say that it is alive and that it wants the information kept. Without this periodic assurance, the object might conclude that the remote service has vanished or is somehow unreachable, and that it should discard the information about it.

Leases are a very general mechanism for allowing one service to have confidence in the existence of the other for a limited period. Because they are general, they allow for a great deal of flexibility in use. Because of the possible variety of services, some parts of the Jini lease mechanism cannot be completely defined and must be left as interfaces for applications to fill in. This generality means that all of the details are not filled in for you, as your own requirements cannot be completely predicted in advance.

A lease is given as an interface, and any agent that wishes to grant leases must implement this interface.

```
package net.jini.core.lease;
import java.rmi.RemoteException;
public interface Lease {
    long FOREVER;
    long ANY;
    long getExpiration();
    void cancel() throws UnknownLeaseException, RemoteException;
    void renew(long duration)
        throws LeaseDeniedException, UnknownLeaseException,
            RemoteException;
    void setSerialFormat(int format);
    int getSerialFormat();
    LeaseMap createLeaseMap(long duration);
    boolean canBatch(Lease lease);
}
```

Jini provides three implementations: an AbstractLease, and a subclass of this, a LandlordLease, which in turn has a subclass ConstrainableLandlordLease.

The main issues in implementing a particular lease class lie in setting a policy for handling the initial request for a lease period and in deciding what to do when a renewal request comes in. Some simple possibilities are as follows:

- Always grant the requested time.

- Ignore the requested time and always grant a fixed time.

Of course, there are many more possibilities based on the lessor's expected TTL, system load, and so forth.

There are other issues, though. Any particular lease will need a timeout mechanism. Also, a group of leases can be managed together, and this can reduce the amount of overhead of managing individual leases.

Abstract Lease

An *abstract lease* gives a basic implementation of a lease that can almost be used for simple leases.

```
package com.sun.jini.lease;
public abstract class AbstractLease implements Lease, java.io.Serializable {
    protected AbstractLease(long expiration);
    public long getExpiration();
    public int getSerialFormat();
    public void setSerialFormat(int format);
    public void renew(long duration);
    protected abstract long doRenew(long duration);
}
```

This class supplies straightforward implementations of much of the Lease interface, with three provisos:

- The constructor is protected, so that constructing a lease with a specified duration is devolved to a subclass. This means that lease duration policy must be set by this subclass.

- The renew() method calls into the abstract doRenew() method, again to force a subclass to implement a renewal policy.

- The Lease interface does not implement the cancel() and createLeaseMap() methods, so these must also be left to a subclass.

Thus, this class implements the easy things and leaves all matters of policy to concrete subclasses.

Landlord Package

The *landlord* is a package that allows more complex leasing systems to be built. It is not part of the Jini specification, but is supplied as a set of classes and interfaces. The set is not complete in itself—some parts are left as interfaces and need to have class implementations. These will be supplied by a particular application.

A landlord looks after a set of leases. Leases are identified to the landlord by a *cookie*, which is a unique identifier (Uuid) for each lease. A landlord does not need to create leases itself; it can use a *landlord lease factory* to do this. (But of course the landlord *can* create leases, depending on how an implementation is done.) When a client wishes to cancel or renew a lease, it asks the lease to perform the cancellation or renewal, and in turn the lease asks its landlord to perform the action. A client is unlikely to ask the landlord directly, as it will only have been given a lease, not a landlord.

The principal classes and interfaces in the landlord package are shown in Figure 8-2, where the interfaces are shown in italic font and the classes in normal font.

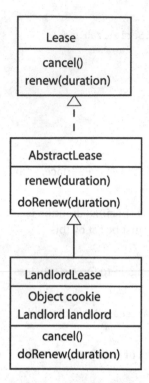

Figure 8-2. *Class diagram in the landlord package*

The interfaces assume that they will be implemented in certain ways, in that each implementation class will contain a reference to certain other interfaces. This doesn't show in the interface specifications, but can be inferred from the method calls.

For example, suppose we wish to develop a lease mechanism for a Foo resource. We would create a FooLandlord to create and manage leases for Foo objects. A minimal structure for this could be as shown in Figure 8-3.

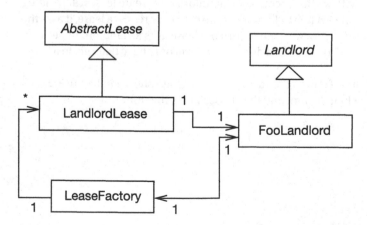

Figure 8-3. *Class diagram of a minimal landlord implementation*

The landlord creates a lease factory and asks it to create leases. Each lease contains a reference to its landlord. When requests are made of the lease, such as renew( ), these are passed to the landlord to make a decision. However, the renew( ) request to the landlord does *not* pass in the lease, but just its UUID.

Information missing from Figure 8-3 includes how the resource itself is dealt with, where leases end up, and how leasing granting and renewal decisions are made:

- Leases are given to the client that is requesting a lease. Calls such as renew( ) are remote calls to the landlord. The landlord doesn't need a copy of the lease, but does need some representation of it, and that is the purpose of the cookie: it acts as a lessor-side representation of the lease.

- The resource being leased has a representation on the lessor. For example, a lookup service would have the marshalled form of the service proxy to manage. The lessor needs to have this representation plus the lease handle (the cookie) and information such as the lease duration and expiration. This information is given in an implementation of the LeasedResource interface.

- Decisions about granting or renewing leases would need to be made using the LeasedResource. While these decisions could be made by the landlord, it is cleaner to hand such a task to a separate object concerned with such policy decisions, which is the function of LeasePeriodPolicy objects. For example, the FixedLeasePeriodPolicy has a simple policy that grants lease times based on a fixed default and maximum lease.

These considerations lead to a more complex class diagram involving the resource and the policy classes, shown in Figure 8-4.

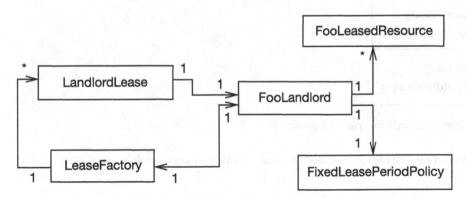

Figure 8-4. *Class diagram in a landlord implementation*

In this context, let's now consider some of these classes in more detail.

LandlordLease Class

The LandlordLease class extends AbstractLease. This class has the private fields cookie and landlord, as shown in Figure 8-5.

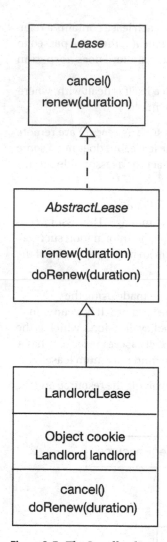

Figure 8-5. *The LandlordLease class diagram*

Implementation of the cancel() and doRenew() methods in LandlordLease is deferred to its landlord.

```
public void cancel() {
    landlord.cancel(cookie);
}
protected long doRenew(long renewDuration) {
    return landlord.renew(cookie, renewDuration);
}
```

The LandlordLease class can be used as is, with no subclassing needed. Note that the landlord system produces these leases, but does not actually keep them anywhere; they are passed on to clients, which then use the lease to call the landlord and hence interact with the landlord lease system. Within the landlord system, the cookie is used as an identifier for the lease.

LeasedResource Interface

A LeasedResource is a convenience wrapper around a resource that includes extra information about a lease and methods for use by landlords. It defines an interface as follows:

```
public interface LeasedResource {
    public void setExpiration(long newExpiration);
    public long getExpiration();
    public Uuid getCookie();
}
```

This interface includes the cookie, a unique identifier for a lease within a landlord system, as well as expiration information for the lease. This is all the information maintained about the lease that has been given out to a client.

An implementation of LeasedResource will typically include the resource that is leased, plus a method of setting the cookie. The following code shows an example:

```
/**
 * FooLeasedResource.java
 */
package foolandlord;
import com.sun.jini.landlord.LeasedResource;
import net.jini.id.Uuid;
import net.jini.id.UuidFactory;
public class FooLeasedResource implements LeasedResource  {

    protected Uuid cookie;
    protected Foo foo;
    protected long expiration = 0;
    public FooLeasedResource(Foo foo) {
        this.foo = foo;
        cookie = UuidFactory.generate();
    }
    public void setExpiration(long newExpiration) {
        this.expiration = newExpiration;
    }
    public long getExpiration() {
        return expiration;
    }
    public Uuid getCookie() {
        return cookie;
    }
    public Foo getFoo() {
        return foo;
    }
} // FooLeasedResource
```

LeasePeriodPolicy Interface

A lease policy is used when a lease is first granted, and when it tries to renew itself. The time requested may be granted, modified, or denied. A lease policy is specified by the LeasePeriodPolicy interface.

```
package com.sun.jini.landlord;
public interface LeasePeriodPolicy {
    LeasePeriodPolicy.Result grant(LeasedResource resource, long requestedDuration);
    LeasePeriodPolicy.Result renew(LeasedResource resource, long requestedDuration);
}
```

An implementation of this policy is given by the FixedLeasePeriodPolicy. The constructor takes maximum and default lease values. It uses these to grant and renew leases.

Landlord Interface

The Landlord is the final interface in the package that we need for a basic landlord system. Other classes and interfaces, such as LeaseMap, are for handling of leases in batches, and will not be dealt with here. The Landlord interface is as follows:

```
package com.sun.jini.lease.landlord;
public interface Landlord extends Remote {
    public long renew(Uuid cookie, long extension)
        throws LeaseDeniedException, UnknownLeaseException, RemoteException;
    public void cancel(Uuid cookie)
        throws UnknownLeaseException, RemoteException;
    public RenewResults renewAll(Object[] cookies, long[] durations)
        throws RemoteException;

    public Map cancelAll(Uuid[] cookies)
        throws RemoteException;
}
```

The renew() and cancel() methods are usually called from the renew() and cancel() methods of a particular lease. An implementation of Landlord, such as FooLandlord, will probably have a table of LeasedResource objects indexed by the Uuid, so that it can work out which resource the request is about.

For any implementation of the Landlord interface, the methods renewAll() and cancelAll() will clearly just loop through the cookies and call renew() and cancel(), respectively, on each cookie. A convenience class, LandlordUtil, has the methods renewAll() and cancelAll(), which just do that, saving the programmer from having to write the same code for each implementation. This utility class needs to have an object that implements just renew() and cancel(), and the LocalLandlord interface has these two methods. So by making our FooLandlord also implement this interface, we can use the utility class to reduce the code we need to write.

The landlord won't make decisions itself about renewals. The renew() method needs to use a policy object to ask for renewal. In the FooManager implementation, it uses a FixedLeasePeriodPolicy.

There must be a method to ask for a new lease for a resource, and this is not specified by the landlord package. This request will probably be made on the lease-granting side, and this should have access to the landlord object, which forms a central point for lease management. So the FooLandlord will quite likely have a method such as the following:

```
public Lease newFooLease(Foo foo, long duration);
```

which will give a lease for a resource.

The lease used in the landlord package is a LandlordLease. This contains a private field, which is a reference to the landlord itself. The lease is given to a client as a result of newFooLease(), and this client will usually be a remote object. Giving the lease to the client will involve serializing the lease and sending it to this remote client. While serializing the lease, the landlord field will also be serialized and sent to the client.

When the client methods such as renew() are called, the implementation of the LandlordLease will make a call to the landlord, which by then will be remote from its origin. So the landlord object invoked by the lease will need to be a remote object making a remote call. In Jini 1.2, this would have been done by making FooLandlord a subclass of UnicastRemoteObject. In Jini 2.0, this is preferably done by explicitly exporting the landlord to get a proxy object. The code that follows uses a BasicJeriExporter (for simplicity), but it would be better to use a configuration.

Putting all this together for the FooLandlord class gives us this:

```
/**
 * FooLandlord.java
 */
package foolandlord;
import net.jini.core.lease.UnknownLeaseException;
import net.jini.core.lease.LeaseDeniedException;
import net.jini.core.lease.Lease;
import net.jini.jeri.BasicJeriExporter;
import net.jini.jeri.BasicILFactory;
import net.jini.jeri.tcp.TcpServerEndpoint;
import net.jini.export.*;
import java.rmi.Remote;
import java.rmi.RemoteException;
import java.util.Map;
import java.util.HashMap;
import net.jini.id.Uuid;
import com.sun.jini.landlord.Landlord;
import com.sun.jini.landlord.LeaseFactory;
import com.sun.jini.landlord.LeasedResource;
import com.sun.jini.landlord.FixedLeasePeriodPolicy;
import com.sun.jini.landlord.LeasePeriodPolicy;
import com.sun.jini.landlord.LeasePeriodPolicy.Result;
import com.sun.jini.landlord.Landlord.RenewResults;
import com.sun.jini.landlord.LandlordUtil;
import com.sun.jini.landlord.LocalLandlord;
import net.jini.id.UuidFactory;
```

```
public class FooLandlord implements Landlord, LocalLandlord {
    private static final long MAX_LEASE = Lease.FOREVER;
    private static final long DEFAULT_LEASE = 1000*60*5; // 5 minutes
    private Map leasedResourceMap = new HashMap();
    private LeasePeriodPolicy policy = new
        FixedLeasePeriodPolicy(MAX_LEASE, DEFAULT_LEASE);
    private Uuid myUuid = UuidFactory.generate();
    private LeaseFactory factory;
    public FooLandlord() throws java.rmi.RemoteException {
        Exporter exporter = new
            BasicJeriExporter(TcpServerEndpoint.getInstance(0),
                            new BasicILFactory());
        Landlord proxy = (Landlord) exporter.export(this);
        factory = new LeaseFactory(proxy, myUuid);
    }

    public void cancel(Uuid cookie) throws UnknownLeaseException {
        if (leasedResourceMap.remove(cookie) == null) {
            throw new UnknownLeaseException();
        }
    }
    public Map cancelAll(Uuid[] cookies) {
        return LandlordUtil.cancelAll(this, cookies);
    }
    public long renew(Uuid cookie,
                    long extension) throws LeaseDeniedException,
                                        UnknownLeaseException {
        LeasedResource resource = (LeasedResource)
            leasedResourceMap.get(cookie);
        LeasePeriodPolicy.Result result = null;
        if (resource != null) {
            result = policy.renew(resource, extension);
        } else {
            throw new UnknownLeaseException();
        }
        return result.duration;
    }
    public Landlord.RenewResults renewAll(Uuid[] cookies, long[] durations) {
        return LandlordUtil.renewAll(this, cookies, durations);
    }
    public LeasePeriodPolicy.Result grant(LeasedResource resource,
                                        long requestedDuration)
        throws LeaseDeniedException {
        Uuid cookie = resource.getCookie();
        try {
            leasedResourceMap.put(cookie, resource);
        } catch(Exception e) {
```

```
                throw new LeaseDeniedException(e.toString());
        }
        return policy.grant(resource, requestedDuration);
    }
    public Lease newFooLease(Foo foo, long duration)
        throws LeaseDeniedException {
        FooLeasedResource resource = new FooLeasedResource(foo);
        Uuid cookie = resource.getCookie();
        // find out how long we should grant the lease for
        LeasePeriodPolicy.Result result = grant(resource, duration);
        long expiration = result.expiration;
        resource.setExpiration(expiration);
        Lease lease = factory.newLease(cookie, expiration);
        return lease;
    }
    public static void main(String[] args) throws RemoteException,
                                         LeaseDeniedException,
                                         UnknownLeaseException {
        // simple test harness

        long DURATION = 2000; // 2 secs;

        FooLandlord landlord = new FooLandlord();
        Lease lease = landlord.newFooLease(new Foo(), DURATION);
        long duration = lease.getExpiration() - System.currentTimeMillis();
        System.out.println("Lease granted for " + duration + " msecs");
        try {
            Thread.sleep(1000);
        } catch(InterruptedException e) {
            // ignore
        }
        lease.renew(5000);
        duration = lease.getExpiration() - System.currentTimeMillis();
        System.out.println("Lease renewed for " + duration + " msecs");
        lease.cancel();
        System.out.println("Lease cancelled");
    }
} // FooLandlord
```

The Ant file for this is similar to those given before. I only give the parts that are different this time:

```
<!-- Source files for the server -->
<property name="src.files"
        value="
                foolandlord/Foo.java
                foolandlord/FooLeasedResource.java
```

```
                    foolandlord/FooLandlord.java
                "/>
<!-- Class files to run the server -->
<property name="class.files"
        value="
                foolandlord/Foo.class
                foolandlord/FooLeasedResource.class
                foolandlord/FooLandlord.class
                "/>
<!-- Class files for the client to download -->
<property name="class.files.dl"
        value="
                "/>
```

Summary

Leasing allows resources to be managed without complex garbage collection mechanisms. Leases received from services can be dealt with easily using LeaseRenewalManager. Entities that need to hand out leases can use a system, such as the landlord system, to handle these leases.

■ ■ ■

CHAPTER 9

A Simple Example

This chapter looks at a simple problem to give a complete example of a Jini service and client.

Before a Jini service can be built, common knowledge must be defined about the type of service that will be offered. This involves designing a set of "well-known" classes and interfaces. Based on a well-known interface, a client can be written to search for and use services implementing the interface.

The client can use either a unicast or multicast search to find services, but it will be uninterested in how any particular service is implemented. This chapter looks at building clients using both methods, and these clients will be heavily reused throughout the rest of the book.

The service, on the other hand, is implemented by each vendor in a different way. This chapter discusses a simple choice, with alternatives being dealt with in Chapter 11. It is difficult to get a Jini service and client functioning correctly, as there are many configuration issues to be dealt with. These are discussed in some detail.

By the end of this chapter you should be able to build a client and a service, and configure your system so that they are able to run and communicate with each other.

Problem Description

Applications often need to work out the type of a file, to see if it is a text file, an HTML document, an executable, and so forth. This can be done in two ways:

- By examining the file's name

- By examining the file's contents

Utilities such as the Unix file command use the second method and have a complex description file (such as /etc/magic or /usr/share/magic) to aid in this. Many other applications, such as web browsers, mail readers, and even some operating systems, use the first method and work out a file's type based on its name.

A common way of classifying files is into MIME types, such as text/plain and image/gif. There are tables of "official" MIME types (unofficial ones can be added on an ad hoc basis), and there are also tables of mappings from file name endings to corresponding MIME types. These tables have entries such as these:

```
application/postscript      ai eps ps
application/rtf             rtf
application/zip             zip
image/gif                  gif
```

```
image/jpeg                      jpeg jpg jpe
text/html                       html htm
text/plain                      txt
```

These tables are stored in files for applications to access.

Storing these tables separately from the applications that would use them is considered bad from the object-oriented point of view, since each application would need to have code to interpret the tables. Also, the multiplicity of these tables and the ability of users to modify them makes this a maintenance problem. It would be better to encapsulate at least the file name to a MIME type mapping table in an object.

We could define a MIME class as follows:

```java
package common;
import java.io.Serializable;
/**
 * MIMEType.java
 */
public class MIMEType implements Serializable {
    /**
     * A MIME type is made up of 2 parts
     * contentType/subtype
     */
    private String contentType;
    private String subType;
    public MIMEType() {
        // empty constructor required just in case
        // we want to use this as a Java Bean
    }
    public MIMEType(String type) {
        int slash = type.indexOf('/');
        contentType = type.substring(0, slash-1);
        subType = type.substring(slash+1, type.length());
    }

    public MIMEType(String contentType, String subType) {
        this.contentType = contentType;
        this.subType = subType;
    }
    public String toString() {
        return contentType + "/" + subType;
    }
    /**
     * Accessors/setters
     */
    public String getContentType() {
        return contentType;
```

```
    }
    public void setContentType(String type) {
        contentType = type;
    }
    public String getSubType() {
        return subType;
    }
    public void setSubType(String type) {
        subType = type;
    }
} // MIMEType
```

We could then define a mapping class like this:

```
package standalone;

/**
 * FileClassifier.java
 */

public class FileClassifier  {

    static MIMEType getMIMEType(String fileName) {
        if (fileName.endsWith(".gif")) {
            return new MIMEType("image", "gif");
        } else if (fileName.endsWith(".jpeg")) {
            return new MIMEType("image", "jpeg");
        } else if (fileName.endsWith(".mpg")) {
            return new MIMEType("video", "mpeg");
        } else if (fileName.endsWith(".txt")) {
            return new MIMEType("text", "plain");
        } else if (fileName.endsWith(".html")) {
            return new MIMEType("text", "html");
        } else
            // fill in lots of other types,
            // but eventually give up and
            return null;
    }
} // FileClassifier
```

This mapping class has no constructors, because it justs acts as a lookup table via its static method getMIMEType().

Applications can make use of these classes as they stand, by simply compiling them and having the class files available at runtime. This would still result in duplication throughout JVMs, possible multiple copies of the class files, and potentially severe maintenance problems if applications need to be recompiled, so it may be better to have the FileClassifier as a network service. Let's consider what would be involved in this.

Service Specification

If we wish to make a version of FileClassifier available across the network, there are a number of possibilities. The client will be asking for an instance of a class, and generally will not care too much about the details of this instance. For example, it will want an instance of a DiskDrive or a Calendar. Usually it will not care which drive it gets or which calendar. If it requires further specification, it can either ask for a subclass instance (such as a SeagateDiskDrive) or use an Entry object for this additional information.

Services will have particular implementations and will upload these to the service locators. The uploaded service will be of a specific class and may have associated entries.

The client can use several options when trying to locate a suitable service:

- This is the silly option: push the entire implementation up to the lookup service and make the client ask for it by its class. Then the client might just as well create the classifier as a local object, because it has all the information needed! This doesn't lend itself to flexibility with new unknown services coming along, because the client already has to know the details. So this option is not feasible.

- Let the client ask for a superclass of the service. This option is better than the previous one, as it allows new implementations of a service to just be implemented as new subclasses. It is not ideal, however, as classes have implementation code, and if this changes over time, there is a maintenance issue with the possibility of version "skew." This option can be used for Jini; it just isn't the best way.

- Separate the interface completely from the implementation. Make the interface available to the client, and upload the implementation to the lookup service. Then, when the client asks for an instance object that implements the interface, it will get *any* object for this interface. This will reduce maintenance: if the client is coded just in terms of the interface, then it will not need recompilation even if the implementation changes. Note that these words will translate straight into Java terms; the client knows about a Java interface, whereas the service provider deals in terms of a Java class that implements the interface.

The ideal mechanism in the Jini world is to specify services by Java interfaces and have all clients know this interface. Then each service can be an implementation of this interface. This is simple in Java terms, simple in specification terms, and simple for maintenance. This is not the complete set of choices for the service, but it is enough to allow a service to be specified and to get on with building the client. One possibility for service implementation is looked at later in this chapter, and Chapter 11 is devoted to the full range of possibilities.

Although I do not wish to get involved in discussions about which middleware is "best," I would like to note that consistent use of Java throughout Jini, and in particular its use for both specification and implementation, avoids many of the "mismatch" problems that can occur when specification and implementation occur in different languages. For example, Web Services use XML data types, and this is a very rich system distinct from the Java type system. It is not possible to represent all XML types in Java, nor all Java types in XML. This leads to either compromises with a "least common denominator" approach or to services that cannot be written or specified properly.

Common Classes

The client and any implementations of a service must share some common classes. For a file classification service, the common classes are the classifier itself (which can be implemented as many different services) and the return value, the MIMEType. These have to change very slightly from their stand-alone form.

MIMEType

The MIMEType class is known to the client and to any file classifier service. The MIMEType class files can be expected to be known to the JVMs of all clients and services. That is, these class files need to be in the CLASSPATH of every file classifier service and of every client that wants to use a file classifier service.

The getMIMEType() method will return an object from the file classifer service. Implementation possibilities that can affect this object are as follows:

- If the service runs in the client's JVM, then nothing special needs to be done.

- If the service is implemented remotely and runs in a separate JVM, then the MIMEType object must be serialized for transport to the client JVM. For this to be possible, it must implement the Serializable interface. Note that while the class files are accessible to both client and service, the instance data of the MIMEType object needs to be serializable to move the object from one machine to the other.

There can be differences in the object depending on possible implementations. If it implements Serializable, it can be used in both the remote and local cases, but if it doesn't, then it can only be used in the local case.

Making decisions about interfaces based on future implementation concerns is traditionally considered to be poor design. In particular, the philosophy behind remote procedure calls is that they hide the network as much as possible and make the calls behave as though they were local calls. With this philosophy, there is no need to make a distinction between local and remote calls at design time. However, a document from Sun, "A Note on Distributed Computing," by Jim Waldo and others, argues that this is wrong, particularly in the case of distributed objects. The basis of their argument is that the network brings in a host of other factors, in particular that of *partial failure*. That is, part of the network itself may fail, or a component on the network may fail without all of the network or all of the components failing. If other components do not make allowance for this possible (or maybe even likely) behavior, then the system as a whole will not be robust and could be brought down by the failure of a single component.

According to this document, it is important to determine whether the objects could be running remotely and to adjust interfaces and classes accordingly at the design stage. Doing so enables you to take into account possible extra failure modes of methods, and in this case, an extra requirement on the object. This important paper is reprinted in *The Jini Specifications*, *Second Edition*, edited by Ken Arnold (Addison-Wesley Professional, 2000), and is also at http://www.sun.com/research/techrep/1994/abstract_29.html.

These considerations lead to an interface that adds the Serializable interface to the original version of the MIMEType class, as objects of this class could be sent across the network. The objects sent are copies of the one on the server, not references to one that remains on the server.

```java
package common;
import java.io.Serializable;
/**
 * MIMEType.java
 */
public class MIMEType implements Serializable {
    /**
     * A MIME type is made up of 2 parts
     * contentType/subtype
     */
    private String contentType;
    private String subType;
    public MIMEType() {
        // empty constructor required just in case
        // we want to use this as a Java Bean
    }
    public MIMEType(String type) {
        int slash = type.indexOf('/');
        contentType = type.substring(0, slash-1);
        subType = type.substring(slash+1, type.length());
    }

    public MIMEType(String contentType, String subType) {
        this.contentType = contentType;
        this.subType = subType;
    }
    public String toString() {
        return contentType + "/" + subType;
    }
    /**
     * Accessors/setters
     */
    public String getContentType() {
        return contentType;
    }
    public void setContentType(String type) {
        contentType = type;
    }
    public String getSubType() {
        return subType;
    }
    public void setSubType(String type) {
        subType = type;
    }
} // MIMEType
```

FileClassifier Interface

Changes have to be made to the file classifier interface as well. First, interfaces cannot have static methods, so we will have to turn the getMIMEType() method into a public instance method.

In addition, all methods are defined to throw a java.rmi.RemoteException. This type of exception is used throughout Java (not just the RMI component) to mean "a network error has occurred." This error could be a lost connection, a missing server, a class not downloadable, and so on. There is a little subtlety here, related to the java.rmi.Remote class: the methods of Remote must all throw a RemoteException, but a class is not required to be Remote if its methods throw RemoteException. If all the methods of a class throw RemoteException, it does not mean the class implements or extends Remote; it only means that an implementation *may* be implemented as a remote (distributed) object, and this implementation may also use the RMI Remote interface.

There are some very fine points to this, which you can skip if you like. Basically, though, you can't go wrong if every method of a Jini interface throws RemoteException and the interface does not extend Remote. In fact, prior to JDK 1.2.2, making the interface extend Remote would force each implementation of the interface to actually be a remote object. At JDK 1.2.2, however, the semantics of Remote were changed a little, and this requirement was relaxed. From JDK 1.2.2 onward, an interface can extend Remote without implementation consequences. At least, that is almost the case: "unusual" ways of implementing RMI, such as over IIOP (IIOP is the transport protocol for CORBA, and RMI can use this), have not yet caught up to this. So for maximum flexibility, just throw RemoteException from each method and don't extend Remote.

Doing so gives the following interface:

```
package common;
/**
 * FileClassifier.java
 */
public interface FileClassifier {

    public MIMEType getMIMEType(String fileName)
        throws java.rmi.RemoteException;

} // FileClasssifier
```

Why does this interface throw a java.rmi.RemoteException in the getMIMEType() method? Well, an interface is supposed to be above all possible implementations and should never change. The implementation discussed later in this chapter does not throw such an exception. However, other implementations in other sections use a Remote implementation, and this will require that the method throws a java.rmi.RemoteException. Since it is not possible to just add a new exception in a subclass or interface implementation, the possibility must be added in the interface specification.

There is nothing Jini-specific about these classes. They can be compiled using any Java compiler with no special flags. For example, the following code shows a compilation using the JDK compiler:

```
javac common/MIMEType.java common/FileClassifier.java
```

The Client

The client is the same for all of the possible server implementations discussed throughout this book. The client does not care how the service implementation is done, just as long as it gets a service that it wants, and it specifies this by asking for a FileClassifier interface.

Unicast Client

If there is a known service locator that will know about the service, then there is no need to search for the service locator. This doesn't mean that the location of the service is known, only the location of the locator. For example, there might be a (fictitious) organization "All About Files" at http://www.all_about_files.com that would know about various file services, keeping track of them as they come online, move, disappear, and so on. A client would ask the service locator running on this site for the service, wherever it is. This client uses the unicast lookup techniques:

```
package client;
import common.FileClassifier;
import common.MIMEType;
import net.jini.core.discovery.LookupLocator;
import net.jini.core.lookup.ServiceRegistrar;
import net.jini.core.lookup.ServiceItem;
import net.jini.core.lookup.ServiceRegistration;
import java.rmi.RMISecurityManager;
import net.jini.core.lookup.ServiceTemplate;
/**
 * TestUnicastFileClassifier.java
 */
public class TestUnicastFileClassifier {
    public static void main(String argv[]) {
        new TestUnicastFileClassifier();
    }
    public TestUnicastFileClassifier() {
        LookupLocator lookup = null;
        ServiceRegistrar registrar = null;
        FileClassifier classifier = null;
        try {
            // lookup = new LookupLocator("jini://www.all_about_files.com");
            lookup = new LookupLocator("jini://192.168.1.13");
        } catch(java.net.MalformedURLException e) {
```

```
                System.err.println("Lookup failed: " + e.toString());
                System.exit(1);
            }
            System.setSecurityManager(new RMISecurityManager());
            try {
                registrar = lookup.getRegistrar();
            } catch (java.io.IOException e) {
                System.err.println("Registrar search failed: " + e.toString());
                System.exit(1);
            } catch (java.lang.ClassNotFoundException e) {
                System.err.println("Registrar search failed: " + e.toString());
                System.exit(1);
            }
            Class[] classes = new Class[] {FileClassifier.class};
            ServiceTemplate template = new ServiceTemplate(null, classes, null);
            try {
                classifier = (FileClassifier) registrar.lookup(template);
            } catch(java.rmi.RemoteException e) {
                e.printStackTrace();
                System.exit(1);
            }
            if (classifier == null) {
                System.out.println("Classifier null");
                System.exit(2);
            }
            MIMEType type;
            try {
                type = classifier.getMIMEType("file1.txt");
                System.out.println("Type is " + type.toString());
            } catch(java.rmi.RemoteException e) {
                System.err.println(e.toString());
            }
            System.exit(0);
    }
} // TestUnicastFileClassifier
```

The client's JVM looks like Figure 9-1. Figure 9-1 shows a UML class diagram, surrounded by the JVM in which the objects exist.

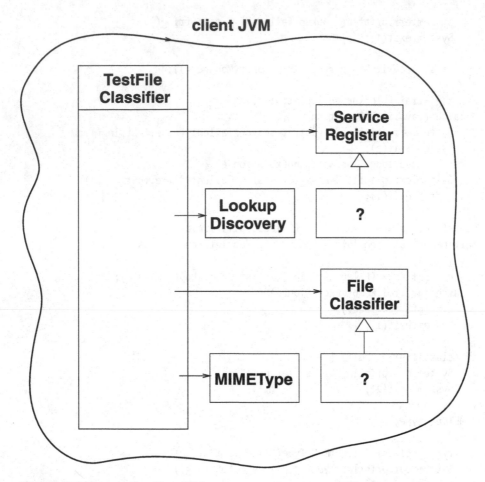

Figure 9-1. *Objects in the client JVM*

The client has a main TestFileClassifier class, which has two objects of types LookupDiscovery and MIMEType. It also has objects that implement the interfaces ServiceRegistrar and FileClassifier, but it doesn't know (or need to know) what classes they are. These objects have come across the network as implementation objects of the two interfaces.

Figure 9-2 shows the situation when the lookup service's JVM is added in. The lookup service has an object implementing ServiceRegistrar, and this is the object exported to the client.

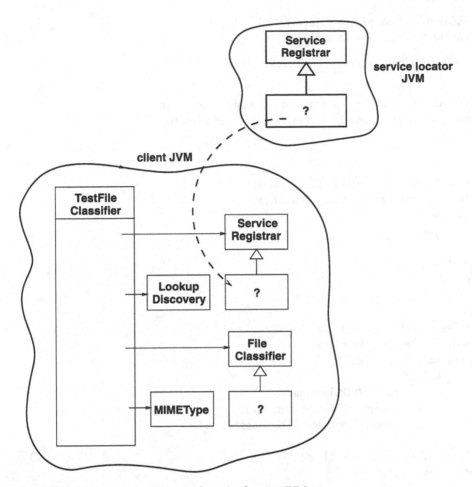

Figure 9-2. *Objects in the client and service locator JVMs*

Figure 9-2 shows that the client gets its registrar from the JVM of the service locator. This registrar object is not specified in detail. Sun supplies a service locator known as reggie, which implements the ServiceRegistrar using an implementation that neither clients nor services are expected to know. The classes that implement the ServiceRegistrar object are contained in the reggie-dl.jar file and are downloaded to the clients and services using (typically) an HTTP server.

The figure also shows a question mark for the object in the client implementing FileClassifier. The source of this object is not yet shown; it will get the object from a service, but we haven't yet discussed any of the possible implementations of a FileClassifier service.

The unicast client uses a number of Jini classes. These classes must be in the CLASSPATH of the compiler. The classes are in the Jini lib directory in the jsk-platform.jar and jsk-lib.jar files. These files need to be in the CLASSPATH for any compiler, for example:

```
javac -classpath .../jsk-platform.jar:.../jsk-lib.jar \
      client/TestUnicastFileClassifier.java
```

An Ant file to build this client is client.TestUnicastFileClassifier.xml:

```
<!--
    Project name must be the same as the filename which must
    be the same as the main.class. Builds jar files with the
    same name
  -->


<project name="client.TestUnicastFileClassifier">
    <!-- Inherits properties from ../build.xml:
        jini.home
        jini.jars
        src
        dist
        build
        httpd.classes
      -->
    <!-- files for this project -->
    <!-- Source files for the client -->
    <property name="src.files"
            value="
                    common/MIMEType.java,
                    common/FileClassifier.java,
                    client/TestUnicastFileClassifier.java
                    "/>
    <!-- Class files to run the client -->
    <property name="class.files"
            value="
                    common/MIMEType.class,
                    common/FileClassifier.class,
                    client/TestUnicastFileClassifier.class
                    "/>
    <!-- Class files for the client to download -->
    <property name="class.files.dl"
            value="
                    "/>
    <!-- Uncomment if no class files downloaded to the client -->
    <property name="no-dl" value="true"/>
    <!-- derived names - may be changed -->
    <property name="jar.file"
            value="${ant.project.name}.jar"/>
```

```xml
    <property name="jar.file.dl"
            value="${ant.project.name}-dl.jar"/>
    <property name="main.class"
            value="${ant.project.name}"/>
    <!-- targets -->
    <target name="all" depends="compile"/>
    <target name="compile">
        <javac destdir="${build}" srcdir="${src}"
            classpath="${jini.jars}"
            includes="${src.files}">
        </javac>
    </target>
    <target name="dist" depends="compile"
            description="generate the distribution">
        <jar jarfile="${dist}/${jar.file}"
            basedir="${build}"
            includes="${class.files}"/>
        <antcall target="dist-jar-dl"/>
    </target>
    <target name="dist-jar-dl" unless="no-dl">
        <jar jarfile="${dist}/${jar.file.dl}"
            basedir="${build}"
            includes="${class.files.dl}"/>
    </target>
    <target name="build" depends="dist,compile"/>
    <target name="run" depends="build">
        <java classname="${main.class}"
            fork="true"
            classpath="${jini.jars}:${dist}/${jar.file}">
            <jvmarg value="-Djava.security.policy=${res}/policy.all"/>
        </java>
    </target>
    <target name="deploy" depends="dist" unless="no-dl">
        <copy file="${dist}/${jar.file.dl}"
            todir="${httpd.classes}"/>
    </target>
</project>
```

Multicast Client

We have looked at the unicast client, where the location of the service locator is already known. However, it is more likely that a client will need to search through all of the service locators until it finds one holding a service it is looking for. It would need to use a multicast search for this. If it needs only one occurrence of the service, then it can exit after using the service. More complex behavior will be illustrated in later examples.

   In this situation, the client does not need to have long-term persistence, but it does need a user thread to remain in existence for long enough to find service locators and find a suitable service. Therefore, in main() a user thread sleeps for a short period (ten seconds).

```java
package client;
import common.FileClassifier;
import common.MIMEType;
import java.rmi.RMISecurityManager;
import net.jini.discovery.LookupDiscovery;
import net.jini.discovery.DiscoveryListener;
import net.jini.discovery.DiscoveryEvent;
import net.jini.core.lookup.ServiceRegistrar;
import net.jini.core.lookup.ServiceTemplate;
/**
 * TestFileClassifier.java
 */
public class TestFileClassifier implements DiscoveryListener {
    public static void main(String argv[]) {
        new TestFileClassifier();
        // stay around long enough to receive replies
        try {
            Thread.currentThread().sleep(100000L);
        } catch(java.lang.InterruptedException e) {
            // do nothing
        }
    }
    public TestFileClassifier() {
        System.setSecurityManager(new RMISecurityManager());
        LookupDiscovery discover = null;
        try {
            discover = new LookupDiscovery(LookupDiscovery.ALL_GROUPS);
        } catch(Exception e) {
            System.err.println(e.toString());
            System.exit(1);
        }
        discover.addDiscoveryListener(this);
    }

    public void discovered(DiscoveryEvent evt) {
        ServiceRegistrar[] registrars = evt.getRegistrars();
        Class [] classes = new Class[] {FileClassifier.class};
        FileClassifier classifier = null;
```

```java
        ServiceTemplate template = new ServiceTemplate(null, classes,
                                                 null);

        for (int n = 0; n < registrars.length; n++) {
            System.out.println("Lookup service found");
            ServiceRegistrar registrar = registrars[n];
            try {
                classifier = (FileClassifier) registrar.lookup(template);
            } catch(java.rmi.RemoteException e) {
                e.printStackTrace();
                continue;
            }
            if (classifier == null) {
                System.out.println("Classifier null");
                continue;
            }
            // Use the service to classify a few file types
            MIMEType type;
            try {
                String fileName;
                fileName = "file1.txt";
                type = classifier.getMIMEType(fileName);
                printType(fileName, type);
                fileName = "file2.rtf";
                type = classifier.getMIMEType(fileName);
                printType(fileName, type);
                fileName = "file3.abc";
                type = classifier.getMIMEType(fileName);
                printType(fileName, type);
            } catch(java.rmi.RemoteException e) {
                System.err.println(e.toString());
                continue;
            }
            // success
            System.exit(0);
        }
    }
    private void printType(String fileName, MIMEType type) {
        System.out.print("Type of " + fileName + " is ");
        if (type == null) {
            System.out.println("null");
        } else {
            System.out.println(type.toString());
        }
    }
```

```
    }
    public void discarded(DiscoveryEvent evt) {
        // empty
    }
} // TestFileClassifier
```

The multicast client uses a number of Jini classes. These classes must be in the CLASSPATH of the compiler. The classes are in the Jini lib directory in the jsk-platform.jar and jsk-lib.jar files. These need to be in the CLASSPATH for any compiler, for example:

```
javac -classpath .../jsk-platform.jar:.../jsk-lib.jar client/TestFileClassifier.java
```

An Ant file to build this client is client.TestFileClassifier.xml:

```
<!--
    Project name must be the same as the filename which must
    be the same as the main.class. Builds jar files with the
    same name
  -->

<project name="client.TestFileClassifier">
    <!-- Inherits properties from ../build.xml:
        jini.home
        jini.jars
        src
        dist
        build
        httpd.classes
      -->
    <!-- files for this project -->
    <!-- Source files for the client -->
    <property name="src.files"
            value="
                    common/MIMEType.java,
                    common/FileClassifier.java,
                    client/TestFileClassifier.java
                    "/>
    <!-- Class files to run the client -->
    <property name="class.files"
            value="
                    common/MIMEType.class,
                    common/FileClassifier.class,
                    client/TestFileClassifier.class
                    "/>
```

```xml
<!-- Class files for the client to download -->
<property name="class.files.dl"
          value="
                 "/>
<!-- Uncomment if no class files downloaded to the client -->
<property name="no-dl" value="true"/>
<!-- derived names - may be changed -->
<property name="jar.file"
          value="${ant.project.name}.jar"/>
<property name="jar.file.dl"
          value="${ant.project.name}-dl.jar"/>
<property name="main.class"
          value="${ant.project.name}"/>
<!-- targets -->
<target name="all" depends="compile"/>
<target name="compile">
    <javac destdir="${build}" srcdir="${src}"
           classpath="${jini.jars}"
           includes="${src.files}">
    </javac>
</target>
<target name="dist" depends="compile"
        description="generate the distribution">
    <jar jarfile="${dist}/${jar.file}"
         basedir="${build}"
         includes="${class.files}"/>
    <antcall target="dist-jar-dl"/>
</target>
<target name="dist-jar-dl" unless="no-dl">
    <jar jarfile="${dist}/${jar.file.dl}"
         basedir="${build}"
         includes="${class.files.dl}"/>
</target>
<target name="build" depends="dist,compile"/>
<target name="run" depends="build">
    <java classname="${main.class}"
          fork="true"
          classpath="${jini.jars}:${dist}/${jar.file}">
        <jvmarg value="-Djava.security.policy=${res}/policy.all"/>
    </java>
</target>
<target name="deploy" depends="dist" unless="no-dl">
    <copy file="${dist}/${jar.file.dl}"
```

```
                    todir="${httpd.classes}"/>
    </target>
</project>
```

Exception Handling

A Jini program can generate a huge number of exceptions, often related to the network nature of Jini. This is not accidental, but lies at the heart of the Jini approach to network programming. Services can disappear because the link to them has vanished, the server machine has crashed, or the service provider has died. Class files can disappear for similar problems with the HTTP server that delivers them. Timeouts can occur due to unpredictable network delays. Many of these exceptions have their own exception types, such as LookupUnmarshalException, which can occur when unmarshalling objects. Many others are simply wrapped in a RemoteException, which has a detail field for the wrapped exception.

Since many Jini calls can generate exceptions, these must be handled somehow. Many Java programs (or rather, their programmers!) adopt a somewhat cavalier attitude to exceptions: catch them, maybe put out an error message, and continue—Java makes it easy to handle errors! More seriously, whenever an exception occurs, the following questions have to be asked: Can the program continue, or has its state been corrupted but not so badly that it cannot recover? Or has the program state been damaged so much that the program must exit?

The multicast TestFileClassifier of the last section can throw exceptions at a number of places:

- The LookupDiscovery constructor can fail. This is indicative of some serious network error. The created discover object is needed to add a listener, and if this cannot be done, then the program really can't do anything. So it is appropriate to exit with an error value.

- The ServiceRegistrar.lookup() method can fail. This is indicative of some network error in the connection with a particular service locator. While this connection may have failed, it is possible that other network connections may succeed. The application can restore a consistent state by skipping the rest of the code in this iteration of the for() loop by using a continue statement.

- The FileClassifier.getMIMEType() method can fail. This can be caused by a network error, or perhaps the service has simply gone away. Regardless, consistent state can again be restored by skipping the rest of this loop iteration.

Finally, if one part of a program can exit with an abnormal (nonzero) error value, then a successful exit should signal its success with an exit value of 0. If this is not done, then the exit value becomes indeterminate and is of no value to other processes that may wish to know whether or not the program exited successfully.

The Service Proxy

A service will be delivered from out of a service provider. That is, a server will be started to act as a service provider. It will create one or more objects, which between them will implement the service. Among these objects will be a distinguished object: the service object. The service provider will register the service object with service locators and then wait for network requests to come in for the service. What the service provider will actually export as service object is usually a proxy for the service. The *proxy* is an object that will eventually run in a client, and it will usually make calls back across the network to *service back-end* objects. These back-end objects running within the server actually complete the implementation of the service.

The proxy and the service back-end objects are tightly integrated; they must communicate using a protocol known to them both, and they must exchange information in an agreed-upon manner. However, the relative *size* of each is up to the designer of a service and its proxy. For example, the proxy may be "fat" (or "smart"), which means it does a lot of processing on the client side. Back-end object(s) within the service provider itself are then typically "thin," not doing much at all. Alternatively, the proxy may be "thin," doing little more (or nothing more) than passing requests between the client and "fat" back-end objects, and most processing will be done by these back-end objects running in the service provider.

As well as this choice of size, there is also a choice of communication mechanisms between the client and service provider objects. Client/server systems often have the choice of message-based or remote procedure call (RPC) communications. These choices are also available between a Jini proxy and its service. Since they are both in Java, there is a standard RPC-like mechanism called Remote Method Invocation (RMI), and this can be used if wanted. There is no need to use RMI, but many implementations of Jini proxies will do so because it is easy. RMI does force a particular choice of thin proxy to fat service back-end, though, and this may not be ideal for all situations.

This chapter looks at one possibility only, where the proxy is fat and is the whole of the service implementation (the service back-end is an empty set of objects). Chapter 11 covers the other possibilities in more detail.

Uploading a Complete Service

The file classifier service does not rely on any particular properties of its host—it is not hardware or operating system dependent, and it does not make use of any files on the host side. In this case, it is possible to upload the entire service to the client and let it run there. The proxy is the service, and no processing elements need to be left on the server.

FileClassifier Implementation

The implementation of the FileClassifier is straightforward:

```
package complete;
import common.MIMEType;
import common.FileClassifier;
/**
 * FileClassifierImpl.java
 */
public class FileClassifierImpl implements FileClassifier, java.io.Serializable {
    public MIMEType getMIMEType(String fileName) {
        if (fileName.endsWith(".gif")) {
```

```
                return new MIMEType("image", "gif");
            } else if (fileName.endsWith(".jpeg")) {
                return new MIMEType("image", "jpeg");
            } else if (fileName.endsWith(".mpg")) {
                return new MIMEType("video", "mpeg");
            } else if (fileName.endsWith(".txt")) {
                return new MIMEType("text", "plain");
            } else if (fileName.endsWith(".html")) {
                return new MIMEType("text", "html");
            } else
                // fill in lots of other types,
                // but eventually give up and
                return null;
        }
        public FileClassifierImpl() {
            // empty
        }
    } // FileClassifierImpl
```

This implementation consists of ordinary Java code and does not require any special libraries. It does need the FileClassifier and MIMEType in its classpath. The implementation can be compiled by a simple command:

```
javac complete/FileClassifierImpl.java
```

Other implementations may require other packages to be included, of course.

FileClassifierServer Implementation

The service provider for the file classifier service needs to create an instance of the exportable service object, register this, and keep the lease alive. In the discovered() method, it not only registers the service but also adds it to a LeaseRenewalManager, to keep the lease alive "forever." This manager runs its own threads to keep reregistering the leases, but these are daemon threads. So in the main() method, the user thread goes to sleep for as long as you want the server to stay around.

The following code uses an "unsatisfied wait" condition that will sleep forever until interrupted. Note that if the server does terminate, then the lease will fail to be renewed and the exported service object will be discarded from lookup locators even though the server is not required for delivery of the service.

The serviceID is initially set to null. This may be the first time this service is ever run, or at least the first time it is ever run with this particular implementation. Since a service ID is issued by lookup services, it must remain null until at least the first registration. Then the service ID can be extracted from the registration and reused for all further lookup services. In addition, the service ID can be saved in some permanent form so that if the server crashes and restarts, the service ID can be retrieved from permanent storage and used. The following server code saves and retrieves this value in a FileClassifier.id file. Note that we get the service ID from the registration, not the registrar.

```java
package complete;
import java.rmi.RMISecurityManager;
import net.jini.discovery.LookupDiscovery;
import net.jini.discovery.DiscoveryListener;
import net.jini.discovery.DiscoveryEvent;
import net.jini.core.lookup.ServiceRegistrar;
import net.jini.core.lookup.ServiceItem;
import net.jini.core.lookup.ServiceRegistration;
import net.jini.core.lease.Lease;
import net.jini.core.lookup.ServiceID ;
import net.jini.lease.LeaseListener;
import net.jini.lease.LeaseRenewalEvent;
import net.jini.lease.LeaseRenewalManager;
import java.io.*;
/**
 * FileClassifierServer.java
 */
public class FileClassifierServer implements DiscoveryListener,
                                    LeaseListener {

    protected LeaseRenewalManager leaseManager = new LeaseRenewalManager();
    protected ServiceID serviceID = null;
    protected          FileClassifierImpl impl;
    public static void main(String argv[]) {
        FileClassifierServer s = new FileClassifierServer();

        // keep server running forever to
        // - allow time for locator discovery and
        // - keep re-registering the lease
        Object keepAlive = new Object();
        synchronized(keepAlive) {
            try {
                keepAlive.wait();
            } catch(java.lang.InterruptedException e) {
                // do nothing
            }
        }
    }
    public FileClassifierServer() {
        // Create the service
        impl = new FileClassifierImpl();
        // Try to load the service ID from file.
        // It isn't an error if we can't load it, because
        // maybe this is the first time this service has run
        DataInputStream din = null;
        try {
```

```java
            din = new DataInputStream(new FileInputStream("FileClassifier.id"));
            serviceID = new ServiceID(din);
        } catch(Exception e) {
            // ignore
        }
        System.setSecurityManager(new RMISecurityManager());
        LookupDiscovery discover = null;
        try {
            discover = new LookupDiscovery(LookupDiscovery.ALL_GROUPS);
        } catch(Exception e) {
            System.err.println("Discovery failed " + e.toString());
            System.exit(1);
        }
        discover.addDiscoveryListener(this);
    }

    public void discovered(DiscoveryEvent evt) {
        ServiceRegistrar[] registrars = evt.getRegistrars();
        for (int n = 0; n < registrars.length; n++) {
            ServiceRegistrar registrar = registrars[n];
            ServiceItem item = new ServiceItem(serviceID,
                                               impl,
                                               null);
            ServiceRegistration reg = null;
            try {
                reg = registrar.register(item, Lease.FOREVER);
            } catch(java.rmi.RemoteException e) {
                System.err.println("Register exception: " + e.toString());
                continue;
            }
            System.out.println("Service registered with id " + reg.getServiceID());
            // set lease renewal in place
            leaseManager.renewUntil(reg.getLease(), Lease.FOREVER, this);
            // set the serviceID if necessary
            if (serviceID == null) {
                serviceID = reg.getServiceID();
                // try to save the service ID in a file
                DataOutputStream dout = null;
                try {
                    dout = new DataOutputStream(
                            new FileOutputStream("FileClassifier.id"));
                    serviceID.writeBytes(dout);
                    dout.flush();
```

```
                } catch(Exception e) {
                    // ignore
                }
            }
        }
    }
    public void discarded(DiscoveryEvent evt) {
    }
    public void notify(LeaseRenewalEvent evt) {
        System.out.println("Lease expired " + evt.toString());
    }
} // FileClassifierServer
```

Figure 9-3 shows the server by itself running in its JVM.

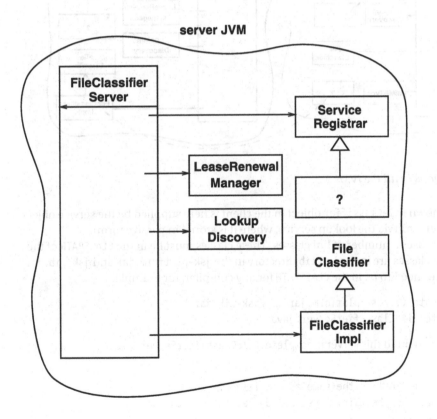

Figure 9-3. *Objects in the server JVM*

The server receives an object implementing ServiceRegistrar from the service locator (such as reggie). Adding in the service locator and the client in their JVMs is shown in Figure 9-4.

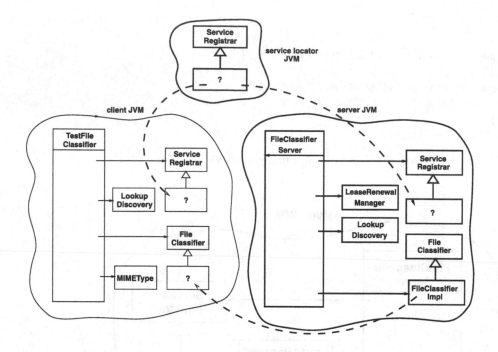

Figure 9-4. *Objects in all the JVMs*

The unknown FileClassifier object in the client is here supplied by the service object FileClassifierImpl (via the lookup service, where it is stored in passive form).

The server uses a number of Jini classes. These classes must be in the CLASSPATH of the compiler. The classes are in the Jini lib directory in the jsk-platform.jar and jsk-lib.jar files. These files need to be in the CLASSPATH for any compiler, for example:

```
javac -classpath .../jsk-platform.jar:.../jsk-lib.jar \
    complete/FileClassifierServer.java
```

An Ant file to build this server is complete.FileClassifierServer.xml:

```
<!--
    Project name must be the same as the filename which must
    be the same as the main.class. Builds jar files with the
    same name
  -->

<project name="complete.FileClassifierServer">
    <!-- Inherits properties from ../build.xml:
        jini.home
        jini.jars
```

```
       src
       dist
       build
       httpd.classes
       localhost
  -->
<!-- files for this project -->
<!-- Source files for the server -->
<property name="src.files"
          value="
                  common/MIMEType.java,
                  common/FileClassifier.java,
                  complete/FileClassifierImpl.java,
                  complete/FileClassifierServer.java
                  "/>
<!-- Class files to run the server -->
<property name="class.files"
          value="
                  common/MIMEType.class,
                  common/FileClassifier.class,
                  complete/FileClassifierImpl.class,
                  complete/FileClassifierServer.class
                  "/>
<!-- Class files for the client to download -->
<property name="class.files.dl"
          value="
                  common/MIMEType.class,
                  common/FileClassifier.class,
                  complete/FileClassifierImpl.class
                  "/>
<!-- Uncomment if no class files downloaded to the client -->
<!-- <property name="no-dl" value="true"/> -->
<!-- derived names - may be changed -->
<property name="jar.file"
          value="${ant.project.name}.jar"/>
<property name="jar.file.dl"
          value="${ant.project.name}-dl.jar"/>
<property name="main.class"
          value="${ant.project.name}"/>
<property name="codebase"
          value="http://${localhost}/classes/${jar.file.dl}"/>
<!-- targets -->
<target name="all" depends="compile"/>
<target name="compile">
    <javac destdir="${build}" srcdir="${src}"
           classpath="${jini.jars}"
           includes="${src.files}">
```

```
            </javac>
        </target>
        <target name="dist" depends="compile"
                description="generate the distribution">
            <jar jarfile="${dist}/${jar.file}"
                basedir="${build}"
                includes="${class.files}"/>
            <antcall target="dist-jar-dl"/>
        </target>
        <target name="dist-jar-dl" unless="no-dl">
            <jar jarfile="${dist}/${jar.file.dl}"
                basedir="${build}"
                includes="${class.files.dl}"/>
        </target>
        <target name="build" depends="dist,compile"/>
        <target name="run" depends="build,deploy">
            <java classname="${main.class}"
                fork="true"
                classpath="${jini.jars}:${dist}/${jar.file}">
                <jvmarg value="-Djava.security.policy=${res}/policy.all"/>
                <jvmarg value="-Djava.rmi.server.codebase=${codebase}"/>
            </java>
        </target>
        <target name="deploy" depends="dist" unless="no-dl">
            <copy file="${dist}/${jar.file.dl}"
                todir="${httpd.classes}"/>
        </target>
</project>
```

Client Implementation

The client for this service was discussed earlier in the section "The Client." The client does not need any special information about this implementation of the service and so can remain quite generic.

What Classes Need to Be Where?

In this chapter, we have defined the following classes:

- common.MIMEType

- common.FileClassifier

- complete.FileClassifierImpl

- complete.FileClassifierServer

- client.TestFileClassifier

Instance objects of these classes could be running on up to four different machines:

- The server machine for FileClassifier.

- The machine for the lookup service.

- The machine running the client TestFileClassifier.

- An HTTP server will need to run somewhere to deliver the class file definition of FileClassifierImpl to clients.

What classes need to be known to which machines? The term "known" can refer to different things:

- The class may be in the CLASSPATH of a JVM.

- The class may be loadable across the network.

- The class may be accessible by an HTTP server.

Service Provider

The server running FileClassifierServer needs to know the following classes and interfaces:

- The common.FileClassifier interface

- The common.MIMEType class

- The complete.FileClassifierServer class

- The complete.FileClassifierImpl class

These classes all need to be in the CLASSPATH of the server.

HTTP Server

The complete.FileClassifierImpl class will need to be accessible to an HTTP server, as discussed in the next section.

Lookup Service

The lookup service does not need to know any of these classes. It just deals with them in the form of a java.rmi.MarshalledObject.

Client

The client needs to know the following:

- The common.FileClassifier interface

- The common.MIMEType class

- The client.TestFileClassifier class

These all need to be in the CLASSPATH of the client. In addition, the client will need to know the class files for complete.FileClassifierImpl. However, these will come across the network as part of the discovery process, and this will be invisible to the client's programmer.

Running the FileClassifier

We now have a FileClassifierServer service and a TestFleClassifier client to run. There should also be at least one lookup locator already running. The CLASSPATH should be set for each to include the classes discussed in the last section, in addition to the standard ones.

A serialized instance of complete.FileClassifierImpl will be passed from the server to the locator and then to the client. Once on the client, it will need to be able to run the class file for this service object, and so will need to load its class file from an HTTP server. The location of this class file relative to the server's DocumentRoot will need to be specified by the service invocation. For example, if it is stored in /DocumentRoot/classes/complete/FileClassifierImpl.class, then the server will also be downloading a registrar object from the lookup service, so it will need a security policy. The service will be started as follows:

```
java -Djava.rmi.server.codebase=http://hostname/classes \
    -Djava.security.policy=policy.all \
    complete.FileClassifierServer
```

In this command, hostname is the name of the host the server is running on. Note that this hostname cannot be localhost, because the localhost for the server will not be the localhost for the client!

In this case, we only need to put one file, FileClassifierImpl.class, on the HTTP server. Although the implementation relies on the MIMEType and the FileClassifier interface, the client has copies of these. In more complex situations, the implementation may consist of more classes, some of which will not be known to the client. All of these class files may be put individually on the HTTP server, but it has become common practice to put them all into a .jar file with a name including -dl (for *download*), such as FileClassifierImpl-dl.jar. I should also point out that service browsers will not know about the classes used by the implementation, so for them to be able to examine the service, the .jar file should include all classes that the service depends on—that is, the .jar file should be created as follows:

```
jar cf FileClassifierImpl-dl.jar \
    common/MIMEType.class \
    common/FileClassifier.class \
    complete/FileClassifierImpl.class
```

and the server would then be run as follows:

```
java -Djava.rmi.server.codebase=http://hostname/classes/FileClassifierImpl-dl.jar \
    -Djava.security.policy=policy.all \
    complete.FileClassifierServer
```

The client will be loading a class definition across the network. It will need to allow this in a security policy file with the following statement:

```
java -Djava.security.policy=policy.all client.TestFileClassifier
```

The client does *not* need to know anything about the implementation classes. It just needs to know the FileClassifier interface, the MIMEType class, and the standard Jini classes. All other classes are downloaded as needed from the HTTP server specified by the service.

Summary

In this chapter, the material presented in the previous chapters was put together in a simple example. We discussed the requirements of class structures for a Jini system, and we also covered the classes that need to be available to each component of a Jini system.

■■■

CHAPTER 10

Jini Extensible Remote
Invocation

Jini Extensible Remote Invocation, or Jeri, is an alternative to the Java Remote Method Protocol (JRMP) used by "traditional" RMI. It incorporates lessons learned from RMI over IIOP and other transports.

Jini is middleware for distributed processing. As such, it relies on a number of mechanisms for distributed processing. One of these is the ability of proxies and services to communicate, so that client calls on the proxy can result in remote invocations of service methods.

Initial versions of Jini often used the Java remote method invocation (RMI). In RMI, an object stays on a server and a dumb proxy is sent to a client. The client makes method calls on this proxy. The proxy just transmits calls across the network to the server, which calls the original object. The result of this method call is then sent back to the proxy, which returns the result to the client. This is an object-oriented version of remote procedure calls. It is somewhat similar to CORBA remote references, except that the proxy is a Java object that runs in the client and does not require the "backplane" support of CORBA.

The original implementation of RMI used JRMP, a particular protocol built directly on TCP. Since then, a number of other ways of doing RMI have emerged, such as RMI over HTTP (the web transport protocol), RMI over IIOP (the CORBA transport protocol), and RMI over Secure Socket Layer (SSL). There is even an implementation of RMI on FireWire (IEEE 1394), the high-speed transport layer designed for audio/visual data such as high-definition TV.

The different ways of doing RMI each have their own programmatic interface, with specialized classes. This should be abstracted to one mechanism, with configurations used to select the actual protocol implementation used. For example, a configuration file could specify whether to use RMI over TCP or RMI over IIOP. Then the application could be written in an implementation-independent way, with the protocol chosen at runtime based on runtime configuration information. This is what Jini has now done, and Sun has developed a new protocol, Jeri, which also solves some other issues.

In this chapter, we'll cover this new protocol and look at the changes that are needed compared to traditional RMI. While some parts seem more complex than RMI, Jeri provides a more coherent programming model with greater flexibility. Jeri supports the standard RMI semantics but is designed to be more flexible than existing RMI implementations such as JRMP and RMI-over-IIOP. It can support the following:

- The new Jini trust model

- Elimination of the compile-time generation of stubs

- Non-TCP transports

- More flexible distributed garbage collection

- Much greater customization

Traditional RMI

Most books on Java include a section on RMI, and there are complete books devoted to this topic. In traditional RMI, a class typically subclasses UnicastRemoteObject. After compilation, the RMI compiler rmic is run on the class file to produce a proxy object. When the service is run, this proxy object must be made network-visible in some way so that external clients can locate it. This visibility may be to an RMI Naming service to a Jini registry or to other directory services. Then a client can use the directory to find the proxy object, and use the proxy object to make remote calls on the original service object.

A little bit of chicanery takes place before an object is made network-visible: a class registers itself with the Java runtime by an operation called *exporting*, and then methods that should use the proxy object instead use the original service object. The Java runtime looks out for a UnicastRemoteObject instance and substitutes the proxy object in its place. This means that the programmer does not deal explicitly with the proxy at all, and seemingly writes code that does not use proxies; the Java runtime takes care of substituting the proxy when necessary. However, this process may be confusing, and it certainly does not make clear exactly what is going on: this kind of trick is not one that will be in most programmers' experience.

The most common way to use RMI is simply to declare an object that extends UnicastRemoteObject and implements the Remote interface:

```
package jeri;
import java.rmi.*;
import java.rmi.server.*;
public class RmiImplicitExportDemo extends UnicastRemoteObject implements Remote {
    public static void main(String[] args) throws Exception {
        // this exports the RMI stub to the Java runtime
        // a thread is started to keep the stub alive
        new RmiImplicitExportDemo();
        System.out.println("Proxy is now exported");
        // this application will then stay alive until killed by the user
    }
    // An empty constructor is needed for the runtime to construct
    // the proxy stub
    public RmiImplicitExportDemo() throws java.rmi.RemoteException {
    }
}
```

A UnicastRemoteObject does lots of things in the constructor behind the scenes: it uses the class name to construct a proxy object using the zero args constructor, it starts an extra thread to keep things alive, and it registers the object as a remote object requiring special attention. While the intention is to keep things simple, these activities can prove somewhat unsettling.

The code in `RmiImplicitExportDemo` does not mention a proxy object. The runtime will create the proxy when it constructs the `RmiImplicitExportDemo` object. But just like most other Java objects, it needs to have a class definition for the proxy. The proxy class is created using the `rmic` compiler. This needs to be run on the implementation class file, for example:

```
javac jeri/RmiImplicitExportDemo.java
rmic -v1.2 jeri.RmiImplicitExportDemo
```

This will create an `RmiImplicitDemo_Stub.class` proxy.

An alternative approach makes some of the actions dealing with proxies more explicit:

```
package jeri;
import java.rmi.*;
import java.rmi.server.*;
public class RmiExplicitExportDemo implements Remote {
    public static void main(String[] args) throws Exception {
        Remote demo = new RmiExplicitExportDemo();
        // this exports the RMI stub to the Java runtime
        RemoteStub stub = UnicastRemoteObject.exportObject(demo);
        System.out.println("Proxy is " + stub.toString());

        // This application will stay alive until killed by the user,
        // or it does a System.exit()
        // or it unexports the proxy
        // Note that the demo is "apparently" unexported, not the proxy
        UnicastRemoteObject.unexportObject(demo, true);
    }
}
```

Traditionally, this mechanism has only been used when the class has to inherit from some other class and cannot also inherit from `UnicastRemoteObject`. Again, the proxy class has to be created by running the `rmic` compiler.

```
javac jeri/RmiExplicitExportDemo.java
rmic -v1.2 jeri.RmiExplicitExportDemo
```

Exporter Class

From Jini 2.0 onward, exporting and unexporting are made into explicit operations, using static methods of an `Exporter` class. So, for example, to export an object using JRMP, an exporter of type `JRMPExporter` is created and used:

```
package jeri;
import java.rmi.*;
import net.jini.export.*;
import net.jini.jrmp.JrmpExporter;
public class ExportJrmpDemo implements Remote {
    public static void main(String[] args) throws Exception {
        Exporter exporter = new JrmpExporter();
```

```
        // export an object of this class
        Remote proxy = exporter.export(new ExportJrmpDemo());
        System.out.println("Proxy is " + proxy.toString());
        // now unexport it once finished
        exporter.unexport(true);
    }
}
```

An exporter can export only one object. To export two objects, create two exporters and use each one to export an object. The proxy classes have to be generated using rmic again.

To export an object using IIOP, an exporter of type IIOPExporter is used:

```
package jeri;
import java.rmi.*;
import net.jini.export.*;
import net.jini.iiop.IiopExporter;
public class ExportIiopDemo implements Remote {
    public static void main(String[] args) throws Exception {

        Exporter exporter = new IiopExporter();
        // export an object of this class
        Remote proxy = exporter.export(new ExportIiopDemo());
        System.out.println("Proxy is " + proxy.toString());

        // now unexport it once finished
        exporter.unexport(true);
    }
}
```

Jeri Exporter

The standard exporter for Jeri is BasicJeriExporter. Its constructor takes parameters that specify the transport protocol (e.g., TCP on an arbitrary port) and an invocation object that handles the details of RMI, such as marshalling and unmarshalling parameters and return values, and specifying methods and exceptions. Other Jeri exporters can wrap around this class. The most common use is to create a TCP-based exporter:

```
package jeri;
import java.rmi.*;
import net.jini.export.*;
import net.jini.jeri.BasicJeriExporter;
import net.jini.jeri.BasicILFactory;
import net.jini.jeri.tcp.TcpServerEndpoint;
public class ExportJeriDemo implements Remote {
    public static void main(String[] args) throws Exception {
        Exporter exporter = new BasicJeriExporter(TcpServerEndpoint.getInstance(0),
                                            new BasicILFactory());
        // export an object of this class
        Remote proxy = exporter.export(new ExportJeriDemo());
```

```
        System.out.println("Proxy is " + proxy.toString());
        // now unexport it once finished
        exporter.unexport(true);
    }
}
```

Note that there is no need to generate the proxy class as part of the compile-time build. The proxy is generated at runtime by the Jeri system.

Exported Interfaces

The exported object, the proxy, is declared to be of the Remote interface. In fact, the specification says that the proxy will implement all of the remote interfaces of the original Remote object. In the preceding examples there are none, but in general a remote object will implement one or more Remote interfaces, and so will the proxy.

This last point is worth expanding on. Suppose we have an interface, Iface, that does *not* extend Remote. The interface RemoteIface extends both Iface and Remote. From there, we could have the implementations RemoteIfaceImpl and IfaceImpl, and we could generate proxies from each of these using Exporter. The class names of the proxies are automatically generated (and are obscure), so let's call these classes RemoteIfaceImplProxy and IfaceImplProxy, respectively. The resulting class diagram (with the nonstandard dotted arrow showing the generation of the proxies) is shown in Figure 10-1.

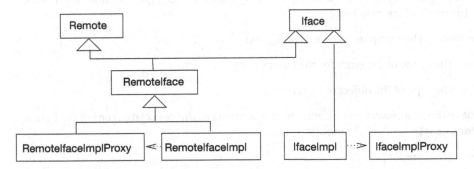

Figure 10-1. *Proxies generated by Exporter*

Since IfaceImpl does not implement any remote interfaces, then neither does IfaceImplProxy (strictly, it *may* implement some additional ones, but probably not ones we are interested in here). There are no inheritance lines leading to IfaceImplProxy. But since RemoteIfaceImpl does implement a remote interface, then so does its proxy.

The most notable consequence of this is that the IfaceImplProxy cannot be cast to an Iface, whereas IfaceRemoteImplProxy can:

```
Iface iface = (Iface) ifaceImplProxy        // class cast error
Iface iface = (Iface) ifaceRemoteImplProxy  // okay
```

Thus, it will be important to include a remote interface somewhere in the interface hierarchy for any implementation.

Failure to include the Remote interface will mean that you can't look up the object. You won't be able to look up an Iface proxy object if it is just derived from an Iface object; it needs to be a proxy object derived from a RemoteIface object.

Configuration

The choices of transport protocol (TCP, FireWire, etc.) and invocation protocol (JRMP, IIOP, Jeri) are usually hard-coded into an application. That is, they are made as *compile-time* choices. More flexibility is gained if they are left as *runtime* choices. Jini 2.0 onward supports a configuration mechanism that allows a single compile-time object to be customized at runtime. The general mechanism is explored in more detail in Chapter 19. It is recommended that you use it for exporting objects.

The configuration mechanism uses a number of levels of indirection to gain a single compile-time object customized in different ways at runtime. First, it gains its Exporter from a Configuration object, which can contain a variety of runtime configuration information. The Configuration object is obtained from a ConfigurationProvider. The ConfigurationProvider can be set to return a custom Configuration, but it defaults to a ConfigurationFile, which takes a configuration file as parameter.

The ConfigurationFile object has a constructor, ConfigurationFile(String[] args). The first element of this list is a file name for a configuration file. The list is passed to the ConfigurationFile constructor from the ConfigurationProvider.getInstance(args) method. Once a configuration object is found, configurable objects can be extracted from it by the Configuration.getEntry(String component, String name, Class type) method. The parameters for this method are as follows:

- component: The component being configured

- name: The name of the entry for the component

- type: The type of the object to be returned

To make this framework more concrete, the contents of the jeri/jrmp.config configuration file for a ConfigurationFile may be as follows:

```
import net.jini.jrmp.*;
JeriExportDemo {
    exporter = new JrmpExporter();
}
```

This file specifies an Exporter object constructed from a component name JeriExportDemo with the name exporter, of type JrmpExporter (which is a subclass of Exporter). This configuration file specifies that traditional RMI using JRMP is being used.

The configuration used can be changed by modifying the contents of the file or by using different files. To specify the IIOP protocol, change the configuration file to jeri/iiop.config:

```
import net.jini.iiop.*;
JeriExportDemo {
    exporter = new IiopExporter();
}
```

Or you can use a file with multiple entries, such as jeri/many.config, and different component names to select which one is used:

```
import net.jini.jrmp.*;
import net.jini.iiop.*;
JrmpExportDemo {
    exporter = new JrmpExporter();
}
IiopExportDemo {
    exporter = new IiopExporter();
}
```

To use the new Jeri protocol, use the configuration file jeri/jeri.config:

```
import net.jini.jeri.BasicILFactory;
import net.jini.jeri.BasicJeriExporter;
import net.jini.jeri.tcp.TcpServerEndpoint;
JeriExportDemo {
    exporter = new BasicJeriExporter(TcpServerEndpoint.getInstance(0),
                              new BasicILFactory());
}
```

Once an Exporter has been found, an object can be exported to the Java runtime by the Exporter.export() method. This method takes the implementation object and returns a proxy that can be registered with a lookup service or any other remote directory.

The program to export an object using this configuration mechanism is as follows:

```
package jeri;
import java.rmi.*;
import net.jini.config.*;
import net.jini.export.*;
public class ConfigExportDemo implements Remote {
    // We are using an explicit config file here so you can see
    // where the Configuration is coming from. Really, another
    // level of indirection (such as a command-line argument)
    // should be used
    private static String CONFIG_FILE = "jeri/jeri.config";
    public static void main(String[] args) throws Exception {
        String[] configArgs = new String[] {CONFIG_FILE};
        // get the configuration (by default a FileConfiguration)
        Configuration config = ConfigurationProvider.getInstance(configArgs);
        System.out.println("Configuration: " + config.toString());
        // and use this to construct an exporter
        Exporter exporter = (Exporter) config.getEntry( "JeriExportDemo",
                                                   "exporter",
                                                   Exporter.class);

        // export an object of this class
        Remote proxy = exporter.export(new ConfigExportDemo());
        System.out.println("Proxy is " + proxy.toString());
```

```
            // now unexport it once finished
            exporter.unexport(true);
        }
    }
```

Garbage Collection

Jini is a distributed system. Any JVM will have references to local objects and to remote objects. In addition, remote JVMs will have references to objects running in any particular JVM. In earlier versions of Jini that used "traditional" RMI, remote references to local objects were enough to keep the local objects from being garbage collected—a thread created by RMI did this. This often led to "sloppy" code, where objects would be created and then apparently all (local) references to those objects would go out of scope. Nevertheless, RMI would often keep these objects alive, and they would not be garbage collected.

Java distinguishes between "strong" and "weak" references. Objects that have only weak references to them may be garbage collected, while objects with strong references to them cannot be garbage collected. If there is an explicit reference to an object from another one that in turn has strong references, then the first object cannot be garbage collected. Objects with only weak references may be garbage collected. Earlier versions of this book (up to Jini 1.2) had service objects that did not have strong references. While those examples ran OK under Jini 1.2, that is no longer the case with Jini 2; running examples unchanged may result in this error when the client tries to invoke the service:

```
java.rmi.NoSuchObjectException: no such object in table
```

The solution is to make strong references to service objects. For example, the server's main() method will have a (static) reference to the server object, which in turn will have a reference to the service.

To make this a little more concrete, the FileClassifierServer of Chapter 9 used to have code that looked like this:

```
public class FileClassifierServer {
    public static void main(String argv[]) {
        new FileClassifierServer();
        ...
    }
    public FileClassifierServer() {
        // Create the service
        new FileClassifierImpl();
        ...
    }
}
```

No reference was kept to the server or to the implementation. This didn't matter in Jini 1.2, because the RMI runtime system would keep a reference to the implementation alive. Since Jini 2.0, explicit references should be kept:

```
public class FileClassifierServer {

    protected FileClassifierImpl impl;
    public static void main(String argv[]) {
        FileClassifierServer s = new FileClassifierServer();
        ... // sleep forever
        }
    }
    public FileClassifierServer() {
        // Create the service
        impl = new FileClassifierImpl
        ...
    }
}
```

Then as long as the main() method remains alive, there will be strong references kept to the implementation.

Proxy Accessor

In most of the examples in this book, a server will create a service and then create a proxy for it, export the proxy, and use the proxy later for such tasks as registration with a lookup service. But there are some occasions (such as activation) where it will not be feasible for the server to create the proxy; instead, the service itself will need to create the proxy.

If the service creates its own proxy, then the server may still need to get access to it, such as in registration with a lookup service. The server will then need to ask the service for its proxy. The service can signal that it is able to do this—and supply an access method—by implementing the ProxyAccessor interface:

```
interface ProxyAccessor {
    Object getProxy();
}
```

The service will return a suitable proxy when this method is called. You'll see examples of this in use occasionally.

Summary

This chapter covered the new model for remote invocation, called Jeri. The chapter showed how Jeri differs from the traditional RMI, and also how to deal with the explicit exporter model it uses. Jeri is the preferred mechanism in Jini for remote objects.

Note For more information on the topics covered in this chapter, see Frank Sommers' article titled "Call on extensible RMI: An introduction to JERI" at http://www.javaworld.com/javaworld/jw-12-2003/jw-1219-jiniology.html.

■ ■ ■

CHAPTER 11

Choices for Service Architecture

A client will only be looking for an implementation of an interface, and the implementation can be done in many different ways, as discussed in this chapter. In Chapter 9, we discussed the roles of the service proxy and service back-end, and briefly talked about how different implementations could place different amounts of processing in the proxy or back-end. This can lead to situations such as a thin proxy communicating to a fat back-end using RMI, or at the other end of the scale, to a fat proxy and a thin back-end. Chapter 9 showed one implementation: a fat proxy with a back-end so thin that it did not exist. This chapter fills in some of the other possibilities.

Proxy Choices

A Jini service will be implemented using a proxy on the client side and a service back-end on the service provider side. In RPC-like systems there is little choice: the proxy must be thin and the back-end must be fat. Message-based client/server systems allow choices in the distribution of processing, so that one or other side can be fat or thin, or they can equally share. Jini allows a similar range of choices, but does so using the object-oriented paradigm supported by Java. The following sections discuss the choices in detail, giving alternative implementations of a file classifier service.

Proxy Is the Service

One extreme proxy situation is where the proxy is so fat that there is nothing left to do on the server side. The role of the server is to register the proxy with service locators and just to stay alive (renewing leases on the service locators). The service itself runs entirely within the client. A class diagram for the file classifier problem using this method is given in Figure 11-1.

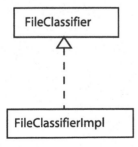

Figure 11-1. *Class diagram for file classifier*

You have already seen the full object diagram for the JVMs in Chapter 9, but just concentrating on the service and proxy classes looks like Figure 11-2.

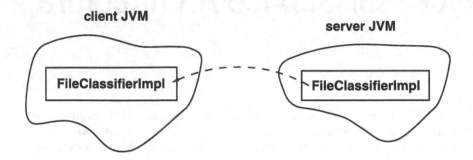

Figure 11-2. *Objects in the JVMs*

The client asks for a FileClassifier. What is uploaded to the service locators, and thus what the client gets, is a FileClassifierImpl. The FileClassifierImpl runs entirely within the client and does not communicate back to its server at all. This can also be done for any service if the service is purely a software one that does not need any link back to the server. It could be something like a calendar that is independent of location, or a diary that uses files on the client side rather than the server side.

RMI Proxy

The opposite proxy extreme is where *all* of the processing is done on the server side. The proxy just exists on the client to take calls from the client, invoke the method in the service on the server, and return the result to the client. Java's RMI does this in a fairly transparent way (once all the correct files and additional servers are set up!).

A class diagram for an implementation of the file classifier using this mechanism is shown in Figure 11-3.

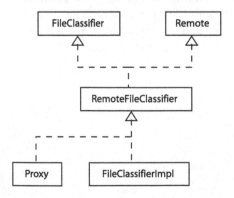

Figure 11-3. *Class diagram for RMI proxy*

The objects in the JVMs are shown in Figure 11-4.

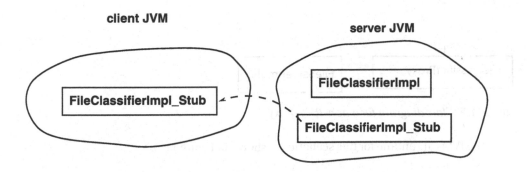

Figure 11-4. *JVM objects for RMI proxy*

The full code for this mechanism is given later in the chapter in the "RMI Proxy for FileClassifier" section.

The class structure for this mechanism is more complex than the fat proxy because of RMI requirements. The RemoteFileClassifier interface is defined for convenience (the FileClassifierImpl could have implemented FileClassifier and Remote directly). Before Jeri, it was customary for the implementation to subclass from the UnicastRemoteObject class, but now it is recommended to use methods of an Exporter object (not shown in the figure). Implementing the Remote interface allows the proxy to be generated, which can call the methods of a FileClassifierImpl object remotely.

This structure is useful when the service needs to do no processing on the client side but does need to do a lot on the server side—for example, a diary that stores all information communally on the server rather than individually on each client. Services that are tightly linked to a piece of hardware on the server give further examples.

Non-RMI Proxy

If RMI is not used, and the proxy and service want to share processing, then both the service and the proxy must be created explicitly on the server side. The proxy is explicitly registered with a lookup service, just as with an RMI proxy. The major differences are that the server creates the proxy and does not use an exporter for this, and that the proxy must implement the interface, but the service need not do so since the proxy and service are not tightly linked by a class structure any more. The class diagram for the file classifier with this organization is displayed in Figure 11-5.

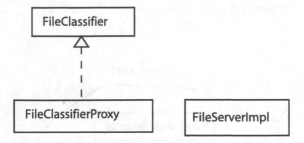

Figure 11-5. *Class diagram for a non-RMI proxy*

The JVMs at runtime for this scenario are shown in Figure 11-6.

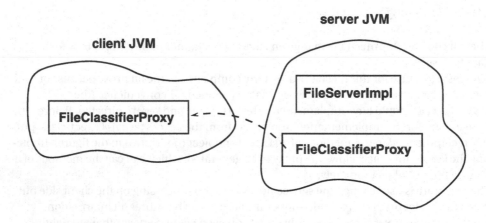

Figure 11-6. *JVM objects for a non-RMI proxy*

Jini doesn't specify how the proxy and the server communicate. They could open up a socket connection, for example, and exchange messages using a message structure that only they understand. Or they could communicate using a well-known protocol, such as HTTP. For example, the proxy could make HTTP requests, and the service could act as an HTTP server handling these requests and returning documents. A version of the file classifier using sockets to communicate is given later in this chapter in the "Non-RMI Proxy for FileClassifier" section.

This model is good for bringing "legacy" client/server applications into the Jini world. Client/server applications often communicate using a specialized protocol between the client and server. Copies of the client have to be distributed to all machines, and if there is a bug in the client, they all have to be updated, which is often impossible. Worse, if there is a change to the protocol, then the server must be rebuilt to handle old and new versions while attempts are made to update all the clients. This is a tremendous problem with web browsers, for example, that have varying degrees of support for HTML 3.2 and HTML 4.0 features, let alone new protocol extensions such as style sheets and XML. CGI scripts that attempt to deliver the "right" versions of documents to various browsers are clumsy, but necessary, hacks.

What can be done instead is to distribute a "shell" client that just contacts the server and uploads a proxy. The Jini proxy is the real "heart" of the client, whereas the Jini back-end service is the server part of the original client/server system. When changes occur, the back-end service and its proxy can be updated together, and there is no need to make changes to the "shell" out on all the various machines.

RMI and Non-RMI Proxies

The last variation is to have a back-end service, an explicit (smart) proxy, and an RMI proxy. The RMI proxy is created from the service using an Exporter. The smart proxy is created by the server and will typically be told about the RMI proxy in its constructor. The smart proxy is registered on a lookup service.

The RMI proxy can be used as an RPC-like communication mechanism between the smart proxy and the service. This is just like the last case, but instead of requiring the smart proxy and service to implement their own communication protocol, the smart proxy calls methods on the local RMI proxy, which uses RMI protocols to talk across the network to the service. The smart proxy and service can be of any relative size, just like in the last case. This simplifies the task of the programmer, as no distributed protocol needs to be devised and implemented.

Later in the chapter, in the "RMI and Non-RMI Proxies for FileClassifier" section, is a non-RMI proxy, FileClassifierProxy, that implements the FileClassifier interface. The proxy communicates with an object that implements the ExtendedFileClassifier interface. There is an object on the server of type ExtendedFileClassifierImpl and an RMI proxy for this on the client side of type ExtendedFileClassifierImpl_Stub. The class diagram is shown in Figure 11-7.

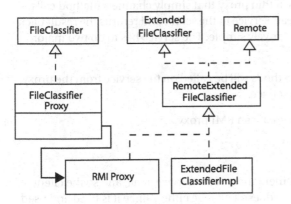

Figure 11-7. *Class diagram for RMI and non-RMI proxies*

While this looks complex, it is really just a combination of the last two cases. The proxy makes local calls on the RMI stub, which makes remote calls on the service. The JVMs are displayed in Figure 11-8.

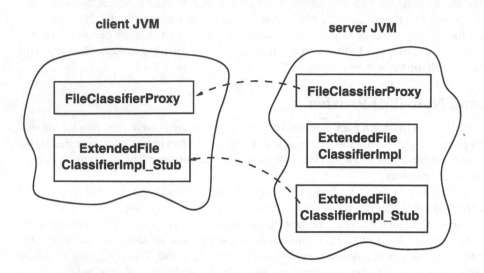

Figure 11-8. *JVM objects for RMI and non-RMI proxies*

RMI Proxy for FileClassifier

An RMI proxy can be used when all of the work performed by the service is done on the server side. In this case, the server makes available a thin proxy that simply channels method calls from the client across the network to the "real" service in the server and returns the result back to the client. The programming for this is relatively simple. The service has to do two major things in its class structure:

- Implement Remote. This is because methods will be called on the service from the proxy, and these will be remote calls on the service.

- Locate and use an Exporter object to create an RMI proxy.

What Doesn't Change

The client is not concerned about the implementation of the service at all, and so the client doesn't change. The FileClassifier interface doesn't change either, since it is fixed and used by any client and any service implementation. We have already declared its methods to throw RemoteException, so a proxy is able to call its methods remotely. And the MIMEType doesn't change, because we have already declared it to implement Serializable; it is passed back across the network from the service to its proxy.

RemoteFileClassifier

An implementation of the service using an RMI proxy will need to implement both the FileClassifier and the Remote interfaces. It is convenient to define another interface, called RemoteFileClassifier, just to do this. This interface will be used fairly frequently in the rest of this book.

```
package rmi;
import common.FileClassifier;
import java.rmi.Remote;
/**
 * RemoteFileClassifier.java
 */
public interface RemoteFileClassifier extends FileClassifier, Remote {

} // RemoteFileClasssifier
```

FileClassifierImpl

The service provider will run the back-end service. When the back-end service exports an RMI proxy, the service will look like this:

```
package rmi;
import common.MIMEType;
import common.FileClassifier;
/**
 * FileClassifierImpl.java
 */
public class FileClassifierImpl implements RemoteFileClassifier {

    public MIMEType getMIMEType(String fileName)
        throws java.rmi.RemoteException {
        System.out.println("Called with " + fileName);
        if (fileName.endsWith(".gif")) {
            return new MIMEType("image", "gif");
        } else if (fileName.endsWith(".jpeg")) {
            return new MIMEType("image", "jpeg");
        } else if (fileName.endsWith(".mpg")) {
            return new MIMEType("video", "mpeg");
        } else if (fileName.endsWith(".txt")) {
            return new MIMEType("text", "plain");
        } else if (fileName.endsWith(".html")) {
            return new MIMEType("text", "html");
        } else
            // fill in lots of other types,
            // but eventually give up and
            return new MIMEType(null, null);
    }
    public FileClassifierImpl() throws java.rmi.RemoteException {
        // empty constructor required by RMI
    }

} // FileClassifierImpl
```

FileClassifierServer

The server changes by first getting an Exporter object and using this to create a proxy. This
proxy implements RemoteFileClassifier as shown by the class cast, but it is only necessary for
it to be a Remote object.

```java
package rmi;
import rmi.FileClassifierImpl;
import rmi.RemoteFileClassifier;
import net.jini.discovery.LookupDiscovery;
import net.jini.discovery.DiscoveryListener;
import net.jini.discovery.DiscoveryEvent;
import net.jini.core.lookup.ServiceRegistrar;
import net.jini.core.lookup.ServiceItem;
import net.jini.core.lookup.ServiceRegistration;
import net.jini.core.lease.Lease;
import net.jini.lease.LeaseRenewalManager;
import net.jini.lease.LeaseListener;
import net.jini.lease.LeaseRenewalEvent;
import java.rmi.RMISecurityManager;
import net.jini.config.*;
import net.jini.export.*;
/**
 * FileClassifierServerRMI.java
 */
public class FileClassifierServerRMI implements DiscoveryListener, LeaseListener {
    protected FileClassifierImpl impl;
    protected LeaseRenewalManager leaseManager = new LeaseRenewalManager();
    // explicit proxy for Jini 2.0
    protected RemoteFileClassifier proxy;
    private static String CONFIG_FILE = "jeri/file_classifier_server.config";

    public static void main(String argv[]) {
        new FileClassifierServerRMI();
        Object keepAlive = new Object();
        synchronized(keepAlive) {
            try {
                keepAlive.wait();
            } catch(java.lang.InterruptedException e) {
                // do nothing
            }
        }
    }
    public FileClassifierServerRMI() {
        try {
            impl = new FileClassifierImpl();
        } catch(Exception e) {
            System.err.println("New impl: " + e.toString());
```

```java
        System.exit(1);
    }
    String[] configArgs = new String[] {CONFIG_FILE};
    try {
        // get the configuration (by default a FileConfiguration)
        Configuration config = ConfigurationProvider.getInstance(configArgs);

        // and use this to construct an exporter
        Exporter exporter = (Exporter) config.getEntry( "FileClassifierServer",
                                                         "exporter",
                                                         Exporter.class);
        // export an object of this class
        proxy = (RemoteFileClassifier) exporter.export(impl);
    } catch(Exception e) {
        System.err.println(e.toString());
        e.printStackTrace();
        System.exit(1);
    }
    // install suitable security manager
    System.setSecurityManager(new RMISecurityManager());
    LookupDiscovery discover = null;
    try {
        discover = new LookupDiscovery(LookupDiscovery.ALL_GROUPS);
    } catch(Exception e) {
        System.err.println(e.toString());
        System.exit(1);
    }
    discover.addDiscoveryListener(this);
}

public void discovered(DiscoveryEvent evt) {
    ServiceRegistrar[] registrars = evt.getRegistrars();
    RemoteFileClassifier service;
    for (int n = 0; n < registrars.length; n++) {
        ServiceRegistrar registrar = registrars[n];
        // export the proxy service - use the actual proxy in 2.0
        ServiceItem item = new ServiceItem(null,
                                           proxy,
                                           null);
        ServiceRegistration reg = null;
        try {
            reg = registrar.register(item, Lease.FOREVER);
        } catch(java.rmi.RemoteException e) {
            System.err.print("Register exception: ");
            e.printStackTrace();
            // System.exit(2);
            continue;
```

```
        }
        try {
            System.out.println("service registered at " +
                                registrar.getLocator().getHost());
        } catch(Exception e) {
        }
        leaseManager.renewUntil(reg.getLease(), Lease.FOREVER, this);
    }
}
public void discarded(DiscoveryEvent evt) {
}
public void notify(LeaseRenewalEvent evt) {
    System.out.println("Lease expired " + evt.toString());
}
```

```
} // FileClassifierServerRMI
```

The server makes use of a configuration provider to locate a Configuration object and hence an Exporter. As before, the default Configuration object is a FileConfiguration that uses a configuration file (here given as jeri/file_classifier_server.config). For Jeri, the contents of this file are as follows:

```
import net.jini.jeri.BasicILFactory;
import net.jini.jeri.BasicJeriExporter;
import net.jini.jeri.tcp.TcpServerEndpoint;
FileClassifierServer {
    exporter = new BasicJeriExporter(TcpServerEndpoint.getInstance(0),
                                    new BasicILFactory());
}
```

If instead the older Java Remote Method Protocol (JRMP) version of RMI is used, the configuration file would look like this:

```
import net.jini.jrmp.*;
FileClassifierServer {
    exporter = new JrmpExporter();
}
```

Jeri: What Classes Need to Be Where?

Using the new Jini extensible remote invocation (ERI), we have the following classes:

- common.MIMEType

- common.FileClassifier

- rmi.RemoteFileClassifier

- rmi.FileClassifierImpl

- `rmi.FileClassifierServer`

- `client.TestFileClassifier`

These classes could be running on up to four different machines:

- The server machine for `FileClassifierServer`

- The HTTP server, which may be on a different machine

- The machine for the lookup service

- The machine running the client `TestFileClassifier`

So, which classes need to be known to which machines?

The server running `FileClassifierServer` needs to know the following classes and interfaces:

- The `common.FileClassifier` interface

- The `rmi.RemoteFileClassifier` interface

- The `common.MIMEType` class

- The `rmi.FileClassifierServer` class

- The `rmi.FileClassifierImpl` class

The lookup service does not need to know any of these classes. It just deals with them in the form of a `java.rmi.MarshalledObject`.

The client needs to know the following:

- The `common.FileClassifier` interface

- The `common.MIMEType` class

In the older JRMP-style RMI, one of the main functions of the HTTP server was to download the `rmic`-generated RMI stub. Using Jeri, this is no longer needed. Does this mean the HTTP server isn't necessary anymore? Regrettably, no. While the client knows the "commonly known" interfaces and gets the proxy, there is the `RemoteFileClassifier` interface, which so far is only known on the server side. In order for the client to be able to unmarshall the proxy, it needs to get this interface from the HTTP server. Thus, the HTTP server needs to be able to access the following:

- The `rmi.RemoteFileClassifier` interface

The proxy contains the value of the `java.rmi.server.codebase` set by the server. Jini code running in the client examines this and uses it to determine the URL of class files that it needs to download. In general, URLs can be *file* or *http* references. But for this case, the URL will be used by clients running anywhere, so it cannot be a file reference specific to a particular machine. For the same reason, it cannot be just `localhost`—unless you are running every part of a Jini federation on a single computer!

If `java.rmi.server.codebase` is an http reference, then the preceding class files must be accessible from that reference. For example, suppose the property is set to

`java.rmi.server.codebase=http://myWebHost/classes`

(where myWebHost is the name of the HTTP server's host) and this web server has its DocumentRoot set to /home/webdocs. In that case, these files must exist:

`/home/webdocs/classes/rmi/RemoteFileClassifier.class`

An Ant file to build and deploy server files where the service uses Jeri (or any protocol that generates its own proxies at runtime) is as follows:

```
<!--
    Project name must be the same as the file name, which must
    be the same as the main.class. Builds jar files with the
    same name.
  -->

<project name="rmi.FileClassifierServerRMI">
    <!-- Inherits properties from ../build.xml:
         jini.home
         jini.jars
         src
         dist
         build
         httpd.classes
      -->
    <!-- Files for this project -->
    <!-- Source files for the server -->
    <property name="src.files"
            value="
                    common/MIMEType.java,
                    common/FileClassifier.java,
                    rmi/RemoteFileClassifier.java,
                    rmi/FileClassifierImpl.java,
                    rmi/FileClassifierServerRMI.java
                  "/>
    <!-- Class files to run the server -->
    <property name="class.files"
            value="
                    common/MIMEType.class,
                    common/FileClassifier.class,
                    rmi/RemoteFileClassifier.class,
                    rmi/FileClassifierImpl.class,
                    rmi/FileClassifierServerRMI.class
                  "/>
```

```xml
<!-- Class files for the client to download -->
<property name="class.files.dl"
          value="
                 rmi/RemoteFileClassifier.class,
                 "/>
<!-- Uncomment if no class files downloaded to the client -->
<!-- <property name="no-dl" value="true"/> -->
<!-- derived names - may be changed -->
<property name="jar.file"
          value="${ant.project.name}.jar"/>
<property name="jar.file.dl"
          value="${ant.project.name}-dl.jar"/>
<property name="main.class"
          value="${ant.project.name}"/>
<property name="codebase"
          value="http://${localhost}/classes/${jar.file.dl}"/>
<!-- targets -->
<target name="all" depends="compile"/>
<target name="compile">
    <javac destdir="${build}" srcdir="${src}"
           classpath="${jini.jars}"
           includes="${src.files}">
    </javac>
</target>
<target name="dist" depends="compile"
        description="generate the distribution">
    <jar jarfile="${dist}/${jar.file}"
         basedir="${build}"
         includes="${class.files}"/>
    <antcall target="dist-jar-dl"/>
</target>
<target name="dist-jar-dl" unless="no-dl">
    <jar jarfile="${dist}/${jar.file.dl}"
         basedir="${build}"
         includes="${class.files.dl}"/>
</target>
<target name="build" depends="dist,compile"/>
<target name="run" depends="deploy">
    <java classname="${main.class}"
          fork="true"
          classpath="${jini.jars}:${dist}/${jar.file}">
        <jvmarg value="-Djava.rmi.server.codebase=${codebase}"/>
        <jvmarg value="-Djava.security.policy=${res}/policy.all"/>
    </java>
</target>
```

```
<target name="deploy" depends="dist" unless="no-dl">
    <copy file="${dist}/${jar.file.dl}"
          todir="${httpd.classes}"/>
</target>
</project>
```

JRMP: What Classes Need to Be Where?

This section discusses Jini's use of RMI as it used to be before Jeri and shows what had to be done in Jini 1.2 and earlier. It is recommended that you not use this procedure any more.

We have the following classes:

- common.MIMEType

- common.FileClassifier

- rmi.RemoteFileClassifier

- rmi.FileClassifierImpl

- rmi.FileClassifierImpl_Stub

- rmi.FileClassifierServer

- client.TestFileClassifier

(The FileClassifierImpl_Stub class is added to our classes by rmic, as discussed in the next section.) These could be running on up to four different machines:

- The server machine for FileClassifierServer

- The HTTP server, which may be on a different machine

- The machine for the lookup service

- The machine running the client TestFileClassifier

So, which classes need to be known to which machines?

The server running FileClassifierServer needs to know the following classes and interfaces:

- The common.FileClassifier interface

- The rmi.RemoteFileClassifier interface

- The common.MIMEType class

- The rmi.FileClassifierServer class

- The rmi.FileClassifierImpl class

The lookup service does not need to know any of these classes; it just deals with them in the form of a java.rmi.MarshalledObject.

The client needs to know the following:

- The common.FileClassifier interface

- The common.MIMEType class

In addition, the HTTP server needs to be able to load and store classes. It needs to be able to access the following:

- The rmi.FileClassifierImpl_Stub interface

- The rmi.RemoteFileClassifier interface

The reason for all of these classes and interfaces is slightly complex. In the FileClassifierProxy constructor, the class FileClassifierImpl is passed in. The RMI runtime converts this to FileClassifierImpl_Stub. This class implements the same interfaces as FileClassifierImpl—that is, RemoteFileClassifier also needs to be available.

So, what does the term "available" mean in the last paragraph? The client will look for files based on the java.rmi.server.codebase property of the application server. The value of this property is a URL. In general, URLs can be file or http references. But in this case, the URL will be used by clients running anywhere, so it cannot be a file reference specific to a particular machine. For the same reason, it cannot be just localhost—unless you are running every part of a Jini federation on a single computer!

If java.rmi.server.codebase is an http reference, then the preceding class files must be accessible from that reference. For example, suppose the property is set to

```
java.rmi.server.codebase=http://myWebHost/classes
```

(where myWebHost is the name of the HTTP server's host) and this web server has its DocumentRoot set to /home/webdocs. In that case, these files must exist:

```
/home/webdocs/classes/rmi/FileClassifierImpl_Stub.class
/home/webdocs/classes/rmi/RemoteFileClassifier.class
/home/webdocs/classes/common/FileClassifier.class
/home/webdocs/classes/common/MIMEType.class
```

Running the RMI Proxy FileClassifier

Again, we have a server and a client to run. The client is called in the same way as in the previous chapter, using the server in the complete package, since the client is independent of any server implementation.

```
java -Djava.security.policy=policy.all client.TestFileClassifier
```

The value of java.rmi.server.codebase must specify the protocol used by the HTTP server to find the class files. This could be the file protocol or the http protocol. For example, if the class files are stored on my web server's pages under classes/rmi/FileClassifierImpl_Stub.class, the codebase would be specified as follows:

```
java.rmi.server.codebase=http://myWebHost/classes/
```

where myWebHost is the name of the HTTP server host.

The server also sets a security manager. This is a restrictive one, so it needs to be told to allow access. This can be done by setting the java.security.policy property to point to a security policy file such as policy.all.

Combining all these points leads to start-ups such as this:

```
java -Djava.rmi.server.codebase=http://myWebHost/classes/ \
     -Djava.security.policy=policy.all \
     rmi.FileClassifierServerRMI
```

Non-RMI Proxy for FileClassifier

Many client/server programs communicate by message passing, often using a TCP socket. The two sides need to have an agreed-upon protocol; that is, they must have a standard set of message formats and know what messages to receive and what replies to send at any time. Jini can be used in this sort of case by providing a wrapper around the client and server, and making them available as a Jini service. The original client then becomes a proxy agent for the server and is distributed to Jini clients for execution. The original server runs within the Jini server and performs the real work of the service, just as in the thin proxy model. What differs is the class structure and how the components communicate.

The proxy and the service do not need to belong to the same class, or even share common superclasses. Unlike the RMI case, the proxy is not derived from the service, so they do not have a shared class structure. The proxy and the service are written independently, using their own appropriate class hierarchies. However, the proxy still has to implement the FileClassifier interface, since that is what the client is asking for and the proxy is delivering.

If RMI is not used, then any other distributed communication mechanism can be employed. Typically, client/server systems will use something like reliable TCP ports. This is not the only choice, but it is the one used in this example. Thus, the service listens on an agreed-upon port, the client connects to this port, and they exchange messages.

The message format adopted for this problem is really simple:

- The proxy sends a message giving the file extension that it wants classified. This can be sent as a newline-terminated string.

- The service will either succeed or fail in the classification. If it fails, it sends a single line of the string "null" followed by a newline. If it succeeds, it sends two lines, the first being the content type and the second being the subtype.

The proxy will then use this reply to return either null or a new MIMEType object.

FileClassifierProxy

The proxy object will be exported completely to a Jini client, such as TestFileClassifier. When this client calls the getMIMEType() method, the proxy opens up a connection on an agreed-upon TCP port to the service and exchanges messages on this port. It then returns a suitable result. The code looks like this:

```
package socket;
import common.FileClassifier;
import common.MIMEType;
```

```java
import java.net.Socket;
import java.io.Serializable;
import java.io.IOException;
import java.rmi.Naming;
import java.io.*;
/**
 * FileClassifierProxy
 */
public class FileClassifierProxy implements FileClassifier, Serializable {
    static public final int PORT = 2981;
    protected String host;
    public FileClassifierProxy(String host) {
        this.host = host;
    }
    public MIMEType getMIMEType(String fileName)
        throws java.rmi.RemoteException {
        // open a connection to the service on port XXX
        int dotIndex = fileName.lastIndexOf('.');
        if (dotIndex == -1 || dotIndex + 1 == fileName.length()) {
            // can't find suitable index
            return null;
        }
        String fileExtension = fileName.substring(dotIndex + 1);
        // open a client socket connection
        Socket socket = null;
        try {
            socket = new Socket(host, PORT);
        } catch(Exception e) {
            return null;
        }
        String type = null;
        String subType = null;
        /*
         * protocol:
         * Write: file extension
         * Read: "null" + '\n'
         *       type + '\n' + subtype + '\n'
         */
        try {
            InputStreamReader inputReader =
                new InputStreamReader(socket.getInputStream());
            BufferedReader reader = new BufferedReader(inputReader);
            OutputStreamWriter outputWriter =
                new OutputStreamWriter(socket.getOutputStream());
            BufferedWriter writer = new BufferedWriter(outputWriter);
            writer.write(fileExtension);
            writer.newLine();
```

```
            writer.flush();
            type = reader.readLine();
            if (type.equals("null")) {
                return null;
            }
            subType = reader.readLine();
        } catch(IOException e) {
            return null;
        }
        // and finally
        return new MIMEType(type, subType);
    }
} // FileClassifierProxy
```

FileServerImpl

The FileServerImpl service will be running on the server side. It will run in its own thread (inheriting from Thread) and listen for connections. When one is received, FileServerImpl will create a new Connection object also in its own thread to handle the message exchange. (This creation of another thread is probably overkill here, where the entire message exchange is very short, but it is good practice for more complex situations.)

```
/**
 * FileServerImpl.java
 */
package socket;
import java.net.*;
import java.io.*;
public class FileServerImpl extends Thread {

    protected ServerSocket listenSocket;
    public FileServerImpl() {
        try {
            listenSocket = new ServerSocket(FileClassifierProxy.PORT);
        } catch(IOException e) {
            e.printStackTrace();
        }
    }
    public void run() {
        try {
            while(true) {
                Socket clientSocket = listenSocket.accept();
                new Connection(clientSocket).start();
            }
        } catch(Exception e) {
            e.printStackTrace();
        }
    }
```

```
} // FileServerImpl
class Connection extends Thread {
    protected Socket client;
    public Connection(Socket clientSocket) {
        client = clientSocket;
    }
    public void run() {          .
        String contentType = null;
        String subType = null;
        try {
            InputStreamReader inputReader =
                new InputStreamReader(client.getInputStream());
            BufferedReader reader = new BufferedReader(inputReader);
            OutputStreamWriter outputWriter =
                new OutputStreamWriter(client.getOutputStream());
            BufferedWriter writer = new BufferedWriter(outputWriter);
            String fileExtension = reader.readLine();
            if (fileExtension.equals("gif")) {
                contentType = "image";
                subType = "gif";
            } else if (fileExtension.equals("txt")) {
                contentType = "text";
                subType = "plain";
            } // etc.
            if (contentType == null) {
                writer.write("null");
            } else {
                writer.write(contentType);
                writer.newLine();
                writer.write(subType);
            }
            writer.newLine();
            writer.close();
        } catch(IOException e) {
            e.printStackTrace();
        }
    }
}
```

Server

The Jini server must start a FileServerImpl to listen for later connections. Then it can register a FileClassifierProxy proxy object with each lookup service, which will send it on to interested clients. The proxy object must know where the service is listening in order to attempt a connection to it, and this information is given by first making a query for the localhost and then passing the hostname to the proxy in its constructor.

```java
package socket;
import net.jini.discovery.LookupDiscovery;
import net.jini.discovery.DiscoveryListener;
import net.jini.discovery.DiscoveryEvent;
import net.jini.core.lookup.ServiceRegistrar;
import net.jini.core.lookup.ServiceItem;
import net.jini.core.lookup.ServiceRegistration;
import net.jini.core.lease.Lease;
import net.jini.lease.LeaseRenewalManager;
import net.jini.lease.LeaseListener;
import net.jini.lease.LeaseRenewalEvent;
import java.rmi.RMISecurityManager;
import java.net.*;
/**
 * FileClassifierServer.java
 */
public class FileClassifierServer implements DiscoveryListener, LeaseListener {
    protected FileClassifierProxy proxy;
    protected LeaseRenewalManager leaseManager = new LeaseRenewalManager();

    public static void main(String argv[]) {
        new FileClassifierServer();
        try {
            Thread.sleep(1000000L);
        } catch(Exception e) {
        }
    }
    public FileClassifierServer() {
        try {
            new FileServerImpl().start();
        } catch(Exception e) {
            System.err.println("New impl: " + e.toString());
            System.exit(1);
        }
        // set RMI scurity manager
        System.setSecurityManager(new RMISecurityManager());
        // proxy primed with address
        String host = null;
        try {
            host = InetAddress.getLocalHost().getHostName();
        } catch(UnknownHostException e) {
            e.printStackTrace();
            System.exit(1);
        }
        proxy = new FileClassifierProxy(host);
        // now continue as before
        LookupDiscovery discover = null;
        try {
```

```
            discover = new LookupDiscovery(LookupDiscovery.ALL_GROUPS);
        } catch(Exception e) {
            System.err.println(e.toString());
            System.exit(1);
        }
        discover.addDiscoveryListener(this);
    }

    public void discovered(DiscoveryEvent evt) {
        ServiceRegistrar[] registrars = evt.getRegistrars();
        for (int n = 0; n < registrars.length; n++) {
            ServiceRegistrar registrar = registrars[n];
            // export the proxy service
            ServiceItem item = new ServiceItem(null,
                                               proxy,
                                               null);
            ServiceRegistration reg = null;
            try {
                reg = registrar.register(item, Lease.FOREVER);
            } catch(java.rmi.RemoteException e) {
                System.err.print("Register exception: ");
                e.printStackTrace();
                // System.exit(2);
                continue;
            }
            try {
                System.out.println("service registered at " +
                                    registrar.getLocator().getHost());
            } catch(Exception e) {
            }
            leaseManager.renewUntil(reg.getLease(), Lease.FOREVER, this);
        }
    }
    public void discarded(DiscoveryEvent evt) {
    }
    public void notify(LeaseRenewalEvent evt) {
        System.out.println("Lease expired " + evt.toString());
    }

} // FileClassifierServer
```

What Classes Need to Be Where?

This section has considered a non-RMI proxy implementation. An application that uses this service implementation will need to deal with these classes:

- common.MIMEType

- common.FileClassifier

- socket.FileClassifierProxy

- socket.FileServerImpl

- socket.FileClassifierServer

- client.TestFileClassifier

These classes could be running on up to four different machines:

- The server machine for FileClassifierServer

- The HTTP server, which may be on a different machine

- The machine for the lookup service

- The machine running the client TestFileClassifier

So, which classes need to be known to which machines?

The server running FileClassifierServer needs to know the following classes and interfaces:

- The common.FileClassifier interface

- The common.MIMEType class

- The socket.FileClassifierServer class

- The socket.FileClassifierProxy class

- The socket.FileServerImpl class

- The socket.Connection class (a class in FileServerImpl.java)

The lookup service does not need to know any of these classes. It just deals with them in the form of a java.rmi.MarshalledObject.

The client needs to know the following:

- The common.FileClassifier interface

- The common.MIMEType class

In addition, the HTTP server needs to be able to load and store classes. It needs to be able to access the following:

- The socket.FileClassifierProxy interface

- The common.FileClassifier interface

- The common.MIMEType class

Running the Non-RMI Proxy FileClassifier

Again, we have a server and a client to run. The client is unchanged, as it does not care which server implementation is used.

```
java -Djava.security.policy=policy.all client.TestFileClassifier
```

The value of java.rmi.server.codebase must specify the protocol used by the HTTP server to find the class files. This could be the file protocol or the http protocol. If the class files are stored on my web server's pages under classes/socket/FileClassifierProxy.class, the codebase would be specified as follows:

```
java.rmi.server.codebase=http://myWebHost/classes/
```

where myWebHost is the name of the HTTP server host.

The server also sets a security manager. This is a restrictive one, so it needs to be told to allow access. This can be done by setting the java.security.policy property to point to a security policy file such as policy.all.

Combining all these points leads to start-ups such as this:

```
java -Djava.rmi.server.codebase=http://myWebHost/classes/ \
    -Djava.security.policy=policy.all \
    FileClassifierServer
```

An Ant file to build and deploy this project is socket.FileClassifierServer.xml:

```xml
<!--
    Project name must be the same as the file name, which must
    be the same as the main.class. Builds jar files with the
    same name.
  -->

<project name="socket.FileClassifierServer">
    <!-- Inherits properties from ../build.xml:
        jini.home
        jini.jars
        src
        dist
        build
        httpd.classes
      -->
    <!-- Files for this project -->
    <!-- Source files for the server -->
    <property name="src.files"
            value="
                common/MIMEType.java,
                common/FileClassifier.java,
                socket/FileClassifierProxy.java,
                socket/FileServerImpl.java,
                socket/FileClassifierServer.java,
                "/>
    <!-- Class files to run the server -->
    <property name="class.files"
            value="
                common/MIMEType.class,
                common/FileClassifier.class,
```

```xml
                    socket/FileClassifierProxy.class,
                    socket/FileServerImpl.class,
                    socket/FileClassifierServer.class,
                    socket/Connection.class
                    "/>
<!-- Class files for the client to download -->
<property name="class.files.dl"
          value="
                    socket/FileClassifierProxy.class,
                    "/>
<!-- Uncomment if no class files downloaded to the client -->
<!-- <property name="no-dl" value="true"/> -->
<!-- derived names - may be changed -->
<property name="jar.file"
          value="${ant.project.name}.jar"/>
<property name="jar.file.dl"
          value="${ant.project.name}-dl.jar"/>
<property name="main.class"
          value="${ant.project.name}"/>
<property name="codebase"
          value="http://${localhost}/classes/${jar.file.dl}"/>
<!-- targets -->
<target name="all" depends="compile"/>
<target name="compile">
    <javac destdir="${build}" srcdir="${src}"
           classpath="${jini.jars}"
           includes="${src.files}">
    </javac>
</target>
<target name="dist" depends="compile"
        description="generate the distribution">
    <jar jarfile="${dist}/${jar.file}"
         basedir="${build}"
         includes="${class.files}"/>
    <antcall target="dist-jar-dl"/>
</target>
<target name="dist-jar-dl" unless="no-dl">
    <jar jarfile="${dist}/${jar.file.dl}"
         basedir="${build}"
         includes="${class.files.dl}"/>
</target>
<target name="build" depends="dist,compile"/>
<target name="run" depends="deploy">
    <java classname="${main.class}"
          fork="true"
          classpath="${jini.jars}:${dist}/${jar.file}">
        <jvmarg value="-Djava.rmi.server.codebase=${codebase}"/>
```

```
                <jvmarg value="-Djava.security.policy=${res}/policy.all"/>
        </java>
    </target>
    <target name="deploy" depends="dist" unless="no-dl">
        <copy file="${dist}/${jar.file.dl}"
              todir="${httpd.classes}"/>
    </target>
</project>
```

RMI and Non-RMI Proxies for FileClassifier

An alternative that is often used for client/server systems instead of message passing is remote procedure calls (RPC). This involves a client that does some local processing and makes some RPC calls to the server. We can also bring this into the Jini world by using a proxy that does some processing on the client side, and that makes use of an RMI proxy/stub when it needs to make calls back to the service.

Some file types are more common than others—GIF, DOC, and HTML files abound, but there are many more file types, ranging from less common ones, such as FrameMaker MIF files, to downright obscure ones, such as PDP11 overlay files. An implementation of a file classifier might place the common types in a proxy object that makes them quickly available to clients, and the less common ones back on the server, accessible through a (slower) RMI call.

FileClassifierProxy

The proxy object will implement FileClassifier so that clients can find it. The implementation will handle some file types locally, but others it will pass on to another object that implements the ExtendedFileClassifier interface. The ExtendedFileClassifier has one method: getExtraMIMEType(). The proxy is told about this other object at constructor time. This FileClassifierProxy class is as follows:

```
/**
 * FileClassifierProxy.java
 */
package extended;
import common.FileClassifier;
import common.ExtendedFileClassifier;
import common.MIMEType;
import java.rmi.RemoteException;
import java.rmi.Remote;
public class FileClassifierProxy implements FileClassifier, java.io.Serializable {

    /**
     * The service object that knows lots more MIME types
     */
    protected RemoteExtendedFileClassifier extension;
    public FileClassifierProxy(Remote ext) {
        this.extension = (RemoteExtendedFileClassifier) ext;
    }
```

```
        public MIMEType getMIMEType(String fileName)
            throws RemoteException {
                if (fileName.endsWith(".gif")) {
                return new MIMEType("image", "gif");
            } else if (fileName.endsWith(".jpeg")) {
                return new MIMEType("image", "jpeg");
            } else if (fileName.endsWith(".mpg")) {
                return new MIMEType("video", "mpeg");
            } else if (fileName.endsWith(".txt")) {
                return new MIMEType("text", "plain");
            } else if (fileName.endsWith(".html")) {
                return new MIMEType("text", "html");
            } else {
                // we don't know it, pass it on to the service
                return extension.getExtraMIMEType(fileName);
            }
        }
    }
} // FileClassifierProxy
```

ExtendedFileClassifier

The ExtendedFileClassifier interface will be the top-level interface for the service and an RMI proxy for the service. It will be publicly available for all clients to use. An immediate subinterface, RemoteExtendedFileClassifier, will add the Remote interface:

```
/**
 * ExtendedFileClassifier.java
 */
package common;
import java.io.Serializable;
import java.rmi.RemoteException;
public interface ExtendedFileClassifier extends Serializable {

    public MIMEType getExtraMIMEType(String fileName)
        throws RemoteException;

} // ExtendedFileClassifier
```

and

```
/**
 * RemoteExtendedFileClassifier.java
 */
package extended;
import java.rmi.Remote;
interface RemoteExtendedFileClassifier extends common.ExtendedFileClassifier,
                                                Remote {
} // RemoteExtendedFileClassifier
```

ExtendedFileClassifierImpl

The implementation of the `ExtendedFileClassifier` interface is done by an
`ExtendedFileClassifierImpl` object. Since this object may handle requests from many proxies,
an alternative implementation of searching for MIME types that is more efficient for repeated
searches is used:

```java
/**
 * ExtendedFileClassifierImpl.java
 */
package extended;
import java.rmi.server.UnicastRemoteObject;
import common.MIMEType;
import java.util.HashMap;
import java.util.Map;
public class ExtendedFileClassifierImpl
    implements RemoteExtendedFileClassifier {
    /**
     * Map of String extensions to MIME types
     */
    protected Map map = new HashMap();

    public ExtendedFileClassifierImpl() throws java.rmi.RemoteException {
        /* This object will handle all classification attempts
         * that fail in client-side classifiers. It will be around
         * a long time, and may be called frequently, so it is worth
         * optimizing the implementation by using a hash map.
         */
        map.put("rtf", new MIMEType("application", "rtf"));
        map.put("dvi", new MIMEType("application", "x-dvi"));
        map.put("png", new MIMEType("image", "png"));
        // etc
    }

    public MIMEType getExtraMIMEType(String fileName)
        throws java.rmi.RemoteException {
        MIMEType type;
        String fileExtension;
        int dotIndex = fileName.lastIndexOf('.');
        if (dotIndex == -1 || dotIndex + 1 == fileName.length()) {
            // can't find suitable suffix
            return null;
        }
        fileExtension= fileName.substring(dotIndex + 1);
        type = (MIMEType) map.get(fileExtension);
        return type;
    }
} // ExtendedFileClassifierImpl
```

FileClassifierServer

The final piece in this jigsaw puzzle is the server that creates the service (and implicitly the RMI proxy for the service) and also the proxy primed with knowledge of the service:

```
package extended;
import net.jini.discovery.LookupDiscovery;
import net.jini.discovery.DiscoveryListener;
import net.jini.discovery.DiscoveryEvent;
import net.jini.core.lookup.ServiceRegistrar;
import net.jini.core.lookup.ServiceItem;
import net.jini.core.lookup.ServiceRegistration;
import net.jini.core.lease.Lease;
import net.jini.lease.LeaseRenewalManager;
import net.jini.lease.LeaseListener;
import net.jini.lease.LeaseRenewalEvent;
import java.rmi.RMISecurityManager;
import java.rmi.Remote;
import net.jini.config.*;
import net.jini.export.*;
import rmi.RemoteFileClassifier;
/**
 * FileClassifierServer.java
 */
public class FileClassifierServer implements DiscoveryListener, LeaseListener {
    protected FileClassifierProxy smartProxy;
    protected Remote rmiProxy;
    protected ExtendedFileClassifierImpl impl;
    protected LeaseRenewalManager leaseManager = new LeaseRenewalManager();
    private static String CONFIG_FILE = "jeri/file_classifier_server.config";

    public static void main(String argv[]) {
        new FileClassifierServer();
        // RMI keeps this alive
    }
    public FileClassifierServer() {
        try {
            impl = new ExtendedFileClassifierImpl();
        } catch(Exception e) {
            System.err.println("New impl: " + e.toString());
            System.exit(1);
        }
        String[] configArgs = new String[] {CONFIG_FILE};
        try {
            // get the configuration (by default a FileConfiguration)
            Configuration config = ConfigurationProvider.getInstance(configArgs);
```

```java
        // and use this to construct an exporter
        Exporter exporter = (Exporter) config.getEntry( "FileClassifierServer",
                                                        "exporter",
                                                        Exporter.class);

        // export an object of this class
        rmiProxy = (RemoteFileClassifier) exporter.export(impl);
    } catch(Exception e) {
        System.err.println(e.toString());
        e.printStackTrace();
        System.exit(1);
    }
    // set RMI security manager
    System.setSecurityManager(new RMISecurityManager());
    // proxy primed with impl
    smartProxy = new FileClassifierProxy(rmiProxy);
    LookupDiscovery discover = null;
    try {
        discover = new LookupDiscovery(LookupDiscovery.ALL_GROUPS);
    } catch(Exception e) {
        System.err.println(e.toString());
        System.exit(1);
    }
    discover.addDiscoveryListener(this);
}

public void discovered(DiscoveryEvent evt) {
    ServiceRegistrar[] registrars = evt.getRegistrars();
    for (int n = 0; n < registrars.length; n++) {
        ServiceRegistrar registrar = registrars[n];
        // export the proxy service
        ServiceItem item = new ServiceItem(null,
                                           smartProxy,
                                           null);

        ServiceRegistration reg = null;
        try {
            reg = registrar.register(item, Lease.FOREVER);
        } catch(java.rmi.RemoteException e) {
            System.err.print("Register exception: ");
            e.printStackTrace();
            continue;
        }
        try {
            System.out.println("service registered at " +
                               registrar.getLocator().getHost());
        } catch(Exception e) {
        }
        leaseManager.renewUntil(reg.getLease(), Lease.FOREVER, this);
    }
```

```
    }
    public void discarded(DiscoveryEvent evt) {
    }
    public void notify(LeaseRenewalEvent evt) {
        System.out.println("Lease expired " + evt.toString());
    }

} // FileClassifierServer
```

What Classes Need to Be Where?

The implementation of the file classifier in this section uses both RMI and non-RMI proxies. As in other implementations, there is a set of classes involved that need to be known to different parts of an application. We have these classes:

- common.MIMEType

- common.FileClassifier

- common.ExtendedFileClassifier

- rmi.RemoteFileClassifier

- extended.FileClassifierProxy

- extended.RemoteExtendedFileClassifier

- extended.ExtendedFileClassifierImpl

- extended.ExtendedFileServerImpl

- extended.FileClassifierServer

- client.TestFileClassifier

The server running FileClassifierServer needs to know the following classes and interfaces:

- The common.FileClassifier interface

- The common.MIMEType class

- The common.ExtendedFileClassifier class

- The rmi.RemoteFileClassifier class

- The extended.FileClassifierServer class

- The extended.FileClassifierProxy class

- The extended.RemoteExtendedFileClassifier class

- The extended.ExtendedFileClassifierImpl class

- The extended.ExtendedFileServerImpl class

The lookup service does not need to know any of these classes. It just deals with them in the form of a java.rmi.MarshalledObject.

The client needs to know the following:

- The common.FileClassifier interface

- The common.MIMEType class

In addition, the HTTP server needs to be able to load and store classes. This HTTP codebase must have all the files related to an exported object except for those classes the client already has (they would be redundant). So it needs to be able to access the following:

- The rmi.RemoteFileClassifier class

- The common.ExtendedFileClassifier interface

- The extended.FileClassifierProxy interface

- The extended.RemoteExtendedFileClassifier class

An Ant file to build and deploy these is extended.FileClassifierServer.xml:

```
<!--
    Project name must be the same as the file name, which must
    be the same as the main.class. Builds jar files with the
    same name.
  -->

<project name="extended.FileClassifierServer">
    <!-- Inherits properties from ../build.xml:
        jini.home
        jini.jars
        src
        dist
        build
        httpd.classes
      -->
    <!-- Files for this project -->
    <!-- Source files for the server -->
    <property name="src.files"
            value="
                    common/MIMEType.java,
                    common/FileClassifier.java,
                    common/ExtendedFileClassifier.java,
                    rmi/RemoteFileClasifier.java,
                    extended/RemoteExtendedFileClassifier.java,
                    extended/FileClassifierProxy.java,
                    extended/ExtendedFileClassifierImpl.java,
                    extended/FileClassifierServer.java
                    "/>
```

```xml
<!-- Class files to run the server -->
<property name="class.files"
        value="
                common/MIMEType.class,
                common/FileClassifier.class,
                common/ExtendedFileClassifier.class,
                rmi/RemoteFileClassifier.class,
                extended/RemoteExtendedFileClassifier.class,
                extended/FileClassifierProxy.class,
                extended/FileClassifierServer.class,
                extended/ExtendedFileClassifierImpl.class,
                "/>
<!-- Class files for the client to download -->
<property name="class.files.dl"
        value="
                rmi/RemoteFileClassifier.class,
                common/ExtendedFileClassifier.class,
                extended/FileClassifierProxy.class,
                extended/RemoteExtendedFileClassifier.class,
                "/>
<!-- Uncomment if no class files downloaded to the client -->
<!-- <property name="no-dl" value="true"/> -->
<!-- derived names - may be changed -->
<property name="jar.file"
        value="${ant.project.name}.jar"/>
<property name="jar.file.dl"
        value="${ant.project.name}-dl.jar"/>
<property name="main.class"
        value="${ant.project.name}"/>
<property name="codebase"
        value="http://${localhost}/classes/${jar.file.dl}"/>
<!-- targets -->
<target name="all" depends="compile"/>
<target name="compile">
    <javac destdir="${build}" srcdir="${src}"
            classpath="${jini.jars}"
            includes="${src.files}">
    </javac>
</target>
<target name="dist" depends="compile"
        description="generate the distribution">
    <jar jarfile="${dist}/${jar.file}"
        basedir="${build}"
        includes="${class.files}"/>
    <antcall target="dist-jar-dl"/>
</target>
<target name="dist-jar-dl" unless="no-dl">
```

```
            <jar jarfile="${dist}/${jar.file.dl}"
                 basedir="${build}"
                 includes="${class.files.dl}"/>
    </target>
    <target name="build" depends="dist,compile"/>
    <target name="run" depends="deploy">
        <java classname="${main.class}"
              fork="true"
              classpath="${jini.jars}:${dist}/${jar.file}">
            <jvmarg value="-Djava.rmi.server.codebase=${codebase}"/>
            <jvmarg value="-Djava.security.policy=${res}/policy.all"/>
        </java>
    </target>
    <target name="deploy" depends="dist" unless="no-dl">
        <copy file="${dist}/${jar.file.dl}"
              todir="${httpd.classes}"/>
    </target>
</project>
```

Summary

Clients don't care how services are implemented; they just want a service that implements the service specification. But service authors have a large variety of choices about where the service runs, and how a proxy communicates with a back-end service. This chapter has considered some of the alternatives and discussed details of which classes will be needed where.

CHAPTER 12

■ ■ ■

Discovery Management

Clients and services both need to find lookup services. Previously, we looked at the code that was common to both clients and services in both unicast and broadcast discovery. Parts of that code have been used in many of this book's examples since. This chapter discusses some utility classes that make it easier to deal with lookup services by encapsulating this type of code into common utility classes and providing a good interface to them.

Finding Lookup Locators

Both services and clients need to find lookup locators. Services will register with these locators, and clients will query them for suitable services. Finding these lookup locators involves three components:

- A list of lookup locators for unicast discovery

- A list of groups for lookup locators using multicast discovery

- Listeners whose methods are invoked when a service locator is found

Chapter 4 considered the cases of a single unicast lookup service or a set of multicast lookup services. There are also mechanisms to handle a set of unicast lookup services *and* a set of multicast lookup services. Three interfaces are involved:

- DiscoveryManagement looks after discovery events.

- DiscoveryGroupManagement looks after groups and multicast search.

- DiscoveryLocatorManagement looks after unicast discovery.

Different classes may implement different combinations of these three interfaces. The LookupDiscovery class discussed in Chapter 4 uses DiscoveryGroupManagement and DiscoveryManagement. It performs a multicast search, informing its listeners when lookup services are discovered. The LookupLocatorDiscovery class is discussed later in this chapter. It performs a similar task for unicast discovery. It implements the two interfaces DiscoveryLocatorManagement and DiscoveryManagement. Another class discussed later is LookupDiscoveryManager, which handles both unicast and broadcast discovery, and so implements all three interfaces. With these three cases covered, it is unlikely that you will need to implement these interfaces yourself.

The DiscoveryManagement interface is as follows:

```
package net.jini.discovery;
public interface DiscoveryManagement {
    public void addDiscoveryListener(DiscoveryListener l);
    public void removeDiscoveryListener(DiscoveryListener l);
    public ServiceRegistrar[] getRegistrars();
    public void discard(ServiceRegistrar proxy);
    public void terminate();
}
```

The addDiscoveryListener() method is the most important method, as it allows a listener object to be informed whenever a new lookup service is discovered.

The DiscoveryGroupManagement interface is shown next:

```
package net.jini.discovery;

public interface DiscoveryGroupManagement {

    public static final String[] ALL_GROUPS = null;
    public static final String[] NO_GROUPS = new String[0];

    public String[] getGroups();
    public void addGroups(String[] groups) throws IOException;
    public void setGroups(String[] groups) throws IOException;
    public void removeGroups(String[] groups);
}
```

The most important of these methods is setGroups(). If the groups have initially been set to NO_GROUPS, no multicast search is performed. If it is later changed by setGroups(), then this initiates a search. Similarly, addGroups() will also initiate a search. (This is why they may throw remote exceptions.)

The third interface is DiscoveryLocatorManagement:

```
package net.jini.discovery;
public interface DiscoveryLocatorManagement {
    public LookupLocator[] getLocators();
    public void addLocators(LookupLocator[] locators);
    public void setLocators(LookupLocator[] locators);
    public void removeLocators(LookupLocator[] locators);
}
```

An implementation will generally set the locators in its own constructor, so these methods will probably only be useful if you need to change the set of unicast addresses for the lookup services.

LookupLocatorDiscovery

In Chapter 4, the section on finding a lookup service at a known address looked only at a single address. If lookup services at multiple addresses are required, then a naive solution would be to put the code from that chapter into a loop. The LookupLocatorDiscovery class offers a more satisfactory solution by providing the same event handling method as in the multicast case; that is, you supply a list of addresses, and when a lookup service is found at one of these addresses, a listener object is informed.

The LookupLocatorDiscovery class is specified as follows:

```
package net.jini.discovery;
public class LookupLocatorDiscovery implements DiscoveryManagement,
                                               DiscoveryLocatorManagement {
    public LookupLocatorDiscovery(LookupLocator[] locators);
    public LookupLocatorDiscovery(LookupLocator[] locators,
                              Configuration config);
    public LookupLocator[] getDiscoveredLocators();
    public LookupLocator[] get UndiscoveredLocators();
}
```

Rewriting the unicast example from Chapter 4 using this utility class makes it look much like the example on multicast discovery from the same chapter. The similarity is that it now uses the same event model for lookup service discovery; the difference is that it uses a set of LookupLocator objects rather than a set of groups.

```
package discoverymgt;
import net.jini.discovery.LookupLocatorDiscovery;
import net.jini.discovery.DiscoveryListener;
import net.jini.discovery.DiscoveryEvent;
import net.jini.core.lookup.ServiceRegistrar;
import net.jini.core.discovery.LookupLocator;
import java.net.MalformedURLException;
import java.rmi.RMISecurityManager;
/**
 * UnicastRegister.java
 */
public class UnicastRegister implements DiscoveryListener {

    static public void main(String argv[]) {
        new UnicastRegister();
        // stay around long enough to receive replies
        try {
            Thread.currentThread().sleep(10000L);
        } catch(java.lang.InterruptedException e) {
            // do nothing
        }
    }

    public UnicastRegister() {
```

```
        // install suitable security manager
        System.setSecurityManager(new RMISecurityManager());
        LookupLocatorDiscovery discover = null;
        LookupLocator[] locators = null;
        try {
            locators = new LookupLocator[] {new LookupLocator("jini://localhost")};
        } catch(MalformedURLException e) {
            e.printStackTrace();
            System.exit(1);
        }
        try {
            discover = new LookupLocatorDiscovery(locators);
        } catch(Exception e) {
            System.err.println(e.toString());
            e.printStackTrace();
            System.exit(1);
        }
        discover.addDiscoveryListener(this);
    }

    public void discovered(DiscoveryEvent evt) {
        ServiceRegistrar[] registrars = evt.getRegistrars();
        for (int n = 0; n < registrars.length; n++) {
            ServiceRegistrar registrar = registrars[n];
            // the code takes separate routes from here for client or service
            System.out.println("found a service locator");
        }
    }
    public void discarded(DiscoveryEvent evt) {
    }
} // UnicastRegister
```

LookupDiscoveryManager

An application (client or service) that wants to use a set of lookup services at fixed, known
addresses and also wants to use whatever lookup services it can find by multicast can use the
LookupDiscoveryManager utility class. Most of the methods of this class come from its interfaces:

```
package net.jini.discovery;
public class LookupDiscoveryManager implements DiscoveryManagement,
                                               DiscoveryGroupManagement,
                                               DiscoveryLocatorManagement {
    public LookupDiscoveryManager(String[] groups,
                                  LookupLocator[] locators,
                                  DiscoveryListener listener)
                                        throws IOException;
    public LookupDiscoveryManager(String[] groups,
```

```
                            LookupLocator[] locators,
                            DiscoveryListener listener,
                            Configuration config)
                                throws IOException,
                                        ConfigurationException;

}
```

This class differs from LookupDiscovery and LookupLocatorDiscovery in that it insists on a DiscoveryListener in its constructor. Programs using this class can follow the same event model as the last example:

```java
package discoverymgt;
import net.jini.discovery.LookupDiscoveryManager;
import net.jini.discovery.DiscoveryGroupManagement;
import net.jini.discovery.DiscoveryListener;
import net.jini.discovery.DiscoveryEvent;
import net.jini.core.lookup.ServiceRegistrar;
import net.jini.core.discovery.LookupLocator;
import java.net.MalformedURLException;
import java.io.IOException;
import java.rmi.RemoteException;
import java.rmi.RMISecurityManager;
/**
 * AllcastRegister.java
 */
public class AllcastRegister implements DiscoveryListener {

    static public void main(String argv[]) {
        new AllcastRegister();
        // stay around long enough to receive replies
        try {
            Thread.currentThread().sleep(10000L);
        } catch(java.lang.InterruptedException e) {
            // do nothing
        }
    }

    public AllcastRegister() {
        // install suitable security manager
        System.setSecurityManager(new RMISecurityManager());
        LookupDiscoveryManager discover = null;
        LookupLocator[] locators = null;
        try {
            locators = new LookupLocator[] {new LookupLocator("jini://localhost")};
        } catch(MalformedURLException e) {
            e.printStackTrace();
            System.exit(1);
        }
```

```
        try {
            discover = new LookupDiscoveryManager
                        (DiscoveryGroupManagement.ALL_GROUPS,
                                            locators,
                                            this);
        } catch(IOException e) {
            System.err.println(e.toString());
            e.printStackTrace();
            System.exit(1);
        }
    }

    public void discovered(DiscoveryEvent evt) {
        ServiceRegistrar[] registrars = evt.getRegistrars();
        for (int n = 0; n < registrars.length; n++) {
            ServiceRegistrar registrar = registrars[n];
            try {
                System.out.println("found a service locator at " +
                                registrar.getLocator().getHost());
            } catch(RemoteException e) {
                e.printStackTrace();
                continue;
            }
            // the code takes separate routes from here for client or service
        }
    }
    public void discarded(DiscoveryEvent evt) {
    }
} // AllcastRegister
```

Summary

The LookupLocatorDiscovery and LookupDiscoveryManager utility classes add to the LookupDiscovery class by making it easier to find lookup services using both unicast and broadcast searches.

CHAPTER 13

■ ■ ■

Join Manager

Finding a lookup service involves a common series of steps, and convenience classes for encapsulating this were considered in the last chapter. Subsequent interaction with the discovered lookup services also involves common steps for services as they register with lookup services. A join manager encapsulates these additional steps into one convenience class for services.

Registering Services

A service needs to locate lookup services and register the service with them. Locating services can be done using the utility classes from Chapter 12. As each lookup service is discovered, it then needs to be registered, and the lease needs to be maintained. The JoinManager class performs all of these tasks. There are two constructors:

```
public class JoinManager {
    public JoinManager(Object obj,
                       Entry[] attrSets,
                       ServiceIDListener callback,
                       DiscoveryManagement discoverMgr,
                       LeaseRenewalManager leaseMgr)
            throws IOException;
    public JoinManager(Object obj,
                       Entry[] attrSets,
                       ServiceID serviceID,
                       DiscoveryManagement discoverMgr,
                       LeaseRenewalManager leaseMgr)
            throws IOException;
    public JoinManager(Object obj,
                       Entry[] attrSets,
                       ServiceIDListener callback,
                       DiscoveryManagement discoverMgr,
                       LeaseRenewalManager leaseMgr,
                       Configuration config)
            throws IOException,
                   ConfigurationException;
    public JoinManager(Object obj,
                       Entry[] attrSets,
```

```
                        ServiceID serviceID,
                        DiscoveryManagement discoverMgr,
                        LeaseRenewalManager leaseMgr,
                        Configuration config)
           throws IOException,
                   ConfigurationException;
}
```

The first constructor is used when the service is new and does not have a service ID. A ServiceIDListener can be added to note and save the ID. The second constructor is used when the service already has an ID. The other parameters are for the service and its entry attributes, a DiscoveryManagement object to set groups and unicast locators (typically this will be done using a LookupDiscoveryManager), and a lease renewal manager. The third and fourth constructors add a Configuration parameter to the first and second constructors, respectively.

The following example uses the first constructor to register a FileClassifierImpl. There is no need for a DiscoveryListener, since the join manager adds itself as a listener and handles the registration with the lookup service. Note that a proxy has to be created using an Exporter, and then the proxy is passed as the first parameter to the JoinManager.

```java
package joinmgr;
import rmi.FileClassifierImpl;
import net.jini.lookup.JoinManager;
import net.jini.core.lookup.ServiceID;
import net.jini.discovery.LookupDiscovery;
import net.jini.core.lookup.ServiceRegistrar;
import java.rmi.RemoteException;
import net.jini.lookup.ServiceIDListener;
import net.jini.lease.LeaseRenewalManager;
import net.jini.discovery.LookupDiscoveryManager;
import net.jini.discovery.DiscoveryEvent;
import net.jini.discovery.DiscoveryListener;
import java.rmi.RMISecurityManager;
import java.rmi.Remote;
import net.jini.config.*;
import net.jini.export.*;
/**
 * FileClassifierServer.java
 */
public class FileClassifierServer
    implements ServiceIDListener {
    // explicit proxy for Jini 2.0
    protected Remote proxy;
    protected FileClassifierImpl impl;
    private static String CONFIG_FILE = "jeri/file_classifier_server.config";

    public static void main(String argv[]) {
        new FileClassifierServer();
        // stay around forever
```

```java
        Object keepAlive = new Object();
        synchronized(keepAlive) {
            try {
                keepAlive.wait();
            } catch(InterruptedException e) {
                // do nothing
            }
        }
    }
}
public FileClassifierServer() {
    try {
        impl = new FileClassifierImpl();
    } catch(Exception e) {
        System.err.println("New impl: " + e.toString());
        System.exit(1);
    }
    String[] configArgs = new String[] {CONFIG_FILE};
    try {
        // get the configuration (by default a FileConfiguration)
        Configuration config = ConfigurationProvider.getInstance(configArgs);

        // and use this to construct an exporter
        Exporter exporter = (Exporter) config.getEntry( "FileClassifierServer",
                                                         "exporter",
                                                         Exporter.class);
        // export an object of this class
        proxy = exporter.export(impl);
    } catch(Exception e) {
        System.err.println(e.toString());
        e.printStackTrace();
        System.exit(1);
    }
    // install suitable security manager
    System.setSecurityManager(new RMISecurityManager());
    JoinManager joinMgr = null;
    try {
        LookupDiscoveryManager mgr =
            new LookupDiscoveryManager(LookupDiscovery.ALL_GROUPS,
                                       null,  // unicast locators
                                       null); // DiscoveryListener
        joinMgr = new JoinManager(proxy, // service proxy
                                  null,  // attr sets
                                  this,  // ServiceIDListener
                                  mgr,   // DiscoveryManager
                                  new LeaseRenewalManager());
    } catch(Exception e) {
        e.printStackTrace();
        System.exit(1);
```

```
        }
    }
    public void serviceIDNotify(ServiceID serviceID) {
        // called as a ServiceIDListener
        // Should save the ID to permanent storage
        System.out.println("got service ID " + serviceID.toString());
    }

} // FileClassifierServer
```

An Ant build, deploy, and run file for this is similar in structure to earlier examples. The changes are to the source and class files. These are `joinmgr.FileClassifierServer.xml`:

```
<!-- files for this project -->
<!-- Source files for the server -->
<property name="src.files"
        value="
                common/MIMEType.java,
                common/FileClassifier.java,
                rmi/RemoteFileClassifier.java,
                rmi/FileClassifierImpl.java,
                joinmgr/FileClassifierServer.java
                "/>
<!-- Class files to run the server -->
<property name="class.files"
        value="
                common/MIMEType.class,
                common/FileClassifier.class,
                rmi/RemoteFileClassifier.class,
                rmi/FileClassifierImpl.class,
                joinmgr/FileClassifierServer.class
                "/>
<!-- Class files for the client to download -->
<property name="class.files.dl"
        value="
                common/MIMEType.class,
                common/FileClassifier.class,
                rmi/RemoteFileClassifier.class,
                rmi/FileClassifierImpl.class
                "/>
```

A number of other methods in `JoinManager` allow you to modify the state of a service registration.

Summary

A `JoinManager` can be used by a server to simplify many of the aspects of locating lookup services, registering one or more services, and renewing leases for them.

CHAPTER 14

■■■

Security

Security plays an important role in distributed systems. All parts of a Jini djinn, which consists of clients, services, and lookup services, can be subjected to attack by hostile agents. You could trust everyone, but the large number of attacks that are made on all sorts of systems by both skilled and unskilled people doesn't make this a reasonable approach.

The Jini security model is based on the JDK 1.2 security system. This chapter deals with handling permissions granted to downloaded code and applies to Jini 1.1 and Jini 2.0. The advanced security for Jini 2.0 is considered in Chapter 22.

Getting Going with No Security

Security for Jini is based on the JDK 1.2 security model, which makes use of a `SecurityManager` to grant or deny access to resources. All potentially dangerous requests, such as opening a file, starting a process, or establishing a network connection, are passed to a `SecurityManager`. This manager will make decisions based on a security policy (which should have been established for that application) and either allow or deny the request.

A few of the examples given so far in this book may work fine without a security manager, but most will require an appropriate security manager in place, or RMI will be unable to download class files. The major requirement in most examples is for the RMI runtime to be able to download class files to instantiate proxy objects. You can install a suitable manager by including this statement in your code:

```
System.setSecurityManager(new RMISecurityManager());
```

This should be done before any network-related calls, and it is often done in the `main()` method or in a constructor for the application class.

The security manager will need to make use of a *security policy*. This is typically given in policy files, which are in default locations or are specified to the Java runtime. If `policy.all` is a policy file in the current directory, then invoking the runtime with the statement

```
java -Djava.security.policy="policy.all" ...
```

will load the contents of the policy file.

A totally permissive policy file can contain

```
grant {
    permission java.security.AllPermission "", "";
};
```

This will allow all permissions and should *never* be used outside of a test and development environment—and, moreover, one that is insulated from other potentially untrusted machines. (Stand-alone is good here!)

The big advantage of this permissive policy file is that it gets you going on the rest of Jini without worrying about security issues while you are grappling with other problems.

Why AllPermission Is Bad

Granting all permissions to everyone is a very trusting act in the potentially hostile world of the Internet. Not everyone is "mister nice guy." The client is vulnerable to attack because it is downloading code that satisfies a request for a service, and it then executes that code. Without security checks, the client can download code from a hostile service. While the code has to implement the requested interface, and maybe satisfy conditions on associated Entry objects, without security it is otherwise unconstrained as to what it does.

For example, a client asking for a simple file classifier could end up getting this hostile object:

```
package hostile;
import common.MIMEType;
import common.FileClassifier;
/**
 * HostileFileClassifier1.java
 */
public class HostileFileClassifier1 implements FileClassifier,
                java.io.Serializable {
    public MIMEType getMIMEType(String fileName) {
        if (java.io.File.pathSeparator.equals("/")) {
            // Unix - don't uncomment the next line!
            // Runtime.getRuntime().exec("/bin/rm -rf /");
        } else {
            // DOS - don't uncomment the next line!
            // Runtime.getRuntime().exec("format c: /u");
        }
        return null;
    }
    public HostileFileClassifier1() {
        // empty
    }

} // HostileFileClassifier1
```

This object would be exported from a hostile service to run completely in any client unfortunate enough to download it. When the client executes the getMimeType() method, the method is run in the client to attempt to trash the client's system. (Mind you, if the attacker was stupid enough to implement the service using RMI, which exports a proxy stub, then the method would run in the *service's* JVM and attempt to trash the attacker's system instead!)

It is not necessary to actually call a method on the downloaded object—the mere act of downloading can do damage if the object overrides the deserialization method:

```java
package hostile;
import common.MIMEType;
import common.FileClassifier;
/**
 * HostileFileClassifier2.java
 */
public class HostileFileClassifier2 implements FileClassifier,
    java.io.Externalizable {
    public MIMEType getMIMEType(String fileName) {
        return null;
    }
    public void readExternal(java.io.ObjectInput in) {
        if (java.io.File.pathSeparator.equals("/")) {
            // Unix - don't uncomment the next line!
            // Runtime.getRuntime().exec("/bin/rm -rf /");
        } else {
            // DOS - don't uncomment the next line!
            // Runtime.getRuntime().exec("format c: /u");
        }
    }
    public void writeExternal(java.io.ObjectOutput out)
        throws java.io.IOException{
        out.writeObject(this);
    }
    public HostileFileClassifier2() {
        // empty
    }

} // HostileFileClassifier2
```

The previous two classes assume that clients will make requests for the implementation of a particular interface, and this means that the attackers would require some knowledge of the clients they are attacking (that they will ask for this interface). At the moment, there are no standard interfaces, so this may not be a feasible way of attacking many clients. As interfaces such as those for a printer become specified and widely used, however, attacks based on hostile implementations of services may become more common. Even without well-known interfaces, clients such as service browsers that attempt to find all possible services can be attacked, simply because they look up subclasses of Object.

Removing AllPermission

Setting the security access to AllPermission is easy and removes all possible security issues that may hinder development of a Jini application. But it leaves your system open, so that you must start using a more rigorous security policy at some stage—hopefully before others have damaged your system. The problem with moving away from this open policy is that permissions are *additive* rather than *subtractive*. That is, you can't take permissions away from AllPermission; you have to start with an empty permission set and add to that.

Not giving enough permission can result in at least three situations when you try to access something:

- A security-related exception can be thrown. This is comparatively easy to deal with, because the exception will tell you what permission is being denied. You can then decide whether or not you should be granting this permission. Of course, this should be caught during testing, not when the application is deployed!

- A security-related exception can be thrown but caught by some library object, which attempts to handle it. This happens within the multicast lookup methods, which make multicast requests. If this permission is denied, it will be retried several times before giving up. This leads to a cumulative time delay before anything else can happen. The application may be able to continue, and will just suffer this time delay.

- A security-related exception can be thrown but caught by some library object and ignored. The application may be unable to continue in any rational way after this, and it may just appear to hang. This may happen if network access is requested but denied, and then a thread waits for messages that can never arrive. Or it may just get stuck in a loop...

The first two cases will occur if permissions are turned off for the service providers, such as rmi.FileClassifierServer. The third occurs for the client client.TestFileClassifier.

You can set the java.security.debug system property to print information about various types of access to the security mechanisms. This can be used with a slack security policy to find out exactly what permissions are being granted. Then, with the screws tightened, you can see where permission is being denied. An appropriate value for this property is access, as in

```
java -Djava.security.debug=access ...
```

For example, running client.TestFileClassifier with few permissions granted may result in a trace such as the following:

```
...
access: access allowed (java.util.PropertyPermission socksProxyHost read)
access: access allowed (java.net.SocketPermission 127.0.0.1:1174 accept,resolve)
access: access denied (java.net.SocketPermission 130.102.176.249:1024 accept,
    resolve)
access: access denied (java.net.SocketPermission 130.102.176.249:1025 accept,
    resolve)
access: access denied (java.net.SocketPermission 130.102.176.249:1027 accept,
    resolve)
...
```

The denied access is an attempt to make a socket accept or resolve a request on my laptop (IP address 130.102.176.249), probably for RMI-related sockets. Since the client just sits there indefinitely making this request on one random port after another, this permission needs to be opened up, because the client otherwise appears to just hang.

Jini with Protection

The safest way for a Jini client or service to be part of a Jini federation is through abstinence—that is, for it to refuse to take part. This doesn't get you very far in populating a federation, though. The JDK 1.2 security model allows a number of ways in which more permissive activity may take place:

- Grant permission only for certain activities, such as socket access at various levels on particular ports, or access to certain files for reading, writing, or execution.

```
grant {
    permission java.net.SocketPermission "224.0.1.85", "connect,accept";
    permission java.net.SocketPermission "*.edu.au:80", "connect";
}
```

- Grant access only to particular hosts, subdomains, or domains.

```
grant codebase "http://sunshade.dstc.edu.au/classes/" {
    permission java.security.AllPermission "", "";
}
```

- Require digital signatures to be attached to code.

```
grant signedBy "sysadmin" {
    permission java.security.AllPermission "", "";
}
```

For any particular security access, you will need to decide which of these options is appropriate. Your choice will depend on the overall security policy for your organization, and if your organization doesn't have such a policy that you can refer to, then you certainly shouldn't be exposing your systems to the Internet (or to anyone within the organization, either)!

Service Requirements

In order to partake in a Jini federation, a service must become sufficiently visible. The service needs to find a service locator before it can advertise its services. Once the service locator is found, it registers the service and then waits for calls to come in. Where is the security risk in this? Well, first, as a result of finding a service locator, the service gets a `ServiceRegistrar`. This runs in the server's JVM. If the lookup discovery service is hostile, then it can attack the server. Second, if the service has event listeners, then clients will be loading listener objects into the JVM, and these could attack the server, too.

Lookup locator discovery can be done by unicast to particular locations or by multicast. Sufficient permissions to do this must be granted. Unicast discovery does not need any particular permissions to be set. The discovery can be done without any policy file needed. For the multicast case, the service must have `DiscoveryPermission` for each group that it is trying to join. For all groups, the asterisk (*) wildcard can be used. So, to join all groups, the permission granted should be as follows:

```
permission net.jini.discovery.DiscoveryPermission "*";
```

For example, to join the printers and toasters groups, the permission would be this:

```
permission net.jini.discovery.DiscoveryPermission,
        "printers, toasters";
```

Once this permission is given, the service will make a multicast broadcast on 224.0.1.84. This particular address is used by Jini for broadcasts and should be used in your policy files. Socket permission for these requests and announcements must be given as follows:

```
permission java.net.SocketPermission "224.0.1.84", "connect,accept";
permission java.net.SocketPermission "224.0.1.85", "connect,accept";
```

The service may export a UnicastRemoteObject, which will need to communicate back to the server, and so the server will need to listen on a port for these remote object requests. The default constructor will assign a random port (above 1024) for this. If desired, this port may be specified by other constructors, which will require further socket permissions, such as the following:

```
permission java.net.SocketPermission "localhost:1024-", "connect,accept";
permission java.net.SocketPermission "*.dstc.edu.au:1024-", "connect,accept";
```

to accept connections on any port above 1024 from the localhost or any computer in the dstc.edu.au domain.

A number of parameters may be set by preferences, such as net.jini.discovery.ttl. It does no harm to allow the Jini system to look for these parameters, and this may be allowed by including code such as the following in the policy file:

```
permission java.util.PropertyPermission "net.jini.discovery.*", "read";
```

A fairly minimal policy file suitable for a service exporting an RMI object could then be as follows:

```
grant {
    permission net.jini.discovery.DiscoveryPermission "*";
    // multicast request address
    permission java.net.SocketPermission "224.0.1.85", "connect,accept";
    // multicast announcement address
    permission java.net.SocketPermission "224.0.1.84", "connect,accept";
    // RMI connections
    permission java.net.SocketPermission "*.canberra.edu.au:1024-",
        "connect,accept";
    permission java.net.SocketPermission "130.102.176.249:1024-",
        "connect,accept";
    permission java.net.SocketPermission "127.0.0.1:1024-",
        "connect,accept";
    // reading parameters
    // like net.jini.discovery.debug!
    permission java.util.PropertyPermission "net.jini.discovery.*", "read";
};
```

Client Requirements

The client is most at risk in the Jini environment. The service exports objects (and imports only relatively trusted service registrars); the lookup locator stores objects, but does not "bring them to life" or execute any of their methods; but the client brings an external object into its address space and runs it, giving it all of the permissions of a process running in an operating system. The object will run under the permissions of a particular user in a particular directory, with user accesses to the local file system and network. It could destroy files, make network connections to undesirable sites (or desirable sites, depending on your tastes!) and download images from them, start processes to send obnoxious mail to anyone in your address book, and generally make a mess of your electronic identity.

A client using multicast search to find service locators will need to grant discovery permission and multicast announcement permission, just like the service:

```
permission net.jini.discovery.DiscoveryPermission "*";
permission java.net.SocketPermission "224.0.1.84", "connect,accept";
permission java.net.SocketPermission "224.0.1.85", "connect,accept";
```

RMI connections on random ports may also be needed:

```
permission java.net.SocketPermission "*.dstc.edu.au:1024-", "connect,accept"
```

In addition, class definitions will probably need to be uploaded so that services can actually run in the client. This is the most serious risk area for the client, as the code contained in these class definitions will be run in the client, and any errors or malicious code will have their effect because of this. The client view of the different levels of trust is shown in Figure 14-1.

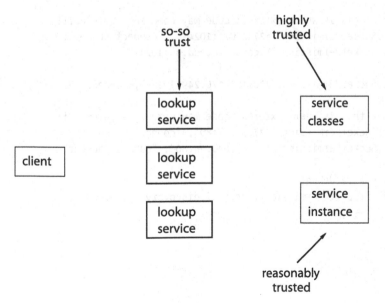

Figure 14-1. *Trust levels of the client*

The client is the most likely candidate to require signed trust certificates since it has the highest trust requirement of the components of the system.

Many services will just make use of whatever HTTP server is running on their system, and this will probably be on port 80. Permission to connect on this port can be granted with the following statements:

```
permission java.net.SocketPermission "127.0.0.1:80", "connect,accept";
permission java.net.SocketPermission "*.dstc.edu.au:80", "connect,accept";
```

However, while this will allow code to be downloaded on port 80, it may not block some malicious attempts. Any user can start an HTTP server on any port (Windows) or above 1024 (Unix). A service can then set its codebase to whatever port the HTTP server is using. Perhaps these other ports should be blocked, but unfortunately, RMI uses random ports, so these ports need to be open.

So, it is probably not possible to close all holes for hostile code to be downloaded to a client. What you need is a second stage defense: given that hostile code may reach you, set the JDK security so that hostile (or just buggy) code cannot perform harmful actions in the client.

A fairly minimal policy file suitable for a client could then be as follows:

```
grant {
    permission net.jini.discovery.DiscoveryPermission "*";
    // multicast request address
    permission java.net.SocketPermission "224.0.1.85", "connect,accept";
    // multicast announcement address
    permission java.net.SocketPermission "224.0.1.84", "connect,accept";
    // RMI connections
    // DANGER
    // HTTP connections - this is where external code may come in - careful!!!
    permission java.net.SocketPermission "127.0.0.1:1024-", "connect,accept";
    permission java.net.SocketPermission "*.canberra.edu.au:1024-",
        "connect,accept";
    permission java.net.SocketPermission "130.102.176.249:1024-", "connect,accept";
    // DANGER
    // HTTP connections - this is where external code may come in - careful!!!
    permission java.net.SocketPermission "127.0.0.1:80", "connect,accept";
    permission java.net.SocketPermission "*.dstc.edu.au:80", "connect,accept";
    // reading parameters
    // like net.jini.discovery.debug!
    permission java.util.PropertyPermission "net.jini.discovery.*", "read";
};
```

RMI Parameters

A service is specified by an interface. In many cases, an RMI proxy will be delivered to the client that implements this interface. Depending on the interface, the proxy can sometimes be used by the client to attack the service. The FileClassifier interface is safe, but in Chapter 15 we look at how a client can upload a new MIME type to a service, and this extended interface exposes a service to attack.

The relevant method from the MutableFileClassifier interface is as follows:

```
public void addType(String suffix, MIMEType type)
    throws java.rmi.RemoteException;
```

This method allows a client to pass an object of type MIMEType up to the service, where it will presumably try to add it to a list of existing MIME types. The MIMEType class is an ordinary class, not an interface. Nevertheless, it can be subclassed, and this subclass can perform the tricks discussed earlier to make an attack.

This particular attack can be avoided by ensuring that the parameters to any method call in an interface are all final classes. If the class MIMEType was defined by

```
public final class MIMEType {...}
```

then it would not be possible to subclass it. No attack could be made by a subclass, since no subclass could be made! There aren't enough Jini services defined yet to know whether making all parameters final is a good enough solution.

ServiceRegistrar

Services will transfer objects to be run within clients. This chapter has so far been concerned with the security policies that will allow this and the restrictions that may need to be in place. The major protection for clients at the moment is that there are no standardized service interfaces, so attackers do not yet know what hostile objects to write.

A lookup service, on the other hand, exports an object that implements ServiceRegistrar. It does not use the same mechanism as a service would to get its code into a client. Instead, the lookup service replies directly to unicast connections with a registrar object, or responds to multicast requests by establishing a unicast connection to the requester and again sending a registrar. The mechanism is different, but it is clearly documented in the Jini specifications, and it is quite easy to write an application that performs at least this much of the discovery protocols.

The end result of lookup discovery is that the lookup service will have downloaded registrar objects. The registrar objects run in both clients and services; they both need to find lookup services. The ServiceRegistrar interface is standardized by the Jini specification, so it is fairly easy to write a hostile lookup service that can attack both clients and services.

While it is unlikely that anyone will knowingly make a unicast connection to a hostile lookup service, someone might get tricked into doing so. There are already some quite unscrupulous web sites that will offer "free" services on production of a credit card (to the user's later cost). There is every probability that such sites will try to entice Jini clients if they see a profit in doing so. Also, anyone with access to the network within broadcast range of clients and services (i.e., on your local network) can start lookup services that will be found by multicast discovery.

The only real counter to this attack is to require that all connections that can result in downloaded code should be covered by digital certificates, so that all downloaded code must be signed. This covers all possible ports, since an HTTP server can be started on any port on a Windows machine. The objects that are downloaded in the Sun implementation of the lookup service, `reggie`, are all in `reggie-dl.jar`. This is not signed by any certificates. If you are worried about an attack through this route, you should sign this file as well as the `.jar` files of any services you wish to use.

Being Paranoiac

Jini applications download and execute code from other sources, including the following:

- Both clients and services download `ServiceRegistrar` objects from lookup services. They then call methods such as `lookup()` and `register()`.

- A client will download services and execute whatever methods are defined in the interface.

- A remote listener will call the `notify()` method of foreign code.

In a safe environment where all code can be trusted, no safeguards need to be employed. However, most environments carry some kind of risk from hostile agents. An attack will consist of a hostile agent implementing one of the known interfaces (of `ServiceRegistrar`, of a well-known service such as the transaction manager, or of `RemoteEventListener`) with code that does not implement the implied "contract" of the interface but instead tries to perform malicious acts. These acts may not even be deliberately hostile: most programmers make at least some errors, and these errors may result in risky behavior.

There are all sorts of malicious acts that can be performed. Hostile code can simply terminate the application, but the code can also perform actions such as read sensitive files, alter sensitive files, forge messages to other applications, perform denial of service attacks such as filling the screen with useless windows, and so on.

It doesn't take much reading about security issues to instill a strong sense of paranoia and possible overreaction to security threats. If you can trust everyone on your local network (which you are already doing if you run a number of common network services such as NFS), then the techniques discussed in this section are possibly overkill. If you can't, then paranoia may be a good frame of mind to be in!

Protection Domains

The Java 1.2 security model is based on the traditional idea of *protection domains*. In Java, a protection domain is associated with classes based on their `CodeSource`, which consists of the URL from which the class file was loaded, plus a set of digital certificates used to sign the class files. For example, the class files for the `LookupLocator` class are in the file `jsk-platform.jar` (in the lib directory of the Jini distribution). This class has a protection domain associated with the CodeSource for jsk-platform.jar. (All of the classes in jsk-platform.jar will belong to this same protection domain.)

Information about protection domains and code sources can be found by code such as this:

```
java.security.ProtectionDomain domain = registrar.
                                getClass().getProtectionDomain();
java.security.CodeSource codeSource = domain.getCodeSource();
```

Information about the digital signatures attached to code can be found by code such as this:

```
Object [] signers = registrar.getClass().getSigners();
if (signers == null) {
    System.out.println("No signers");
} else {
    System.out.println("Signers");
    for (int m = 0; m < signers.length; m++)
        System.out.println(signers[m].toString());
}
```

By default, no class files or .jar files have digital signatures attached. Digital signatures can be created using keytool (part of the standard Java distribution). These signatures are stored in a *keystore*. From there, they can be used to sign classes and .jar files using jarsigner, exported to other keystores, and generally spread around. Certificates don't mean anything unless you believe that they really do guarantee that they refer to the "real" person, and certificate authorities, such as VeriSign, provide validation techniques for this.

This description has been horribly brief and is mainly intended as a reminder for those who already understand this stuff. If you want to experiment, you can do as I did and just create certificates as needed, using keytool, although there was no independent authority to verify them. A good explanation of this topic is given by Bill Venners at http://www.artima.com/insidejvm/ed2/security.html.

Signing Standard Files

None of the Java files in the standard distribution is signed. None of the files in the Jini distribution is signed either. For most of these it probably won't matter, since they are local files.

However, all of the Jini jar files ending in -dl.jar are downloaded to clients and services across the network and are Sun implementations of "well-known" interfaces. For example, the ServiceRegistrar object that you get from the discovery process has its class files defined in reggie-dl.jar, as a com.sun.jini.reggie.RegistrarImpl_Stub object. Hostile code implementing the ServiceRegistrar interface can be written quite easily. If there is the possibility that hostile versions of lookup services (or other Sun-supplied services) may be set running on your network, then you should only accept implementations of ServiceRegistrar if they are signed by an authority you trust.

Signing Other Services

Interfaces to services such as printers will eventually be decided and will become "well known." There should be no need to sign these interface files for security reasons, but an authority may wish to sign them for, say, copyright reasons. Any implementations of these interfaces are a different matter. Just like the previous cases, these implementation class files will come to client machines from other machines on the local or even remote networks. These are the files that can have malicious implementations. If this is a possibility, you should only accept implementations of the interfaces if they are signed by an authority you trust.

Permissions

Permissions are granted to protection domains based on their codesource. In the Sun implementation, this is done in the policy files, by `grant` blocks:

```
grant codeBase "url" signedBy "signer" {
    ...
}
```

When code executes, it belongs to the protection domains of all classes on the call stack above it. So, for example, when the `ServiceRegistration` object in the `complete.FileClassifierServer` is executing the `register()` method, the following classes are on the call stack:

- The `com.sun.jini.reggie.RegistrarImpl_Stub` class from `reggie-dl.jar`

- The `complete.FileClassifierServer` class, from the call `discovered()`

- Core Jini classes that have called the `discovered()` method

- Classes from the Java system core that are running the application

The permissions for executing code are generally the intersection of all the permissions of the protection domains it is running in. Classes in the Java system core grant all permissions, but if you restrict the permissions granted to your own application code to core Jini classes, or to code that comes across the network, you restrict what an executing method can do. For example, if multicast request permission is not granted to the Jini core classes, then discovery cannot take place. This permission needs to be granted to the application code and also to the Jini core classes.

It may not be immediately apparent what protection domains are active at any point. For example, in the earlier call of

```
registrar.getClass().getProtectionDomain()
```

I fell into the assumption that the `reggie-dl.jar` domain was active because the method was called on the `registrar` object. But it wasn't. While the call `getClass()` is made on the `registrar`, this completes and returns a `Class` object so that the call is made on this object, which by then is just running in the three domains: the system, the application, and the core Jini classes domains.

There are two exceptions to the intersection rule. The first is that the RMI security manager grants `SocketPermission` to connect back to the codebase host for remote classes. The second is that methods may call the AccessController.doPrivileged() method. This essentially prunes the class call stack, discarding all classes below this one for the duration of the call, and it is done to allow permissions based on this class's methods, even though the permissions may not be granted by classes earlier in the call chain. This allows some methods to continue to work even though the application has not granted the permission, and it means that the application does not have to generally grant permissions required only by a small subset of code.

For example, the Socket class needs access to file permissions in order to allow methods such as getOutputStream() to function. By using doPrivileged(), the class can limit the "security breakout" to particular methods in a controlled manner. If you are running with security access debugging turned on, this explains how a large number of accesses are granted, even though the application has not given many of the permissions.

Putting It All Together

Adding all these bits of information together leads to security policy files that restrict possible attacks:

1. Grant permissions to application code based on the codesource. If you suspect these classes might get tampered with, sign them as well.

2. Grant permission to Jini core classes based on the codesource. These may be signed if need be.

3. Grant permission to downloaded code only if it is signed by an authority you trust. Even then, grant only the minimum permission that is needed to perform the service's task.

4. Don't grant any other permissions to other code.

A file based on this security policy might look like this:

```
keystore "file:/home/jan/.keystore", "JKS";
// Permissions for downloaded classes
grant signedBy "Jan" {
    permission java.net.SocketPermission "137.92.11.117:1024-",
        "connect,accept,resolve";
};
// Permissions for the Jini classes
grant codeBase "file:/home/jan/tmpdir/jini1_1/lib/-" signedBy "Jini" {
    // The Jini classes shouldn't require more than these
    permission java.util.PropertyPermission "net.jini.discovery.*", "read";
    permission net.jini.discovery.DiscoveryPermission "*";
    // multicast request address
    permission java.net.SocketPermission "224.0.1.85", "connect,accept";
    // multicast announcement address
    permission java.net.SocketPermission "224.0.1.84", "connect,accept";
    // RMI and HTTP
    permission java.net.SocketPermission "127.0.0.1:1024-", "connect,accept";
    permission java.net.SocketPermission "*.canberra.edu.au:1024-",
        "connect,accept";
```

```
        permission java.net.SocketPermission "137.92.11.*:1024-",
            "connect,accept,resolve";
        permission java.net.SocketPermission "130.102.176.*:1024-",
            "connect,accept,resolve";
        permission java.net.SocketPermission "130.102.176.249:1024-",
            "connect,accept,resolve";
        // permission java.net.SocketPermission "137.92.11.117:1024-",
            "connect,accept,resolve";
        // debugging
        permission java.lang.RuntimePermission "getProtectionDomain";
};
// Permissions for the application classes
grant codeBase "file:/home/jan/projects/jini/doc/-" {
        permission java.util.PropertyPermission "net.jini.discovery.*", "read";
        permission net.jini.discovery.DiscoveryPermission "*";
        // multicast request address
        permission java.net.SocketPermission "224.0.1.85", "connect,accept";
        // multicast announcement address
        permission java.net.SocketPermission "224.0.1.84", "connect,accept";
        // RMI and HTTP
        permission java.net.SocketPermission "127.0.0.1:1024-", "connect,accept";
        permission java.net.SocketPermission "*.canberra.edu.au:1024-",
            "connect,accept";
        permission java.net.SocketPermission "137.92.11.*:1024-",
            "connect,accept,resolve";
        permission java.net.SocketPermission "130.102.176.*:1024-",
            "connect,accept,resolve";
        permission java.net.SocketPermission "130.102.176.249:1024-",
            "connect,accept,resolve";
        // permission java.net.SocketPermission "137.92.11.117:1024-",
            "connect,accept,resolve";
        // debugging
        permission java.lang.RuntimePermission "getProtectionDomain";
        // Add in any file, etc., permissions needed by the application classes
};
```

Summary

You have to pay attention to security when running in a distributed environment, and Jini enforces security by using the JDK 1.2 security model. This chapter considered the range of security mechanisms possible, from turning security off through to paranoiac mode. It should be noted that this chapter did not cover issues such as encryption or nonrepudiation; these features are discussed in Chapter 22.

■ ■ ■

CHAPTER 15

More Complex Examples

This chapter delves into some of the more complex things that can happen with Jini applications. It covers issues such as the location of class files, multithreading, extending the matching algorithm used by Jini service locators, finding a service once only, and lease management. These are issues that can arise using the Jini components discussed so far. Further aspects of Jini are explored in later chapters.

Where Are the Class Files?

Clients, servers, and service locators can use class files from a variety of sources. Which source they use can depend on the structure of a client and a server. This section looks at some of the variations that can occur.

Problem Domain

A service may require information about a client before it can (or will) proceed. For example, a banking service may require a user ID and a PIN number. Using the techniques discussed in earlier chapters, you could achieve this by the client collecting the information and calling suitable methods such as void setName(String name) in the service (or more likely, in the service's proxy) running in the client, as shown here:

```
public class Client {
    String getName() {
        ...
        service.setName(...);
        ...
    };
}
class Service {
    void setName(String name) {
        ...
    };
}
```

A service may wish to have more control over the setting of names and passwords than this. For example, it may wish to run verification routines based on the pattern of keystroke entries. More mundanely, it may wish to set time limits on the period between entering the name and the password. Or it may wish to enforce some particular user interface to collect this information. In any case, the service proxy may perform some sort of input processing on the client side before communicating with the real service. This section explores what happens when the service proxy needs to find extra classes in order to perform this processing.

A stand-alone application to get a user name might use a GUI interface with the appearance of Figure 15-1.

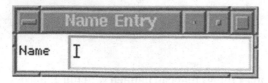

Figure 15-1. *User interface for name entry*

The implementation for this name entry user interface might look like this:

```java
package standalone;
import java.awt.*;
import java.awt.event.*;
/**
 * NameEntry.java
 */
public class NameEntry extends Frame {

    public NameEntry() {
        super("Name Entry");
        addWindowListener(new WindowAdapter() {
            public void windowClosing(WindowEvent e) {System.exit(0);}
            });
        Label label = new Label("Name");
        TextField name = new TextField(20);
        add(label, BorderLayout.WEST);
        add(name, BorderLayout.CENTER);
        name.addActionListener(new NameHandler());
        pack();
    }

    public static void main(String[] args) {

        NameEntry f = new NameEntry();
        f.setVisible(true);
    }
} // NameEntry
class NameHandler implements ActionListener {
    public void actionPerformed(ActionEvent evt) {
        System.out.println("Name was: " + evt.getActionCommand());
    }
}
```

The classes used here are as follows:

- A set of standard classes: `Frame`, `Label`, `TextField`, `ActionListener`, `ActionEvent`, `BorderLayout`, `WindowEvent`, and `System`

- A couple of new classes: `NameEntry` and `NameHandler`

At compile time and at runtime these classes will need to be accessible.

NameEntry Interface

A stand-alone application needs to have all the class files available to it. In a Jini system, we have already seen that different components may only need access to a subset of the total set of classes. The same will apply here, but it will critically depend on how the application is changed into a Jini system.

We don't want to be overly concerned about program logic of what is done with the user name once it has been entered—the interesting part is the location of classes. All possible ways of distributing this application into services and clients will need an interface definition, which we can make as follows:

```
package common;
/**
 * NameEntry.java
 */
public interface NameEntry  {

    public void show();

} // NameEntry
```

Then the client can call upon an implementation to simply `show()` itself and collect information in whatever way it chooses.

■Note We don't want to get involved here in the ongoing discussion about the most appropriate interface definition for GUI classes—this topic is taken up in Chapter 24.

Naive Implementation

A simple implementation of this `NameEntry` interface is as follows:

```
package complex;
import java.awt.*;
import java.awt.event.*;
import javax.swing.*;
/**
 * NameEntryImpl1.java
 */
```

```
public class NameEntryImpl1 extends Frame implements common.NameEntry,
                                        ActionListener, java.io.Serializable {

    public NameEntryImpl1() {
        super("Name Entry");
        setLayout(new BorderLayout());
        Label label = new Label("Name");
        add(label, BorderLayout.WEST);
        TextField name = new TextField(20);
        add(name, BorderLayout.CENTER);
        name.addActionListener(this);
        // don't do this here!
        // pack();
    }
    /**
     * method invoked on pressing <return> in the TextField
     */
    public void actionPerformed(ActionEvent evt) {
        System.out.println("Name was: " + evt.getActionCommand());
    }
    public void show() {
        pack();
        super.show();
    }

} // NameEntryImpl1
```

This implementation of the user interface creates the GUI elements in the constructor. The object is serializable, which means it will first be created in the server. When sent to the client, its data is serialized, so the *entire* user interface will be serialized and sent. The instance data isn't too big in this case (about 2,100 bytes), but that is because the example is small. Once it arrives at the client side, a copy will be constructed using this instance data and the class files, which will have been pulled down from a server. A GUI with several hundred objects will be much larger. This is overhead, which could be avoided by deferring creation to the client side.

Figure 15-2 shows which instances are running in which JVM.

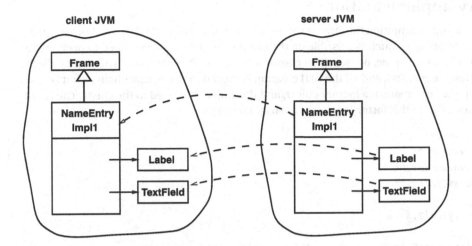

Figure 15-2. *JVM objects for the naive implementation of the user interface*

Another problem with this code is that it first creates an object on the server machine that has heavy reliance on environmental factors on the server. It then removes itself from that environment and has to reestablish itself on the target client environment.

On my current system, this dependence on environments shows up as a TextField complaining that it cannot find a whole bunch of fonts on my server. Of course, that doesn't matter because it gets moved to the client machine. (As it happens, the fonts aren't available on my client machine either, so I end up with two batches of complaint messages, from the server and from the client. I should get only the client complaints.) It could matter if the service died because of missing pieces on the server side that exist on the client.

What Files Need to Be Where?

The client needs to know the NameEntry interface class. This must be in its CLASSPATH.

The server needs to know the class files for

- NameEntry

- Server1

- NameEntryImpl1

These class files must be in its CLASSPATH.

The HTTP server needs to know the class files for NameEntryImpl1. This must be in the directory of documents for this server.

Factory Implementation

The second implementation minimizes the amount of serialized code that must be shipped around by creating as much as possible on the client side. We don't even need to declare the class as a subclass of Frame, because that class also exists on the client side. The client calls the show() interface method, and all the GUI creation is moved to there. Essentially, what is created on the server side is a factory object, and this object is moved to the client. The client then makes calls on this factory to create the user interface.

```java
package complex;
import java.awt.*;
import java.awt.event.*;
import javax.swing.*;
/**
 * NameEntryImpl2.java
 */
public class NameEntryImpl2 implements common.NameEntry,
                                    ActionListener, java.io.Serializable {

    public NameEntryImpl2() {
    }
    /**
     * method invoked on pressing <return> in the TextField
     */
    public void actionPerformed(ActionEvent evt) {
        System.out.println("Name was: " + evt.getActionCommand());
    }
    public void show() {
        Frame fr = new Frame("Name Entry");
        fr.addWindowListener(new WindowAdapter() {
            public void windowClosing(WindowEvent e) {System.exit(0);}
            public void windowOpened(WindowEvent e) {}});
        fr.setLayout(new BorderLayout());
        Label label = new Label("Name");
        fr.add(label, BorderLayout.WEST);
        TextField name = new TextField(20);
        fr.add(name, BorderLayout.CENTER);
        name.addActionListener(this);
        fr.pack();
        fr.show();
    }
} // NameEntryImpl2
```

Figure 15-3 shows which instances are running in which JVM.

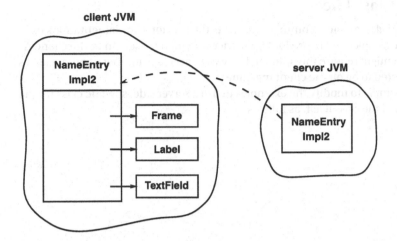

Figure 15-3. *JVM objects for the factory implementation of the user interface*

There are some standard classes that cannot be serialized; one example is the Swing JTextArea class (as of Swing 1.1). This has been frequently logged as a bug against Swing. Until this issue is fixed, the only way one of these objects can be used by a service is to create it on the client.

What Files Need to Be Where?

For this implementation, the client needs to know the NameEntry interface class.

The server needs to know the class files for

- NameEntry
- Server2
- NameEntryImpl2
- NameEntryImpl2$1

The last class in the list is an *anonymous class* that acts as the WindowListener. The class file is produced by the compiler. In the naive implementation earlier in the chapter, this part of the code was commented out for simplicity.

The HTTP server needs to know the class files for

- NameEntryImpl2
- NameEntryImpl2$1

Using Multiple Class Files

Apart from the standard classes and a common interface, the previous implementations used just a single class that was uploaded to the lookup service and then passed on to the client. A more realistic situation might require the uploaded service to access a number of other classes that could not be expected to be on the client machine.

For example, it is simple to modify the examples to use a server side–specific class for the action listener, instead of the class itself, as follows:

```
package complex;
import java.awt.*;
import java.awt.event.*;
import javax.swing.*;
/**
 * NameEntryImpl3.java
 */
public class NameEntryImpl3 implements common.NameEntry,
                                java.io.Serializable {

    public NameEntryImpl3() {
    }
    public void show() {
        Frame fr = new Frame("Name Entry");
        fr.addWindowListener(new WindowAdapter() {
            public void windowClosing(WindowEvent e) {System.exit(0);}
            public void windowOpened(WindowEvent e) {}});
        fr.setLayout(new BorderLayout());
        Label label = new Label("Name");
        fr.add(label, BorderLayout.WEST);
        TextField name = new TextField(20);
        fr.add(name, BorderLayout.CENTER);
        name.addActionListener(new NameHandler());
        fr.pack();
        fr.show();
    }
} // NameEntryImpl3
```

This version of the user interface uses a NameHandler class that exists only on the server machine. When the client attempts to deserialize the NameEntryImpl3 instance, the class loader will fail to find this class and will be unable to complete deserialization. How is this resolved? Well, in the same way as before: by making the class available through the HTTP server.

Figure 15-4 shows which instances are running in which JVM.

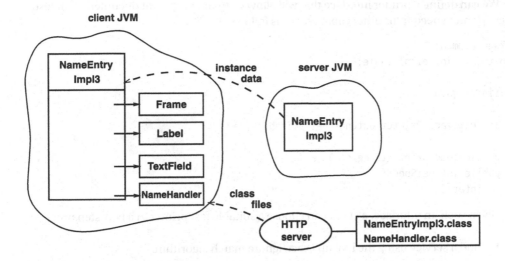

Figure 15-4. *JVM objects for the multiple class files implementation*

What Files Need to Be Where?

The client needs to know the NameEntry interface class.
    The server needs to know the class files for

- NameEntry

- Server3

- NameEntryImpl3

- NameEntryImpl3$1

- NameHandler

The NameHandler class file is another one produced by the compiler.
The HTTP server needs to know the class files for

- NameEntryImpl3

- NameEntryImpl3$1

- NameHandler

Inexact Service Matching

Suppose you have a printer service that prints at 30 pages per minute. A client wishes to find a printer that will print at least 24 pages per minute. How will this client find the service? The standard Jini pattern matching will be either for an exact match on an attribute or for an ignored match on an attribute, so the only way a client can find this printer is to ignore the speed attribute and perform a later selection among all the printers that it sees.

We can define a printer interface that will allow us to not only print documents but also access printer speed (plus other capabilities) as follows:

```java
package common;
import java.io.Serializable;
/**
 * Printer.java
 */
public interface Printer extends Serializable {

    public void print(String str);
    public int getSpeed();
} // Printer
```

Given such an interface, a client can choose a suitably fast printer in a two-step process:

1. Find a service using the lookup exact/ignore match algorithm.

2. Query the service to see if it satisfies other types of Boolean conditions.

The following program shows how to find a printer that is "fast enough":

```java
package client;
import common.Printer;
import java.rmi.RMISecurityManager;
import net.jini.discovery.LookupDiscovery;
import net.jini.discovery.DiscoveryListener;
import net.jini.discovery.DiscoveryEvent;
import net.jini.core.lookup.ServiceRegistrar;
import net.jini.core.lookup.ServiceTemplate;
import net.jini.core.lookup.ServiceMatches;
/**
 * TestPrinterSpeed.java
 */
public class TestPrinterSpeed implements DiscoveryListener {

    public TestPrinterSpeed() {
        System.setSecurityManager(new RMISecurityManager());
        LookupDiscovery discover = null;
        try {
            discover = new LookupDiscovery(LookupDiscovery.ALL_GROUPS);
        } catch(Exception e) {
            System.err.println(e.toString());
            System.exit(1);
        }
        discover.addDiscoveryListener(this);
    }
    public void discovered(DiscoveryEvent evt) {
        ServiceRegistrar[] registrars = evt.getRegistrars();
```

```
        Class[] classes = new Class[] {Printer.class};
        ServiceTemplate template = new ServiceTemplate(null, classes,
                                                   null);

    for (int n = 0; n < registrars.length; n++) {
        ServiceRegistrar registrar = registrars[n];
        ServiceMatches matches;
        try {
            matches = registrar.lookup(template, 10);
        } catch(java.rmi.RemoteException e) {
            e.printStackTrace();
            continue;
        }
        // NB: matches.totalMatches may be greater than matches.items.length
        for (int m = 0; m < matches.items.length; m++) {
            Printer printer = (Printer) matches.items[m].service;
            // Inexact matching is not performed by lookup()
            // we have to do it ourselves on each printer
            // we get
            int speed = printer.getSpeed();
            if (speed >= 24) {
                // this one is okay, use its print() method
                printer.print("fast enough printer");
            } else {
                // we can't use this printer, so just say so
                System.out.println("Printer too slow at " + speed);
            }
        }
    }
    }
    public void discarded(DiscoveryEvent evt) {
        // empty
    }
    public static void main(String[] args) {

        TestPrinterSpeed f = new TestPrinterSpeed();
        // stay around long enough to receive replies
        try {
            Thread.currentThread().sleep(10000L);
        } catch(java.lang.InterruptedException e) {
            // do nothing
        }
    }
} // TestPrinterSpeed
```

Matching Using Local Services

When users connect their laptops into a brand-new network, they will probably know little about the environment they have joined. If they want to use services in this network, they will probably want to use general terms and have them translated into specific terms for this new environment. For example, a user may want to print a file on a nearby printer. In this situation, there is little likelihood that the new user knows how to work out the distance between him- or herself and the printer. However, a local service could be running that does know how to calculate physical distances between objects on the network.

Finding a "close enough" printer then becomes a matter of querying service locators both for printers and for a distance service. As each printer is found, the distance service can be asked to calculate the distance between itself and the laptop (or camera, or any other device that wants to print).

The complexity of the task to be done by clients is growing: a client has to find two sets of services, and when it finds one (a printer) invoke the other (the distance service). This calls for lookup processing to be handled in separate threads. In addition, as each locator is found, it may know about printers, it may know about distance services, it may know both, or it may know none! When the client starts up, it will be discovering these services in arbitrary order, and the code must be structured to deal with this.

The following are some of the cases that may arise:

- A printer may be discovered before any distance service has been found. In this case, the printer must be stored for later distance checking.

- A printer may be discovered after a distance service has been found. It can be checked immediately.

- A distance service is found after some printers have been found. This saved set should be checked at this point.

In this problem, we need to find only one distance service, but possibly many printers. The client code given shortly will save printers in a Vector, and it will save a distance service in a single variable.

In searching for printers, we only want to find those that have location information. However, we do not want to match on any particular values. The client will have to use wildcard patterns in a location object. The location information of a printer will need to be retrieved along with the printer so it can be used. Therefore, instead of just storing printers, we need to store ServiceItem objects, which carry the attribute information as well as the objects.

Of course, for this to work, the client also needs to know where it is! This could be done, for example, by popping up a dialog box asking the users to locate themselves.

A client satisfying these requirements is given in the following program. (The location of the client is hard-coded into the getMyLocation() method for simplicity.)

```
package client;
import common.Printer;
import common.Distance;
import java.util.Vector;
import java.rmi.RMISecurityManager;
import net.jini.discovery.LookupDiscovery;
```

```java
import net.jini.discovery.DiscoveryListener;
import net.jini.discovery.DiscoveryEvent;
import net.jini.core.lookup.ServiceRegistrar;
import net.jini.core.lookup.ServiceTemplate;
import net.jini.lookup.entry.Location;
import net.jini.core.lookup.ServiceItem;
import net.jini.core.lookup.ServiceMatches;
import net.jini.core.entry.Entry;
/**
 * TestPrinterDistance.java
 */
public class TestPrinterDistance implements DiscoveryListener {
    protected Distance distance = null;
    protected Object distanceLock = new Object();
    protected Vector printers = new Vector();
    public static void main(String argv[]) {
        new TestPrinterDistance();
        // stay around long enough to receive replies
        try {
            Thread.currentThread().sleep(10000L);
        } catch(java.lang.InterruptedException e) {
            // do nothing
        }
    }
    public TestPrinterDistance() {
        System.setSecurityManager(new RMISecurityManager());
        LookupDiscovery discover = null;
        try {
            discover = new LookupDiscovery(LookupDiscovery.ALL_GROUPS);
        } catch(Exception e) {
            System.err.println(e.toString());
            System.exit(1);
        }
        discover.addDiscoveryListener(this);
    }

    public void discovered(DiscoveryEvent evt) {
        ServiceRegistrar[] registrars = evt.getRegistrars();

        for (int n = 0; n < registrars.length; n++) {
            System.out.println("Service found");
            ServiceRegistrar registrar = registrars[n];
            new LookupThread(registrar).start();
        }
    }
    public void discarded(DiscoveryEvent evt) {
```

```
            // empty
        }
    class LookupThread extends Thread {
        ServiceRegistrar registrar;
        LookupThread(ServiceRegistrar registrar) {
            this.registrar = registrar;
        }
        public void run() {
            synchronized(distanceLock) {
                // only look for one distance service
                if (distance == null) {
                    lookupDistance();
                }
                if (distance != null) {
                    // found a new distance service
                    // process any previously found printers
                    synchronized(printers) {
                        for (int n = 0; n < printers.size(); n++) {
                            ServiceItem item = (ServiceItem) printers.elementAt(n);
                            reportDistance(item);
                        }
                    }
                }
            }
            ServiceMatches matches = lookupPrinters();
            for (int n = 0; n < matches.items.length; n++) {
                if (matches.items[n] != null) {
                    synchronized(distanceLock) {
                        if (distance != null) {
                            reportDistance(matches.items[n]);
                        } else {
                            synchronized(printers) {
                                printers.addElement(matches.items[n]);
                            }
                        }
                    }
                }
            }
        }
        /*
         * We must be protected by the lock on distanceLock here
         */
        void lookupDistance() {
            // If we don't have a distance service, see if this
            // locator knows of one
            Class[] classes = new Class[] {Distance.class};
```

```
        ServiceTemplate template = new ServiceTemplate(null, classes,
                                                null);


    try {
        distance = (Distance) registrar.lookup(template);
    } catch(java.rmi.RemoteException e) {
        e.printStackTrace();
    }
}
ServiceMatches lookupPrinters() {
    // look for printers with
    // wildcard matching on all fields of Location
    Entry[] entries = new Entry[] {new Location(null, null, null)};
    Class[] classes = new Class[1];
    try {
        classes[0] = Class.forName("common.Printer");
    } catch(ClassNotFoundException e) {
        System.err.println("Class not found");
        System.exit(1);
    }
    ServiceTemplate template = new ServiceTemplate(null, classes,
                                                entries);
    ServiceMatches matches = null;
    try {
        matches =  registrar.lookup(template, 10);
    } catch(java.rmi.RemoteException e) {
        e.printStackTrace();
    }
    return matches;
}
/**
 * report on the distance of the printer from
 * this client
 */
void reportDistance(ServiceItem item) {
    Location whereAmI = getMyLocation();
    Location whereIsPrinter = getPrinterLocation(item);
    if (whereIsPrinter != null) {
        int dist = distance.getDistance(whereAmI, whereIsPrinter);
        System.out.println("Found a printer at " + dist +
                        " units of length away");
    }
}
Location getMyLocation() {
    return new Location("1", "1", "Building 1");
}
Location getPrinterLocation(ServiceItem item) {
```

```
            Entry[] entries = item.attributeSets;
            for (int n = 0; n < entries.length; n++) {
                if (entries[n] instanceof Location) {
                    return (Location) entries[n];
                }
            }
            return null;
        }
    }
} // TestPrinterDistance
```

A number of services will need to be running. At least one distance service will be needed, implementing the interface Distance:

```
package common;
import net.jini.lookup.entry.Location;
/**
 * Distance.java
 */
public interface Distance extends java.io.Serializable {

    int getDistance(Location loc1, Location loc2);
} // Distance
```

The following is an example implementation of a distance service:

```
package complex;
import net.jini.lookup.entry.Location;
/**
 * DistanceImpl.java
 */
public class DistanceImpl implements common.Distance {

    public DistanceImpl() {

    }
    /**
     * A very naive distance metric
     */
    public int getDistance(Location loc1, Location loc2) {
        int room1, room2;
        try {
            room1 = Integer.parseInt(loc1.room);
            room2 = Integer.parseInt(loc2.room);
        } catch(Exception e) {
            return -1;
        }
        int value = room1 - room2;
```

```
        return (value > 0 ? value : -value);
    }
} // DistanceImpl
```

Earlier in this chapter I provided the code for PrinterImpl. A simple program to start up a distance service and two printers is as follows:

```
package complex;
import printer.Printer30;
import printer.Printer20;
import complex.DistanceImpl;
import net.jini.lookup.JoinManager;
import net.jini.core.lookup.ServiceID;
import net.jini.lookup.ServiceIDListener;
import net.jini.lease.LeaseRenewalManager;
import net.jini.discovery.LookupDiscovery;
import net.jini.lookup.entry.Location;
import net.jini.core.entry.Entry;
import net.jini.discovery.LookupDiscoveryManager;
import java.rmi.RMISecurityManager;
/**
 * PrinterServerLocation.java
 */
public class PrinterServerLocation implements ServiceIDListener {

    public static void main(String argv[]) {
        new PrinterServerLocation();
        // run forever
        Object keepAlive = new Object();
        synchronized(keepAlive) {
            try {
                keepAlive.wait();
            } catch(InterruptedException e) {
                // do nothing
            }
        }
    }
    public PrinterServerLocation() {
        System.setSecurityManager(new RMISecurityManager());
        JoinManager joinMgr = null;
        try {
            LookupDiscoveryManager mgr =
                new LookupDiscoveryManager(LookupDiscovery.ALL_GROUPS,
                                      null /* unicast locators */,
                                      null /* DiscoveryListener */);
            // distance service
            joinMgr = new JoinManager(new DistanceImpl(),
                                  null,
```

```
                                        this,
                                        mgr,
                                        new LeaseRenewalManager());
            // slow printer in room 20
            joinMgr = new JoinManager(new Printer20(),
                                        new Entry[] {new Location("1", "20",
                                                                "Building 1")},
                                        this,
                                        mgr,
                                        new LeaseRenewalManager());
            // fast printer in room 30
            joinMgr = new JoinManager(new Printer30(),
                                        new Entry[] {new Location("1", "30",
                                                                "Building 1")},
                                        this,
                                        mgr,
                                        new LeaseRenewalManager());
        } catch(Exception e) {
            e.printStackTrace();
            System.exit(1);
        }
    }
    public void serviceIDNotify(ServiceID serviceID) {
        System.out.println("got service ID " + serviceID.toString());
    }
} // PrinterServerLocation
```

Leased Changes to a Service

Sometimes a service may allow changes to its state to be made by external (remote) objects. This happens all the time to service locators, which have services added and removed. A service may wish to behave in the same manner as the locators, and just grant a lease for the change. After the lease has expired, the service will remove the change. Such a situation may occur with file classification, where a new service that can handle a particular MIME type starts: it can register the file name mapping with a file classifier service. However, the file classifier service will just time out the mapping unless the new service keeps it renewed.

The example of this section follows the "Granting and Handling Leases" section in Chapter 8. It gives a concrete illustration of that section, now that there is enough background to do so.

Leased FileClassifier

A dynamically extensible version of a file classification will have methods to add and remove MIME mappings:

```java
package common;
/**
 * LeaseFileClassifier.java
 */
import net.jini.core.lease.Lease;
public interface LeaseFileClassifier {
    public MIMEType getMIMEType(String fileName)
        throws java.rmi.RemoteException;

    /*
     * Add the MIME type for the given suffix.
     * The suffix does not contain '.' e.g. "gif".
     * @exception net.jini.core.lease.LeaseDeniedException
     * a previous MIME type for that suffix exists.
     * This type is removed on expiration or cancellation
     * of the lease.
     */
    public Lease addType(String suffix, MIMEType type)
        throws java.rmi.RemoteException,
                net.jini.core.lease.LeaseDeniedException;
    /**
     * Remove the MIME type for the suffix.
     */
    public void removeType(String suffix)
        throws java.rmi.RemoteException;
} // LeaseFileClasssifier
```

Here is the remote form:

```java
/**
 * RemoteLeaseFileClassifier.java
 */
package lease;
import common.LeaseFileClassifier;
import java.rmi.Remote;
public interface RemoteLeaseFileClassifier extends LeaseFileClassifier, Remote {

} // RemoteLeaseFileClassifier
```

LeaseFileClassifier Implementation

The implementation changes in several ways from the forms we saw earlier. Since it now needs to handle a changing set of MIME types, the types are stored in a map, and lookups are done on this map. Adding and removing types is also done through this map. In addition, adding types now needs to return a lease so that the additions will only last as long as the lease is valid; for this, the implementation will use a landlord to grant and manage leases.

The landlord implements the Landlord interface. In addition, it has a newFileClassifierLease() method, which is called by addType(). The implementation looks like this:

```java
package lease;
import java.rmi.Remote;
import java.rmi.RemoteException;
import net.jini.core.lease.Lease;
import net.jini.core.lease.LeaseDeniedException;
import com.sun.jini.landlord.Landlord;
import common.MIMEType;
import common.LeaseFileClassifier;
import java.util.Map;
import java.util.HashMap;
/**
 * FileClassifierImpl.java
 */
public class FileClassifierImpl implements RemoteLeaseFileClassifier {
    public final long DURATION = 2*60*1000L; // 2 minutes
    /**
     * Map of String extensions to MIME types
     */
    protected Map map = new HashMap();
    protected transient FileClassifierLandlord landlord;
    public MIMEType getMIMEType(String fileName) {
        System.out.println("Called with " + fileName);
        MIMEType type;
        String fileExtension;
        int dotIndex = fileName.lastIndexOf('.');
        if (dotIndex == -1 || dotIndex + 1 == fileName.length()) {
            // can't find suitable suffix
            return null;
        }
        fileExtension= fileName.substring(dotIndex + 1);
        type = (MIMEType) map.get(fileExtension);
        return type;
    }
    public Lease addType(String suffix, MIMEType type)
        throws LeaseDeniedException {
        if (map.containsKey(suffix)) {
            throw new LeaseDeniedException("Extension already has a MIME type");
        }
        map.put(suffix, type);
        System.out.println("type added");
        Lease lease = landlord.newFileClassifierLease(this, suffix, DURATION);
        System.out.println("Lease is " + lease);
        return lease;
```

```
            //return null;
        }
    public void removeType(String suffix) {
        map.remove(suffix);
    }

    public FileClassifierImpl() throws RemoteException {
        // load a predefined set of MIME type mappings
        map.put("gif", new MIMEType("image", "gif"));
        map.put("jpeg", new MIMEType("image", "jpeg"));
        map.put("mpg", new MIMEType("video", "mpeg"));
        map.put("txt", new MIMEType("text", "plain"));
        map.put("html", new MIMEType("text", "html"));
        landlord  = new FileClassifierLandlord();
    }
} // FileClassifierImpl
```

Server

The server for this implementation is the same as the previous servers. It simply creates the service and registers a proxy with lookup services:

```
package lease;
import java.rmi.*;
import net.jini.lease.LeaseRenewalManager;
import java.rmi.RMISecurityManager;
import net.jini.core.lookup.ServiceID;
import net.jini.lookup.ServiceIDListener;
import common.LeaseFileClassifier;
import net.jini.lookup.JoinManager;
import net.jini.discovery.LookupDiscovery;
import net.jini.discovery.LookupDiscoveryManager;
import net.jini.export.Exporter;
import net.jini.jeri.BasicJeriExporter;
import net.jini.jeri.BasicILFactory;
import net.jini.jeri.tcp.TcpServerEndpoint;
/**
 * FileClassifierServer.java
 */
public class FileClassifierServer implements ServiceIDListener  {
    protected FileClassifierImpl impl;

    public static void main(String argv[]) throws Exception {
        FileClassifierServer server = new FileClassifierServer();
        // keep server running forever to
        // - allow time for locator discovery and
        // - keep reregistering the lease
        Object keepAlive = new Object();
```

```java
            synchronized(keepAlive) {
                try {
                    keepAlive.wait();
                } catch(java.lang.InterruptedException e) {
                    // do nothing
                }
            }
        }
    }
    public FileClassifierServer() throws Exception {
        System.setSecurityManager(new RMISecurityManager());
        impl = new FileClassifierImpl();
        Exporter exporter = new BasicJeriExporter(TcpServerEndpoint.getInstance(0),
                                            new BasicILFactory());
        // export an object of this class
        Remote proxy = exporter.export(impl);
        JoinManager joinMgr = null;
        try {
            LookupDiscoveryManager mgr =
                new LookupDiscoveryManager(LookupDiscovery.ALL_GROUPS,
                                    null /* unicast locators */,
                                    null /* DiscoveryListener */);
            joinMgr = new JoinManager(proxy,
                                    null,
                                    this,
                                    mgr,
                                    new LeaseRenewalManager());
        } catch(Exception e) {
            e.printStackTrace();
            System.exit(1);
        }
    }

    public void serviceIDNotify(ServiceID serviceID) {
        System.out.println("got service ID " + serviceID.toString());
    }
} // FileClassifierServer
```

FileClassifierLeasedResource Class

The FileClassifierLeasedResource implements the LeasedResource interface. It acts as a wrapper around the actual resource (a LeaseFileClassifier). It adds cookie and time expiration fields around the resource, and it creates a unique cookie for the resource, in addition to making the wrapped resource visible.

```java
/**
 * FileClassifierLeasedResource.java
 */
package lease;
```

```java
import common.LeaseFileClassifier;
import com.sun.jini.landlord.LeasedResource;
import net.jini.id.Uuid;
import net.jini.id.UuidFactory;
public class FileClassifierLeasedResource implements LeasedResource  {

    protected Uuid cookie;
    protected LeaseFileClassifier fileClassifier;
    protected long expiration = 0;
    protected String suffix = null;
    public FileClassifierLeasedResource(LeaseFileClassifier fileClassifier,
                                        String suffix) {
        this.fileClassifier = fileClassifier;
        this.suffix = suffix;
        cookie = UuidFactory.generate();
    }
    public void setExpiration(long newExpiration) {
        this.expiration = newExpiration;
    }
    public long getExpiration() {
        return expiration;
    }
    public Uuid getCookie() {
        return cookie;
    }
    public LeaseFileClassifier getFileClassifier() {
        return fileClassifier;
    }
    public String getSuffix() {
        return suffix;
    }
} // FileClassifierLeasedResource
```

Reaper

When leases expire, something should clean them up. For this, we will use a simple *reaper* thread that scans the map of leased resources regularly, looking for expired leases. When the reaper finds an expired lease, it removes the lease from the map of resources and also calls removeType() on the file classifier implementation.

```java
package lease;
/**
 * Reaper.java
 */
import java.util.Map;
import java.util.Set;
import java.util.Iterator;
import java.rmi.RemoteException;
```

```java
/**
 * Every minute, scan list of resources, remove those that
 */
public class Reaper extends Thread {
    private Map leasedResources;
    public Reaper(Map leasedResources) {
        this.leasedResources = leasedResources;
    } // Reaper constructor

    public void run() {
        while (true) {
            try {
                Thread.sleep(10*1000L);
            } catch (InterruptedException e) {
                // ignore
            }
            Set keys = leasedResources.keySet();
            Iterator iter = keys.iterator();
            System.out.println("Reaper running");
            while (iter.hasNext()) {
                Object key = iter.next();
                FileClassifierLeasedResource res =
                        (FileClassifierLeasedResource) leasedResources.get(key);
                long expires = res.getExpiration() - System.currentTimeMillis();
                if (expires < 0) {
                    leasedResources.remove(key);
                    try {
                        res.getFileClassifier().removeType(res.getSuffix());
                    } catch (RemoteException e) {
                        // ignore
                    }

                }
            }
        }
    }

} // Reaper
```

FileClassifierLandlord Class

The FileClassifierLandlord class is similar to FooLandlord, which was covered in Chapter 8.
However, it also includes a reaper to clean up expired leases.

```java
/**
 * FileClassifierLandlord.java
 */
package lease;
```

```java
import common.LeaseFileClassifier;
import net.jini.core.lease.LeaseDeniedException;
import net.jini.core.lease.Lease;
import net.jini.core.lease.UnknownLeaseException;
import net.jini.id.Uuid;
import net.jini.id.UuidFactory;

import java.rmi.Remote;
import java.rmi.RemoteException;
import java.util.Map;
import java.util.HashMap;
import com.sun.jini.landlord.Landlord;
import com.sun.jini.landlord.LeaseFactory;
import com.sun.jini.landlord.LeasedResource;
import com.sun.jini.landlord.FixedLeasePeriodPolicy;
import com.sun.jini.landlord.LeasePeriodPolicy;
import com.sun.jini.landlord.LeasePeriodPolicy.Result;
import com.sun.jini.landlord.Landlord.RenewResults;
import com.sun.jini.landlord.LandlordUtil;
import com.sun.jini.landlord.LocalLandlord;
import net.jini.jeri.BasicJeriExporter;
import net.jini.jeri.BasicILFactory;
import net.jini.jeri.tcp.TcpServerEndpoint;
import net.jini.export.*;
import java.rmi.Remote;
public class FileClassifierLandlord implements Landlord, LocalLandlord {
    private static final long MAX_LEASE = Lease.FOREVER;
    private static final long DEFAULT_LEASE = 1000*60*5; // 5 minutes
    private Map leasedResourceMap = new HashMap();
    private LeasePeriodPolicy policy = new
        FixedLeasePeriodPolicy(MAX_LEASE, DEFAULT_LEASE);
    private Uuid myUuid = UuidFactory.generate();
    private LeaseFactory factory;
    public FileClassifierLandlord() throws java.rmi.RemoteException {
        Exporter exporter = new
            BasicJeriExporter(TcpServerEndpoint.getInstance(0),
                            new BasicILFactory());
        Landlord proxy = (Landlord) exporter.export(this);
        factory = new LeaseFactory(proxy, myUuid);
        // start a reaper to clean up expired leases
        new Reaper(leasedResourceMap).start();
    }

    public void cancel(Uuid cookie) throws UnknownLeaseException {
        Object value;
        if ((value = leasedResourceMap.remove(cookie)) == null) {
            throw new UnknownLeaseException();
```

```
        }
        FileClassifierLeasedResource resource =
                    (FileClassifierLeasedResource) value;

        try {
            resource.getFileClassifier().removeType(resource.getSuffix());
        } catch (RemoteException e) {
            // ignore??
        }
    }
    public Map cancelAll(Uuid[] cookies) {
        return LandlordUtil.cancelAll(this, cookies);
    }
    public long renew(Uuid cookie,
                    long extension)
        throws net.jini.core.lease.LeaseDeniedException,
              net.jini.core.lease.UnknownLeaseException {
        LeasedResource resource = (LeasedResource)
            leasedResourceMap.get(cookie);
        LeasePeriodPolicy.Result result = null;
        if (resource != null) {
            result = policy.renew(resource, extension);
        } else {
            throw new UnknownLeaseException();
        }
        return result.duration;
    }
    public LeasePeriodPolicy.Result grant(LeasedResource resource,
                                        long requestedDuration)
        throws LeaseDeniedException {
        Uuid cookie = resource.getCookie();
        try {
            leasedResourceMap.put(cookie, resource);
        } catch(Exception e) {
            throw new LeaseDeniedException(e.toString());
        }
        return policy.grant(resource, requestedDuration);
    }
    public Lease newFileClassifierLease(LeaseFileClassifier fileClassifier,
                                        String suffixKey, long duration)
        throws LeaseDeniedException {
        FileClassifierLeasedResource resource =
                        new FileClassifierLeasedResource(fileClassifier,
                                                        suffixKey);
        Uuid cookie = resource.getCookie();
        // find out how long we should grant the lease for
        LeasePeriodPolicy.Result result = grant(resource, duration);
```

```
            long expiration = result.expiration;
            resource.setExpiration(expiration);
            Lease lease = factory.newLease(cookie, expiration);
            return lease;
    }
    public Landlord.RenewResults renewAll(Uuid[] cookies,
                                          long[] durations) {
        return LandlordUtil.renewAll(this, cookies, durations);
    }
} // FileClassifierLandlord
```

Lease Client

A sample client finds the service and adds a new type to it, getting a lease in return. It renews the lease and finally lets it expire.

```
package client;
import common.LeaseFileClassifier;
import common.MIMEType;
import java.rmi.RMISecurityManager;
import net.jini.discovery.LookupDiscovery;
import net.jini.discovery.DiscoveryListener;
import net.jini.discovery.DiscoveryEvent;
import net.jini.core.lookup.ServiceRegistrar;
import net.jini.core.lookup.ServiceTemplate;
import net.jini.core.lease.Lease;
/**
 * TestFileClassifierLease.java
 */
public class TestFileClassifierLease implements DiscoveryListener {
    public static void main(String argv[]) {
        new TestFileClassifierLease();
        // stay around long enough to receive replies
        try {
            Thread.currentThread().sleep(20*60*1000L);
        } catch(java.lang.InterruptedException e) {
            // do nothing
        }
        System.out.println("Exiting normally");
    }
    public TestFileClassifierLease() {
        System.setSecurityManager(new RMISecurityManager());
        LookupDiscovery discover = null;
        try {
            discover = new LookupDiscovery(LookupDiscovery.ALL_GROUPS);
        } catch(Exception e) {
            System.err.println(e.toString());
            System.exit(1);
```

```java
            }
        discover.addDiscoveryListener(this);
    }

    public void discovered(DiscoveryEvent evt) {
        ServiceRegistrar[] registrars = evt.getRegistrars();
        Class [] classes = new Class[] {LeaseFileClassifier.class};
        LeaseFileClassifier classifier = null;
        ServiceTemplate template = new ServiceTemplate(null, classes,
                                                       null);

        for (int n = 0; n < registrars.length; n++) {
            System.out.println("Service found");
            ServiceRegistrar registrar = registrars[n];
            try {
                classifier = (LeaseFileClassifier) registrar.lookup(template);
            } catch(java.rmi.RemoteException e) {
                e.printStackTrace();
                System.exit(2);
            }
            if (classifier == null) {
                System.out.println("Classifier null");
                continue;
            }
            MIMEType type;
            try {
                type = classifier.getMIMEType("file1.txt");
                System.out.println("Type of known type file1.txt is " +
                                   type.toString());
                type = classifier.getMIMEType("file1.ps");
                System.out.println("Type of unknown type file1.ps is " + type);
                // Add a type
                Lease lease = classifier.addType("ps",
                                       new MIMEType("text", "postscript"));
                if (lease != null) {
                    System.out.println("Added type for ps");
                    System.out.println("lease for " +
                                       (lease.getExpiration() -
                                        System.currentTimeMillis())/1000 +
                                       " seconds");
                    type = classifier.getMIMEType("file1.ps");
                    System.out.println("Type for now known type file1.ps is " +
                                       type.toString());
                    // sleep for 1 min and try again
                    System.out.println("Sleeping for 1 min");
                    Thread.sleep(1*60*1000L);
                    type = classifier.getMIMEType("file1.ps");
```

```
                        System.out.println("Type for still known type file1.ps is " +
                                        type.toString());
                        // renew lease
                        lease.renew(3*60*1000L);
                        System.out.println("renewed lease for " +
                                        (lease.getExpiration() -
                                            System.currentTimeMillis())/1000 +
                                        " seconds");
                        // let lease lapse
                        System.out.println("Sleeping for 4 min to let lease lapse");
                        Thread.sleep(4*60*1000L);
                        type = classifier.getMIMEType("file1.ps");
                        System.out.println("Type for now unknown type file1.ps is " +
                                        type);
                } else {
                    System.err.println("was null");
                }
            } catch(Exception e) {
                e.printStackTrace();
            }
            // System.exit(0);
        }
    }
    public void discarded(DiscoveryEvent evt) {
        // empty
    }
} // TestFileClassifierLease
```

Summary

Jini provides a framework for building distributed applications. Nevertheless, there is still room for variation in how services and clients are written, and some of these are better than others. This chapter has looked at some of the variations that can occur and how to deal with them.

■ ■ ■

CHAPTER 16

Remote Events

Components of a system can change state and may need to inform other components that this change has happened. JavaBeans and user-interface elements such as AWT or Swing objects use events to signal these changes. Jini also has an event mechanism, and this chapter examines the distributed event model that is part of Jini. It looks at how remote event listeners are registered with objects, and how these objects notify their listeners of changes. Event listeners may disappear, and so the Jini event mechanism uses leases to manage listener lists.

This chapter also covers how leases are managed by event sources. Finally, we'll consider how events can be used by applications to monitor when services are registered or discarded from service locators.

Event Models

Java has a number of event models, differing in various subtle ways. All of these involve an object (an *event source*) generating an event in response to some change of state, either in the object itself (for example, if someone has changed a field) or in the external environment (such as when a user moves the mouse). At some earlier stage, a listener (or set of listeners) will have registered interest in this event. When the event source generates an event, it will call suitable methods called on the listeners with the event as parameter. The event models all have their origin in the `Observer` pattern from *Design Patterns*, by Eric Gamma et al. (Addison-Wesley, 1995), but this is modified by other pressures, such as JavaBeans.

There are low-level *input events*, which are generated by user actions when they control an application with a graphical user interface. These events—of type `KeyEvent` and `MouseEvent`—are placed in an *event queue*. They are removed from the queue by a separate thread and dispatched to the relevant objects. In this case, the object that is responsible for generating the event is not responsible for dispatch to listeners, and creation and dispatch of events occurs in different threads.

Input events are a special case caused by the need to listen to user interactions and always deal with them without losing response time. Most events are dealt with in a simpler manner: an object maintains its own list of listeners, generates its own events, and dispatches them directly to its listeners. In this category fall all the *semantic events* generated by the AWT and Swing tool-kits, such as `ActionEvent`, `ListSelectionEvent`, and so on. There is a large range of these event types, and they all call different methods in the listeners, based on the event name. For example, an `ActionEvent` is used in a listener's `actionPerformed()` method of an `ActionListener`. There are naming conventions involved in this, specified by JavaBeans.

JavaBeans is also the influence behind `PropertyChange` events, which get delivered whenever a bean changes a "bound" or "constrained" property value. These are delivered to the

PropertyChangeListener's propertyChange() method and to the VetoableChangeListener's vetoableChange() method. These events are usually used to signal a change in a field of an object, where this change may be of interest to the listeners either for information or for vetoing.

Jini objects may also be interested in changes in other Jini objects, and would like to be listeners for such changes. The networked nature of Jini has led to a particular event model that differs slightly from the other models already in Java. The differences are caused by several factors:

- Network delivery is unreliable; messages may be lost. Synchronous methods requiring a reply may not work here.

- Network delivery is time dependent; messages may arrive at different times to different listeners. As a result, the state of an object as perceived by a listener at any time may be inconsistent with the state of that object as perceived by others. Passing complex object state across the network may be more complex to manage than passing simpler information.

- A remote listener may have disappeared by the time the event occurs. Listeners have to be allowed to time out, like services do.

- JavaBeans can require method names and event types that vary. This requires the availability of classes across the network, which is more complex than a single method on a single event type (the original Observer pattern used a single method, for simplicity).

Remote Events

Unlike the large number of event classes in AWT and Swing (for example), Jini typically uses events of one type, the RemoteEvent, or a small number of subclasses of RemoteEvent. The class has these public methods:

```
package net.jini.core.event;
public class RemoteEvent implements java.io.Serializable {
    public long getID();
    public long getSequenceNumber();
    public java.rmi.MarshalledObject getRegistrationObject();
}
```

Events in JavaBeans and AWT convey complex object state information, and this is enough for the listeners to act with full knowledge of the changes that have caused the event to be generated. Jini events avoid this and convey just enough information to allow state information to be found if needed. A remote event is serializable and can be moved around the network to its listeners. The listeners then have to decide whether or not they need more detailed information than the simple information in each remote event. If they do need more information, they will have to contact the event source to get it.

AWT events, such as MouseEvent, contain an id field that is set to a value such as MOUSE_PRESSED or MOUSE_RELEASED. These fields are not seen by the AWT programmer because the AWT event dispatch system uses the id field to choose an appropriate method, such as mousePressed() or mouseReleased(). Jini does not make these assumptions about event dispatch, and just gives you the identifier. Either the source or the listener (or both) will know what this value means. For example, a file classifier that can update its knowledge of MIME types could have message types ADD_TYPE and REMOVE_TYPE to reflect the sorts of changes it is going through.

In a synchronous system with no losses, both sides of an interaction can keep consistent ideas of state and order of events. In a network system this is not so easy. Jini makes no assumptions about guarantees of delivery and does not even assume that events are delivered in order. The Jini event mechanism does not specify how events get from producer to listener; it could be by RMI calls, but it may be through an unreliable third party. The event source supplies a sequence number that could be used to construct state and ordering information if needed, and this generalizes things such as timestamps on mouse events. For example, a message with an id of ADD_TYPE and a sequence number of 10 could correspond to the state change "added MIME type text/xml for files with suffix .xml." Another event with an id of REMOVE_TYPE and a sequence number of 11 would be taken as a later event, even if it arrived earlier. The event source should be able to supply state information upon request, given the sequence number.

An idea borrowed from systems such as the Xt Intrinsics and Motif is called *handback* data. This is a piece of data that is given by the listener to the event source at the time it registers itself for events. The event source records this handback and then returns it to the listener with each event. This handback can be a reminder of listener state at the time of registration.

This idea can be a little difficult to understand at first. The listener is basically saying to the event source that it wants to be told whenever something interesting happens, but when that does happen, the listener may have forgotten why it was interested in the first place, or what it intended to do with the information. So the listener also gives the event source some extra information that it wants returned as a "reminder."

For example, a Jini taxi-driver might register interest in taxi-booking events from the base station while passing through a geographical area. It registers itself as a listener for booking events, and as part of its registration, it could include its current location. Then, when it receives a booking event, it is told its old location, and it could check to see if it is still interested in events from that old location. A more novel possibility is that one object can register a different object for events; so for example your stock broker could register you for events about stock movements, and when you receive an event, you would also get a reminder about who registered your interest (plus a request for commission . . .).

Event Registration

Jini does not say how to register listeners with objects that can generate events. This is unlike other event models in Java that specify methods like this

```
public void addActionListener(ActionListener listener);
```

for ActionEvent generators. What Jini does do is specify a convenience class as a return value from this registration. This is the convenience class EventRegistration:

```
package net.jini.core.event;
import net.jini.core.lease.Lease;
public class EventRegistration implements java.io.Serializable {
```

```
    public EventRegistration(long eventID, Object source,
                             Lease lease, long seqNum);
    public long getID();
    public Object getSource();
    public Lease getLease();
    public long getSequenceNumber();
}
```

This return object contains information that *may* be of value to the object that registered a listener. Each registration will typically be for only a limited amount of time, and this information may be returned in the Lease object. If the event registration was for a particular type, this may be returned in the id field. A sequence number may also be given. The meaning of these values may depend on the particular system—in other words, Jini gives you a class that is optional in use and whose fields are not tightly specified. This gives you the freedom to choose your own meanings to some extent. Note that in Jini 1, the source object was typically this, and the programmer would rely on Java substituting a proxy. In Jini 2.0, the proxy will have to be explicitly given, for example:

```
new EventRegistration(0L, proxy, null, 0L)
```

The event model means that as the programmer of an event producer, you have to define (and implement) methods such as the following:

```
public EventRegistration addRemoteEventListener(RemoteEventListener listener);
```

There is no standard interface for this.

Listener List

Each listener for remote events must implement the RemoteEventListener interface:

```
public interface RemoteEventListener
            extends java.rmi.Remote, java.util.EventListener {
    public void notify(RemoteEvent theEvent)
            throws UnknownEventException,
                   java.rmi.RemoteException;
}
```

Because it extends Remote, the listener will most likely be something like an RMI stub for a remote object, so that calling notify() will result in a call on the remote object, with the event being passed across to it.

In event generators, there are multiple implementations for handling lists of event listeners all the way through the Java core and extensions. There is no public API for dealing with event-listener lists, so the programmer has to reinvent (or copy) code to pass events to listeners. There are basically two cases:

- Only one listener can be in the list.

- Any number of listeners can be in the list.

Single Listener

The case where there is only one listener allowed can be implemented by using a single-valued variable, as shown in Figure 16-1.

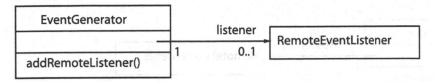

Figure 16-1. *A single listener*

The simplest case of event registration is as follows:

```
protected RemoteEventListener listener = null;
public EventRegistration addRemoteListener(RemoteEventListener listener)
        throws java.util.TooManyListenersException {
    if (this.listener == null {
        this.listener = listener;
    } else {
        throw new java.util.TooManyListenersException();
    }
    return new EventRegistration(0L, proxy, null, 0L);
}
```

This is close to the ordinary Java event registration; no really useful information is returned that wasn't known before. In particular, there is no lease object, so you could probably assume that the lease is being granted "forever," as would be the case with non-networked objects.

When an event occurs, the listener can be informed by the event generator calling fireNotify(). In Jini 2.0, the source object will be a proxy:

```
protected void fireNotify(long eventID,
                          long seqNum) {
    if (listener == null) {
        return;
    }
    RemoteEvent remoteEvent = new RemoteEvent(proxy, eventID,
                                              seqNum, null);
    listener.notify(remoteEvent);
}
```

It is easy to add a handback to this: just add another field to the object, and set and return this in the registration and notify methods. Far more complex is the addition of a non-null lease. First, the event source has to decide on a *lease policy*—that is, for what periods of time is it going to grant leases. Then it has to implement a timeout mechanism to discard listeners when their leases expire. And finally, it has to handle lease renewal and cancellation requests, possibly using its lease policy again to make decisions. The landlord package would be of use here.

Multiple Listeners

For the case where there can be any number of listeners, the convenience class javax.swing.
event.EventListenerList can be used. The object delegates all list handling to the convenience
class, as shown in Figure 16-2.

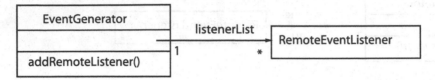

Figure 16-2. *Multiple listeners*

A version suitable for ordinary events is as follows:

```
import javax.swing.event.EventListenerList;
EventListenerList listenerList = new EventListenerList();
public EventRegistration addRemoteListener(RemoteEventListener l) {
    listenerList.add(RemoteListener.class, l);
    return new EventRegistration(OL, proxy, null, OL);
}
public void removeRemoteListener(RemoteEventListener l) {
    listenerList.remove(RemoteListener.class, l);
}
// Notify all listeners that have registered interest for
// notification on this event type.  The event instance
// is lazily created using the parameters passed into
// the fire method.
protected void fireNotify(long eventID,
                          long seqNum) {
    RemoteEvent remoteEvent = null;
    // Guaranteed to return a non-null array
    Object[] listeners = listenerList.getListenerList();
    // Process the listeners last to first, notifying
    // those that are interested in this event
    for (int n = listeners.length - 2; n >= 0; n -= 2) {
        if (listeners[n] == RemoteEventListener.class) {
            RemoteEventListener listener =
                            (RemoteEventListener) listeners[n+1];
            if (remoteEvent == null) {
                remoteEvent = new RemoteEvent(proxy, eventID,
                                              seqNum, null);
            }
            try {
                listener.notify(remoteEvent);
            } catch(UnknownEventException e) {
                e.printStackTrace();
```

```
        } catch(java.rmi.RemoteException e) {
            e.printStackTrace();
        }
    }
  }
}
```

In this case, a source object need only call `fireNotify()` to send the event to all listeners. (You may decide that it is easier to simply use a `Vector` of listeners.)

It is again straightforward to add handbacks to this. The only tricky point is that each listener can have its own handback, so they will need to be stored in some kind of map (say, a `HashMap`) keyed on the listener. Then, before `notify()` is called for each listener, the handback will need to be retrieved for the listener and a new remote event created with that handback.

Listener Source

The ordinary Java event model has all objects in a single address space, so that registration of event listeners and notification of these listeners takes place using objects in the one space. We have already seen that this is not the case with Jini. Jini is a networked federation of objects, and in many cases you are dealing with proxy objects, not the real objects.

This is the same with remote events, except that in this case you often have the direction of proxies reversed. To see what I mean by this, consider what happens if a client wants to monitor any changes in the service. The client will already have a proxy object for the service, and it will use this proxy to register itself as a listener. However, the service proxy will most likely just hand this listener back to the service itself (that is what proxies, such as RMI proxies, do). So we need to get a proxy for the client over to the service.

Consider the file classification problems we looked at in earlier chapters. The file classifier had a hard-coded set of file name extensions built in. However, it may be possible to extend these, if applications come along that know how to define (and maybe handle) such extensions. For example, an application would locate the file classification server, and using an exported method from the file classification interface, it would add the new MIME type and file extension. This is no departure from any standard Java or earlier Jini stuff. It only affects the implementation level of the file classifier, changing it from a static list of file name extensions to a more dynamic one.

What it does affect is the poor application that has been blocked (and is probably sleeping) on an unknown file name extension. When the classifier installs a new type, it can send an event saying so. The blocked application could then try again to see if the extension is now known. If so, it uses it; if not, it blocks again. Note that we don't bother with identifying the actual state change, since it is just as easy to make another query, knowing that the state has changed. More complex situations may require more information to be maintained. However, in order to get to this situation, the application must have registered its interest in events, and the event producer must be able to find the listener.

How this gets resolved is for the client to first find the service in the same way as previously discussed. The client ends up with a proxy object for the service in the client's address space. One of the methods on the proxy will add an event listener, and this method will be called by the client.

For simplicity, assume that the client is being added as a listener to the service. The client will call the add listener method of the proxy, with the client as parameter. The proxy will then call the real object's add listener method, back on its server side. But in doing this, we have made a remote call across the network, and the client, which was local to the call on the proxy, is now remote to the real object, so what the real object is getting is a proxy to the client. When the service makes notification calls to the proxy listeners, the client's proxy can make a remote call back to the client itself. These proxies are shown in Figure 16-3.

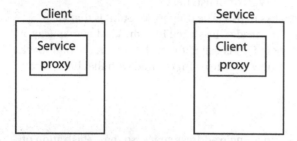

Figure 16-3. *Proxies for services and listeners*

File Classifier with Events

Let's make this discussion more concrete by looking at a new file classifier that can have its set of mappings dynamically updated. In the last chapter, we also considered such a situation, but from the point of view of leasing such additions. In this chapter, we ignore leasing issues and concentrate on generating events as the mappings change.

The first interface required is MutableFileClassifier, which is known to all objects. This interface adds methods to add and remove types, and also to register listeners for events. The event types are labeled with two constants. The listener model is simple, and it does not include handbacks or leases. The sequence identifier must be increasing, so we just add 1 on each event generation, although we don't really need it here: it is easy for a listener to just make MIME type queries again.

```
package common;
import java.io.Serializable;
/**
 * MutableFileClassifier.java
 */
import net.jini.core.event.RemoteEventListener;
import net.jini.core.event.EventRegistration;
public interface MutableFileClassifier extends FileClassifier {
    static final public long ADD_TYPE = 1;
    static final public long REMOVE_TYPE = 2;
    /*
     * Add the MIME type for the given suffix.
     * The suffix does not contain '.' e.g. "gif".
     * Overrides any previous MIME type for that suffix
     */
```

```
    public void addType(String suffix, MIMEType type)
        throws java.rmi.RemoteException;
    /*
     * Delete the MIME type for the given suffix.
     * The suffix does not contain '.' e.g. "gif".
     * Does nothing if the suffix is not known
     */
    public void removeType(String suffix)
        throws java.rmi.RemoteException;
    public EventRegistration addRemoteListener(RemoteEventListener listener)
        throws java.rmi.RemoteException;
} // MutableFileClasssifier
```

The RemoteFileClassifier interface just changes its package and inheritance for any service implementation:

```
package mutable;
import common.MutableFileClassifier;
import java.rmi.Remote;
/**
 * RemoteFileClassifier.java
 */
public interface RemoteFileClassifier extends MutableFileClassifier, Remote {

} // RemoteFileClasssifier
```

The implementation changes from a static list of if...then statements to a dynamic map keyed on file suffixes. It manages the event listener list for multiple listeners in the simple way discussed earlier. It generates events whenever a new suffix/type is added or successfully removed.

There are, however, several subtleties related to proxies. When a listener registers by addListener(), an EventRegistration is returned. This EventRegistration contains the service object (or rather, its proxy). Similarly, when notify() is called on the listener, it is passed a RemoteEvent, and this also contains the service (or rather, its proxy). With the "old" version of RMI, all of the work to do with proxies was looked after by the Java runtime, but with the Jeri model, handling of proxies must be made explicit. This means that the implementation object must know its proxy in order to prepare EventRegistration and RemoteEvent objects.

In all of the servers we have seen so far, the server creates the service and then goes on to create its proxy. This means that the service normally does not know its proxy. One way to overcome this is for the service to implement a method such as setProxy(); another way is for the service to create its own proxy and make it available to the server with a method such as getProxy(). Jini from version 2.0 has an interface, ProxyAccessor, that supports the second method.

```
interface ProxyAccessor {
    public Object getProxy();
}
```

The implementation needs to be passed enough information (e.g., a configuration) in its constructor to create a proxy. The methods addType() and removeType() manipulate the map of MIME types and also call firNotify() to generate events:

```java
package mutable;
import java.rmi.server.UnicastRemoteObject;
import java.rmi.MarshalledObject;
import net.jini.core.event.RemoteEventListener;
import net.jini.core.event.RemoteEvent;
import net.jini.core.event.EventRegistration;
import java.rmi.RemoteException;
import java.rmi.Remote;
import net.jini.core.event.UnknownEventException ;
import javax.swing.event.EventListenerList;
import net.jini.export.*;
import net.jini.jeri.BasicJeriExporter;
import net.jini.jeri.BasicILFactory;
import net.jini.export.ProxyAccessor;
import net.jini.config.*;
import common.MIMEType;
import common.MutableFileClassifier;
import java.util.Map;
import java.util.HashMap;
/**
 * FileClassifierImpl.java
 */
public class FileClassifierImpl implements RemoteFileClassifier, ProxyAccessor {
    /**
     * Map of String extensions to MIME types
     */
    protected Map map = new HashMap();
    /**
     * Listeners for change events
     */
    protected EventListenerList listenerList = new EventListenerList();
    protected long seqNum = OL;
    protected Remote proxy;
    public MIMEType getMIMEType(String fileName)
        throws java.rmi.RemoteException {
        System.out.println("Called with " + fileName);
        MIMEType type;
        String fileExtension;
        int dotIndex = fileName.lastIndexOf('.');
        if (dotIndex == -1 || dotIndex + 1 == fileName.length()) {
            // can't find suitable suffix
            return null;
        }
```

```java
        fileExtension= fileName.substring(dotIndex + 1);
        type = (MIMEType) map.get(fileExtension);
        return type;
    }
public void addType(String suffix, MIMEType type)
    throws java.rmi.RemoteException {
    System.out.println("type added");
    map.put(suffix, type);
    fireNotify(ADD_TYPE);
}
public void removeType(String suffix)
    throws java.rmi.RemoteException {
    System.out.println("Type removed");
    if (map.remove(suffix) != null) {
        fireNotify(REMOVE_TYPE);
    }
}
public EventRegistration addRemoteListener(RemoteEventListener listener)
    throws java.rmi.RemoteException {
    listenerList.add(RemoteEventListener.class, listener);
    return new EventRegistration(0,
                            proxy,
                            null, /* Lease is null for simplicity only.
                                    It should be e.g. a LandlordLease
                                  */
                            0);
}
// Notify all listeners that have registered interest for
// notification on this event type.  The event instance
// is lazily created using the parameters passed into
// the fire method.
protected void fireNotify(long eventID) {
    RemoteEvent remoteEvent = null;

    // Guaranteed to return a non-null array
    Object[] listeners = listenerList.getListenerList();

    // Process the listeners last to first, notifying
    // those that are interested in this event
    for (int i = listeners.length - 2; i >= 0; i -= 2) {
        if (listeners[i] == RemoteEventListener.class) {
            RemoteEventListener listener = (RemoteEventListener) listeners[i+1];
            if (remoteEvent == null) {
                remoteEvent = new RemoteEvent(proxy, eventID,
                                            seqNum++, null);
            }
```

```java
                    try {
                        listener.notify(remoteEvent);
                    } catch(UnknownEventException e) {
                        e.printStackTrace();
                    } catch(RemoteException e) {
                        // Remove this listener from the list due to failure
                        listenerList.remove(RemoteEventListener.class, listener);
                        System.out.println("notification failed, listener removed");
                    }
                }
            }
        }
        // Implementation for ProxyAccessor
        public Object getProxy() {
            return proxy;
        }
        public FileClassifierImpl()  throws java.rmi.RemoteException {
            // empty constructor for proxy generation
        }
        public FileClassifierImpl(String[] configArgs)  throws java.rmi.RemoteException
{
            // load a predefined set of MIME type mappings
            map.put("gif", new MIMEType("image", "gif"));
            map.put("jpeg", new MIMEType("image", "jpeg"));
            map.put("mpg", new MIMEType("video", "mpeg"));
            map.put("txt", new MIMEType("text", "plain"));
            map.put("html", new MIMEType("text", "html"));
            try {
                // get the configuration (by default a FileConfiguration)
                Configuration config = ConfigurationProvider.getInstance(configArgs);

                // and use this to construct an exporter
                Exporter exporter = (Exporter) config.getEntry( "FileClassifierServer",
                                                                "exporter",
                                                                Exporter.class);

                // export an object of this class
                proxy = exporter.export(this);
            } catch(Exception e) {
                System.err.println(e.toString());
                e.printStackTrace();
                System.exit(1);
            }
        }
} // FileClassifierImpl
```

The server changes by passing in configuration information to the implementation's constructor and then getting the proxy from it in order to register the service.

```java
package mutable;
import net.jini.lookup.JoinManager;
import net.jini.core.lookup.ServiceID;
import net.jini.discovery.LookupDiscovery;
import net.jini.core.lookup.ServiceRegistrar;
import java.rmi.RemoteException;
import net.jini.lookup.ServiceIDListener;
import net.jini.lease.LeaseRenewalManager;
import net.jini.discovery.LookupDiscoveryManager;
import net.jini.discovery.DiscoveryEvent;
import net.jini.discovery.DiscoveryListener;
import java.rmi.RMISecurityManager;
import java.rmi.Remote;
import net.jini.config.*;
import net.jini.export.*;
/**
 * FileClassifierServer.java
 */
public class FileClassifierServer
    implements ServiceIDListener {
    // explicit proxy for Jini 2.0
    protected Remote proxy;
    protected FileClassifierImpl impl;
    private static String CONFIG_FILE = "jeri/file_classifier_server.config";

    public static void main(String argv[]) {
        FileClassifierServer server = new FileClassifierServer();
        // stay around forever
        Object keepAlive = new Object();
        synchronized(keepAlive) {
            try {
                keepAlive.wait();
            } catch(InterruptedException e) {
                // do nothing
            }
        }
    }
    public FileClassifierServer() {
        String[] configArgs = new String[] {CONFIG_FILE};
        try {
            impl = new FileClassifierImpl(configArgs);
        } catch(Exception e) {
            System.err.println("New impl: " + e.toString());
            System.exit(1);
        }
        proxy = (Remote) impl.getProxy();
```

```
            // install suitable security manager
            System.setSecurityManager(new RMISecurityManager());
            JoinManager joinMgr = null;
            try {
                LookupDiscoveryManager mgr =
                    new LookupDiscoveryManager(LookupDiscovery.ALL_GROUPS,
                                            null,  // unicast locators
                                            null); // DiscoveryListener
                joinMgr = new JoinManager(proxy, // service proxy
                                        null,  // attr sets
                                        this,  // ServiceIDListener
                                        mgr,   // DiscoveryManager
                                        new LeaseRenewalManager());
            } catch(Exception e) {
                e.printStackTrace();
                System.exit(1);
            }
        }
    public void serviceIDNotify(ServiceID serviceID) {
        // called as a ServiceIDListener
        // Should save the id to permanent storage
        System.out.println("got service ID " + serviceID.toString());
    }
} // FileClassifierServer
```

The client must have an object that implements RemoteEventListener:

```
package client;
import common.MutableFileClassifier;
import common.MIMEType;
import java.rmi.RMISecurityManager;
import net.jini.discovery.LookupDiscovery;
import net.jini.discovery.DiscoveryListener;
import net.jini.discovery.DiscoveryEvent;
import net.jini.core.lookup.ServiceRegistrar;
import net.jini.core.lookup.ServiceTemplate;
import net.jini.core.event.RemoteEventListener;
import net.jini.core.event.RemoteEvent;
import java.rmi.*;
import java.rmi.server.ExportException;
import net.jini.export.Exporter;
import net.jini.jeri.BasicJeriExporter;
import net.jini.jeri.BasicILFactory;
import net.jini.jeri.tcp.TcpServerEndpoint;
/**
 * TestFileClassifierEvent.java
 */
```

```java
public class TestFileClassifierEvent implements DiscoveryListener,
                                                RemoteEventListener {
    public static void main(String argv[]) {
        TestFileClassifierEvent client = new TestFileClassifierEvent();
        // stay around long enough to receive replies
        try {
            Thread.currentThread().sleep(100000L);
        } catch(java.lang.InterruptedException e) {
            // do nothing
        }
    }
    public TestFileClassifierEvent() {
        System.setSecurityManager(new RMISecurityManager());
        LookupDiscovery discover = null;
        try {
            discover = new LookupDiscovery(LookupDiscovery.ALL_GROUPS);
        } catch(Exception e) {
            System.err.println(e.toString());
            System.exit(1);
        }
        discover.addDiscoveryListener(this);
    }

    public void discovered(DiscoveryEvent evt) {
        ServiceRegistrar[] registrars = evt.getRegistrars();
        Class [] classes = new Class[] {MutableFileClassifier.class};
        MutableFileClassifier classifier = null;
        ServiceTemplate template = new ServiceTemplate(null, classes,
                                                       null);

        for (int n = 0; n < registrars.length; n++) {
            System.out.println("Lookup service found");
            ServiceRegistrar registrar = registrars[n];
            try {
                classifier = (MutableFileClassifier) registrar.lookup(template);
            } catch(java.rmi.RemoteException e) {
                e.printStackTrace();
                continue;
            }
            if (classifier == null) {
                System.out.println("Classifier null");
                continue;
            }
            // Add ourselves as an event listener
            Exporter exporter = new BasicJeriExporter(
                                    TcpServerEndpoint.getInstance(0),
                                    new BasicILFactory());
```

```
        // export an object of this class
        RemoteEventListener proxy = null;
        try {
            proxy =  (RemoteEventListener) exporter.export(this);
        } catch (ExportException e) {
            e.printStackTrace();
            continue;
        }
        try {
            classifier.addRemoteListener(proxy);
        } catch (RemoteException e) {
            e.printStackTrace();
            continue;
        }

        // Add some types to the service to generate events
        try {
            classifier.addType("ps", new MIMEType("text", "postscript"));
            classifier.removeType("ps");
        } catch(java.rmi.RemoteException e) {
            System.err.println(e.toString());
            continue;
        }
        }
    }
    public void discarded(DiscoveryEvent evt) {
        // empty
    }
    public void notify(RemoteEvent evt) {
        System.out.println("Event of type " + evt.getID());
    }
} // TestFileClassifier
```

Leasing Event Listeners

The implementation presented in the previous section creates a null object for a lease. This is not correct; it should be a non-null object. However, conceptually there is nothing here that we have not already covered in earlier chapters. See, for example, the section in Chapter 15 titled "Leased Changes to a Service" for how to add a landlord lease.

Monitoring Changes in Services

Services will start and stop. When they start, they will inform the lookup services, and sometime after they stop, they will be removed from the lookup services. However, many times other services or clients will want to know when services start or are removed. For example, an editor may want to know if a disk service has started so that it can save its file; a graphics display program may want to know when printer services start up; the user interface for a camera may want to track changes in disk and printer services so that it can update the Save and Print buttons; and so on.

A service registrar acts as a generator of ServiceEvent type events, which subclass from RemoteEvent. These events are generated in response to changes in the state of services that match (or fail to match) a template pattern for services. This event type has three categories from the ServiceEvent.getTransition() method:

- TRANSITION_NOMATCH_MATCH: A service has changed state so that whereas it previously did not match the template, now it does. In particular, if it didn't exist before, now it does. This transition type can be used to spot new services starting or detect wanted changes in the attributes of an existing registered service; for example, an offline printer can change attributes to being online, which now makes it a useful service.

- TRANSITION_MATCH_NOMATCH: A service has changed state so that whereas it previously did match the template, now it doesn't. This can be used to detect when services are removed from a lookup service. This transition can also be used to spot changes in the attributes of an existing registered service that are not wanted; for example, an online printer can change attributes to being offline.

- TRANSITION_MATCH_MATCH: A service has changed state, but it matched both before and after. This typically happens when an Entry value changes, and it is used to monitor changes of state such as a printer running out of paper, or a piece of hardware signaling that it is due for maintenance work.

A client that wants to monitor changes of services on a lookup service must first create a template for the types of service it is interested in. A client that wants to monitor all changes could prepare a template such as this:

```
ServiceTemplate templ = new ServiceTemplate(null, null, null); // or
ServiceTemplate templ = new ServiceTemplate(null, new Class[] {},
                                            new Entry[] {}); // or
ServiceTemplate templ = new ServiceTemplate(null, new Class[] {Object.class}, null);
```

It then could set up a transition mask as a bitwise OR of the three service transitions and call notify() on the ServiceRegistrar object. Note that this method expects to receive a proxy object (this was implicit in Jini 1 but needs to be made explicit in Jini 2.0). The following is a program to monitor all changes:

```
/**
 * RegistrarObserver.java
 */
package observer;
import net.jini.core.event.RemoteEventListener;
import net.jini.core.event.RemoteEvent;
import net.jini.core.lookup.ServiceEvent;
import net.jini.core.lookup.ServiceRegistrar;
import net.jini.core.lease.Lease;
import net.jini.core.lookup.ServiceTemplate;
import net.jini.core.lookup.ServiceID;
```

```java
import net.jini.core.event.EventRegistration;
import net.jini.lease.LeaseRenewalManager;
import net.jini.core.lookup.ServiceMatches;
import java.rmi.RemoteException;
import java.rmi.server.UnicastRemoteObject;
import net.jini.core.entry.Entry;
import net.jini.core.event.UnknownEventException;
import net.jini.config.*;
import net.jini.export.*;
import java.rmi.Remote;
public class RegistrarObserver implements RemoteEventListener {

    protected static LeaseRenewalManager leaseManager = new LeaseRenewalManager();
    protected ServiceRegistrar registrar;
    protected final int transitions = ServiceRegistrar.TRANSITION_MATCH_NOMATCH |
                            ServiceRegistrar.TRANSITION_NOMATCH_MATCH |
                            ServiceRegistrar.TRANSITION_MATCH_MATCH;
    public RegistrarObserver() throws RemoteException {
    }
    public RegistrarObserver(Configuration config,
                        ServiceRegistrar registrar) throws RemoteException {
        RemoteEventListener proxy;
        this.registrar = registrar;
        Exporter exporter = null;
        try {
            exporter = (Exporter) config.getEntry( "JeriExportDemo",
                                    "exporter",
                                    Exporter.class);
        } catch(ConfigurationException e) {
            e.printStackTrace();
            return;
        }
        // export an object of this class
        proxy = (RemoteEventListener) exporter.export(this);
        ServiceTemplate templ = new ServiceTemplate(null, null, null);
        EventRegistration reg = null;
        try {
            reg = registrar.notify(templ,
                        transitions,
                        proxy,
                        null,
                        Lease.ANY);
            System.out.println("notifed id " + reg.getID());
        } catch(RemoteException e) {
            e.printStackTrace();
        }
        leaseManager.renewUntil(reg.getLease(), Lease.FOREVER, null);
```

```
        }
    public void notify(RemoteEvent evt)
        throws RemoteException, UnknownEventException {
        try {
            ServiceEvent sevt = (ServiceEvent) evt;
            int transition = sevt.getTransition();
            System.out.println("transition " + transition);
            switch (transition) {
            case ServiceRegistrar.TRANSITION_NOMATCH_MATCH:
                System.out.println("nomatch -> match");
                break;
            case ServiceRegistrar.TRANSITION_MATCH_MATCH:
                System.out.println("match -> match");
                break;
            case ServiceRegistrar.TRANSITION_MATCH_NOMATCH:
                System.out.println("match -> nomatch");
                break;
            }
            System.out.println(sevt.toString());
            if (sevt.getServiceItem() == null) {
                System.out.println("now null");
            } else {
                Object service = sevt.getServiceItem().service;
                System.out.println("Service is " + service.toString());
            }
        } catch(Exception e) {
            e.printStackTrace();
        }
    }
}
} // RegistrarObserver
```

A suitable driver for this is as follows:

```
package client;
import java.rmi.RMISecurityManager;
import java.rmi.RemoteException;
import net.jini.discovery.LookupDiscovery;
import net.jini.discovery.DiscoveryListener;
import net.jini.discovery.DiscoveryEvent;
import net.jini.core.lookup.ServiceRegistrar;
import net.jini.core.lookup.ServiceTemplate;
import net.jini.core.lookup.ServiceMatches;
import net.jini.config.*;
import java.util.Vector;
import observer.RegistrarObserver;
/**
 * ReggieMonitor.java
 */
```

```
public class ReggieMonitor implements DiscoveryListener {
    private Vector observers = new Vector();
    private Configuration config;
    public static void main(String argv[]) {
        new ReggieMonitor(argv);
        // stay around long enough to receive replies
        try {
            Thread.currentThread().sleep(100000L);
        } catch(java.lang.InterruptedException e) {
            // do nothing
        }
    }
    public ReggieMonitor(String[] argv) {
        String[] configArgs = new String[] {argv[0]};
        try {
            // get the configuration (by default a FileConfiguration)
            config = ConfigurationProvider.getInstance(configArgs);
        } catch(Exception e) {
            System.err.println(e.toString());
            e.printStackTrace();
            System.exit(1);
        }
        System.setSecurityManager(new RMISecurityManager());
        LookupDiscovery discover = null;
        try {
            discover = new LookupDiscovery(LookupDiscovery.ALL_GROUPS);
        } catch(Exception e) {
            System.err.println(e.toString());
            System.exit(1);
        }
        discover.addDiscoveryListener(this);
    }

    public void discovered(DiscoveryEvent evt) {
        ServiceRegistrar[] registrars = evt.getRegistrars();

        for (int n = 0; n < registrars.length; n++) {
            System.out.println("Service lookup found");
            ServiceRegistrar registrar = registrars[n];
            if (registrar == null) {
                System.out.println("registrar null");
                continue;
            }
            try {
                System.out.println("Lookup service at " +
                                registrar.getLocator().getHost());
            } catch(RemoteException e) {
```

```
                System.out.println("Lookup service infor unavailable");
            }
            try {
                observers.add(new RegistrarObserver(config, registrar));
            } catch(RemoteException e) {
                System.out.println("adding observer failed");
            }
            ServiceTemplate templ = new ServiceTemplate(null, new
                Class[] {Object.class}, null);
            ServiceMatches matches = null;
            try {
                matches = registrar.lookup(templ, 10);
            } catch(RemoteException e) {
                System.out.println("lookup failed");
            }
            for (int m = 0; m < matches.items.length; m++) {
                if (matches.items[m] != null &&
                    matches.items[m].service != null) {
                    System.out.println("Reg knows about " +
                                    matches.items[m].service.toString() +
                                    " with id " +
                                    matches.items[m].serviceID);
                }
            }
        }
    }
    public void discarded(DiscoveryEvent evt) {
        // remove observer
    }
} // ReggieMonitor
```

Summary

This chapter looked at how the remote event differs from the other event models in Java and at how to create and use remote events. Jini events allow distributed components to inform other components when they change state and to supply enough support information for listeners to determine the nature of the change. This adds an asynchronous state-change mechanism to Jini, which can allow more flexible systems to be built.

■ ■ ■

CHAPTER 17

ServiceDiscoveryManager

Clients and services need to find lookup services. Both can do this using low-level core classes or discovery utilities such as LookupDiscoveryManager. Once a lookup service is found, a service just needs to register with it and try to keep the lease alive for as long as it wants to. A service can make use of the JoinManager class for this.

The ServiceDiscoveryManager class performs client-side functions similar to that of JoinManager for services, and it simplifies the tasks of finding services. It is only available in Jini 1.1 and later.

ServiceDiscoveryManager Interface

The ServiceDiscoveryManager class is a utility class designed to help in the various client-side lookup cases that can occur:

- A client may wish to use a service immediately or later.

- A client may want to use multiple services.

- A client will want to find services by their interfaces, but may also want to apply additional criteria, such as being a "fast enough" printer.

- A client may just wish to use a service if it is available at the time of the request, but alternatively may want to be informed of new services becoming available and to respond to this new availability (e.g., a service browser).

Due to the variety of possible cases, the ServiceDiscoveryManager class is more complex than JoinManager. Its interface includes the following:

```
package net.jini.lookup;
public class ServiceDiscoveryManager {
    public ServiceDiscoveryManager(DiscoveryManagement discoveryMgr,
                            LeaseRenewalManager leaseMgr)
        throws IOException;
    public ServiceDiscoveryManager(DiscoveryManagement discoveryMgr,
                            LeaseRenewalManager leaseMgr,
                            Configuration config)
        throws IOException,
               ConfigurationException;
    LookupCache createLookupCache(ServiceTemplate tmpl,
```

```
                                    ServiceItemFilter filter,
                                    ServiceDiscoveryListener listener);
        ServiceItem[] lookup(ServiceTemplate tmpl,
                        int maxMatches, ServiceItemFilter filter);
        ServiceItem lookup(ServiceTemplate tmpl,
                        ServiceItemFilter filter);
        ServiceItem lookup(ServiceTemplate tmpl,
                        ServiceItemFilter filter, long wait);
        ServiceItem[] lookup(ServiceTemplate tmpl,
                        int minMaxMatch, int maxMatches,
                        ServiceItemFilter filter, long wait);
        void terminate();
}
```

ServiceItemFilter Interface

Most methods of the client lookup manager require a ServiceItemFilter. This is a simple interface designed to be an additional filter on the client side to help in finding services. The primary way for a client to find a service is to ask for an instance of an interface, possibly with additional entry attributes. This matching is performed on the lookup service, and it only involves a form of exact pattern matching. It allows the client to ask for a toaster, for example, that will handle two slices of toast exactly, but not for one that will toast two or more.

Performing arbitrary Boolean matching on the lookup service raises a security issue, as it would involve running some code from the client or service in the lookup service, and it also raises a possible performance issue for the lookup service. This means that enhancing the matching process in the lookup services is unlikely to occur, so any more sophisticated matching must be done by the client. The ServiceItemFilter allows additional Boolean filtering to be performed on the client side, by client code, so these issues are local to the client only.

The ServiceItemFilter interface is as follows:

```
package net.jini.lookup;
public interface ServiceItemFilter {
    boolean check(ServiceItem item);
}
```

A client filter will implement this interface to perform additional checking.

Client-side filtering will not solve all of the problems of locating the "best" service. Some situations will still require other services that know "local" information, such as distances in a building.

Finding a Service Immediately

The simplest scenario for a client is that it wants to find a service immediately, use it, and then (perhaps) terminate. The client will be prepared to wait a certain amount of time before giving up. All issues of discovery can be given to the ServiceDiscoveryManager, and the task of finding a service can be given to a method such as lookup() with a wait parameter. The lookup()

method will block until a suitable service is found or the time limit is reached. If the time limit is reached, a null object will be returned; otherwise, a non-null service object will be returned.

```
package client;
import common.FileClassifier;
import common.MIMEType;
import java.rmi.RMISecurityManager;
import net.jini.discovery.LookupDiscovery;
import net.jini.core.lookup.ServiceTemplate;
import net.jini.discovery.LookupDiscoveryManager;
import net.jini.lookup.ServiceDiscoveryManager;
import net.jini.core.lookup.ServiceItem;
import net.jini.lease.LeaseRenewalManager;
/**
 * ImmediateClientLookup.java
 */
public class ImmediateClientLookup {
    private static final long WAITFOR = 100000L;
    public static void main(String argv[]) {
        new ImmediateClientLookup();
        // stay around long enough to receive replies
        try {
            Thread.currentThread().sleep(2*WAITFOR);
        } catch(java.lang.InterruptedException e) {
            // do nothing
        }
    }
    public ImmediateClientLookup() {
        ServiceDiscoveryManager clientMgr = null;
        System.setSecurityManager(new RMISecurityManager());
        try {
            LookupDiscoveryManager mgr =
                new LookupDiscoveryManager(LookupDiscovery.ALL_GROUPS,
                                    null, // unicast locators
                                    null); // DiscoveryListener
            clientMgr = new ServiceDiscoveryManager(mgr,
                                    new LeaseRenewalManager());
        } catch(Exception e) {
            e.printStackTrace();
            System.exit(1);
        }

        Class [] classes = new Class[] {FileClassifier.class};
        ServiceTemplate template = new ServiceTemplate(null, classes,
                                            null);
        ServiceItem item = null;
```

```java
        // Try to find the service, blocking until timeout if necessary
        try {
            item = clientMgr.lookup(template,
                                    null, // no filter
                                    WAITFOR); // timeout
        } catch(Exception e) {
            e.printStackTrace();
            System.exit(1);
        }
        if (item == null) {
            // couldn't find a service in time
            System.out.println("no service");
            System.exit(1);
        }
        // Get the service
        FileClassifier classifier = (FileClassifier) item.service;
        if (classifier == null) {
            System.out.println("Classifier null");
            System.exit(1);
        }
        // Now we have a suitable service, use it
        MIMEType type;
        try {
            String fileName;

            // Try several file types: .txt, .rtf, .abc
            fileName = "file1.txt";
            type = classifier.getMIMEType(fileName);
            printType(fileName, type);

            fileName = "file2.rtf";
            type = classifier.getMIMEType(fileName);
            printType(fileName, type);

            fileName = "file3.abc";
            type = classifier.getMIMEType(fileName);
            printType(fileName, type);
        } catch(java.rmi.RemoteException e) {
            System.err.println(e.toString());
        }
        System.exit(0);
    }
    private void printType(String fileName, MIMEType type) {
        System.out.print("Type of " + fileName + " is ");
        if (type == null) {
            System.out.println("null");
        } else {
```

```
            System.out.println(type.toString());
        }
    }
} // ImmediateClientLookup
```

Using a Filter

An example in Chapter 15 discussed how to select a printer with a speed greater than a certain value. This type of problem is well suited to the ServiceDiscoveryManager using a ServiceItemFilter. The ServiceItemFilter interface has a check() method, which is called on the client side to perform additional filtering of services. This method can accept or reject a service based on criteria supplied by the client. The following program illustrates how this check() method can be used to select only printer services with a speed of greater than 24 pages per minute.

```
package client;
import common.Printer;
import java.rmi.RMISecurityManager;
import net.jini.discovery.LookupDiscovery;
import net.jini.core.lookup.ServiceTemplate;
import net.jini.discovery.LookupDiscoveryManager;
import net.jini.lookup.ServiceDiscoveryManager;
import net.jini.core.lookup.ServiceItem;
import net.jini.lease.LeaseRenewalManager;
import net.jini.lookup.ServiceItemFilter;
/**
 * TestPrinterSpeedFilter.java
 */
public class TestPrinterSpeedFilter implements ServiceItemFilter {
    private static final long WAITFOR = 100000L;

    public TestPrinterSpeedFilter() {
        ServiceDiscoveryManager clientMgr = null;
        System.setSecurityManager(new RMISecurityManager());
        try {
            LookupDiscoveryManager mgr =
                new LookupDiscoveryManager(LookupDiscovery.ALL_GROUPS,
                                           null,  // unicast locators
                                           null); // DiscoveryListener
            clientMgr = new ServiceDiscoveryManager(mgr,
                                           new LeaseRenewalManager());
        } catch(Exception e) {
            e.printStackTrace();
            System.exit(1);
        }
        Class[] classes = new Class[] {Printer.class};
```

```
            ServiceTemplate template = new ServiceTemplate(null, classes,
                                                            null);
            ServiceItem item = null;
            try {
                item = clientMgr.lookup(template,
                                        this,      // filter
                                        WAITFOR); // timeout
            } catch(Exception e) {
                e.printStackTrace();
                System.exit(1);
            }
            if (item == null) {
                // couldn't find a service in time
                System.exit(1);
            }
            Printer printer = (Printer) item.service;
            // Now use the printer
            // ...
        }
        public boolean check(ServiceItem item) {
            // This is the filter
            Printer printer = (Printer) item.service;
            if (printer.getSpeed() > 24) {
                return true;
            } else {
                return false;
            }
        }
        public static void main(String[] args) {

            TestPrinterSpeed f = new TestPrinterSpeed();
            // stay around long enough to receive replies
            try {
                Thread.currentThread().sleep(2*WAITFOR);
            } catch(java.lang.InterruptedException e) {
                // do nothing
            }
        }
} // TestPrinterSpeed
```

Building a Cache of Services

A client may wish to make use of a service multiple times. If the client simply found a suitable
reference to a service, then before each use it would have to check that the reference was still
valid, and if not, it would need to find another one. The client may also want to use minor vari-
ants of a service, such as a fast printer one time and a slow one the next. While this management
can be done easily enough in each case, the ServiceDiscoveryManager can supply a cache of

services that will do this work for you. This cache will monitor lookup services to keep the cache as up to date as possible.

The cache is defined as an interface:

```
package net.jini.lookup;

public interface LookupCache {
    public ServiceItem lookup(ServiceItemFilter filter);
    public ServiceItem[] lookup(ServiceItemFilter filter,
                                int maxMatches);
    public void addListener(ServiceDiscoveryListener l);
    public void removeListener(ServiceDiscoveryListener l);
    public void discard(Object serviceReference);
    void terminate();
}
```

A suitable implementation object can be created by the ServiceDiscoveryManager method:

```
LookupCache createLookupCache(ServiceTemplate tmpl,
                              ServiceItemFilter filter,
                              ServiceDiscoveryListener listener);
```

We will ignore the ServiceDiscoveryListener until the next section of this chapter. It can be set to null in createLookupCache().

The LookupCache created by createLookupCache() takes a template for matching against interface and entry attributes. It also takes a filter to perform additional client-side Boolean filtering of services. The cache will then maintain a set of references to services matching the template and passing the filter. These references are all local to the client and consist of the service proxies and their attributes downloaded to the client. Searching for a service can then be done by local methods: LookupCache.lookup(). These can take an additional filter that can be used to further refine the set of services returned to the client.

The search in the cache is done directly on the proxy services and attributes already found by the client, and it does not involve querying lookup services. Essentially, this involves a tradeoff of lookup service activity while the client is idle to produce fast local response when the client is active.

There are versions of ServiceDiscoveryManager.lookup() with a time parameter, which block until a service is found or the method times out. These methods do not use polling, but instead use event notification because they are trying to find services based on remote calls to lookup services. The lookup() methods of LookupCache do not implement such a blocking call because the methods run purely locally, and it is reasonable to poll the cache for a short time if need be.

Here is a version of the file classifier client that creates and examines the cache for suitable service:

```
package client;
import common.FileClassifier;
import common.MIMEType;
import java.rmi.RMISecurityManager;
import net.jini.discovery.LookupDiscovery;
```

```java
import net.jini.core.lookup.ServiceTemplate;
import net.jini.discovery.LookupDiscoveryManager;
import net.jini.lookup.ServiceDiscoveryManager;
import net.jini.lookup.LookupCache;
import net.jini.core.lookup.ServiceItem;
import net.jini.lease.LeaseRenewalManager;
/**
 * CachedClientLookup.java
 */
public class CachedClientLookup {
    private static final long WAITFOR = 100000L;
    public static void main(String argv[]) {
        new CachedClientLookup();
        // stay around long enough to receive replies
        try {
            Thread.currentThread().sleep(WAITFOR);
        } catch(java.lang.InterruptedException e) {
            // do nothing
        }
    }

    public CachedClientLookup() {
        ServiceDiscoveryManager clientMgr = null;
        LookupCache cache = null;
        System.setSecurityManager(new RMISecurityManager());
        try {
            LookupDiscoveryManager mgr =
                new LookupDiscoveryManager(LookupDiscovery.ALL_GROUPS,
                                           null,  // unicast locators
                                           null); // DiscoveryListener
            clientMgr = new ServiceDiscoveryManager(mgr,
                                           new LeaseRenewalManager());
        } catch(Exception e) {
            e.printStackTrace();
            System.exit(1);
        }

        Class [] classes = new Class[] {FileClassifier.class};
        ServiceTemplate template = new ServiceTemplate(null, classes,
                                                       null);
        try {
            cache = clientMgr.createLookupCache(template,
                                           null,  // no filter
                                           null); // no listener
        } catch(Exception e) {
            e.printStackTrace();
            System.exit(1);
        }
```

```java
        // loop until we find a service
        ServiceItem item = null;
        while (item == null) {
            System.out.println("no service yet");
            try {
                Thread.currentThread().sleep(1000);
            } catch(java.lang.InterruptedException e) {
                // do nothing
            }
            // see if a service is there now
            item = cache.lookup(null);
        }
        FileClassifier classifier = (FileClassifier) item.service;
        if (classifier == null) {
            System.out.println("Classifier null");
            System.exit(1);
        }
        // Now we have a suitable service, use it
        MIMEType type;
        try {
            String fileName;

            fileName = "file1.txt";
            type = classifier.getMIMEType(fileName);
            printType(fileName, type);

            fileName = "file2.rtf";
            type = classifier.getMIMEType(fileName);
            printType(fileName, type);

            fileName = "file3.abc";
            type = classifier.getMIMEType(fileName);
            printType(fileName, type);
        } catch(java.rmi.RemoteException e) {
            System.err.println(e.toString());
        }
        System.exit(0);
    }
    private void printType(String fileName, MIMEType type) {
        System.out.print("Type of " + fileName + " is ");
        if (type == null) {
            System.out.println("null");
        } else {
            System.out.println(type.toString());
        }
    }
} // CachedClientLookup
```

Running the CachedClientLookup

While it is OK to poll the local cache, the cache itself must get its contents from lookup services, and in general it is not OK to poll these because doing so involves possibly heavy network traffic. The cache gets its information by registering itself as a listener for service events from the lookup services. The lookup services will then call notify() on the cache listener. This is a remote call from the remote lookup service to the local cache, done (probably) using an RMI stub. In fact, the Sun implementation of ServiceDiscoveryManager uses a nested class, ServiceDiscoveryManager.LookupCacheImpl.LookupListener, which has an RMI stub.

In order for the cache to actually work, it is necessary to set the RMI codebase property java.rmi.server.codebase to a suitable location for the class files (such as an HTTP server), and to make sure that the class net/jini/lookup/ServiceDiscoveryManager$LookupCacheImpl$ LookupListener_Stub.class is accessible from this codebase. The stub file may be found in the library lib/jini-ext.jar in the Jini 1.1 distribution. It has to be extracted from there and placed in the codebase using a command such as this:

```
unzip jini-ext.jar \
'net/jini/lookup/ \
ServiceDiscoveryManager$LookupCacheImpl$LookupListener_Stub.class' \
-d /home/WWW/htdocs/classes
```

Note that the specification just says this type of thing has to be done but does not descend to details about the class name—that is left to the documentation of the ServiceDiscoveryManager as implemented by Sun. If another implementation is made of the Jini classes, then it would probably use a different remote class.

Monitoring Changes to the Cache

The cache uses remote events to monitor the state of lookup services. It includes a local mechanism to pass some of these changes to a client by means of the ServiceDiscoveryListener interface:

```
package net.jini.lookup;
interface ServiceDiscoveryListener {
    void serviceAdded(ServiceDiscoveryEvent event);
    void serviceChanged(ServiceDiscoveryEvent event);
    void serviceRemoved(ServiceDiscoveryEvent event);
}
```

with event

```
package net.jini.lookup;
class ServiceDiscoveryEvent extends EventObject {
    ServiceItem getPostEventServiceItem();
    ServiceItem getPreEventServiceItem();
}
```

Clients are not likely to be interested in all events generated by lookup services, even for services in which they are interested. For example, if a new service registers itself with ten lookup services, they will all generate transition events from NO_MATCH to MATCH, but the client will usually only be interested in seeing the first of these—the other nine are just repeated information. Similarly, if a service's lease expires from one lookup service, then that doesn't matter much, but if it expires from all lookup services that the client knows of, then it does matter, because the service is no longer available to it. The cache consequently prunes events so that the client gets information about the real services rather than information about the lookup services.

From Chapter 16, recall the example involving monitoring changes to services from a lookup service viewpoint, reporting each change to lookup services. A client-oriented view just monitors changes in services themselves, which can be done easily using ServiceDiscoveryEvent objects:

```java
package client;
import java.rmi.RMISecurityManager;
import net.jini.discovery.LookupDiscovery;
import net.jini.lookup.ServiceDiscoveryListener;
import net.jini.lookup.ServiceDiscoveryEvent;
import net.jini.core.lookup.ServiceTemplate;
import net.jini.core.lookup.ServiceItem;
import net.jini.lookup.ServiceDiscoveryManager;
import net.jini.discovery.LookupDiscoveryManager;
import net.jini.lease.LeaseRenewalManager;
import net.jini.lookup.LookupCache;
/**
 * ServiceMonitor.java
 */
public class ServiceMonitor implements ServiceDiscoveryListener {
    public static void main(String argv[]) {
        new ServiceMonitor();
        // stay around long enough to receive replies
        try {
            Thread.currentThread().sleep(100000L);
        } catch(java.lang.InterruptedException e) {
            // do nothing
        }
    }

    public ServiceMonitor() {
        ServiceDiscoveryManager clientMgr = null;
        LookupCache cache = null;
        System.setSecurityManager(new RMISecurityManager());
        try {
            LookupDiscoveryManager mgr =
                new LookupDiscoveryManager(LookupDiscovery.ALL_GROUPS,
                                    null, // unicast locators
                                    null); // DiscoveryListener
            clientMgr = new ServiceDiscoveryManager(mgr,
                                    new LeaseRenewalManager());
        } catch(Exception e) {
            e.printStackTrace();
            System.exit(1);
```

```
        }

        ServiceTemplate template = new ServiceTemplate(null, null,
                                                        null);
        try {
            cache = clientMgr.createLookupCache(template,
                                            null,  // no filter
                                            this); // listener
        } catch(Exception e) {
            e.printStackTrace();
            System.exit(1);
        }
    }
    // methods for ServiceDiscoveryListener
    public void serviceAdded(ServiceDiscoveryEvent evt) {
        // evt.getPreEventServiceItem() == null
        ServiceItem postItem = evt.getPostEventServiceItem();
        System.out.println("Service appeared: " +
                        postItem.service.getClass().toString());
    }
    public void serviceChanged(ServiceDiscoveryEvent evt) {
        ServiceItem preItem = evt.getPostEventServiceItem();
        ServiceItem postItem = evt.getPreEventServiceItem() ;
        System.out.println("Service changed: " +
                        postItem.service.getClass().toString());
    }
    public void serviceRemoved(ServiceDiscoveryEvent evt) {
        // evt.getPostEventServiceItem() == null
        ServiceItem preItem = evt.getPreEventServiceItem();
        System.out.println("Service disappeared: " +
                        preItem.service.getClass().toString());
    }

} // ServiceMonitor
```

Summary

Clients searching for services have varying requirements. Clients may wish to block until a service is found, or continue doing something while a cache of services is built. Or they may wish to filter the services using more complex logic than just service type and Entry values. The service discovery manager is a complex class that can be used for many of these different situations, and it makes it easier to write clients with nontrivial service requirements.

■ ■ ■

CHAPTER 18

Example: Flashing Clocks

One of the early promises of Jini was that it would find its way into all sorts of devices that could advertise their presence. However, Jini does not run on the really small JVMs such as the KVM. But if it could, how would it be used?

Most people have a number of electronic clocks in their homes: alarm clocks, a clock on the oven, another clock on the microwave, and so on. When the electricity resumes after a power failure, all of these clocks start flashing, and you have to go to each one and reset it manually. Wouldn't it be nice if you had to reset only one of these clocks (or if it got a value from a time server somewhere) and all the others reset themselves from it?

In this chapter, we'll look at this "flashing clocks" problem from a Jini viewpoint, to see what a Jini solution might look like. This example uses `JoinManager` and `ServiceDiscoveryManager` to advertise and discover services.

Note On my site (`http://jan.netcomp.monash.edu.au/internetdevices/upnp/`
`upnp-more-programming.html`) is an alternative solution using UPnP, a middleware system that is gaining more ground in the area of small devices than Jini is, probably due to lighter resource requirements and an active coordinating body.

Timer

Each clock is available as a service called a `Timer`. A timer has methods to get and set the time, and in addition it knows if it has a valid time or if it has an invalid time (and so should be shown flashing). A timer can have its time set; when it does, it becomes valid and the display stops flashing.

The interface for a timer is as follows:

```
/**
 * Timer service
 */
package clock.service;
import java.rmi.Remote;
import java.rmi.RemoteException;
import java.util.Date;
public interface Timer extends Remote {
```

```
    public void setTime(Date t) throws RemoteException;
    public Date getTime() throws RemoteException;
    public boolean isValidTime() throws RemoteException;
}
```

TickerTimer

I'll give two implementations of this service. The first is given in this section and is the "dumb" one: when the timer starts, it guesses at a start time and enters an invalid state. It uses a separate thread (a "ticker") to keep increasing its time every second (approximately). When its time is set, it becomes valid, but it will probably drift from the correct time due to its use of a sleep to keep changing the time.

The dumb ticker timer is as follows:

```java
package clock.service;
import java.util.Date;
import java.rmi.RemoteException;
public class TickerTimer implements Timer {
    private Date time;
    private boolean isValid;
    private Ticker ticker;
    /**
     * Constructor with no starting time has
     * invalid timer and any time
     */
    public TickerTimer() {
        time = new Date(0);
        isValid = false;
        ticker = new Ticker(time);
        ticker.start();
    }
    public TickerTimer(Date t) {
        time = t;
        isValid = true;
        ticker = new Ticker(time);
        ticker.start();
    }

    public void setTime(Date t) {
        System.out.println("Setting time to " + t);
        time = t;
        isValid = true;
        if (ticker != null) {
            ticker.stopRunning();
        }
        ticker = new Ticker(time);
        ticker.start();
    }
```

```java
        public Date getTime() {
            return ticker.getTime();
        }
        public boolean isValidTime() {
            if (isValid) {
                return true;
            } else {
                return false;
            }
        }
    }
}
class Ticker extends Thread {
    private Date time;
    private boolean keepRunning = true;
    public Ticker(Date t) {
        time = t;
    }
    public Date getTime() {
        return time;
    }
    public void run() {
        while (keepRunning) {
            try {
                sleep(1000);
            } catch(InterruptedException e) {
            }
            time = new Date(time.getTime() + 1000);
        }
    }
    public void stopRunning() {
        keepRunning = false;
    }
}
```

ComputerTimer

This section describes the second implementation of a timer. This timer uses the computer's internal clock to always return the correct time on request. It is always valid.

```java
package clock.service;
import java.util.Date;
import net.jini.core.event.*;
import java.util.Vector;
import java.rmi.RemoteException;
public class ComputerTimer implements Timer {
    public ComputerTimer() {
    }
    public void setTime(Date t) {
```

```
        // void
    }
    public Date getTime() {
        return new Date();
    }
    public boolean isValidTime() {
        return true;
    }
}
```

ClockFrame

To make the clocks more visual, we can put the timers into a Swing frame and watch them ticking away. The following code is based on that of Satoshi Konno for UPnP.

A clock pane is as follows:

```
/**
 * Copyright (C) Satoshi Konno 2002
 * Minor changes Jan Newmarch
 */
package clock.clock;
import clock.device.*;
import java.io.*;
import java.awt.*;
import java.awt.geom.*;
import java.awt.image.*;
import javax.swing.*;
import javax.imageio.ImageIO;
import java.rmi.RemoteException;
import java.util.Date;
import java.text.DateFormat;
import java.text.SimpleDateFormat;
public class ClockPane extends JPanel
{
    private ClockDevice clockDev;
    private Color lastBlink = Color.BLACK;
    private DateFormat dateFormat = new SimpleDateFormat("kk:mm:ss");
    public ClockPane(ClockDevice clockDev)
    {
        this.clockDev = clockDev;
        loadImage();
        initPanel();
    }


    /////////////////////////////////////////////////
    //          Background
    /////////////////////////////////////////////////
```

```java
    private final static int DEFAULT_WIDTH = 200;
    private final static int DEFAULT_HEIGHT = 60;
    private final static String CLOCK_PANEL_IMAGE = "images/clock.jpg";
    private final static String CLOCK_PANEL_IMAGE_FILE = "resources/" +
                                                CLOCK_PANEL_IMAGE;

    private Image panelmage;
    private int imageWidth = DEFAULT_WIDTH;
    private int imageHeight = DEFAULT_HEIGHT;

    private void loadImage()
    {
        // Try to get the image form the local file system
        File f = new File(CLOCK_PANEL_IMAGE_FILE);
        try {
            panelmage = ImageIO.read(f);
            imageWidth = ((BufferedImage) panelmage).getWidth();
            imageHeight = ((BufferedImage) panelmage).getHeight();
            return;
        }
        catch (Exception e) {
            // Not in local file system
        }
        // Try to get the image from classpath jar files
        java.net.URL url = getClass().getClassLoader().
                                getResource(CLOCK_PANEL_IMAGE);
        if (url != null) {
            ImageIcon icon = new ImageIcon(url);
            panelmage = icon.getImage();
            imageWidth = icon.getIconWidth();
            imageHeight = icon.getIconHeight();
            return;
        }

        // couldn't find an image, leave panelmage as null
    }

    private Image getPaneImage()
    {
        return panelmage;
    }

    //////////////////////////////////////////////
    //          Background
    //////////////////////////////////////////////

    private void initPanel()
    {
```

```java
        Image panelmage = getPaneImage();
        setPreferredSize(new Dimension(imageWidth, imageHeight));
    }


    /////////////////////////////////////////////////
    //          Font
    /////////////////////////////////////////////////

    private final static String DEFAULT_FONT_NAME = "Lucida Console";
    private final static int DEFAULT_TIME_FONT_SIZE = 48;
    private final static int DEFAULT_DATE_FONT_SIZE = 18;
    private final static int DEFAULT_SECOND_BLOCK_HEIGHT = 8;
    private final static int DEFAULT_SECOND_BLOCK_FONT_SIZE = 10;

    private Font timeFont = null;
    private Font dateFont = null;
    private Font secondFont = null;

    private Font getFont(Graphics g, int size)
    {
        Font font = new Font(DEFAULT_FONT_NAME, Font.PLAIN, size);
        if (font != null)
            return font;
        return g.getFont();
    }

    private Font getTimeFont(Graphics g)
    {
        if (timeFont == null)
            timeFont = getFont(g, DEFAULT_TIME_FONT_SIZE);
        return timeFont;
    }

    private Font getDateFont(Graphics g)
    {
        if (dateFont == null)
            dateFont = getFont(g, DEFAULT_DATE_FONT_SIZE);
        return dateFont;
    }

    private Font getSecondFont(Graphics g)
    {
        if (secondFont == null)
            secondFont = getFont(g, DEFAULT_SECOND_BLOCK_FONT_SIZE);
        return secondFont;
    }
```

```
///////////////////////////////////////////////
//       paint
///////////////////////////////////////////////

private void drawClockInfo(Graphics g)
{
    int winWidth = getWidth();
    int winHeight = getHeight();

    boolean valid = false;
    try {
        valid = clockDev.isValidTime();
    } catch(RemoteException e) {
        // valid is already false
    }
    if (valid) {
        g.setColor(Color.BLACK);
    } else {
        if (lastBlink == Color.WHITE) {
            g.setColor(Color.BLACK);
            lastBlink = Color.BLACK;
        } else {
            g.setColor(Color.WHITE);
            lastBlink = Color.WHITE;
        }
    }

    //// Time String ////
    Date now = null;
    try {
        now = clockDev.getTime();
    } catch(RemoteException e) {
        now = new Date(0);
    }
    String timeStr = dateFormat.format(now);

    Font timeFont = getTimeFont(g);
    g.setFont(timeFont);

    FontMetrics timeFontMetric = g.getFontMetrics();
    Rectangle2D timeStrBounds = timeFontMetric.getStringBounds(timeStr, g);

    int timeStrWidth = (int)timeStrBounds.getWidth();
    int timeStrHeight = (int)timeStrBounds.getHeight();
    int timeStrX = (winWidth-timeStrWidth)/2;
    int timeStrY = (winHeight+timeStrHeight)/2;
    int timeStrOffset = timeStrHeight/8/2;
```

```java
            g.drawString(
                        timeStr,
                        timeStrX,
                        timeStrY);

            //// Date String ////

            String dateStr = "Time";

            Font dateFont = getDateFont(g);
            g.setFont(dateFont);

            FontMetrics dateFontMetric = g.getFontMetrics();
            Rectangle2D dateStrBounds = dateFontMetric.getStringBounds(dateStr, g);

            g.drawString(
                        dateStr,
                        (winWidth-(int)dateStrBounds.getWidth())/2,
                        timeStrY-timeStrHeight-timeStrOffset);

    }

    private void clear(Graphics g)
    {
        g.setColor(Color.GRAY);
        g.clearRect(0, 0, getWidth(), getHeight());
    }


    private void drawPanelImage(Graphics g)
    {
        if (getPaneImage() == null) {
            return;
        }
        g.drawImage(getPaneImage(), 0, 0, null);
    }

    public void paint(Graphics g)
    {
        clear(g);
        drawPanelImage(g);
        drawClockInfo(g);
    }
}
```

Here's a clock frame:

```java
/**
 * Copyright (C) Satoshi Konno 2002-2003
 * Minor changes Jan Newmarch
 */
package clock.clock;
import clock.device.*;
import java.awt.*;
import java.awt.event.*;
import javax.swing.*;
public class ClockFrame extends JFrame implements Runnable, WindowListener
{
    private final static String DEFAULT_TITLE = "Sample Clock";
    private ClockDevice clockDev;
    private ClockPane clockPane;
    public ClockFrame(ClockDevice clockDev) {
        this(clockDev, DEFAULT_TITLE);
    }
    public ClockFrame(ClockDevice clockDev, String title)
    {
        super(title);
        this.clockDev = clockDev;

        getContentPane().setLayout(new BorderLayout());

        clockPane = new ClockPane(clockDev);
        getContentPane().add(clockPane, BorderLayout.CENTER);

        addWindowListener(this);

        pack();
        setVisible(true);
    }

    public ClockPane getClockPanel()
    {
        return clockPane;
    }

    public ClockDevice getClockDevice()
    {
        return clockDev;
    }


    /////////////////////////////////////////////////
    //          run
    /////////////////////////////////////////////////
```

```java
private Thread timerThread = null;

public void run()
{
    Thread thisThread = Thread.currentThread();

    while (timerThread == thisThread) {
        // getClockDevice().update();
        getClockPanel().repaint();
        try {
            Thread.sleep(1000);
        }
        catch(InterruptedException e) {}
    }
}

public void start()
{
    // clockDev.start();

    timerThread = new Thread(this);
    timerThread.start();
}

public void stop()
{
    // clockDev.stop();
    timerThread = null;
}

/////////////////////////////////////////////////
//        main
/////////////////////////////////////////////////

public void windowActivated(WindowEvent e)
{
}

public void windowClosed(WindowEvent e)
{
}

public void windowClosing(WindowEvent e)
{
    stop();
    System.exit(0);
}
```

```
    public void windowDeactivated(WindowEvent e)
    {
    }

    public void windowDeiconified(WindowEvent e)
    {
    }

    public void windowIconified(WindowEvent e)
    {
    }

    public void windowOpened(WindowEvent e)
    {
    }
}
```

TickerTimer Driver

A driver for the ticker timer in the preceding frame is as follows:

```
package clock.clock;
import clock.device.*;
import clock.service.*;
public class TickerClock {

    public static void main(String args[])
    {
        ClockDevice clockDev = new ClockDevice();
        clockDev.setTimer(new TickerTimer());
        ClockFrame clock;
        if (args.length > 0) {
            clock= new ClockFrame(clockDev, args[0]);
        } else {
            clock = new ClockFrame(clockDev);
        }
        clock.start();
    }
}
```

This driver can be run with the following:

```
java clock.clock.TickerClock "Ticking Clock"
```

ComputerTimer Driver

A driver for the computer timer in the preceding frame is as follows:

```
package clock.clock;
import clock.device.*;
import clock.service.*;
public class ComputerClock {

    public static void main(String args[])
    {
        ClockDevice clockDev = new ClockDevice();

        clockDev.setTimer(new ComputerTimer());
        ClockFrame clock;
        if (args.length > 0) {
            clock= new ClockFrame(clockDev, args[0]);
        } else {
            clock = new ClockFrame(clockDev);
        }
        clock.start();    }
}
```

This driver can be run with the following:

```
java clock.clock.ComputerClock "Computer Clock"
```

Multiple Clocks

Two (or more) clocks can be started. If ticking clocks are started, then they will all be flashing. Once a computer clock is started, though, the clocks will discover each other. Either the computer clock will discover ticking clocks and reset them, or the ticking clocks will discover the computer clock and reset themselves. I don't know which scenario occurs, and it doesn't matter.

When running, two clocks look like Figure 18-1.

Figure 18-1. *A ticking clock and a computer clock*

ClockDevice

The final part of the code for each clock is to advertise each timer as a Jini service, to try to locate other timer services and to listen to events from each one. This is handled by the clock device (really, it is what we have been calling a Jini server; we have just adopted the UPnP). The device has a timer installed by setTimer(), and it advertises this using a JoinManager. In the meantime, it uses a ServiceDiscoveryManager to find other timers.

```
package clock.device;
import clock.service.*;
import java.io.*;
import java.util.Date;
import java.rmi.*;
import java.rmi.server.ExportException;
import net.jini.export.*;
import net.jini.jeri.BasicJeriExporter;
import net.jini.jeri.BasicILFactory;
import net.jini.jeri.tcp.TcpServerEndpoint;
import net.jini.lookup.JoinManager;
import net.jini.core.lookup.ServiceID;
import net.jini.discovery.LookupDiscovery;
import net.jini.core.lookup.ServiceRegistrar;
import java.rmi.RemoteException;
import net.jini.lookup.ServiceIDListener;
import net.jini.lease.LeaseRenewalManager;
import net.jini.discovery.LookupDiscoveryManager;
import net.jini.lookup.ServiceDiscoveryListener;
import net.jini.lookup.ServiceDiscoveryEvent;
import net.jini.core.lookup.ServiceTemplate;
```

```java
import net.jini.core.lookup.ServiceItem;
import net.jini.lookup.ServiceDiscoveryManager;
import net.jini.discovery.LookupDiscoveryManager;
import net.jini.lease.LeaseRenewalManager;
import net.jini.lookup.LookupCache;
public class ClockDevice implements ServiceIDListener, ServiceDiscoveryListener {
    private Timer timer;
    public ClockDevice() {
        System.setSecurityManager(new RMISecurityManager());
        // Build a cache of all discovered clocks and monitor changes
        ServiceDiscoveryManager serviceMgr = null;
        LookupCache cache = null;
        Class [] classes = new Class[] {Timer.class};
        ServiceTemplate template = new ServiceTemplate(null, classes,
                                                            null);

        try {
            LookupDiscoveryManager mgr =
                new LookupDiscoveryManager(LookupDiscovery.ALL_GROUPS,
                                    null,  // unicast locators
                                    null); // DiscoveryListener
            serviceMgr = new ServiceDiscoveryManager(mgr,
                                            new LeaseRenewalManager());
        } catch(Exception e) {
            e.printStackTrace();
            System.exit(1);
        }

        try {
            cache = serviceMgr.createLookupCache(template,
                                        null,  // no filter
                                        this); // listener
        } catch(Exception e) {
            e.printStackTrace();
            System.exit(1);
        }
    }
    public void setTimer(Timer t) {
        timer = t;
        System.out.println("Our timer service is " + t);
        Exporter exporter = new BasicJeriExporter(TcpServerEndpoint.getInstance(0),
                                new BasicILFactory());
        // export a Timer proxy
        Remote proxy = null;
        try {
            proxy = exporter.export(timer);
        } catch(ExportException e) {
            System.exit(1);
```

```
    }
    // Register with all lookup services as they are discovered
    JoinManager joinMgr = null;
    try {
        LookupDiscoveryManager mgr =
            new LookupDiscoveryManager(LookupDiscovery.ALL_GROUPS,
                                    null, // unicast locators
                                    null); // DiscoveryListener
        joinMgr = new JoinManager(proxy, // service proxy
                                null,  // attr sets
                                this,  // ServiceIDListener
                                mgr,   // DiscoveryManager
                                new LeaseRenewalManager());
    } catch(Exception e) {
        e.printStackTrace();
        System.exit(1);
    }
}

public void serviceIDNotify(ServiceID serviceID) {
    // called as a ServiceIDListener
    // Should save the ID to permanent storage
    System.out.println("got service ID " + serviceID.toString());
}
public void serviceAdded(ServiceDiscoveryEvent evt) {
    // evt.getPreEventServiceItem() == null
    ServiceItem postItem = evt.getPostEventServiceItem();
    System.out.println("Service appeared: " +
                        postItem.service.getClass().toString());
    tryClockValidation((Timer) postItem.service);
}
public void serviceChanged(ServiceDiscoveryEvent evt) {
    ServiceItem preItem = evt.getPostEventServiceItem();
    ServiceItem postItem = evt.getPreEventServiceItem() ;
    System.out.println("Service changed: " +
                        postItem.service.getClass().toString());
}
public void serviceRemoved(ServiceDiscoveryEvent evt) {
    // evt.getPostEventServiceItem() == null
    ServiceItem preItem = evt.getPreEventServiceItem();
    System.out.println("Service disappeared: " +
                        preItem.service.getClass().toString());
}
private void tryClockValidation(Timer otherTimer) {
    try {
        if (timer.isValidTime() &&  ! otherTimer.isValidTime()) {
```

```
                    // other clock needs to be set by us
                    otherTimer.setTime(timer.getTime());
                } else if (! timer.isValidTime() && otherTimer.isValidTime()) {
                    // we need to be set from the other clock
                    timer.setTime(otherTimer.getTime());
                }
            } catch(RemoteException e) {
                // ignore other timer!
            }
        }
    }
    public void setTime(Date t) throws RemoteException {
        timer.setTime(t);
    }
    public Date getTime()  throws RemoteException {
        return timer.getTime();
    }
    public boolean isValidTime()  throws RemoteException {
        return timer.isValidTime();
    }
}
```

Runtime Behavior

If several clocks are started, they will advertise themselves and also attempt to find other clocks. When one clock finds another, it tries to determine its state. If one is valid and the other is invalid, then either the valid one sets the time on the invalid one, or the invalid one gets the correct time from the valid one. Which procedure takes place depends on whether the valid one discovers the invalid one or vice versa; it doesn't matter, since the result is the same. Two valid clocks do nothing to each other, as do two invalid ones.

The Ant file `clock.clock.xml` runs a ticker clock, pauses 60 seconds, and then runs a computer clock. When one clock discovers the other, the ticker clock has its time reset.

Summary

This chapter looked at a common household problem to show how Jini could be used in such a situation. The solution uses many of the features of Jini that we have covered so far. When running, it gives a visual demonstration of Jini service discovery and invocation techniques.

CHAPTER 19

■ ■ ■

Configuration

Many Jini programs end up with hard-coded strings, objects, and classes. It is becoming more common in complex systems to separate out runtime parameters from compile-time code. Java programs have long been able to provide properties to give runtime configuration, but this is very simplistic and only allows strings to be given. The Jini Configuration class allows values to be passed into a Jini program at runtime. These values are not just limited to strings, but can be Java objects. In this chapter, we discuss how configurations can be specified, what they can contain, and how a Jini program can use them at runtime.

Runtime Configuration

Most applications have runtime configuration mechanisms. For example, most web browsers allow you to set the home page, choose which proxy server is used, select the default font sizes, and so on. When an application starts, it must be able to pick up these configuration options somehow. They are generally specified on the command line, put in a file, or picked up from a database.

Options on a command line are usually very simple and of the form vbl=value. For example, Sun's Java compiler takes command-line options of the form -Dproperty=value. Configuration values stored in files can be more complex; while many applications will just use lines of vbl=value, it is possible to have complete programs in an interpreted programming language. For example, Netscape stores configuration values in liprefs.js as JavaScript function calls.

Jini 2.0 has mechanisms for support of runtime configuration. It offers a spectrum of choices ranging from simple values to a full programming language. From the programmer's viewpoint, accessing configuration information is basically restricted to getting the value of parameters by methods such as the following:

```
Object Configuration.getEntry(String component, String name, Class type)
```

While simple, this mechanism is still quite powerful. You don't just get strings (like you get from Java properties or from command-line arguments); you get full Java objects. These could be URL objects for specifying unicast lookup services, protocol objects such as JrmpExporter, or any other Java objects, such as arrays of hashmaps.

Configuration is an interface. You get an implementation of this interface by calling ConfigurationProvider.getInstance(configArgs), for example:

```
        String[] configArgs = new String[] {...};
        Configuration config = ConfigurationProvider.getInstance(configArgs);
        Exporter exporter = (Exporter) config.getEntry( "JeriExportDemo",
                                                        "exporter",
                                                        Exporter.class);
```

The implementation could support anything from simple variable/value pairs to a full programming language. The default implementation is a ConfigurationFile.

ConfigurationFile

The ConfigurationFile is the middle ground between variable/value pairs and a full programming language. It uses a syntax based on Java with the following capabilities:

- Values can be assigned to variables.

- Objects can be created.

- Static methods can be called.

- Some access to the calling environment is allowed.

Procedural constructs such as loops and conditional statements are not in this language. While constructors and calling static methods are included, general method calls are not. The full syntax is given in the API documentation for ConfigurationFile.

For example, the file jeri/jeri.config contains the following:

```
import net.jini.jeri.BasicILFactory;
import net.jini.jeri.BasicJeriExporter;
import net.jini.jeri.tcp.TcpServerEndpoint;
JeriExportDemo {
    exporter = new BasicJeriExporter(TcpServerEndpoint.getInstance(0),
                                     new BasicILFactory());
}
```

This configuration file imports all classes needed. It defines a component, JeriExportDemo, and within this component is an entry defining the identifier exporter. The identifier is assigned an expression that contains two constructors, BasicJeriExporter() and BasicILFactory(). It also contains a static method call, TcpServerEndpoint.getInstance().

This mechanism is not restricted to getting an exporter for RMI proxies. It can be used for any other configurable properties. For example, suppose a program wishes to use a particular URL. Instead of passing it as a command-line parameter, it can be placed in the configuration file:

```
import net.jini.jrmp.*;
import java.net.URL;
ConfigDemo {
    exporter = new JrmpExporter();
    url = new URL("http://jan.netcomp.monash.edu.au/internetdevices/jmf/test.wav");
}
```

and used by

```
url = (URL) config.getEntry("ConfigDemo",
                            "url",
                            URL.class);
```

In a similar manner, a configuration can also be used to specify other strings and objects to a program. It can be used to specify arrays of objects, though the syntax gets a little more complex. For example, suppose a set of Entry objects is required for a service. Since they are by definition additional information for a service, they should not be hard-coded into a program. OK, so put them in the configuration file:

```
import net.jini.jrmp.*;
import java.net.URL;
import net.jini.core.entry.Entry;
import net.jini.lookup.entry.*;
ConfigDemo {
    exporter = new JrmpExporter();
    url = new URL("http://localhost/internetdevices/jmf/test.wav");
    entries = new Entry[] {new Name("Jan Newmarch"),
                           new Comment("Author of Jini book")};
}
```

The hard part is getting the array out of the configuration; the last argument to getEntry() is a Class object, which here has to be a class object for an array. The simplest way to accomplish this is as follows:

```
Class cls = Entry[].class;
```

Retrieval follows the same pattern:

```
entries = (Entry []) config.getEntry("ConfigDemo",
                                     "entries",
                                     cls);
```

Specifying the Configuration

The default configuration implementation is a ConfigurationFile. In order to find this implementation, the ConfigurationProvider.getInstance() method has to be given a file name as a parameter. But there are other possibilities: the configuration could be stored in a database, in which case the argument to ConfigurationProvider.getInstance() should be a database handle. Or it could be stored on a web site, in which case it should be a URL. None of these other possibilities is at present supported, but there are hooks so that Jini (or any programmer) can provide implementations of Configuration that have these other behaviors.

To avoid tying down an implementation by explicitly hard-coding a file name into an application, the file name too should be left as a runtime parameter. But of course, we can't use configuration to specify a configuration; we need a bootstrapping mechanism. For this, we could fall back to command-line arguments or Java properties.

Using a command line where the configuration file is given as the first command-line argument, code would look like this:

```
if (args.length == 0) {
    System.err.println("No configuration specified");
    System.exit(1);
}
String[] configArgs = new String[] {args[0]};
Configuration config = ConfigurationProvider.getInstance(configArgs);
Exporter exporter = (Exporter) config.getEntry( "JeriExportDemo",
                                                 "exporter",
                                                 Exporter.class);
```

Storing the Service ID

A recommended practice is for a service to have a persistent service ID. Even if it stops and restarts, it should have the same ID (unless a restart really represents a distinct service). The JoinManager class has different constructors to support this: a constructor for first-time registration and a constructor that supplies an earlier ID.

A service can get its service ID from several places. It may be presupplied by a vendor, but it is most likely generated by the first lookup service it is registered with. The ServiceIDListener interface is provided for a service to determine what ID it has been assigned. Once it has an ID, the service is expected to save it in persistent storage and reuse it later. The details of this persistent storage are, of course, unspecified by Jini. In Chapter 9, a binary representation of the service ID was stored in an .id file and retrieved (if possible) when the service was restarted.

Hard-coding the .id file name is imposing a compile-time decision on what should be a runtime option. So the file name could be stored in a configuration file and extracted from there.

The configuration mechanism makes it tempting to store the ID in the configuration file and pull it out of there. If it is not in the file, then ask a lookup service for the ID and rewrite the file to store it there for next time. This is quite a tall order for a general-purpose system, especially since configurations may not be stored in files at all!

A better way is to store the persistent storage *file name* in the configuration. A configuration file could look like this:

```
import java.io.*;
ServiceIdDemo {
    serviceIdFile = new File("serviceId.id");
}
```

and a program using this configuration could be as follows:

```
package config;
import java.rmi.RMISecurityManager;
import net.jini.discovery.LookupDiscovery;
import net.jini.discovery.DiscoveryListener;
import net.jini.discovery.DiscoveryEvent;
```

```java
import net.jini.core.lookup.ServiceRegistrar;
import net.jini.core.lookup.ServiceItem;
import net.jini.core.lookup.ServiceRegistration;
import net.jini.core.lease.Lease;
import net.jini.core.lookup.ServiceID ;
import net.jini.lease.LeaseListener;
import net.jini.lease.LeaseRenewalEvent;
import net.jini.lease.LeaseRenewalManager;
import net.jini.config.Configuration;
import net.jini.config.ConfigurationException;
import net.jini.config.ConfigurationProvider;
import java.io.*;
/**
 * FileClassifierServerIDConfig.java
 */
public class FileClassifierServerIDConfig implements DiscoveryListener,
                                LeaseListener {

    protected LeaseRenewalManager leaseManager = new LeaseRenewalManager();
    protected ServiceID serviceID = null;
    protected complete.FileClassifierImpl impl;
    protected File serviceIdFile;
    public static void main(String args[]) {
        FileClassifierServerIDConfig s = new FileClassifierServerIDConfig(args);

        // keep server running forever to
        // - allow time for locator discovery and
        // - keep re-registering the lease
        Object keepAlive = new Object();
        synchronized(keepAlive) {
            try {
                keepAlive.wait();
            } catch(java.lang.InterruptedException e) {
                // do nothing
            }
        }
    }
    public FileClassifierServerIDConfig(String[] args) {
        // Create the service
        impl = new complete.FileClassifierImpl();
        if (args.length == 0) {
            System.err.println("No configuration specified");
            System.exit(1);
        }
        String[] configArgs = new String[] {args[0]};
        Configuration config = null;
```

```
        try {
            config = ConfigurationProvider.getInstance(configArgs);
            serviceIdFile = (File) config.getEntry("ServiceIdDemo",
                                            "serviceIdFile",
                                            File.class);
        } catch(ConfigurationException e) {
            System.err.println("Configuration error: " + e.toString());
            System.exit(1);
        }
        // Try to load the service ID from file.
        // It isn't an error if we can't load it, because
        // maybe this is the first time this service has run
        DataInputStream din = null;
        try {
            din = new DataInputStream(new FileInputStream(serviceIdFile));
            serviceID = new ServiceID(din);
            System.out.println("Found service ID in file " + serviceIdFile);
            din.close();
        } catch(Exception e) {
            // ignore
        }
        System.setSecurityManager(new RMISecurityManager());
        LookupDiscovery discover = null;
        try {
            discover = new LookupDiscovery(LookupDiscovery.ALL_GROUPS);
        } catch(Exception e) {
            System.err.println("Discovery failed " + e.toString());
            System.exit(1);
        }
        discover.addDiscoveryListener(this);
    }

    public void discovered(DiscoveryEvent evt) {
        ServiceRegistrar[] registrars = evt.getRegistrars();
        for (int n = 0; n < registrars.length; n++) {
            ServiceRegistrar registrar = registrars[n];
            ServiceItem item = new ServiceItem(serviceID,
                                            impl,
                                            null);
            ServiceRegistration reg = null;
            try {
                reg = registrar.register(item, Lease.FOREVER);
            } catch(java.rmi.RemoteException e) {
                System.err.println("Register exception: " + e.toString());
                continue;
            }
            System.out.println("Service registered with id " + reg.getServiceID());
```

```
                // set lease renewal in place
                leaseManager.renewUntil(reg.getLease(), Lease.FOREVER, this);
                // set the serviceID if necessary
                if (serviceID == null) {
                    System.out.println("Getting service ID from lookup service");
                    serviceID = reg.getServiceID();
                    // try to save the service ID in a file
                    DataOutputStream dout = null;
                    try {
                        dout = new DataOutputStream(
                                new FileOutputStream(serviceIdFile));
                        serviceID.writeBytes(dout);
                        dout.flush();
                        dout.close();
                        System.out.println("Service id saved in " + serviceIdFile);
                    } catch(Exception e) {
                        // ignore
                    }
                }
            }
        }
    }
    public void discarded(DiscoveryEvent evt) {
    }
    public void notify(LeaseRenewalEvent evt) {
        System.out.println("Lease expired " + evt.toString());
    }
}

} // FileClassifierServerIDConfig
```

This program could be run as follows:

```
java FileClassifierServerIDConfig config/serviceid.config
```

Specifying the Codebase

A Jini service needs to specify the java.rmi.server.codebase property so that clients can pick up class definitions. In previous chapters where the command line to start a service has been shown, this has always been done by specifying a property at the command line:

```
java -Djava.rmi.server.codebase=http://... ...
```

The Java runtime handles parsing the command line, extracting the property and its value, and using these to set the property value.

Properties can also be set by using the configuration mechanism. While this approach is more cumbersome than using a command-line parameter, it ensures that all runtime options are stored and handled in the same way. A server can pick up the codebase as follows:

```
package config;
import java.rmi.RMISecurityManager;
```

```java
import net.jini.discovery.LookupDiscovery;
import net.jini.discovery.DiscoveryListener;
import net.jini.discovery.DiscoveryEvent;
import net.jini.core.lookup.ServiceRegistrar;
import net.jini.core.lookup.ServiceItem;
import net.jini.core.lookup.ServiceRegistration;
import net.jini.core.lease.Lease;
import net.jini.core.lookup.ServiceID ;
import net.jini.lease.LeaseListener;
import net.jini.lease.LeaseRenewalEvent;
import net.jini.lease.LeaseRenewalManager;
import net.jini.config.Configuration;
import net.jini.config.ConfigurationException;
import net.jini.config.ConfigurationProvider;
import java.io.*;
/**
 * FileClassifierServerConfig.java
 */
public class FileClassifierServerCodebaseConfig implements DiscoveryListener,
                                            LeaseListener {

    protected LeaseRenewalManager leaseManager = new LeaseRenewalManager();
    protected complete.FileClassifierImpl impl;
    protected File serviceIdFile;
    public static void main(String args[]) {
        FileClassifierServerCodebaseConfig s = new FileClassifierServerCodebaseConfig(args);

        // keep server running forever to
        // - allow time for locator discovery and
        // - keep re-registering the lease
        Object keepAlive = new Object();
        synchronized(keepAlive) {
            try {
                keepAlive.wait();
            } catch(java.lang.InterruptedException e) {
                // do nothing
            }
        }
    }
    public FileClassifierServerCodebaseConfig(String[] args) {
        // Create the service
        impl = new complete.FileClassifierImpl();
        if (args.length == 0) {
            System.err.println("No configuration specified");
            System.exit(1);
        }
```

```
        String[] configArgs = new String[] {args[0]};
        Configuration config = null;
        String codebase = null;
        try {
            config = ConfigurationProvider.getInstance(configArgs);
            codebase = (String) config.getEntry("ServiceCodebaseDemo",
                                                "codebase",
                                                String.class);
        } catch(ConfigurationException e) {
            System.err.println("Configuration error: " + e.toString());
            System.exit(1);
        }
        System.setProperty("java.rmi.manager.codebase", codebase);
        System.setSecurityManager(new RMISecurityManager());
        LookupDiscovery discover = null;
        try {
            discover = new LookupDiscovery(LookupDiscovery.ALL_GROUPS);
        } catch(Exception e) {
            System.err.println("Discovery failed " + e.toString());
            System.exit(1);
        }
        discover.addDiscoveryListener(this);
    }

    public void discovered(DiscoveryEvent evt) {
        ServiceRegistrar[] registrars = evt.getRegistrars();
        for (int n = 0; n < registrars.length; n++) {
            ServiceRegistrar registrar = registrars[n];
            ServiceItem item = new ServiceItem(null,
                                               impl,
                                               null);
            ServiceRegistration reg = null;
            try {
                reg = registrar.register(item, Lease.FOREVER);
            } catch(java.rmi.RemoteException e) {
                System.err.println("Register exception: " + e.toString());
                continue;
            }
            System.out.println("Service registered with id " + reg.getServiceID());
            // set lease renewal in place
            leaseManager.renewUntil(reg.getLease(), Lease.FOREVER, this);
        }
    }
    public void discarded(DiscoveryEvent evt) {
    }
    public void notify(LeaseRenewalEvent evt) {
        System.out.println("Lease expired " + evt.toString());
```

```
    }

} // FileClassifierServerCodebaseConfig
```

Using localhost

In a development environment, it is quite common to build clients and services all on the same machine. My main computer is my laptop, and I keep moving from one IP domain to another, so my IP address keeps changing, and when I upload code to another machine it changes again. In these circumstances, it is quite common to use localhost for the current machine. But as soon as you distribute an application, use of localhost often breaks: *my*localhost is not *your*localhost, and distributed applications will often get confused.

Within an application, localhost can always be resolved to a "real" hostname:

```
InetAddress localhost = InetAdress.getLocalHost();
String loclaHostName = localhost.getHostName();
```

However, this code cannot be used in configuration files since it involves a call to an instance method, and only static method calls are allowed.

Jini 2.0 includes a ConfigUtils class that wraps this particular instance method with a static method, ConfigUtils.getHostName(). It also includes a static method to concatenate strings (which would otherwise be done by "+" on instance objects). I would expect the methods in this class to grow as more uses are made of Jini configuration. This class is in the com.sun.jini.config package, so it is not a finalized part of Jini.

A configuration to set the codebase to localhost might contain the following:

```
codebase = ConfigUtil.concat(new String[] {
                               "http://",
                               ConfigUtil.getHostName(),
                               ":80/classes"
                   }
               );
```

A Generic Server

The configuration mechanism can be used to place all runtime information in a configuration file. This can even include the service—all that the server needs to know is that the service implements the Remote interface. For example, information about the service could be given in a file such as config/generic.config:

```
import net.jini.jeri.BasicILFactory;
import net.jini.jeri.BasicJeriExporter;
import net.jini.jeri.tcp.TcpServerEndpoint;
import com.sun.jini.config.ConfigUtil;
import net.jini.core.discovery.LookupLocator;
import net.jini.core.entry.Entry;
import net.jini.lookup.entry.*;
import java.io.File;
```

```
GenericServer {
    // If the HTTP server for classes is running on the
    // local machine, use this for the codebase
    localhost = ConfigUtil.getHostName();
    port = "80";
    directory = "/classes";
    // codebase = http://"localhost":80/classes
    codebase =   ConfigUtil.concat(new String[] {
                                        "http://",
                                        localhost,
                                        ":",
                                        port,
                                        directory
                                    }
                            );
    exporter = new BasicJeriExporter(TcpServerEndpoint.getInstance(0),
                            new BasicILFactory());
    /* Groups to join
     * Could be e.g.
     *     groups  = new String[] {"admin", "sales"};
     */
    groups = LookupDiscovery.ALL_GROUPS;
    /* Unicast lookup services
     */
    unicastLocators = new LookupLocator[] { // empty
                                        };
    /* Entries
     */
    entries = new Entry[] {new Name("Jan Newmarch"),
                            new Comment("Author of Jini book")
                        };
    /* Service ID file
     */
    serviceIdFile = new File("serviceId.id");
    /* The service
     */
    service = new rmi.FileClassifierImpl();
}
```

A server using such a configuration file could be as follows:

```
package config;
import net.jini.lookup.JoinManager;
import net.jini.core.lookup.ServiceID;
import net.jini.core.discovery.LookupLocator;
import net.jini.core.entry.Entry;
import net.jini.lookup.ServiceIDListener;
import net.jini.lease.LeaseRenewalManager;
```

```java
import net.jini.discovery.LookupDiscoveryManager;
import java.rmi.RMISecurityManager;
import java.rmi.Remote;
import net.jini.export.Exporter;
import net.jini.core.lookup.ServiceID;
import java.io.*;
import net.jini.config.*;
/**
 * GenericServer.java
 */
public class GenericServer
    implements ServiceIDListener {
    private static final String SERVER = "GenericServer";
    private Remote proxy;
    private Remote impl;
    private Exporter exporter;
    private String[] groups;
    private Entry[] entries;
    private LookupLocator[] unicastLocators;
    private File serviceIdFile;
    private String codebase;
    private ServiceID serviceID;
    public static void main(String args[]) {
        new GenericServer(args);
        // stay around forever
        Object keepAlive = new Object();
        synchronized(keepAlive) {
            try {
                keepAlive.wait();
            } catch(InterruptedException e) {
                // do nothing
            }
        }
    }
    public GenericServer(String[] args) {
        if (args.length == 0) {
            System.err.println("No configuration specified");
            System.exit(1);
        }
        String[] configArgs = new String[] {args[0]};
        getConfiguration(configArgs);
        // set codebase
        System.setProperty("java.rmi.manager.codebase", codebase);
        // export a service object
        try {
            proxy = exporter.export(impl);
        } catch(java.rmi.server.ExportException e) {
```

```java
                e.printStackTrace();
                System.exit(1);
            }
            // install suitable security manager
            System.setSecurityManager(new RMISecurityManager());

            tryRetrieveServiceId();
            JoinManager joinMgr = null;
            try {
                LookupDiscoveryManager mgr =
                    new LookupDiscoveryManager(groups,
                                        unicastLocators, // unicast locators
                                        null); // DiscoveryListener

                if (serviceID != null) {
                    joinMgr = new JoinManager(proxy, // service proxy
                                        entries, // attr sets
                                        serviceID, // ServiceID
                                        mgr,    // DiscoveryManager
                                        new LeaseRenewalManager());
                } else {
                    joinMgr = new JoinManager(proxy, // service proxy
                                        entries, // attr sets
                                        this, // ServiceIDListener
                                        mgr,    // DiscoveryManager
                                        new LeaseRenewalManager());
                }
            } catch(Exception e) {
                e.printStackTrace();
                System.exit(1);
            }
        }
    public void tryRetrieveServiceId() {
        // Try to load the service ID from file.
        // It isn't an error if we can't load it, because
        // maybe this is the first time this service has run
        DataInputStream din = null;
        try {
            din = new DataInputStream(new FileInputStream(serviceIdFile));
            serviceID = new ServiceID(din);
            System.out.println("Found service ID in file " + serviceIdFile);
            din.close();
        } catch(Exception e) {
            // ignore
        }
    }
    public void serviceIDNotify(ServiceID serviceID) {
        // called as a ServiceIDListener
```

```
        // Should save the ID to permanent storage
        System.out.println("got service ID " + serviceID.toString());

        // try to save the service ID in a file
        if (serviceIdFile != null) {
            DataOutputStream dout = null;
            try {
                dout = new DataOutputStream(new FileOutputStream(serviceIdFile));
                serviceID.writeBytes(dout);
                dout.flush();
            dout.close();
            System.out.println("Service id saved in " +  serviceIdFile);
            } catch(Exception e) {
                // ignore
            }
        }
    }
    private void getConfiguration(String[] configArgs) {
        Configuration config = null;
        // We have to get a configuration file or
        // we can't continue
        try {
            config = ConfigurationProvider.getInstance(configArgs);
        } catch(ConfigurationException e) {
            System.err.println(e.toString());
            e.printStackTrace();
            System.exit(1);
        }

        // The config file must have an exporter, a service, and a codebase
        try {
            exporter = (Exporter) config.getEntry(SERVER,
                                                  "exporter",
                                                  Exporter.class);
            impl = (Remote) config.getEntry(SERVER,
                                            "service",
                                            Remote.class);
            codebase = (String) config.getEntry(SERVER,
                                                "codebase",
                                                String.class);
        } catch(NoSuchEntryException  e) {
            System.err.println("No config entry for " + e);
            System.exit(1);
        } catch(Exception e) {
            System.err.println(e.toString());
            e.printStackTrace();
            System.exit(2);
```

```
        }
        // These fields can fall back to a default value
        try {
            unicastLocators = (LookupLocator[])
                config.getEntry("GenericServer",
                                "unicastLocators",
                                LookupLocator[].class,
                                null); // default

            entries = (Entry[])
                config.getEntry("GenericServer",
                                "entries",
                                Entry[].class,
                                null); // default
            serviceIdFile = (File)
                config.getEntry("GenericServer",
                                "serviceIdFile",
                                File.class,
                                null); // default
        } catch(Exception e) {
            System.err.println(e.toString());
            e.printStackTrace();
            System.exit(2);
        }
    }

} // GenericServer
```

Summary

Jini has a configuration system that can be used to supply runtime parameters. It is not limited to strings, and it can specify Java objects. This chapter has looked at how you can specify configurations, what they contain, and how a Jini program can use them.

CHAPTER 20

■ ■ ■

Logging

Jini 2.0 introduced use of the `java.util.logging` package. This package can be used for auditing, or possibly for debugging, and it allows an application to write to named logs. Typically, the name of a log is a package name. For example, the log for `LookupDiscovery` objects is `net.jini.discovery.LookupDiscovery`. Each object will write a record of its activities to the class log. These messages will have levels such as `SEVERE`, `INFO`, and so on down to `FINEST`. For example, `LookupDiscovery` objects will write these messages, among others:

- `SEVERE` when a network interface is bad or not configured for multicast

- `INFO` when any exception other than an `InterruptedIOException` occurs while attempting unicast discovery

- `FINEST` when a discovered, discarded, or changed event is sent

To see what is put into a log, a `Handler` must be added to the log. There are several supplied handlers, including the following:

- `ConsoleHandler`: This handler writes all log messages to the console that have `INFO` level or above. The format is given by the `SimpleFormatter` object, and just gives brief readable messages.

- `FileHandler`: This handler writes all messages to a file, using an XML format. If you only want simple messages, this can be set to be a `SimpleFormatter`.

In this chapter, we'll discuss how this is used in a typical Jini object and how you can log events from such an object.

Logging LookupDiscovery

A program to log activities of a `LookupDiscovery` object is given by this program, which just adds logging to the earlier `MulticastRegister` program:

```
package basic;
import net.jini.discovery.LookupDiscovery;
import net.jini.discovery.DiscoveryListener;
import net.jini.discovery.DiscoveryEvent;
import net.jini.core.lookup.ServiceRegistrar;
import java.lang.reflect.*;
import java.util.logging.*;
```

```java
/**
 * MulticastRegisterLogger.java
 */
public class MulticastRegisterLogger implements DiscoveryListener {
    static final String DISCOVERY_LOG = "net.jini.discovery.LookupDiscovery";
    static final Logger logger = Logger.getLogger(DISCOVERY_LOG);
    private static FileHandler fh;

    static public void main(String argv[]) {
        new MulticastRegisterLogger();
        // stay around long enough to receive replies
        try {
            Thread.currentThread().sleep(10000L);
        } catch(java.lang.InterruptedException e) {
            // do nothing
        }
    }

    public MulticastRegisterLogger() {
        try {
            // this handler will save ALL log messages in the file
            fh = new FileHandler("mylog.txt");
            // the format is simple rather than XML
            fh.setFormatter(new SimpleFormatter());
            logger.addHandler(fh);
        } catch(Exception e) {
            e.printStackTrace();
        }
        // this handler will write all INFO and
        // above messages to the console
        logger.addHandler(new ConsoleHandler());
        System.setSecurityManager(new java.rmi.RMISecurityManager());
        LookupDiscovery discover = null;
        try {
            discover = new LookupDiscovery(LookupDiscovery.ALL_GROUPS);
        } catch(Exception e) {
            System.err.println(e.toString());
            e.printStackTrace();
            System.exit(1);
        }
        discover.addDiscoveryListener(this);
    }

    public void discovered(DiscoveryEvent evt) {
        ServiceRegistrar[] registrars = evt.getRegistrars();
        for (int n = 0; n < registrars.length; n++) {
            ServiceRegistrar registrar = registrars[n];
```

```
            // the code takes separate routes from here for client or service
            System.out.println("found a service locator");
        }
    }
    public void discarded(DiscoveryEvent evt) {
    }
} // MulticastRegister
```

When this program is run, a few messages will be printed to the console. A great deal more will be written to the mylog.txt file, including a line like this whenever a lookup locator is found:

```
FINEST:    discovered locator  = jini://jannote.jan.edu.au/
```

Summary

This short chapter has looked at the logging package and its use in the core Jini classes. It has shown how logging information collected by a Jini object can be used by a program to give extra information about what the Jini object is doing.

CHAPTER 21

ServiceStarter

A service is created by a server and registered with lookup services. The server has a fairly standard format, usually varying only in small details: the actual service, its entry attributes, the number of services, and so on. The ServiceStarter class can help with some of this by placing much of the information in configuration files. It is used by Sun for its tools, such as reggie.

ServiceDescriptor

In Chapter 19, we looked at how a metaserver might be written that would get information from a configuration file describing a service, and use that information to build the service. In order to make a service available for use, a number of parameters must be set up, including the following:

- The service class and how to construct it

- The transport protocol (Jeri/JRMP)

- The proxy for the service

- The codebase for the proxy files

- The classpath for the local files

- A security policy to run the server for this service

- Entry/attribute information

- Unicast locators of lookup services

- The group to join on lookup services

- The service item ID

Some of these items belong to the service, some to its proxy, some to the containing server, and others are advertisement parameters for joining lookup services.

Jini has an interface, ServiceDescriptor, that gives a standard way of handling some of these items. This class is in the com.sun.jini.start package, which is not specified by Jini and may change or even disappear in later versions of Jini.

```
interface ServiceDescriptor {
        Object create(Configuration config); }
```

There are a number of implementations of ServiceDescriptor:

- NonActivatableServiceDescriptor

- SharedActivatableServiceDescriptor

- SharedActivationGroupDescriptor

The first implementation is useful for the most common situation described in this book: a nonactivatable service. The meat of the NonActivatableServiceDescriptor class is in its constructors:

```
class NonActivatableServiceDescriptor {
    NonActivatableServiceDescriptor(String codebase,
                                    String policy,
                                    String classpath,
                                    String implClassName,
                                    String[] serverConfigArgs);

    NonActivatableServiceDescriptor(String codebase,
                                    String policy,
                                    String classpath,
                                    String implClassName,
                                    String[] serverConfigArgs,
                                    LifeCycle lifeCycle);
}
```

The codebase is a URL of a directory or .jar file of the proxy classes on an HTTP server; policy is the file name of the policy for this service within the context of the policy existing for the server; classpath is the classpath for the service run by the server; and serverConfigArgs is an array of configuration parameters (typically just a single file name). It is not yet clear what lifeCycle is or how it is used.

It is notable what the constructor does—and does not—describe. It describes the service's class and its classpath—that is, how to run it. It describes the environment for the proxy, but not how to create it. The constructor does not describe the entry information, the service ID, or the groups to which this service belongs. The parameters in the constructor for NonActivatableServiceDescriptor describe the service's runtime/deployment environment. They do not describe the service's advertisement environment.

The NonActivatableServiceDescriptor class provides an implementation of the create() method. This is defined in the interface to return an Object, but the class actually returns a com.sun.jini.start.NonActivatableServiceDescriptor.Created. This has no methods, just two public fields:

```
public class Created {
    public Object impl;
    public Object proxy;
}
```

From a Created object, you can extract the implementation and its proxy.

There are further wrinkles in using NonActivatableServiceDescriptor. The implementation object must be constructed from its class. The constructor has two parameters: the serverConfigArgs string array and a lifecycle object. At present, it is not clear what role this object is expected to play, and it is sufficient to use a default value, NoOpLifeCycle.

In addition to creating the implementation object, the create() method must create a proxy object for the implementation in order to return a Created object. This is done by requiring the implementation to support one of the two interfaces ServiceProxyAccessor or ProxyAccessor, and calling getServiceProxy() or getProxy() respectively on the implementation. That is, the service must include the method getServiceProxy() (or getProxy()), and within this method it will probably create the proxy (possibly using the configuration information) object and return it.

Pseudocode for a service description is as follows:

```
codebase = ...
policy = ...
classpath = ...
implClass = ...
configArgs = ...
create a NonActivatableServiceDescriptor
call create() on this, returning "created" object
impl = created.impl
proxy = created.proxy
```

while the service will have a constructor

```
Service(String[] config, Lifecyle lc) {
    proxy = ...
}
```

and method

```
getServiceProxy() {
    return proxy
}
```

Starting a Nonactivatable Service

The implementation must be Remote, and it must be able to create a proxy. In the implementation's constructor, it is handed a configuration array, so this may as well be used to find an exporter to get the proxy. The starter.FileClassifierStarterImpl class inherits from rmi. FileClassifierImpl and adds ServiceProxyAccessor to the basic file classifier:

```
package starter;
import rmi.FileClassifierImpl;
import com.sun.jini.start.ServiceProxyAccessor;
import com.sun.jini.start.LifeCycle;
import net.jini.config.*;
import net.jini.export.*;
```

```java
import java.rmi.Remote;
import java.rmi.RemoteException;
public class FileClassifierStarterImpl extends FileClassifierImpl
    implements ServiceProxyAccessor {
    Remote proxy;
    public FileClassifierStarterImpl(String[] configArgs, LifeCycle lifeCycle)
        throws RemoteException {
        super();
        try {
            // get the configuration (by default a FileConfiguration)
            Configuration config = ConfigurationProvider.getInstance(configArgs);

            // and use this to construct an exporter
            Exporter exporter = (Exporter) config.getEntry( "FileClassifierServer",
                                                            "exporter",
                                                            Exporter.class);
            // export an object of this class
            proxy = exporter.export(this);
        } catch(Exception e) {
            // empty
        }
    }
    public Object getServiceProxy() {
        return proxy;
    }
}
```

A configuration file suitable for using Jeri with the preceding FileClassifierStarterImpl is resources/starter/file_classifier.config:

```java
import net.jini.jeri.BasicILFactory;
import net.jini.jeri.BasicJeriExporter;
import net.jini.jeri.tcp.TcpServerEndpoint;
FileClassifierServer {
    exporter = new BasicJeriExporter(TcpServerEndpoint.getInstance(0),
                                     new BasicILFactory());
}
```

The server to start this service needs to set various parameters for the ServiceDescriptor. The preceding pseudocode set these explicitly. However, since they describe the runtime and deployment environment, they are better set in another configuration file, such as resources/starter/serviceDesc.config:

```java
import net.jini.core.discovery.LookupLocator;
import net.jini.discovery.LookupDiscovery;
import net.jini.core.entry.Entry;
import java.io.File;
import com.sun.jini.config.ConfigUtil;
ServiceDescription {
```

```
    localhost = ConfigUtil.getHostName();
    port = "80";
    directory = "/classes";
    file = "starter.ServiceDescription-dl.jar";
    codebase =   ConfigUtil.concat(new String[] {
                                    "http://",
                                    localhost,
                                    ":",
                                    port,
                                    directory,
                                    "/",
                                    file
                                }
                            );
    policy = "policy.all";
    classpath = "/.../starter.ServiceDescription-start.jar";
    implClass = "starter.FileClassifierStarterImpl";
    serverConfigArgs = new String[] {
         "/home/httpd/html/java/jini/tutorial/resources/starter/
file_classifier.config"
        };
}
AdvertDescription {
    entries = new Entry[] {};
    groups = LookupDiscovery.ALL_GROUPS;
    unicastLocators = new LookupLocator[] { // empty
                                    };
    serviceIdFile = new File("serviceId.id");
}
```

This configuration file contains two sets of configurations: one for the ServiceDescription component and one for the AdvertDescription component (discussed shortly).

The resources/starter/serviceDesc.config configuration file uses two .jar files: starter.ServiceDescription-dl.jar for the service codebase and starter.Service➡ Description-start.jar for the server's classpath. The contents of these files are as follows:

- The starter.ServiceDescription-dl.jar contains all the files that need to be downloaded to a client:

```
common/MIMEType.class
common/FileClassifier.class
rmi/RemoteFileClassifier.class
```

- The starter.ServiceDescription-start.jar contains all the files that are needed for the server to create the service:

```
common/FileClassifier.class
common/MIMEType.class
rmi/FileClassifierImpl.class
rmi/RemoteFileClassifier.class
starter/FileClassifierStarterImpl.class
```

A server that picks up the values from this configuration file and creates the service and its proxy follows. The program essentially uses two parts: one to build the service using a ServiceDescriptor and its configuration entries, and the other to advertise the service using JoinManager and its associated AdvertDescription configuration entries. (Although JoinManager has a constructor that will take a configuration, this does not support any of the entries we specified earlier.)

```java
package starter;
import java.rmi.RMISecurityManager;
import net.jini.config.Configuration;
import net.jini.config.ConfigurationException;
import net.jini.config.ConfigurationProvider;
import com.sun.jini.start.ServiceDescriptor;
import com.sun.jini.start.NonActivatableServiceDescriptor;
import com.sun.jini.start.NonActivatableServiceDescriptor.Created;
import net.jini.lookup.JoinManager;
import net.jini.core.lookup.ServiceID;
import net.jini.lookup.ServiceIDListener;
import net.jini.core.discovery.LookupLocator;
import net.jini.core.entry.Entry;
import net.jini.lease.LeaseRenewalManager;
import net.jini.discovery.LookupDiscoveryManager;
import net.jini.discovery.LookupDiscovery;
import java.rmi.Remote;
import java.io.*;
/**
 * ServiceDescription.java
 */
public class ServiceDescription implements ServiceIDListener {

    private Object impl;
    private Remote proxy;
    private File serviceIdFile;
    private Configuration config;
    private ServiceID serviceID;
    public static void main(String args[]) {
        if (System.getSecurityManager() == null) {
            System.setSecurityManager(new RMISecurityManager());
        }
```

```
    ServiceDescription s =
        new ServiceDescription(args);

    // keep server running forever to
    // - allow time for locator discovery and
    // - keep re-registering the lease
    Object keepAlive = new Object();
    synchronized(keepAlive) {
        try {
            keepAlive.wait();
        } catch(java.lang.InterruptedException e) {
            // do nothing
        }
    }
}
public ServiceDescription(String[] args) {
    if (args.length == 0) {
        System.err.println("No configuration specified");
        System.exit(1);
    }
    try {
        config = ConfigurationProvider.getInstance(args);
    } catch(ConfigurationException e) {
        System.err.println("Configuration error: " + e.toString() +
                          " in file " + args[0]);
        System.exit(1);
    }
    startService();
    advertiseService();
}
private void startService() {
    String codebase = null;
    String policy = null;
    String classpath = null;
    String implClass = null;
    String[] serverConfigArgs = null;
    try {
        codebase = (String) config.getEntry("ServiceDescription",
                                            "codebase",
                                             String.class);
        policy = (String) config.getEntry("ServiceDescription",
                                          "policy",
                                           String.class);
        classpath = (String) config.getEntry("ServiceDescription",
                                              "classpath",
                                               String.class);
        implClass = (String) config.getEntry("ServiceDescription",
```

```
                                                "implClass",
                                                String.class);
            serverConfigArgs = (String[]) config.getEntry("ServiceDescription",
                                                        "serverConfigArgs",
                                                        String[].class);
        } catch(ConfigurationException e) {
            System.err.println("Configuration error: " + e.toString());
            System.exit(1);
        }
        // Create the new service descriptor
        ServiceDescriptor desc =
            new NonActivatableServiceDescriptor(codebase,
                                                policy,
                                                classpath,
                                                implClass,
                                                serverConfigArgs);
        // and create the service and its proxy
        Created created = null;
        try {
            created = (Created) desc.create(config);
        } catch(Exception e) {
            e.printStackTrace();
            System.exit(1);
        }
        impl = created.impl;
        proxy = (Remote) created.proxy;
    }
    private void advertiseService() {
        Entry[] entries = null;
        LookupLocator[] unicastLocators = null;
        File serviceIdFile = null;
        String[] groups = null;
        // Now go on to register the proxy with lookup services, using
        // e.g., JoinManager.
        // This will need additional parameters: entries, unicast
        // locators, group and service ID
        try {
            unicastLocators = (LookupLocator[])
                config.getEntry("AdvertDescription",
                                "unicastLocators",
                                LookupLocator[].class,
                                null); // default

            entries = (Entry[])
                config.getEntry("AdvertDescription",
                                "entries",
                                Entry[].class,
```

```
                                        null); // default
            groups = (String[])
                config.getEntry("AdvertDescription",
                                "groups",
                                String[].class,
                                LookupDiscovery.ALL_GROUPS); // default
            serviceIdFile = (File)
                config.getEntry("AdvertDescription",
                                "serviceIdFile",
                                File.class,
                                null); // default
        } catch(Exception e) {
            System.err.println(e.toString());
            e.printStackTrace();
            System.exit(2);
        }
        JoinManager joinMgr = null;
        try {
            LookupDiscoveryManager mgr =
                new LookupDiscoveryManager(groups,
                                        unicastLocators, // unicast locators
                                        null); // DiscoveryListener

            if (serviceID != null) {
                joinMgr = new JoinManager(proxy, // service proxy
                                        entries, // attr sets
                                        serviceID, // ServiceID
                                        mgr,    // DiscoveryManager
                                        new LeaseRenewalManager());
            } else {
                joinMgr = new JoinManager(proxy, // service proxy
                                        entries, // attr sets
                                        this, // ServiceIDListener
                                        mgr,    // DiscoveryManager
                                        new LeaseRenewalManager());
            }
        } catch(Exception e) {
            e.printStackTrace();
            System.exit(1);
        }
    }
    public void tryRetrieveServiceId() {
        // Try to load the service ID from file.
        // It isn't an error if we can't load it, because
        // maybe this is the first time this service has run
        DataInputStream din = null;
        try {
            din = new DataInputStream(new FileInputStream(serviceIdFile));
```

```
                serviceID = new ServiceID(din);
                System.out.println("Found service ID in file " + serviceIdFile);
                din.close();
            } catch(Exception e) {
                // ignore
            }
        }
        public void serviceIDNotify(ServiceID serviceID) {
            // called as a ServiceIDListener
            // Should save the ID to permanent storage
            System.out.println("got service ID " + serviceID.toString());

            // try to save the service ID in a file
            if (serviceIdFile != null) {
                DataOutputStream dout = null;
                try {
                    dout = new DataOutputStream(new FileOutputStream(serviceIdFile));
                    serviceID.writeBytes(dout);
                    dout.flush();
                dout.close();
                System.out.println("Service id saved in " +  serviceIdFile);
                } catch(Exception e) {
                    // ignore
                }
            }
        }
    }
} // ServiceDescription
```

This server may be run from a command line such as

```
java starter.ServiceDescription resources/starter/serviceDesc.config
```

using a classpath that includes starter.ServiceDescription.

Here's a summary of what's going on here:

- The service is started by running a service.ServiceDescription.

- The classpath for service.ServiceDescription must include (for example) a .jar file, starter.ServiceDescription.jar, that contains starter.ServiceDescription.class as well as the standard Jini classes.

- service.ServiceDescription uses a configuration file such as serviceDesc.config, which includes a description of the codebase, and so forth, which are suitable parameters for the constructor of a ServiceDescriptor.

- The serviceDesc.config configuration also contains an advertisement description to register the service with lookup services.

- When the service is started by ServiceDescriptor.create(), it uses its own configuration file, file_classifier.config, which specifies the exporter.

- The classpath used to start the service includes the files in the .jar file
  starter.ServiceDescription-start.jar.

- The codebase used by clients to download the service includes the .jar file
  starter.ServiceDescription-dl.jar.

The Ant file to build and run this is antBuildFiles/starter.ServiceDescription.xml:

```
<project name="starter.ServiceDescription" default="usage">
    <!-- Inherits properties
         jini.home
         jini.jars
         src
         dist
         build
         httpd.classes
      -->
    <!-- files for this project -->
    <property name="src.files"
            value="common/MIMEType.java,
                   common/FileClassifier.java,
                   rmi/RemoteFileClassifier.java,
                   rmi/FileClassifierImpl.java,
                   starter/FileClassifierStarterImpl.java,
                   starter/ServiceDescription.java"/>
    <property name="class.files"
            value="
                   starter/ServiceDescription.class
                   "/>
    <property name="class.files.start"
            value="common/MIMEType.class,
                   common/FileClassifier.class,
                   rmi/RemoteFileClassifier.class,
                   rmi/FileClassifierImpl.class,
                   starter/FileClassifierStarterImpl.class,
                   "/>
    <property name="class.files.dl"
            value="common/MIMEType.class,
                   common/FileClassifier.class,
                   rmi/RemoteFileClassifier.class,
                   "/>
    <!-- <property name="no-dl" value="false"/> -->
    <!-- derived names - may be changed -->
    <property name="jar.file"
            value="${ant.project.name}.jar"/>
    <property name="jar.file.start"
            value="${ant.project.name}-start.jar"/>
    <property name="jar.file.dl"
```

```xml
                    value="${ant.project.name}-dl.jar"/>
    <property name="main.class"
                value="${ant.project.name}"/>
    <property name="jini.jars.start" value="${jini.jars}:${jini.home}/lib/
start.jar"/>
    <!-- targets -->
    <target name="all" depends="compile"/>
    <target name="compile">
        <javac destdir="${build}" srcdir="${src}"
                classpath="${jini.jars.start}"
                includes="${src.files}">
        </javac>
    </target>
    <target name="dist" depends="compile"
            description="generate the distribution">
        <jar jarfile="${dist}/${jar.file}"
            basedir="${build}"
            includes="${class.files}"/>
        <jar jarfile="${dist}/${jar.file.start}"
            basedir="${build}"
            includes="${class.files.start}"/>
        <antcall target="dist-jar-dl"/>
    </target>
    <target name="dist-jar-dl" unless="no-dl">
        <jar jarfile="${dist}/${jar.file.dl}"
            basedir="${build}"
            includes="${class.files.dl}"/>
    </target>
    <target name="build" depends="dist,compile"/>
    <target name="run" depends="build">
        <java classname="${main.class}"
            fork="true"
            classpath="${jini.jars.start}:${dist}/${jar.file}">
            <jvmarg value="-Djava.security.policy=${res}/policy.all"/>
            <arg value="${res}/starter/serviceDesc.config"/>
        </java>
    </target>
    <target name="deploy" depends="dist" unless="no-dl">
        <copy file="${dist}/${jar.file.dl}"
            todir="${httpd.classes}"/>
    </target>
</project>
```

Starting a Nonactivatable Server

The standard tools supplied by Sun, such as reggie, all use the ServiceDescription class. But instead of starting a service, they start a server. So in this case, an application is needed to start the server, which in turn will start the service.

For this purpose, Sun supplies the ServiceStarter class in the com.sun.jini.start package. This package is not specified by Jini and may change or even disappear in later versions of Jini. It has a public main() method, which will take command-line arguments. A configuration can be given as a command-line argument and will be searched for an array of ServiceDescriptor objects. The search is in the com.sun.jini.start component and the descriptors are labeled as serviceDescriptors. The create() method will be called on each descriptor to create a server.

To use the ServiceStarter, you need to write a server and also a configuration file containing a ServiceDescriptor for that server. The server does not need to have a main() method, since the server is started by ServiceStarter, not the server itself.

For example, we could use the FileClasifierServerConfig from Chapter 19. The configuration file for this server remains unaltered as follows:

```
import java.io.*;
ServiceIdDemo {
    serviceIdFile = new File("serviceId.id");
}
```

The server itself need not be altered; its main() method is just not called. If it were being written from scratch, there would be no need to include this method. Here's the code repeated from Chapter 19:

```
package config;
import java.rmi.RMISecurityManager;
import java.rmi.Remote;
import java.rmi.RemoteException;
import java.rmi.server.ExportException;
import net.jini.discovery.LookupDiscovery;
import net.jini.discovery.DiscoveryListener;
import net.jini.discovery.DiscoveryEvent;
import net.jini.core.lookup.ServiceRegistrar;
import net.jini.core.lookup.ServiceItem;
import net.jini.core.lookup.ServiceRegistration;
import net.jini.core.lease.Lease;
import net.jini.core.lookup.ServiceID ;
import net.jini.lease.LeaseListener;
import net.jini.lease.LeaseRenewalEvent;
import net.jini.lease.LeaseRenewalManager;
import net.jini.config.Configuration;
import net.jini.config.ConfigurationException;
import net.jini.config.ConfigurationProvider;
import net.jini.lookup.JoinManager;
import net.jini.id.UuidFactory;
```

```java
import net.jini.id.Uuid;
import net.jini.discovery.LookupDiscoveryManager;
import net.jini.export.Exporter;
import rmi.RemoteFileClassifier;
import rmi.FileClassifierImpl;
import java.io.*;
/**
 * FileClassifierServerConfig.java
 */
public class FileClassifierServerConfig implements  LeaseListener {

    private LeaseRenewalManager leaseManager = new LeaseRenewalManager();
    private ServiceID serviceID = null;
    private RemoteFileClassifier impl;
    private File serviceIdFile;
    private Configuration config;
    public static void main(String args[]) {
        FileClassifierServerConfig s = new FileClassifierServerConfig(args);

        // keep server running forever to
        // - allow time for locator discovery and
        // - keep re-registering the lease
        Object keepAlive = new Object();
        synchronized(keepAlive) {
            try {
                keepAlive.wait();
            } catch(java.lang.InterruptedException e) {
                // do nothing
            }
        }
    }
    public FileClassifierServerConfig(String[] args) {
        System.setSecurityManager(new RMISecurityManager());
        try {
            config = ConfigurationProvider.getInstance(args);
        } catch(ConfigurationException e) {
            System.err.println("Configuration error: " + e.toString());
            System.exit(1);
        }
        Exporter exporter = null;
        try {
            exporter = (Exporter)
                config.getEntry( "config.FileClassifierServerConfig",
                                 "exporter",
                                 Exporter.class);
        } catch(ConfigurationException e) {
            e.printStackTrace();
```

```
                System.exit(1);
        }
        // Create the service and its proxy
        try {
            impl = new rmi.FileClassifierImpl();
        } catch(RemoteException e) {
            e.printStackTrace();
            System.exit(1);
        }
        Remote proxy = null;
        try {
            proxy = exporter.export(impl);
        } catch(ExportException e) {
            e.printStackTrace();
            System.exit(1);
        }
        // register proxy with lookup services
        JoinManager joinMgr = null;
        try {
            LookupDiscoveryManager mgr =
                new LookupDiscoveryManager(LookupDiscovery.ALL_GROUPS,
                                            null,  // unicast locators
                                            null); // DiscoveryListener
            joinMgr = new JoinManager(proxy, // service proxy
                                       null,  // attr sets
                                       serviceID,
                                       mgr,   // DiscoveryManager
                                       new LeaseRenewalManager());
        } catch(Exception e) {
            e.printStackTrace();
            System.exit(1);
        }
    }
    void getServiceID() {
        // Make up our own
        Uuid id = UuidFactory.generate();
        serviceID = new ServiceID(id.getMostSignificantBits(),
                                   id.getLeastSignificantBits());
    }
    public void serviceIDNotify(ServiceID serviceID) {
        // called as a ServiceIDListener
        // Should save the ID to permanent storage
        System.out.println("got service ID " + serviceID.toString());
    }
    public void discarded(DiscoveryEvent evt) {
    }
    public void notify(LeaseRenewalEvent evt) {
```

```
            System.out.println("Lease expired " + evt.toString());
    }

} // FileClassifierServer
```

What is new is a configuration file for ServiceStarter. This could be in resources/ starter/start-transient-fileclassifier.config:

```
import com.sun.jini.start.ServiceDescriptor;
import com.sun.jini.start.NonActivatableServiceDescriptor;
ServiceIdDemo {
    private static codebase =
        "http://192.168.1.13:8080/file-classifier-dl.jar";
    private static policy = "policy.all";
    private static classpath = "file-classifier.jar";
    private static config = "resources/starter/file_classifier.config";
    static serviceDescriptors = new ServiceDescriptor[] {
            new NonActivatableServiceDescriptor(
                    codebase, policy, classpath,
                    "config.FileClassifierServerConfig",
                    new String[] { config })
    };
}
```

The server is set running as follows:

```
        java -jar start.jar ServiceStarter resources/
start-transient-fileclassifier.config
```

A typical descriptor for the reggie service might be this:

```
String codebase = "http://192.168.1.13:8080/reggie-dl.jar";
String policy = "/usr/local/reggie/reggie.policy";
String classpath = "/usr/local/jini2_0/lib/reggie.jar";
String config = "/usr/local/reggie/transient-reggie.config";
ServiceDescriptor desc =
                new NonActivatableServiceDescriptor(
                        codebase, policy, classpath,
                        "com.sun.jini.reggie.TransientRegistrarImpl",
                        new String[] {config})
```

reggie and ServiceStarter

We can now see what is going on when a standard Sun service such as reggie is started. A typical command line is as follows:

```
java -Djava.security.policy=reggie/start.policy -jar \
    start.jar start-transient-reggie.config
```

The configuration file contains information required to start the reggie server, such as this:

```
import com.sun.jini.start.ServiceDescriptor;
import com.sun.jini.start.NonActivatableServiceDescriptor;
import com.sun.jini.config.ConfigUtil;
com.sun.jini.start {
    private static codebase =
                        ConfigUtil.concat(new Object[] {
                                            "http://",
                                             ConfigUtil.getHostName(),
                                             ":8080/reggie-dl.jar"
                                        }
                                    );
    private static policy = "/usr/local/reggie/reggie.policy";
    private static classpath = "/usr/local/jini2_0/lib/reggie.jar";
    private static config = "/usr/local/reggie/transient-reggie.config";
    static serviceDescriptors = new ServiceDescriptor[] {
                new NonActivatableServiceDescriptor(
                        codebase, policy, classpath,
                        "com.sun.jini.reggie.TransientRegistrarImpl",
                         new String[] { config })
    };
}
```

This particular configuration starts a TransientRegistrarImpl.

When the TransientRegistrarImpl begins, it uses a configuration file, too. This was specified to be /usr/local/reggie/transient-reggie.config and contains the following:

```
com.sun.jini.reggie {
    initialMemberGroups = new String[] {};
}
```

Summary

A ServiceDescriptor allows a service to be created with given parameters. It can be used directly or by using the Sun-supplied ServiceStarter. Sun uses this class to start up its own services, such as reggie. These classes are in the com.sun.jini.start package, and as such are not guaranteed to be stable or even to exist in future versions of Jini. But, like JoinManager, they might migrate to the core Jini package in the future.

CHAPTER 22

∎∎∎

Advanced Security

Prior to version 2.0, Jini used the standard Java security mechanism. This mechanism was designed to deal with code downloaded from a remote location, and it was put in place to limit the foreign code in a local virtual machine. In this capability-based security model, the client grants to foreign code the capability to perform certain activities. So, for example, foreign code cannot write to the local file system unless this particular permission has been granted. Chapter 14 covered this topic in detail.

But what Chapter 14 ignored is a range of issues concerning the network transport, for example:

- *Integrity*: Have the classes and instance data reached the client in the form they started, or has someone corrupted them along the way?

- *Authentication*: Did the data come from whom you expected, or did it come from someone else? The client may need to authenticate itself to the server, or vice versa.

- *Authorization*: Once you know from whom the data came, what rights will you grant it? (This was covered in Chapter 14.)

- *Confidentiality*: Has the data been encrypted so that others cannot read it?

These are standard network security concerns; however, Jini gives them some special wrinkles. For example, instance data for a proxy may be sent from a server to a client either directly or via a lookup server. In addition to the instance data, class files often have to be loaded, and these may come from a third-party HTTP server. There are even subtleties in where a service may be running: an activatable service doesn't run in the server that started it, but in a third-party activation service.

In this chapter, we'll discuss the topics of integrity, authentication, and confidentiality, and see how these are managed within Jini.

Invocation Constraints

The security considerations act as *constraints* on normal execution; something that might have been allowed will be restricted. For example, a client may enforce the constraint that communications be encrypted. A client might not want to know many details of how encryption has been done (that sort of detail can be left to the middleware itself). But if encryption hasn't been done, then the client will just not accept the communication.

Jini 2.0 defines a set of objects that specify constraints on behavior. These objects don't specify *how* a constraint is implemented, but *what* the constraint is. Some of these constraints are as follows:

- Integrity.YES: Detect when message contents (both requests and replies) have been altered by third parties and, if message contents have been altered, refuse to process the message and throw an exception.

- Integrity.NO: Do not detect when message contents have been altered by third parties.

Note In between YES and NO is "DON'T CARE". There is no specific object to express this constraint (or lack of it). If you don't care whether it is checked or not, then you don't specify either a YES or NO constraint—just don't mention the constraint at all.

- Confidentiality.YES: Transmit message contents so that they cannot easily be interpreted by third parties (typically by using encryption).

- Confidentiality.NO: Transmit message contents in the clear (no use of encryption).

Note Similarly, in between YES and NO is "DON'T CARE". There is no specific object to express this constraint (or lack of it). You just don't use either the YES or NO object to mean that you don't care if it is confidential or not. This is common to all constraints.

- ClientAuthentication.YES: The client must authenticate to the server.

- ClientAuthentication.NO: Do not authenticate the client to the server. This has a special meaning in that the client will refuse to say who it is—the client remains anonymous. This may be important for applications where participants wish to preserve their privacy.

- ServerAuthentication.YES: Authenticate the server to the client.

- ServerAuthentication.NO: Do not authenticate the server to the client, so that the server remains anonymous.

The Javadoc for InvocationConstraint lists all its subclasses, and within each of these subclasses are constant objects such as the preceding.

Each InvocationConstraint can potentially limit client or server activity. We can make up two sets of constraints: *mandatory* constraints that must be satisfied and *preferred* constraints that should be satisfied if they do not conflict with a mandatory one. For example, if both Integrity.YES and Integrity.NO are specified as mandatory, then any call must fail. If, however, one is specified as mandatory and the other as preferred, then the mandatory one must be satisfied.

An InvocationConstraints (note the plural) takes a set of mandatory and a set of preferred constraints. These can be specified as collections or arrays to a constructor.

```
class InvocationConstraints {
    InvocationConstraints(Collection reqs, Collection prefs);
    InvocationConstraints(InvocationConstraint[] reqs,
                          InvocationConstraint[] prefs);
    InvocationConstraints(InvocationConstraint req,
                          InvocationConstraint pref);
    ...
}
```

Method Constraints

Whenever a method call is made, constraint checks should be made. For example, a bank method withdraw() should always authenticate the caller. It should be done on each call, not just once—a certificate that is valid for one call may not be valid the next time a call is made.

The MethodConstraints interface allows each method to have its own set of constraints. For example, a method that sends credit card details might require encryption, whereas a "browse" request would not. The BasicMethodConstraints class is usually used to implement this interface. In setting constraints, all methods can be set to use the same set of constraints, or constraints can be set up on a per-method basis.

```
class BasicMethodConstraints {
    BasicMethodConstraints(InvocationConstraints constraints);
    BasicMethodConstraints(BasicMethodConstraints.MethodDesc[] descs);
    ...
}
```

Logging

Security is difficult to get right, and it's hard to debug. The Logger is your friend here (see Chapter 20 for details on logging). Security is handled by the net.jini.security.Security, which writes to three loggers:

- net.jini.security.integrity

- net.jini.security.trust

- net.jini.security.policy

The following sample code gets logging information from the client:

```
static final String TRUST_LOG = "net.jini.security.trust";
static final String INTEGRITY_LOG = "net.jini.security.integrity";
static final String POLICY_LOG = "net.jini.security.policy";
static final Logger trustLogger = Logger.getLogger(TRUST_LOG);
static final Logger integrityLogger = Logger.getLogger(INTEGRITY_LOG);
static final Logger policyLogger = Logger.getLogger(POLICY_LOG);
```

```
    private static FileHandler trustFh;
    private static FileHandler integrityFh;
    private static FileHandler policyFh;
    private static void installLoggers() {
        try {
            // this handler will save ALL log messages in the file
            trustFh = new FileHandler("log.client.trust.txt");
            integrityFh = new FileHandler("log.client.integrity.txt");
            policyFh = new FileHandler("log.client.policy.txt");
            // the format is simple rather than XML
            trustFh.setFormatter(new SimpleFormatter());
            integrityFh.setFormatter(new SimpleFormatter());
            policyFh.setFormatter(new SimpleFormatter());
            trustLogger.addHandler(trustFh);
            integrityLogger.addHandler(integrityFh);
            policyLogger.addHandler(policyFh);
            trustLogger.setLevel(java.util.logging.Level.ALL);
            integrityLogger.setLevel(java.util.logging.Level.ALL);
            policyLogger.setLevel(java.util.logging.Level.ALL);
        } catch(Exception e) {
            e.printStackTrace();
        }
    }
}
```

Protocols

A range of different protocols are available to shift data around the network, including TCP, HTTP (which, of course, is layered above TCP), and protocols designed with security in mind, such as HTTPS, SSL (now officially TLS), and others. I'll cover TCP and SSL in the sections that follow.

TCP

A service implements TCP by using a `BasiJeriExporter` with a TCP server. Typically, the exporter will be defined in a configuration file such as the following:

```
import net.jini.jeri.BasicILFactory;
import net.jini.jeri.BasicJeriExporter;
import net.jini.jeri.tcp.TcpServerEndpoint;
security.FileClassifierServer {
    /* class name for the service */
    serviceName = "rmi.FileClassifierImpl";
    exporter = new BasicJeriExporter(TcpServerEndpoint.getInstance(0),
                                     new BasicILFactory());
}
```

TCP does not support any of the security mechanisms of this chapter. So we use it as a "bad example" once and then no longer consider it.

SSL

The server can use Jeri over SSL, with a configuration such as config/security/
jeri-ssl-minimal.config:

```
/* Configuration source file for an SSL server */
import java.security.Permission;
import net.jini.constraint.BasicMethodConstraints;
import net.jini.core.constraint.InvocationConstraint;
import net.jini.core.constraint.InvocationConstraints;
import net.jini.core.constraint.Integrity;
import net.jini.jeri.*;
import net.jini.jeri.ssl.*;
security.FileClassifierServer {
    /* class name for the service */
    serviceName = "rmi.FileClassifierImpl";
    /* Exporter for the server proxy */
    exporter =
        /* Use secure exporter */
        new BasicJeriExporter(
            /* Use SSL transport */
            SslServerEndpoint.getInstance(0),
            new BasicILFactory(
                /* Require integrity for all methods */
                new BasicMethodConstraints(
                    new InvocationConstraints(
                            (InvocationConstraint[]) null,
                            (InvocationConstraint[]) null)),
                /* No Permission */
                null
            )
        );
}
```

SSL is designed to support encryption using a secret key mechanism following open negotiation. It can also support authentication of both the client and server using public key
certificates.

Proxy Preparer

When a client gets a proxy from a server, the server may already have placed some constraints
on it. But any of these constraints are those that the server requires, not those that the client
may require, so the client has to set its own constraints on the service proxy. It does this by
creating a new proxy from the original by adding in its own constraints. The classes the client
uses for setting its own constraints are described by both an interface and sample implementations. The interface is ProxyPreparer:

```
interface ProxyPreparer {
   Object prepareProxy(Object proxy)
                      throws RemoteException;
}
```

And an implementation is `BasicProxyPreparer`:

```
class BasicProxyPreparer {
    BasicProxyPreparer();
    BasicProxyPreparer(boolean verify,
                       MethodConstraints methodConstraints,
                       Permission[] permissions);
    BasicProxyPreparer(boolean verify,
                       Permission[] permissions);
}
```

The second constructor is the one most likely to be used by a client: get a proxy from a service, create a basic proxy preparer with constraints and permissions (and whether or not to verify the proxy; see the later section "Client with Proxy Verification"), and use this to prepare a new proxy with the constraints and permissions. The new proxy is then used for all calls on the service.

A client that finds a file classifier and prepares a new service proxy, taking the proxy preparer from a configuration file, is as follows:

```
package client;
import common.FileClassifier;
import common.MIMEType;
import java.rmi.RMISecurityManager;
import net.jini.discovery.LookupDiscovery;
import net.jini.discovery.DiscoveryListener;
import net.jini.discovery.DiscoveryEvent;
import net.jini.core.lookup.ServiceRegistrar;
import net.jini.core.lookup.ServiceTemplate;
import java.rmi.RemoteException;
import net.jini.security.BasicProxyPreparer;
import net.jini.security.ProxyPreparer;
import net.jini.config.Configuration;
import net.jini.config.ConfigurationException;
import net.jini.config.ConfigurationProvider;
import java.util.logging.*;
/**
 * TestFileClassifierProxyPreparer.java
 */
public class TestFileClassifierProxyPreparer implements DiscoveryListener {
    private Configuration config;
    static final String TRUST_LOG = "net.jini.security.trust";
    static final String INTEGRITY_LOG = "net.jini.security.integrity";
    static final String POLICY_LOG = "net.jini.security.policy";
    static final Logger trustLogger = Logger.getLogger(TRUST_LOG);
```

```java
static final Logger integrityLogger = Logger.getLogger(INTEGRITY_LOG);
static final Logger policyLogger = Logger.getLogger(POLICY_LOG);
private static FileHandler trustFh;
private static FileHandler integrityFh;
private static FileHandler policyFh;
public static void main(String argv[])
    throws ConfigurationException {
    installLoggers();
    new TestFileClassifierProxyPreparer(argv);
    // stay around long enough to receive replies
    try {
        Thread.currentThread().sleep(100000L);
    } catch(java.lang.InterruptedException e) {
        // do nothing
    }
}
public TestFileClassifierProxyPreparer(String[] argv)
    throws ConfigurationException {
    config = ConfigurationProvider.getInstance(argv);
    System.setSecurityManager(new RMISecurityManager());
    LookupDiscovery discover = null;
    try {
        discover = new LookupDiscovery(LookupDiscovery.ALL_GROUPS);
    } catch(Exception e) {
        System.err.println(e.toString());
        System.exit(1);
    }
    discover.addDiscoveryListener(this);
}
private static void installLoggers() {
    try {
        // this handler will save ALL log messages in the file
        trustFh = new FileHandler("log.client.trust.txt");
        integrityFh = new FileHandler("log.client.integrity.txt");
        policyFh = new FileHandler("log.client.policy.txt");
        // the format is simple rather than XML
        trustFh.setFormatter(new SimpleFormatter());
        integrityFh.setFormatter(new SimpleFormatter());
        policyFh.setFormatter(new SimpleFormatter());
        trustLogger.addHandler(trustFh);
        integrityLogger.addHandler(integrityFh);
        policyLogger.addHandler(policyFh);
        trustLogger.setLevel(java.util.logging.Level.ALL);
        integrityLogger.setLevel(java.util.logging.Level.ALL);
        policyLogger.setLevel(java.util.logging.Level.ALL);
    } catch(Exception e) {
        e.printStackTrace();
```

```java
            }
        }
        public void discovered(DiscoveryEvent evt) {
            ServiceRegistrar[] registrars = evt.getRegistrars();
            Class [] classes = new Class[] {FileClassifier.class};
            FileClassifier classifier = null;
            ServiceTemplate template = new ServiceTemplate(null, classes,
                                                           null);

            for (int n = 0; n < registrars.length; n++) {
                System.out.println("Lookup service found");
                ServiceRegistrar registrar = registrars[n];
                try {
                    classifier = (FileClassifier) registrar.lookup(template);
                } catch(java.rmi.RemoteException e) {
                    e.printStackTrace();
                    System.exit(4);
                    continue;
                }
                if (classifier == null) {
                    System.out.println("Classifier null");
                    continue;
                }
                System.out.println("Getting the proxy");
                // Get the proxy preparer
                ProxyPreparer preparer = null;
                try {
                    preparer =
                    (ProxyPreparer) config.getEntry(
                                        "client.TestFileClassifierProxyPreparer",
                                            "preparer", ProxyPreparer.class,
                                            new BasicProxyPreparer());
                } catch(ConfigurationException e) {
                    e.printStackTrace();
                    preparer = new BasicProxyPreparer();
                }
                // Prepare the new proxy
                System.out.println("Preparing the proxy");
                try {
                    classifier = (FileClassifier) preparer.prepareProxy(classifier);
                } catch(RemoteException e) {
                    e.printStackTrace();
                    System.exit(3);
                } catch(java.lang.SecurityException e) {
                    e.printStackTrace();
                    System.exit(6);
                }
```

```
                // Use the service to classify a few file types
                System.out.println("Calling the proxy");
                MIMEType type;
                try {
                    String fileName;
                    fileName = "file1.txt";
                    type = classifier.getMIMEType(fileName);
                    printType(fileName, type);
                    fileName = "file2.rtf";
                    type = classifier.getMIMEType(fileName);
                    printType(fileName, type);
                    fileName = "file3.abc";
                    type = classifier.getMIMEType(fileName);
                    printType(fileName, type);
                } catch(java.rmi.RemoteException e) {
                    System.out.println("Failed to call method");
                    System.err.println(e.toString());
                    System.exit(5);
                    continue;
                }
                // success
                System.exit(0);
        }
    }
    private void printType(String fileName, MIMEType type) {
        System.out.print("Type of " + fileName + " is ");
        if (type == null) {
            System.out.println("null");
        } else {
            System.out.println(type.toString());
        }
    }
    public void discarded(DiscoveryEvent evt) {
        // empty
    }
} // TestFileClassifier
```

A minimal configuration file for this client is config/security/preparer-minimal.config:

```
import java.security.Permission;
import net.jini.core.constraint.InvocationConstraint;
import net.jini.core.constraint.InvocationConstraints;
import net.jini.core.constraint.Integrity;
import net.jini.security.BasicProxyPreparer;
import net.jini.constraint.BasicMethodConstraints;
client.TestFileClassifierProxyPreparer {
    preparer =
        new BasicProxyPreparer(
```

```
                /* Don't verify the proxy. */
                false,
                /* No constraints */
                new BasicMethodConstraints(
                    new InvocationConstraints(
                        (InvocationConstraint[]) null,
                        (InvocationConstraint[]) null
                    )
                ),
                new Permission[] {}
        );
}
```

This file can be run directly with the following:

```
java ... client.TestFileClassifierProxyPreparer \
        config/security/preparer-minimal.config
```

Or it can be run from the Ant build files with this:

```
ant run -DrunFile=client.TestFileClassifierProxyPreparer \
        -Dconfig=config/security/preparer-minimal.config
```

This client will run successfully with any service that does not impose any constraints on the client. So, for example, it will run with any service of the earlier chapters that does not impose any constraints at all. However, using this configuration, it will not run with some of the examples later in this chapter that *do* impose client-side constraints.

File Classifier Server

A file classifier server using configuration was presented in Chapter 19. The version here is almost the same, with the addition of placing the service name in the configuration (since we might need to run different versions of the service for different security requirements).

```
package config;
import java.rmi.RMISecurityManager;
import java.rmi.Remote;
import java.rmi.RemoteException;
import java.rmi.server.ExportException;
import net.jini.discovery.LookupDiscovery;
import net.jini.discovery.DiscoveryListener;
import net.jini.discovery.DiscoveryEvent;
import net.jini.core.lookup.ServiceRegistrar;
import net.jini.core.lookup.ServiceItem;
import net.jini.core.lookup.ServiceRegistration;
import net.jini.core.lease.Lease;
import net.jini.core.lookup.ServiceID ;
import net.jini.lease.LeaseListener;
import net.jini.lease.LeaseRenewalEvent;
```

```java
import net.jini.lease.LeaseRenewalManager;
import net.jini.config.Configuration;
import net.jini.config.ConfigurationException;
import net.jini.config.ConfigurationProvider;
import net.jini.lookup.JoinManager;
import net.jini.id.UuidFactory;
import net.jini.id.Uuid;
import net.jini.discovery.LookupDiscoveryManager;
import net.jini.export.Exporter;
import rmi.RemoteFileClassifier;
import rmi.FileClassifierImpl;
import java.io.*;
/**
 * FileClassifierServerConfig.java
 */
public class FileClassifierServerConfig implements  LeaseListener {

    private LeaseRenewalManager leaseManager = new LeaseRenewalManager();
    private ServiceID serviceID = null;
    private RemoteFileClassifier impl;
    private File serviceIdFile;
    private Configuration config;
    public static void main(String args[]) {
        FileClassifierServerConfig s = new FileClassifierServerConfig(args);

        // keep server running forever to
        // - allow time for locator discovery and
        // - keep re-registering the lease
        Object keepAlive = new Object();
        synchronized(keepAlive) {
            try {
                keepAlive.wait();
            } catch(java.lang.InterruptedException e) {
                // do nothing
            }
        }
    }
    public FileClassifierServerConfig(String[] args) {
        System.setSecurityManager(new RMISecurityManager());
        try {
            config = ConfigurationProvider.getInstance(args);
        } catch(ConfigurationException e) {
            System.err.println("Configuration error: " + e.toString());
            System.exit(1);
        }
        String serviceName = null;
        try {
```

```
                serviceName = (String)
                    config.getEntry( "security.FileClassifierServer",
                                     "serviceName",
                                     String.class);
            } catch(ConfigurationException e) {
                e.printStackTrace();
                System.exit(1);
            }
            // Create the service and its proxy
            try {
                impl = (RemoteFileClassifier) Class.forName(serviceName).
                                                    newInstance();
            } catch(RemoteException e) {
                e.printStackTrace();
                System.exit(1);
            }
            Remote proxy = null;
            try {
                proxy = exporter.export(impl);
            } catch(ExportException e) {
                e.printStackTrace();
                System.exit(1);
            }
            // register proxy with lookup services
            JoinManager joinMgr = null;
            try {
                LookupDiscoveryManager mgr =
                    new LookupDiscoveryManager(LookupDiscovery.ALL_GROUPS,
                                               null,  // unicast locators
                                               null); // DiscoveryListener
                joinMgr = new JoinManager(proxy, // service proxy
                                          null,  // attr sets
                                          serviceID,
                                          mgr,   // DiscoveryManager
                                          new LeaseRenewalManager());
            } catch(Exception e) {
                e.printStackTrace();
                System.exit(1);
            }
        }
    void getServiceID() {
        // Make up our own
        Uuid id = UuidFactory.generate();
        serviceID = new ServiceID(id.getMostSignificantBits(),
                                  id.getLeastSignificantBits());
    }
```

```
    public void serviceIDNotify(ServiceID serviceID) {
        // called as a ServiceIDListener
        // Should save the id to permanent storage
        System.out.println("got service ID " + serviceID.toString());
    }
    public void discarded(DiscoveryEvent evt) {
    }
    public void notify(LeaseRenewalEvent evt) {
        System.out.println("Lease expired " + evt.toString());
    }

} // FileClassifierServerConfig
```

This server can be run using a configuration file such as a standard Jeri over TCP configuration config/security/jeri-tcp.config:

```
import net.jini.jeri.BasicILFactory;
import net.jini.jeri.BasicJeriExporter;
import net.jini.jeri.tcp.TcpServerEndpoint;
security.FileClassifierServer {
    /* class name for the service */
    serviceName = "rmi.FileClassifierImpl";
    exporter = new BasicJeriExporter(TcpServerEndpoint.getInstance(0),
                                     new BasicILFactory());
}
```

This file can be run from the command line as follows:

```
java ... security.FileClassifierServer \
        config/security/jeri-tcp.config
```

Or it can be run from the Ant build files with this:

```
ant run -DrunFile=security.FileClassifierServer \
        -Dconfig=config/security/jeri-tcp.config
```

The server with the rmi.FileClassifierImpl and config/security/jeri-tcp.config configuration has no security features and will be discarded by a client that imposes any constraints. However, if you change the service class or configuration file, the server can meet various client requirements.

To build the server and run it with various configuration files, I use the Ant file security.FileClassifierServer.xml. This configuration file is a bit trickier than ones presented earlier in that it needs to set different parameters for different situations. For example, in the following section, "Integrity," ordinary HTTP URLs can be used, but in the later section called "Proxy Trust," a different type of URL, HTTPMD, must be used. The URL used is controlled by various command-line *defines*, which can run specialized targets such as httpmd if the Ant file is run with a command-line define of -Ddo.trust=yes. This sets the property codebase.httpd to an HTTPMD URL. Otherwise, the target is not run and a default value of this property as an HTTP URL is used.

The Ant file is as follows:

```xml
<!--
    Project name must be the same as the file name, which must
    be the same as the main.class. Builds jar files with the
    same name.
  -->

<project name="security.FileClassifierServer">
    <!-- Inherits properties from ../build.xml:
        jini.home
        jini.jars
        src
        dist
        build
        httpd.classes
        localhost
    -->
    <!-- Files for this project -->
    <!-- Source files for the server -->
    <property name="src.files"
            value="
                    common/MIMEType.java,
                    common/FileClassifier.java,
                    complete/FileClassifierImpl.java,
                    rmi/RemoteFileClassifier.java,
                    rmi/FileClassifierImpl.java,
                    security/FileClassifierImpl.java,
                    security/FileClassifierServer.java
                    "/>
    <!-- Class files to run the server -->
    <property name="class.files"
            value="
                    common/MIMEType.class,
                    common/FileClassifier.class,
                    complete/FileClassifierImpl.class,
                    rmi/RemoteFileClassifier.class,
                    rmi/FileClassifierImpl.class,
                    security/FileClassifierImpl.class,
                    security/FileClassifierServer.class
                    "/>
    <!-- Class files for the client to download -->
    <property name="class.files.dl"
            value="
                    common/MIMEType.class,
                    common/FileClassifier.class,
```

```
                    complete/FileClassifierImpl.class
                    rmi/RemoteFileClassifier.class,
                    security/FileClassifierImpl.class,
                    "/>
<!-- Uncomment if no class files downloaded to the client -->
<!-- <property name="no-dl" value="true"/> -->
<!-- derived names - may be changed -->
<property name="jar.file"
         value="${ant.project.name}.jar"/>
<property name="jar.file.dl"
         value="${ant.project.name}-dl.jar"/>
<property name="main.class"
         value="${ant.project.name}"/>
<property name="codebase"
         value="http://${localhost}/classes/${jar.file.dl}"/>
<!-- targets -->
<target name="all" depends="compile"/>
<target name="compile">
    <javac destdir="${build}" srcdir="${src}"
           classpath="${jini.jars}"
           includes="${src.files}">
    </javac>
</target>
<target name="dist" depends="compile"
        description="generate the distribution">
    <jar jarfile="${dist}/${jar.file}"
         basedir="${build}"
         includes="${class.files}"/>
    <antcall target="dist-jar-dl"/>
</target>
<target name="dist-jar-dl" unless="no-dl">
    <jar jarfile="${dist}/${jar.file.dl}"
         basedir="${build}"
         includes="${class.files.dl}"/>
</target>
<target name="build" depends="dist,compile"/>
<!-- run the "httpmd" target only if ant is run with -Ddo.trust=yes.
     This is used to calculate an HTTPMD URL for the "run" target -->
<target name="httpmd" if="do.trust" depends="deploy">
    <!-- do a calculation of the MD5 hash and the HTTPMD codebase -->
    <java classname="PrintDigest"
          fork="true"
          failonerror="false"
          classpath="${jini.jars}:."
          dir="."
          outputproperty="hash">
        <arg value="${codebase}"/>
```

```
        </java>
        <property name="codebase.httpmd"
                value="httpmd://${localhost}/classes/${jar.file.dl};md5=${hash}"/>
    </target>
    <target name="run" depends="httpmd,build,deploy">
        <!-- sets the codebase.httpmd to default codebase
            if not already set by the "httpmd" target
          -->
        <property name="codebase.httpmd"
            value="${codebase}"/>
        <!-- now we can run with an HTTP or HTTPMD codebase -->
        <java classname="${main.class}"
            fork="true"
            classpath="${jini.jars}:${dist}/${jar.file}">
            <jvmarg value="-Djava.security.policy=${res}/policy.all"/>
            <jvmarg value="-Djava.rmi.server.codebase=${codebase.httpmd}"/>
            <jvmarg value="-Djava.protocol.handler.pkgs=net.jini.url"/>
            <arg value="${config}"/>
        </java>
    </target>
    <target name="deploy" depends="dist" unless="no-dl">
        <copy file="${dist}/${jar.file.dl}"
                todir="${httpd.classes}"/>
    </target>
</project>
```

Integrity

Integrity ensures that each method call sent from the client to the server gets to its destination in its original form—that is, it is not altered in any way, and similarly, replies are not altered. Integrity does not guarantee privacy (that is the role of confidentiality); anyone can look at the messages. It also does not guarantee that the entity you are sending messages to is the one you think it is (that is the role of authentication).

In the sections that follow, we'll examine how integrity is enforced in the client, TCP server, and SSL server.

Client

A client can enforce integrity by requiring that the proxy support the Integrity.YES constraint. With the earlier example client, this can be done by using the config/security/preparer-integrity.config configuration file:

```
import java.security.Permission;
import net.jini.core.constraint.InvocationConstraint;
import net.jini.core.constraint.InvocationConstraints;
import net.jini.core.constraint.Integrity;
import net.jini.security.BasicProxyPreparer;
```

```
import net.jini.constraint.BasicMethodConstraints;
client.TestFileClassifierProxyPreparer {
    preparer =
        new BasicProxyPreparer(
            /* Don't verify the proxy. */
            false,
            /*
             * Require integrity for all methods.
             */
            new BasicMethodConstraints(
                new InvocationConstraints(
                    new InvocationConstraint[] {
                        Integrity.YES
                    },
                    null
                )
            ),
            new Permission[] {}
        );
}
```

To run the client using this configuration, use the following:

```
java ... client.TestFileClassifierProxyPreparer \
        config/security/preparer-integrity.config
```

or

```
ant run -DrunFile=client.TestFileClassifierProxyPreparer \
        -Dconfig=config/security/preparer-integrity.config
```

instead of

```
java ... client.TestFileClassifierProxyPreparer \
        config/security/preparer-minimal.config
```

or

```
ant run -DrunFile=client.TestFileClassifierProxyPreparer \
        -Dconfig=config/security/preparer-minimal.config
```

Note that only the configuration file has changed.

TCP Server

TCP does not support integrity checking. Using TCP, we can expect integrity to fail. The server can use Jeri over TCP, with a configuration such as config/security/jeri-tcp.config:

```
import net.jini.jeri.BasicILFactory;
import net.jini.jeri.BasicJeriExporter;
```

```
import net.jini.jeri.tcp.TcpServerEndpoint;
security.FileClassifierServer {
    /* class name for the service */
    serviceName = "rmi.FileClassifierImpl";
    exporter = new BasicJeriExporter(TcpServerEndpoint.getInstance(0),
                                      new BasicILFactory());
}
```

This configuration can be run as follows:

```
java ... security.FileClassifierServer config/security/jeri-tcp.config
```

Or it can be run from the Ant file as follows:

```
ant run -DrunFile=security.FileClassifierServer \
         -Dconfig=config/security/jeri-tcp.config
```

The client can find the service and create a new proxy for it. But when it tries to call a method through this proxy, integrity checking will fail. This shows by the client throwing an exception:

```
java.rmi.ConnectIOException: I/O exception connecting to
BasicObjectEndpoint[e42fc746-e7c7-444b-bbc9-b124217439c4,
TcpEndpoint[127.0.0.1:43084]]; nested exception is:
    net.jini.io.UnsupportedConstraintException:
        cannot satisfy constraint: Integrity.YES
```

This exception is thrown when the client attempts to call any method on the proxy. In the preceding example, it occurs in the first method call to the proxy:

```
type = classifier.getMIMEType(fileName)
```

Not only does TCP fail to support integrity checking, but it also fails to support any of the other security mechanisms of this chapter. We will not consider it any further in this chapter.

SSL Server

SSL (or TLS) supports integrity checking. The server can use Jeri over SSL, with a configuration such as config/security/jeri-ssl-minimal.config:

```
import java.security.Permission;
import net.jini.constraint.BasicMethodConstraints;
import net.jini.core.constraint.InvocationConstraint;
import net.jini.core.constraint.InvocationConstraints;
import net.jini.core.constraint.Integrity;
import net.jini.jeri.*;
import net.jini.jeri.ssl.*;
security.FileClassifierServer {
    /* class name for the service */
    serviceName = "rmi.FileClassifierImpl";
    /* Exporter for the server proxy */
```

```
    exporter =
        /* Use secure exporter */
        new BasicJeriExporter(
            /* Use SSL transport */
            SslServerEndpoint.getInstance(0),
            new BasicILFactory(
                /* Require integrity for all methods */
                new BasicMethodConstraints(
                    new InvocationConstraints(
                            (InvocationConstraint[]) null,
                            (InvocationConstraint[]) null)),
                /* No Permission */
                null
            )
        );
}
```

This configuration can be run as follows:

```
  java ... security.FileClassifierServer config/security/jeri-ssl-minimal.config
```

Or it can be run from the Ant file as follows:

```
    ant run -DrunFile=security.FileClassifierServer \
            -Dconfig=config/security/jeri-ssl-minimal.config
```

The service used here is the RMI service discussed in Chapter 11, rmi.FileClassifierImpl:

```java
package rmi;
import common.MIMEType;
import common.FileClassifier;
/**
 * FileClassifierImpl.java
 */
public class FileClassifierImpl implements RemoteFileClassifier {

    public MIMEType getMIMEType(String fileName)
        throws java.rmi.RemoteException {
        System.out.println("Called with " + fileName);
        if (fileName.endsWith(".gif")) {
            return new MIMEType("image", "gif");
        } else if (fileName.endsWith(".jpeg")) {
            return new MIMEType("image", "jpeg");
        } else if (fileName.endsWith(".mpg")) {
            return new MIMEType("video", "mpeg");
        } else if (fileName.endsWith(".txt")) {
            return new MIMEType("text", "plain");
        } else if (fileName.endsWith(".html")) {
```

```
            return new MIMEType("text", "html");
        } else
            // fill in lots of other types,
            // but eventually give up and
            return new MIMEType(null, null);
    }
    public FileClassifierImpl() throws java.rmi.RemoteException {
        // empty constructor required by RMI
    }

} // FileClassifierImpl
```

To satisfy integrity, the service needs no changes—integrity is supplied by the SSL protocol. This service/server/configuration combination works with no exceptions thrown.

This section was a kind of "teaser": *Look how easy it is to implement advanced security! Just add a constraint to the client and use an appropriate protocol for the service!* The following sections look at other aspects of security, and it does get a little more complex.

Proxy Verification

When a client finds a service, it goes through several stages. First, it prepares a service description and asks lookup services if they have any services matching that description. If they do, then the lookup service downloads a MarshalledObject for the service. This object basically contains two things: the instance data for the service and a URL for the class files of the service.

The service places class or .jar files on the HTTP server. The client gets these files from the HTTP server. In Jini 1.2, both the service and client trust the HTTP server. For a secure system, this trust should be demonstrable. The client needs to able to verify that the class files it got from the server are the class files that the service put there. This can be done in many ways, but the Jini team has come up with a neat approach, called HTTPMD.

HTTPMD

There is no integrity or other security aspect involved in getting files from an HTTP server. The standard way of ensuring security uses a protocol such as HTTPS, but this protocol is quite heavyweight and not really suited to the purpose of proxy verification. While we can get a verified document from an HTTPS server, we still don't know whether or not to trust that server!

What we want to get from an HTTP server is a .jar file for the classes that are provided by the service. Only the service knows if the classes are correct or not. That is, it doesn't really matter whether or not the HTTP server can be trusted; what matters is that we can get information from the service to verify the .jar file.

A common way of checking that two files are identical is to use a *hash* of each file. A hash is a number (often 128 bits) that is calculated from the file contents. Hash algorithms are designed with two properties:

- If two files have the same hash, then it is "almost certain" that they are the same file (i.e., have the same contents).

- Given a hash value, it is "nearly impossible" to create a file with that hash value.

So a service can put a `.jar` file on an HTTP server and a client can download it. If the hash calculated by the client is the same as the service thinks it should be, then the client can be "almost certain" that it has the correct file.

There are many hash algorithms. Popular ones are

- Message-Digest algorithm 5 (MD5)

- Secure Hash Algorithm (SHA)

When you get a marshalled object from a lookup service, it contains the URL for the class files. This URL was inserted by the service. If the URL contained the hash for the class files, then it would be possible for a client to verify that it had obtained the correct files. (Of course, this assumes that the lookup service and HTTP server are not in collusion to deliver false hash values—see the section "Proxy Verifier" for information about trusting the lookup service.)

Jini defines an HTTP + Message Digest (HTTPMD) URL that adds the hash value as a component of the URL. The scheme is changed from "http" to "httpmd" and the hash is added as an extra component, along with a statement of the hash algorithm. For example, using the MD5 hash algorithm, a URL of

```
http:jan.netcomp.monash.edu.au/classes/FileClassifierServer-dl.jar
```

would change to

```
httpmd:jan.netcomp.monash.edu.au/
classes/FileClassifierServer-dl.jar;\ md5=7ef2019216d0e9069308cec29b779bc0
```

The service can specify such a URL in its `java.rmi.server.codebase` property. But there is a small hiccup involved: this is a nonstandard protocol that is not recognized by the standard JVM. There is, however, a standard mechanism for adding new handlers to a JVM. The process for doing this is described by Brian Maso in the article "A New Era for Java Protocol Handlers" at `http://java.sun.com/developer/onlineTraining/protocolhandlers`.

The HTTPMD handler is part of the Jini package, and it only needs to be installed into the JVM. This is done by defining an appropriate property:

```
java -Djava.protocol.handler.pkgs=net.jini.url ...
```

which looks for the `net.jini.url.httpmd.Handler` class whenever it needs to handle an HTTPMD document.

Calculating HTTPMD URLs

Many operating systems have tools available for calculating message digests. For example, most Linux distributions include the `md5sum` command for MD5 digests and `shasum` for SHA digests. Use of such tools is operating system-specific, and they must be run by hand or automatically from some sort of script.

A message digest class in the `java.security` package can be used in a platform-independent way. However, it won't directly handle an HTTPMD URL. Jini 2.0 includes the `HttpmdUtil` class, which will calculate digests from a URL and has two methods:

```
class HttpmdUtil {
    static String computeDigest(URL url,
                                String algorithm);
    static String computeDigestCodebase(String sourceDirectory,
                                        String codebase);
}
```

The first method is useful if you already have a .jar file installed in an HTTP server and wish to calculate its digest. So, for example, you could call

```
HttpmdUtil.computeDigest("http://localhost/classes/ClassFiles.jar", "MD5");
```

The resulting digest could be appended to a new URL of type HTTPMD. Note that for this mechanism to be valid, the program using it must trust the HTTP server!

A simple program to calculate and print the hash value of a URL using this mechanism is PrintDigest:

```
import net.jini.url.httpmd.HttpmdUtil;
import java.net.URL;
public class PrintDigest {
    public static void main(String[] args) {
        if (args.length == 0) {
            System.out.println("");
            return;
        }
        String codebase = args[0];
        try {
            System.out.println(HttpmdUtil.computeDigest(
                                            new URL(codebase),
                                            "MD5"));
        } catch(Exception e) {
            System.out.println(codebase);
        }
    }
}
```

I use this program in my Ant files, which assume a local trusted HTTP server.

The second method is useful before deployment of the .jar file to an HTTP server. It returns a new URL for a given URL with a new digest value. For example, the call

```
HttpmdUtil.computeDigestCodebase("dist",
            "httpmd://localhost/classes/ClassFiles.jar;md5=0");
```

strips the scheme, host, and digest value from the URL and appends the directories and .jar file name to the given directory. In this case, it calculates the digest for the local file dist/classes/ClassFiles.jar. It then rebuilds the URL as, for example, httpmd://localhost/classes/ClassFiles.jar;md5=.... This only involves local trust. However, it does rely on a consistent directory convention between local files and HTTP URLs—and I didn't obey that convention.

A third technique is given in the Jini "hello" example: `source/vob/jive/src/com/sun/jini/example/hello`. This sophisticated method is not for the fainthearted. It installs a new `RMIClassLoaderSpi` called `MdClassAnnotationProvider`. The `getClassAnnotation()` method of this class uses the second method of the `HttpmdUtil` to generate an HTTPMD URL on demand from an HTTP URL.

reggie and HTTPMD

The standard setup for `reggie` does not recognize the HTTPMD protocol. I'm not sure why it is looking inside the marshalled objects for this, but it will cause an exception to be thrown in services if it does not understand it. There is an easy fix to this problem: add the property `-Djava.protocol.handler.pkgs=net.jini.url` to the command that starts `reggie`.

Proxy Verifier

When the client gets a proxy for a service, it gets a marshalled object with instance data and a URL for the class files. Assuming that the URL has not been tampered with, it can download the class files from an HTTP server. If it is an HTTPMD URL, then the client can verify that the class files are correct—as long as it trusts the proxy. This is a tricky problem: how do you verify that the proxy is correct when you have a (possibly) false and misleading proxy? Moreover, this possibly antagonistic proxy is the only way you have of talking to the service.

The only entity that can really verify that the proxy is correct is the original service. So, can you send the proxy to the service and get it to tell you? Well, no: if you ask the untrusted proxy to send itself for verification to the service, then it might just lie and claim that, yes, it has done so. What you have to do is get an object from the service that can perform verification locally—under the client's eyes, as it were.

The mechanism adopted by Jini to resolve this issue is to use several levels of proxy: the (untrusted) service proxy is asked to deliver a "bootstrap" proxy that can deliver a verifier. This verifier is the object that will deliver the verdict on whether the proxy can be trusted, so it must be trustworthy itself. Jini ensures this by insisting that the class files for the verifier are local to the client and so are trusted just like any other local code.

The client needs to have a list of local verifiers that it trusts just because they are local. A standard set is given in the Jini library `jsk-platform.jar`. This `.jar` file contains the following verifiers:

- `ConstraintTrustVerifier`

- `BasicJeriTrustVerifier`

- `SslTrustVerifier`

- `KerberosTrustVerifier`

- `ProxyTrustVerifier`

- `ConstrainableLookupLocatorTrustVerifier`

- `DiscoveryConstraintTrustVerifier`

Client with Proxy Verification

To require trust from a service, the client must do three things:

1. Include jsk-platform.jar in its classpath to get a set of proxy verifiers.

2. Install an HTTPMD handler with the runtime property java.protocol.handler.pkgs=net.jini.url.

3. Specify trust checking by setting the first argument of BasicProxyPreparer to true. A configuration file to require trust checking (and nothing else) is config/security/preparer-trust.config:

```
import java.security.Permission;
import net.jini.core.constraint.InvocationConstraint;
import net.jini.core.constraint.InvocationConstraints;
import net.jini.core.constraint.Integrity;
import net.jini.security.BasicProxyPreparer;
import net.jini.constraint.BasicMethodConstraints;
client.TestFileClassifierProxyPreparer {
    preparer =
        new BasicProxyPreparer(
            /* Verify the proxy. */
            true,
            /* No constraints */
            new BasicMethodConstraints(
                new InvocationConstraints(
                    new InvocationConstraint[] {
                    },
                    null
                )
            ),
            new Permission[] {}
        );
}
```

A command line to run this client is as follows:

```
java ... client.TestFileClassifierProxyPreparer \
        config/security/preparer-trust.config
```

Here is the command line using Ant:

```
ant run -DrunFile=client.TestFileClassifierProxyPreparer \
        -Dconfig=config/security/preparer-trust.config
```

SSL Trusted Server

SSL will allow trust checking to be performed by the following mechanisms:

- The service does not need to be adapted, and it can still be the rmi.FileClassifierImpl shown previously.

- The server needs to install an HTTPMD handler with the runtime property java.protocol.handler.pkgs=net.jini.url.

- The security.FileClassiferServer-dl.jar file needs to be created with the contents common/MIMEType.class, common/FileClassifier.class, rmi/RemoteFileClassifier. class, and rmi/FileClassifierImpl.class, and copied to an HTTP server.

- A hash needs to be performed on the security.FileClassiferServer-dl.jar file. In this book, we use the HttpmdUtil to calculate this as explained earlier (we trust the local HTTP server).

- The codebase should be an HTTPMD URL, including the hash value from the previous item.

The service does not need to specify anything other than that it uses SSL for transport (the server supplies the HTTPMD codebase). The server can use the config/security/ jeri-ssl-minimal.config configuration:

```
import java.security.Permission;
import net.jini.constraint.BasicMethodConstraints;
import net.jini.core.constraint.InvocationConstraint;
import net.jini.core.constraint.InvocationConstraints;
import net.jini.core.constraint.Integrity;
import net.jini.jeri.*;
import net.jini.jeri.ssl.*;
security.FileClassifierServer {
    /* class name for the service */
    serviceName = "rmi.FileClassifierImpl";
    /* Exporter for the server proxy */
    exporter =
        /* Use secure exporter */
        new BasicJeriExporter(
            /* Use SSL transport */
            SslServerEndpoint.getInstance(0),
            new BasicILFactory(
                /* Require integrity for all methods */
                new BasicMethodConstraints(
                    new InvocationConstraints(
                            (InvocationConstraint[]) null,
                            (InvocationConstraint[]) null)),
                /* No Permission */
                null
            )
        );
}
```

A command line to run this server is as follows:

```
java ... -Djava.rmi.server.codebase=httpmd://... \
        security.FileClassiferServer \
        config/security/jeri-ssl-minimal.config
```

Here's the command from Ant:

```
ant run -DrunFile=security.FileClassiferServer \
        -Dconfig=config/security/jeri-ssl-minimal.config \
        -Ddo.trust=yes
```

This server/configuration will handle a client that requires trust verification. If the trust logger file for the client is examined, it will contain lines such as the following:

```
FINE: trust verifiers [net.jini.constraint.ConstraintTrustVerifier...]
Aug 16, 2004 9:59:35 PM net.jini.security.Security$Context isTrustedObject
FINE: net.jini.jeri.ssl.SslTrustVerifier@df1832 trusts
        SslEndpoint[127.0.0.1:39693]
Aug 16, 2004 9:59:35 PM net.jini.security.Security$Context isTrustedObject
FINE: net.jini.jeri.BasicJeriTrustVerifier@1a116c9 trusts
        BasicObjectEndpoint[...,SslEndpoint[...]]
Aug 16, 2004 9:59:35 PM net.jini.security.Security$Context isTrustedObject
FINE: net.jini.constraint.ConstraintTrustVerifier@1d1e730 trusts
        InvocationConstraints[reqs: {}, prefs: {}]
Aug 16, 2004 9:59:35 PM net.jini.security.Security$Context isTrustedObject
FINE: net.jini.constraint.ConstraintTrustVerifier@1d1e730 trusts
        BasicMethodConstraints{default => null}
Aug 16, 2004 9:59:35 PM net.jini.security.Security$Context isTrustedObject
FINE: net.jini.jeri.BasicJeriTrustVerifier@1a116c9 trusts
        Proxy[RemoteFileClassifier,
                BasicInvocationHandler[BasicObjectEndpoint[...]]]
```

This code shows that the SslTrustVerifier trusts the SslEndpoint, and because of that, the BasicJeriTrustVerifier trusts the BasicObjectEndpoint, which contains the SslEndpoint. Trust is also applied to the constraints, after which the proxy is declared to be trusted.

It is important to note the limits of what has been achieved in this section. You have downloaded a proxy that you can trust—but whose proxy is it? You have been assured that the code you received has not been tampered with by anyone else, but you could still be getting code from "Antagonistic Alice." All that you know at this point is that you have the code that Alice intended to send to you, and that "Mallory in the Middle" hasn't tampered with it!

Errors

In this section, we'll look at some errors you might encounter when attempting to use proxy verification.

If you forget to include jsk-platform.jar in the client's classpath, then it won't be able to find the standard verifiers and won't be able to verify any proxies. The client will throw a SecurityException:

```
java.lang.SecurityException: object is not trusted:
    Proxy[RemoteFileClassifier,BasicInvocationHandler[
        BasicObjectEndpoint[1c4c3ec0-f91e-46a6-827b-626575702a07,
                            SslEndpoint[127.0.0.1:56641]]]]
    at net.jini.security.Security.verifyObjectTrust(Security.java:268)
    at net.jini.security.BasicProxyPreparer.verify(BasicProxyPreparer.java:309)
```

The trust logger will also show the following:

```
FINE: trust verifiers []
Aug 16, 2004 5:54:27 PM net.jini.security.Security$Context isTrustedObject
FAILED: no verifier trusts Proxy[RemoteFileClassifier,BasicInvocationHandler[Bas
icObjectEndpoint[1c4c3ec0-f91e-46a6-827b-626575702a07,SslEndpoint[127.0.0.1:5664
1]]]]
```

with the failure caused by an empty verifiers list.

If the server uses HTTP URLs instead of HTTPMD URLs, then the client is unable to perform an integrity check. This will result in the client throwing a SecurityException:

```
java.lang.SecurityException: URL does not provide integrity:
    http://192.168.1.13/classes/security.FileClassifierServer-dl.jar
    at net.jini.security.Security.verifyCodebaseIntegrity(Security.java:343)
```

The integrity logger will also show the following:

```
FINE: integrity verifiers [net.jini.url.httpmd.HttpmdIntegrityVerifier@1b5998f,
    net.jini.url.https.HttpsIntegrityVerifier@17494c8,
    net.jini.url.file.FileIntegrityVerifier@d3db51]
Aug 16, 2004 6:01:27 PM net.jini.security.Security verifyCodebaseIntegrity
FAILED: no verifier verifies
        http://192.168.1.13/classes/security.FileClassifierServer-dl.jar
```

It is necessary to install the HTTPMD handler in the server, in the client, and in reggie. If you do not install the handler in the server, then the discovery logger reports this:

```
INFO: exception occurred during unicast discovery
 java.net.MalformedURLException: unknown protocol: httpmd
    at java.net.URL.>init<(URL.java:544)
```

If you leave the handler out of the client, it throws an exception during service discovery:

```
java.rmi.UnmarshalException: error unmarshalling return; nested exception is:
    java.net.MalformedURLException: unknown protocol: httpmd
    at com.sun.jini.reggie.RegistrarProxy.lookup(RegistrarProxy.java:130)
```

If you do not install the HTTPMD handler in reggie, then when the server runs, it gets an error thrown from reggie, which shows in a message from the JoinManager logger:

```
INFO: JoinManager - failure
java.rmi.ServerException: RemoteException in server thread; nested exception is:
    java.rmi.UnmarshalException: unmarshalling method/arguments;
        nested exception is:
    java.net.MalformedURLException: unknown protocol: httpmd
    at net.jini.jeri.BasicInvocationDispatcher.dispatch(...)
```

Confidentiality

A conversation is confidential if no one else can overhear it, or even if someone else can hear the conversation but cannot understand it. Typically, applications use encryption to ensure that messages cannot be read by others. Either a client or a server can specify confidentiality, and we'll look at both methods in this section.

Client

A client specifies confidentiality by adding a `Confidentiality.YES` constraint to the proxy preparer. For example, the `config/security/preparer-conf.config` configuration file can contain the following:

```
import java.security.Permission;
import net.jini.core.constraint.InvocationConstraint;
import net.jini.core.constraint.InvocationConstraints;
import net.jini.core.constraint.Confidentiality;
import net.jini.security.BasicProxyPreparer;
import net.jini.constraint.BasicMethodConstraints;
client.TestFileClassifierProxyPreparer {
    preparer =
        new BasicProxyPreparer(
            /* Don't verify the proxy. */
            false,
            /*
             * Require integrity for all methods.
             */
            new BasicMethodConstraints(
                new InvocationConstraints(
                    new InvocationConstraint[] {
                        Confidentiality.YES
                    },
                    null
                )
            ),
            new Permission[] {}
        );
}
```

To run the client using this configuration, use this:

```
java ... client.TestFileClassifierProxyPreparer \
        config/security/preparer-conf.config
```

or this:

```
ant run -DrunFile=client.TestFileClassifierProxyPreparer \
        -Dconfig=config/security/preparer-conf.config
```

Note that only the configuration file has changed.

SSL Confidential Server

SSL supports confidentiality. Indeed, that is the major purpose behind its design. So all that is needed is for a server to specify that it is using SSL, which can be done using the earlier config/security/jeri-ssl-minimal.config configuration file:

```
import java.security.Permission;
import net.jini.constraint.BasicMethodConstraints;
import net.jini.core.constraint.InvocationConstraint;
import net.jini.core.constraint.InvocationConstraints;
import net.jini.core.constraint.Integrity;
import net.jini.jeri.*;
import net.jini.jeri.ssl.*;
security.FileClassifierServer {
    /* class name for the service */
    serviceName = "rmi.FileClassifierImpl";
    /* Exporter for the server proxy */
    exporter =
        /* Use secure exporter */
        new BasicJeriExporter(
            /* Use SSL transport */
            SslServerEndpoint.getInstance(0),
            new BasicILFactory(
                /* Require integrity for all methods */
                new BasicMethodConstraints(
                    new InvocationConstraints(
                            (InvocationConstraint[]) null,
                            (InvocationConstraint[]) null)),
                /* No Permission */
                null
            )
        );
}
```

A command line to run this server is as follows:

```
java ... security.FileClassiferServer \
        config/security/jeri-ssl-minimal.config
```

Here's the command from Ant:

```
ant run -DrunFile=security.FileClassiferServer \
        -Dconfig=config/security/jeri-ssl-minimal.config
```

Mix and Match

So far we have tried the following security combinations:

- preparer-minimal.config and jeri-tcp.config: No security on either side. This combination works the same way as examples in earlier chapters without security.

- preparer-integrity.config and jeri-tcp.config: This combination fails due to lack of support by TCP for integrity checking.

- preparer-integrity.config and jeri-ssl-minimal.config: This combination succeeds because SSL supports integrity checking.

- preparer-trust.config and jeri-ssl-minimal.config with HTTPMD URLs: This combination works because SSL supports trust of messages and the HTTPMD URLs allow the client to trust the HTTP server.

- preparer-conf.config and jeri-ssl-minimal.config: This combination works because SSL supports confidentiality through encryption.

We can try variations on these combinations—for example, a client that requires trust and integrity with a server that requires encryption. This is just an additive process: add in the extra constraints to the appropriate configuration and ensure that the client or server has the correct runtime to handle the constraints. The client configuration in this case is config/security/preparer-trust-integrity.config:

```
import java.security.Permission;
import net.jini.core.constraint.InvocationConstraint;
import net.jini.core.constraint.InvocationConstraints;
import net.jini.core.constraint.Integrity;
import net.jini.security.BasicProxyPreparer;
import net.jini.constraint.BasicMethodConstraints;
client.TestFileClassifierProxyPreparer {
    preparer =
        new BasicProxyPreparer(
            /* Verify the proxy. */
            true,
            /* No constraints */
            new BasicMethodConstraints(
                new InvocationConstraints(
                    new InvocationConstraint[] {
                        Integrity.YES
                    },
```

```
                        null
                    )
                ),
                new Permission[] {}
            );
}
```

And the server configuration is config/security/jeri-ssl-conf.config:

```
import java.security.Permission;
import net.jini.constraint.BasicMethodConstraints;
import net.jini.core.constraint.InvocationConstraint;
import net.jini.core.constraint.InvocationConstraints;
import net.jini.core.constraint.Confidentiality;
import net.jini.jeri.*;
import net.jini.jeri.ssl.*;
security.FileClassifierServer {
    /* class name for the service */
    serviceName = "rmi.FileClassifierImpl";
    /* Exporter for the server proxy */
    exporter =
        /* Use secure exporter */
        new BasicJeriExporter(
            /* Use SSL transport */
            SslServerEndpoint.getInstance(0),
            new BasicILFactory(
                /* Require confidentiality for all methods */
                new BasicMethodConstraints(
                    new InvocationConstraints(Confidentiality.YES, null)),
                /* No Permission */
                null
            )
        );
}
```

These configurations can be run as follows:

```
java ... client.TestFileClassifierProxyPreparer \
            config/security/preparer-trust-integrity.config
java ... -Djava.rmi.server.codebase=httpmd://... \
        security.FileClassiferServer \
        config/security/jeri-ssl-conf.config
```

They can be run from Ant as follows:

```
ant run -DrunFile=client.TestFileClassifierProxyPreparer \
        -Dconfig=config/security/preparer-trust-integrity.config
ant run -DrunFile=security.FileClassiferServer \
        -Dconfig=config/security/jeri-ssl-.config \
        -Ddo.trust=yes
```

This combination works satisfactorily. The client logs are indicative of what has happened. The trust logger shows the following (with much text elided):

```
FINE: HttpmdIntegrityVerifier verifies httpmd://...
FINE: trust verifiers [...]
FINE: SslTrustVerifier trusts SslEndpoint[...]
FINE: BasicJeriTrustVerifier trusts BasicObjectEndpoint[...]
FINE: ConstraintTrustVerifier trusts Confidentiality.YES
FINE: ConstraintTrustVerifier trusts
        InvocationConstraints[reqs: {Confidentiality.YES}, prefs: {}]
FINE: ConstraintTrustVerifier trusts
        BasicMethodConstraints{default =>
            InvocationConstraints[reqs: {Confidentiality.YES}, prefs: {}]}
FINE: BasicJeriTrustVerifier trusts Proxy[...]
```

This code shows that the HttpmdIntegrityVerifier trusts the HTTPMD URL; the SslTrustVerifier trusts the SslEndpoint; the ConstraintTrustVerifier trusts Confidentiality, and hence the ConstraintTrustVerifier trusts the BasicMethodConstraints; and so on, until finally, the BasicJeriTrustVerifier trusts the proxy.

Similarly, the integrity log shows this:

```
FINE: integrity verifiers [...]
FINE: HttpmdIntegrityVerifier verifies httpmd://...
```

The HttpmdIntegrityVerifier verifies the HTTPMD URL.

By way of contrast, if the client is run with one constraint, and the server is run with its opposite, then the constraints cannot be satisfied. For example, if the client has set Confidentiality.NO and the server has set Confidentiality.YES, then the client will throw an exception:

```
java.rmi.ConnectIOException: I/O exception connecting to
    BasicObjectEndpoint[...,SslEndpoint[...]]; nested exception is:
    net.jini.io.UnsupportedConstraintException: Constraints not supported:
        InvocationConstraints[reqs: {Confidentiality.NO,
                                     Confidentiality.YES}, prefs: {}]
```

Identity Management

If you want to give different individuals different access rights, then you need to be able to verify each individual's identity. This means that they must have some way of expressing what their identity is in a form that you will recognize. People (and things) may have a number of identities: the father of a particular person, staff ID number, driver's license number, name, and so on. Essentially, these are different labels for one entity. The terminology adopted is that the entity is called a *subject*, and in Java this is represented by the Subject class in the javax.security.auth package. The different identities for a subject are called *principals*, and they too have a Java class: Principal.

A subject authenticates itself to a service using a principal and information to verify itself as that principal. For example, you log into a computer using your user name as principal and password for verification, but other mechanisms could be used. A credential is used to authenticate a subject to later services. In the computer world, these include X.509 certificates and Kerberos tickets.

In this section, we'll look at how Jini clients and services can have and demonstrate their identity.

Java Authentication and Authorization Service (JAAS)

A white paper describing JAAS is titled "User Authentication and Authorization in the Java Platform" and can be found at https://java.sun.com/javase/6/docs/technotes/guides/ security/jaas/acsac.html. For further information also see the "Java Authentication and Authorization Service (JAAS) Reference Guide," which should be in the Java distribution directory docs/guide/security/jaas/JAASRefGuide.html, and "JAAS Authentication" at http:// java.sun.com/j2se/1.4.2/docs/guide/security/jgss/tutorials/AcnOnly.html.

JAAS is a framework for verifying common identities, including the following:

- Java Naming and Directory Interface (JNDI)

- Keystore

- Kerberos

- Windows NT

- Unix

Information on these can be found at http://java.sun.com/j2se/1.4.2/docs/guide/ security/jgss/tutorials/LoginConfigFile.html.

JAAS augments the standard Java security model by adding support for principals, so security access is granted not only on the properties of the code itself (signed, etc.), but also on the principals running the code.

To use JAAS, you first need to create a LoginContext. This picks up information from a configuration file to decide which principal it is authenticating as, and how to do it. The configuration file is similar in concept to the Jini configuration files, but the syntax is different and the contents depend upon the mechanism used.

Once you have a context, you attempt to login(). If successful, you are then a recognized entity and a subject with identity. As a subject, you may be able to do more things than if you have no identity. For example, in an SSL interaction, you will be able to present certificates for this identity if required. And the situation is similar with Kerberos: if challenged, you have an identity and a ticket credential to prove it.

You then add the JAAS security checks to code by running it as the privileged subject, like so:

```
LoginContext loginContext =
    new LoginContext("...");
if (loginContext == null) {
    // do some action without JAAS security
} else {
    loginContext.login();
    Subject.doAsPrivileged(
                loginContext.getSubject(),
```

```
                    new PrivilegedExceptionAction() {
                        public Object run() throws Exception {
                                // do the same action, but now
                                // as a particular subject
                                return null;
                        }
                },
                null);
        }
```

Keystores

A *keystore* is a place to store certain types of credentials, such as X.509 certificates, which are used by SSL. A keystore is manipulated by the keytool command. Conventionally, your own private (and associated public keys) are stored in a keystore... file, while public keys from others are stored in a truststore... file.

You can create private keys for the client as follows:

```
keytool -keystore keystore.client -genkey
```

This will prompt for X.509 information, which assumes that you are an individual working for an organization:

```
Enter keystore password:  client
What is your first and last name?
  [Unknown]: Client
What is the name of your organizational unit?
  [Unknown]: IT
What is the name of your organization?
  [Unknown]: Monash
What is the name of your City or Locality?
  [Unknown]: Melbourne
What is the name of your State or Province?
  [Unknown]: Vic
What is the two-letter country code for this unit?
  [Unknown]: AU
Is CN=Client, OU=IT, O=Monash, L=Melbourne, ST=Vic, C=AU correct?
  [no]: yes
Enter key password for <mykey>
        (RETURN if same as keystore password):
```

Similarly, you can set up a keystore for the server:

```
keytool -keystore keystore.server -genkey
Enter keystore password:  server
What is your first and last name?
  [Unknown]: Server
What is the name of your organizational unit?
  [Unknown]: IT
```

```
What is the name of your organization?
  [Unknown]:  Monash
What is the name of your City or Locality?
  [Unknown]:  Melbourne
What is the name of your State or Province?
  [Unknown]:  Vic
What is the two-letter country code for this unit?
  [Unknown]:  AU
Is CN=Server, OU=IT, O=Monash, L=Melbourne, ST=Vic, C=AU correct?
  [no]:  yes
Enter key password for <mykey>
        (RETURN if same as keystore password):
```

You can export the server's public key from the its keystore and import it into the client's truststore under the alias "Server" as follows:

```
keytool -keystore keystore.server -export -file server.cert
Enter keystore password:  server
Certificate stored in file <server.cert>
keytool -keystore truststore.client -import -file server.cert -alias Server
Enter keystore password:  client
Owner: CN=Server, OU=IT, O=Monash, L=Melbourne, ST=Vic, C=AU
Issuer: CN=Server, OU=IT, O=Monash, L=Melbourne, ST=Vic, C=AU
Serial number: 4123f906
Valid from: Thu Aug 19 10:49:10 EST 2004 until: Wed Nov 17 11:49:10 EST 2004
Certificate fingerprints:
        MD5:  6E:24:70:EB:E2:2C:A0:72:C5:B9:9B:95:72:39:87:B1
        SHA1: 2B:AB:0D:80:4F:DF:B8:66:3B:E7:49:66:3D:53:EC:C5:B8:3A:91:5E
Trust this certificate? [no]:  yes
Certificate was added to keystore
```

Similarly, you can export the client's public key and import it into the server's truststore under the alias "Client":

```
keytool -keystore keystore.client -export -file client.cert
Enter keystore password:  client
Certificate stored in file <client.cert>
keytool -keystore truststore.server -import -file client.cert -alias Client
Enter keystore password:  server
Owner: CN=Client, OU=IT, O=Monash, L=Melbourne, ST=Vic, C=AU
Issuer: CN=Client, OU=IT, O=Monash, L=Melbourne, ST=Vic, C=AU
Serial number: 4123f88d
Valid from: Thu Aug 19 10:47:09 EST 2004 until: Wed Nov 17 11:47:09 EST 2004
Certificate fingerprints:
        MD5:  EA:4A:67:E3:A6:58:2D:F4:52:00:FE:CF:2C:AC:7A:6A
        SHA1: 8C:68:E3:9C:E8:08:4A:33:F5:12:E4:9D:73:D6:EF:A4:A5:82:B2:79
Trust this certificate? [no]:  yes
Certificate was added to keystore
```

Authenticating Server

A server that is prepared to authenticate itself must be able to offer suitable credentials when challenged. For SSL, this would be an X.509 certificate; for Kerberos, it would be a Kerberos ticket; and so on. If JAAS is used to provide these credentials, then it must be able to "log in" to get its authentication information.

The server code needs to be modified slightly to get a login context, and then log in using a principal to get a subject. If this succeeds, then the server can run the rest of the code as that subject. The changes to the file classifier server are given as static code to execute before creating the server. The security/FileClassifierServerAuth is as follows:

```
package security;
import java.rmi.RMISecurityManager;
import java.rmi.Remote;
import java.rmi.RemoteException;
import java.rmi.server.ExportException;
import java.security.PrivilegedExceptionAction;
import javax.security.auth.Subject;
import javax.security.auth.login.LoginContext;
import javax.security.auth.login.LoginException;
import java.security.PrivilegedActionException;
import net.jini.discovery.LookupDiscovery;
import net.jini.discovery.DiscoveryListener;
import net.jini.discovery.DiscoveryEvent;
import net.jini.core.lookup.ServiceRegistrar;
import net.jini.core.lookup.ServiceItem;
import net.jini.core.lookup.ServiceRegistration;
import net.jini.core.lease.Lease;
import net.jini.core.lookup.ServiceID ;
import net.jini.lease.LeaseListener;
import net.jini.lease.LeaseRenewalEvent;
import net.jini.lease.LeaseRenewalManager;
import net.jini.config.Configuration;
import net.jini.config.ConfigurationException;
import net.jini.config.ConfigurationProvider;
import net.jini.lookup.JoinManager;
import net.jini.id.UuidFactory;
import net.jini.id.Uuid;
import net.jini.discovery.LookupDiscoveryManager;
import net.jini.export.Exporter;
import rmi.RemoteFileClassifier;
import rmi.FileClassifierImpl;
import java.util.logging.*;
import java.io.*;
/**
 * FileClassifierServerAuth
 */
```

```
public class FileClassifierServerAuth implements  LeaseListener {

    private LeaseRenewalManager leaseManager = new LeaseRenewalManager();
    private ServiceID serviceID = null;
    private RemoteFileClassifier impl;
    private File serviceIdFile;
    private Configuration config;
    static final String TRUST_LOG = "net.jini.security.trust";
    static final String INTEGRITY_LOG = "net.jini.security.integrity";
    static final String POLICY_LOG = "net.jini.security.policy";
    static final Logger trustLogger = Logger.getLogger(TRUST_LOG);
    static final Logger integrityLogger = Logger.getLogger(INTEGRITY_LOG);
    static final Logger policyLogger = Logger.getLogger(POLICY_LOG);
    private static FileHandler trustFh;
    private static FileHandler integrityFh;
    private static FileHandler policyFh;
    private static FileClassifierServerAuth server;
    static final String DISCOVERY_LOG = "net.jini.security.trust";
    static final Logger logger = Logger.getLogger(DISCOVERY_LOG);
    private static FileHandler fh;
    public static void main(String args[]) {
        installLoggers();
        init(args);
        Object keepAlive = new Object();
        synchronized(keepAlive) {
            try {
                keepAlive.wait();
            } catch(java.lang.InterruptedException e) {
                // do nothing
            }
        }
    }
    private static void init(final String[] args) {
        try {
            LoginContext loginContext =
                new LoginContext("security.FileClassifierServerAuth");
            if (loginContext == null) {
                System.out.println("No login context");
                server = new FileClassifierServerAuth(args);
            } else {
                loginContext.login();
                System.out.println("Login succeeded as " +
                                    loginContext.getSubject().toString());
                Subject.doAsPrivileged(
                            loginContext.getSubject(),
                            new PrivilegedExceptionAction() {
```

```
                                        public Object run() throws Exception {
                                            server =
                                                new FileClassifierServerAuth(args);
                                            return null;
                                        }
                                    },
                                    null);
                }
            } catch(LoginException e) {
                e.printStackTrace();
                System.exit(3);
            } catch(PrivilegedActionException e) {
                e.printStackTrace();
                System.exit(3);
            }
        }
        public FileClassifierServerAuth(String[] args) {
            System.setSecurityManager(new RMISecurityManager());
            Exporter exporter = null;
            String serviceName = null;
            try {
                config = ConfigurationProvider.getInstance(args);
                exporter = (Exporter)
                    config.getEntry( "security.FileClassifierServer",
                                     "exporter",
                                     Exporter.class);
                serviceName = (String)
                    config.getEntry( "security.FileClassifierServer",
                                     "serviceName",
                                     String.class);
            } catch(ConfigurationException e) {
                System.err.println("Configuration error: " + e.toString());
                System.exit(1);
            }
            // Create the service and its proxy
            try {
                // impl = new security.FileClassifierImpl();
                impl = (RemoteFileClassifier) Class.forName(serviceName).newInstance();
            } catch(Exception e) {
                e.printStackTrace();
                System.exit(1);
            }
            Remote proxy = null;
            try {
                proxy = exporter.export(impl);
                System.out.println("Proxy is " + proxy.toString());
            } catch(ExportException e) {
```

```
                e.printStackTrace();
                System.exit(1);
        }
        // register proxy with lookup services
        JoinManager joinMgr = null;
        try {
            LookupDiscoveryManager mgr =
                new LookupDiscoveryManager(LookupDiscovery.ALL_GROUPS,
                                        null,  // unicast locators
                                        null); // DiscoveryListener
            joinMgr = new JoinManager(proxy, // service proxy
                                null,  // attr sets
                                serviceID,
                                mgr,   // DiscoveryManager
                                new LeaseRenewalManager());
        } catch(Exception e) {
            e.printStackTrace();
            System.exit(1);
        }
    }
    private static void installLoggers() {
        try {
            // this handler will save ALL log messages in the file
            trustFh = new FileHandler("log.server.trust.txt");
            integrityFh = new FileHandler("log.server.integrity.txt");
            policyFh = new FileHandler("log.server.policy.txt");
            // the format is simple rather than XML
            trustFh.setFormatter(new SimpleFormatter());
            integrityFh.setFormatter(new SimpleFormatter());
            policyFh.setFormatter(new SimpleFormatter());
            trustLogger.addHandler(trustFh);
            integrityLogger.addHandler(integrityFh);
            policyLogger.addHandler(policyFh);
            trustLogger.setLevel(java.util.logging.Level.ALL);
            integrityLogger.setLevel(java.util.logging.Level.ALL);
            policyLogger.setLevel(java.util.logging.Level.ALL);
        } catch(Exception e) {
            e.printStackTrace();
        }
    }
    void getServiceID() {
        // Make up our own
        Uuid id = UuidFactory.generate();
        serviceID = new ServiceID(id.getMostSignificantBits(),
                            id.getLeastSignificantBits());
    }
    public void serviceIDNotify(ServiceID serviceID) {
```

```
        // called as a ServiceIDListener
        // Should save the id to permanent storage
        System.out.println("got service ID " + serviceID.toString());
    }
    public void discarded(DiscoveryEvent evt) {
    }
    public void notify(LeaseRenewalEvent evt) {
        System.out.println("Lease expired " + evt.toString());
    }
```

```
} // FileClassifierServerAuth
```

This login context uses a hard-coded string to specify the name "security.FileClassifier-
ServerAuth" used by JAAS to find information from the JAAS configuration file; this string could
better be given in a Jini configuration file in a production environment.

A few other pieces need to be put in place for this server to authenticate itself:

- The server needs to be run with an additional runtime property. The property
  `java.security.auth.login.config` needs to be set to the login configuration file, as
  follows:

  ```
  java ... -Djava.security.auth.login.config=ssl-server.login ...
  ```

- The JAAS login file specifies how JAAS is to get its credentials. For example, for SSL it will
  need a certificate, which it can get from a keystore. So for an SSL authenticating server,
  the `ssl-server.login` could contain the following:

  ```
  security.FileClassifierServerAuth {
      com.sun.security.auth.module.KeyStoreLoginModule required
          keyStoreAlias="mykey"
          keyStoreURL="file:resources/security/keystore.server"
          keyStorePasswordURL="file:resources/security/password.server";
  };
  ```

  The configuration name "security.FileClassifierServerAuth" is the same as the
  parameter to the `LoginContext` constructor. The file also specifies the alias to be used in
  looking up entries (the default is "mykey," if the alias is not specified during creation of
  the keystore), the keystore, and a file that contains the password to access this keystore.

- The password file `password.server` just contains the password we set earlier: "server".

This server can be run from the command line:

```
java ... security.FileClassiferServerAuth \
        config/security/jeri-ssl-minimal.config
```

or it can be run from Ant:

```
ant run -DrunFile=security.FileClassiferServerAuth \
        -Dconfig=config/security/jeri-ssl-minimal.config
```

The server does not need to set any constraints (since it just authenticates itself), so the minimal server configuration file can be used.

Client Requiring Authentication

The client can require that the server has a proof of identity, or that it identifies itself as a particular subject. This is like asking, "Do you have a card that proves you are over eighteen years old?" versus "Do you have a card that proves you are Joe Bloggs?"

The first case ("Do you have a credential?") can be specified in the client configuration file by just adding the ServerAuthentication.YES constraint:

```
import java.security.Permission;
import net.jini.core.constraint.InvocationConstraint;
import net.jini.core.constraint.InvocationConstraints;
import net.jini.core.constraint.ServerAuthentication;
import net.jini.security.BasicProxyPreparer;
import net.jini.constraint.BasicMethodConstraints;
client.TestFileClassifierProxyPreparer {
    preparer =
        new BasicProxyPreparer(
            /* Don't verify the proxy. */
            false,
            /* Require authentication as anyone  */
            new BasicMethodConstraints(
                new InvocationConstraints(
                    new InvocationConstraint[] {
                        ServerAuthentication.YES
                    },
                    null
                )
            ),
            new Permission[] {}
        );
}
```

The client is the TestFileClassiferProxyPreparer used throughout this chapter. However, although it doesn't look up any certificates, it does seem to need a truststore to be specified—a bug? You can specify a truststore by adding the property to the runtime:

```
-Djavax.net.ssl.trustStore=truststore.client
```

The second case requires specifying which principal(s) the server is required to authenticate as. The most common case is when the client requires a single principal as identity. The ServerMinPrincipal is used for this, with constructors for a single principal or for a set of principals. In order to get an SSL principal, you need to do something like pull it out of a keystore. This involves obtaining the list of users from a keystore and getting a single user from this list. The KeyStores class in Jini allows you to perform these steps from within a configuration file.

The client is still unaltered from TestFileClassifierProxyPreparer. The configuration file is now preparer-auth-server.config:

```
import java.security.Permission;
import net.jini.core.constraint.InvocationConstraint;
import net.jini.core.constraint.InvocationConstraints;
import net.jini.core.constraint.ServerAuthentication;
import net.jini.security.BasicProxyPreparer;
import net.jini.constraint.BasicMethodConstraints;
import com.sun.jini.config.KeyStores;
import net.jini.core.constraint.ServerMinPrincipal;
client.TestFileClassifierProxyPreparer {
    /* Keystore for getting principals */
    private static users=
        KeyStores.getKeyStore("file:resources/security/truststore.client", null);
    private static serverUser =
        KeyStores.getX500Principal("server", users);
    preparer =
        new BasicProxyPreparer(
            /* Don't verify the proxy. */
            false,
            /* Require authentication as "server"  */
            new BasicMethodConstraints(
                new InvocationConstraints(
                    new InvocationConstraint[] {
                        ServerAuthentication.YES,
                        new ServerMinPrincipal(serverUser)
                    },
                    null
                )
            ),
            new Permission[] {}
        );
}
```

Alternative Constraints

Classes such as ServerMinPrincipal can take a set of principals and AND them together, such as "Are you Jan Newmarch AND are you over eighteen AND are you the father of Katy Newmarch?" A client may want to express a set of alternatives, such as "Do you have a driver's license OR do you have a social security card?" The ConstraintAlternatives class can be used to handle these cases.

Authenticating Client

The same mechanism a server uses to authenticate itself is used by the client. That is, the client sets up a login context, logs in, and then runs code as a particular subject. The modified code is client.TestFileClassifierAuth:

```
package client;
import common.FileClassifier;
import common.MIMEType;
import java.security.PrivilegedExceptionAction;
import javax.security.auth.Subject;
import javax.security.auth.login.LoginContext;
import javax.security.auth.login.LoginException;
import java.security.PrivilegedActionException;
import java.rmi.RMISecurityManager;
import net.jini.discovery.LookupDiscovery;
import net.jini.discovery.DiscoveryListener;
import net.jini.discovery.DiscoveryEvent;
import net.jini.core.lookup.ServiceRegistrar;
import net.jini.core.lookup.ServiceTemplate;
import java.rmi.RemoteException;
import net.jini.security.BasicProxyPreparer;
import net.jini.security.ProxyPreparer;
import net.jini.config.Configuration;
import net.jini.config.ConfigurationException;
import net.jini.config.ConfigurationProvider;
import java.util.logging.*;
/**
 * TestFileClassifierAuth.java
 */
public class TestFileClassifierAuth implements DiscoveryListener {
    private Configuration config;
    static final String TRUST_LOG = "net.jini.security.trust";
    static final String INTEGRITY_LOG = "net.jini.security.integrity";
    static final String POLICY_LOG = "net.jini.security.policy";
    static final Logger trustLogger = Logger.getLogger(TRUST_LOG);
    static final Logger integrityLogger = Logger.getLogger(INTEGRITY_LOG);
    static final Logger policyLogger = Logger.getLogger(POLICY_LOG);
    private static FileHandler trustFh;
    private static FileHandler integrityFh;
    private static FileHandler policyFh;
    public static void main(String argv[])
        throws ConfigurationException {
        installLoggers();
        // Become a subject if possible
        init(argv);
        // stay around long enough to receive replies
        try {
            Thread.currentThread().sleep(100000L);
        } catch(java.lang.InterruptedException e) {
            // do nothing
        }
    }
```

```java
        private static void init(final String[] args) {
            try {
                LoginContext loginContext =
                    new LoginContext("security.TestFileClassifierAuth");
                if (loginContext == null) {
                    System.out.println("No login context");
                    new TestFileClassifierAuth(args);
                } else {
                    loginContext.login();
                     System.out.println("Login succeeded as " +
                            loginContext.getSubject().toString());
                    Subject.doAsPrivileged(
                                        loginContext.getSubject(),
                                        new PrivilegedExceptionAction() {
                                            public Object run() throws Exception {
                                                new TestFileClassifierAuth(args);
                                                return null;
                                            }
                                        },
                                        null);
                }
            } catch(LoginException e) {
                e.printStackTrace();
                System.exit(3);
            } catch(PrivilegedActionException e) {
                e.printStackTrace();
                System.exit(3);
            } catch(ConfigurationException e) {
                e.printStackTrace();
                System.exit(3);
            }
        }
        public TestFileClassifierAuth(String[] argv)
            throws ConfigurationException {
            config = ConfigurationProvider.getInstance(argv);
            System.setSecurityManager(new RMISecurityManager());
            LookupDiscovery discover = null;
            try {
                discover = new LookupDiscovery(LookupDiscovery.ALL_GROUPS);
            } catch(Exception e) {
                System.err.println(e.toString());
                System.exit(1);
            }
            discover.addDiscoveryListener(this);
        }
        private static void installLoggers() {
            try {
```

```java
            // this handler will save ALL log messages in the file
            trustFh = new FileHandler("log.client.trust.txt");
            integrityFh = new FileHandler("log.client.integrity.txt");
            policyFh = new FileHandler("log.client.policy.txt");
            // the format is simple rather than XML
            trustFh.setFormatter(new SimpleFormatter());
            integrityFh.setFormatter(new SimpleFormatter());
            policyFh.setFormatter(new SimpleFormatter());
            trustLogger.addHandler(trustFh);
            integrityLogger.addHandler(integrityFh);
            policyLogger.addHandler(policyFh);
            trustLogger.setLevel(java.util.logging.Level.ALL);
            integrityLogger.setLevel(java.util.logging.Level.ALL);
            policyLogger.setLevel(java.util.logging.Level.ALL);
        } catch(Exception e) {
            e.printStackTrace();
        }
    }
}
public void discovered(DiscoveryEvent evt) {
    ServiceRegistrar[] registrars = evt.getRegistrars();
    Class [] classes = new Class[] {FileClassifier.class};
    FileClassifier classifier = null;
    ServiceTemplate template = new ServiceTemplate(null, classes,
                                                    null);

    for (int n = 0; n < registrars.length; n++) {
        System.out.println("Lookup service found");
        ServiceRegistrar registrar = registrars[n];
        try {
            classifier = (FileClassifier) registrar.lookup(template);
        } catch(java.rmi.RemoteException e) {
            e.printStackTrace();
            System.exit(4);
            continue;
        }
        if (classifier == null) {
            System.out.println("Classifier null");
            continue;
        }
        System.out.println("Getting the proxy");
        // Get the proxy preparer
        ProxyPreparer preparer = null;
        try {
            preparer =
            (ProxyPreparer) config.getEntry(
                                    "client.TestFileClassifierProxyPreparer",
                                    "preparer", ProxyPreparer.class,
```

```
                                          new BasicProxyPreparer());
        } catch(ConfigurationException e) {
            e.printStackTrace();
            preparer = new BasicProxyPreparer();
        }
        // Prepare the new proxy
        System.out.println("Preparing the proxy");
        try {
            classifier = (FileClassifier) preparer.prepareProxy(classifier);
        } catch(RemoteException e) {
            e.printStackTrace();
            System.exit(3);
        } catch(java.lang.SecurityException e) {
            e.printStackTrace();
            System.exit(6);
        }
        // Use the service to classify a few file types
        System.out.println("Calling the proxy");
        MIMEType type;
        try {
            String fileName;
            fileName = "file1.txt";
            type = classifier.getMIMEType(fileName);
            printType(fileName, type);
            fileName = "file2.rtf";
            type = classifier.getMIMEType(fileName);
            printType(fileName, type);
            fileName = "file3.abc";
            type = classifier.getMIMEType(fileName);
            printType(fileName, type);
        } catch(java.rmi.RemoteException e) {
            System.out.println("Failed to call method");
            System.err.println(e.toString());
            System.exit(5);
            continue;
        }
        // success
        System.exit(0);
    }
}
private void printType(String fileName, MIMEType type) {
    System.out.print("Type of " + fileName + " is ");
    if (type == null) {
        System.out.println("null");
    } else {
        System.out.println(type.toString());
```

```
        }
    }
    public void discarded(DiscoveryEvent evt) {
        // empty
    }
} // TestFileClassifierAuth
```

As with the server, other pieces need to be in place for this client to authenticate itself:

- The client needs to be run with an additional runtime property. The property `java.security.auth.login.config` needs to be set to the login configuration file, as follows:

  ```
  java ... -Djava.security.auth.login.config=ssl-client.login ...
  ```

- The JAAS login file specifies how JAAS is to get its credentials. For example, for SSL it will need a certificate, which it can get from a keystore. So for an SSL authenticating server, the `ssl-client.login` could contain the following:

  ```
  security.TestFileClassifierAuth {
      com.sun.security.auth.module.KeyStoreLoginModule required
          keyStoreAlias="mykey"
          keyStoreURL="file:resources/security/keystore.client"
          keyStorePasswordURL="file:resources/security/password.client";
  };
  ```

  The configuration name `security.TestFileClassifierAuth` is the same as the parameter to the `LoginContext` constructor. The file also specifies the alias to be used in looking up entries (the default is `mykey` if an alias is not specified during creation of the keystore), the keystore, and a file that contains the password to access this keystore.

- The password file `password.client` just contains the password set earlier: "client".

Server Requiring Authentication

If the server requires the client to authenticate as a particular user, then it can be the `config.FileClassifierServer`. It does not need to have the authentication code itself. It can specify client authentication with the `jeri-ssl-auth-client.config` configuration file:

```
import java.security.Permission;
import net.jini.constraint.BasicMethodConstraints;
import net.jini.core.constraint.InvocationConstraint;
import net.jini.core.constraint.InvocationConstraints;
import net.jini.core.constraint.ClientAuthentication;
import net.jini.core.constraint.ClientMinPrincipal;
import net.jini.jeri.*;
import net.jini.jeri.ssl.*;
import com.sun.jini.config.KeyStores;
security.FileClassifierServer {
    /* class name for the service */
```

```
    serviceName = "rmi.FileClassifierImpl";
/* Keystore for getting principals */
private static users=
    KeyStores.getKeyStore("file:resources/security/truststore.server", null);
private static clientUser =
    KeyStores.getX500Principal("client", users);
/* Exporter for the server proxy */
exporter =
    /* Use secure exporter */
    new BasicJeriExporter(
        /* Use SSL transport */
        SslServerEndpoint.getInstance(0),
        new BasicILFactory(
            /* Require integrity for all methods */
            new BasicMethodConstraints(
                new InvocationConstraints(
                        new InvocationConstraint[] {
                            ClientAuthentication.YES,
                            new ClientMinPrincipal(clientUser)
                        },
                        (InvocationConstraint[]) null)),
            /* No Permission */
            null
        )
    );
}
```

In addition to this, the server needs to be run with a define:

```
-Djavax.net.ssl.trustStore=resources/security/truststore.server
```

To locate the truststore file, it will use verify certificates from the client.

Authorization

Standard Java uses policy files to determine what foreign code is allowed to do. This policy is installed when the application starts, so it is a *static* policy mechanism. In Jini 2.0, when a service is discovered, it may wish to ask for a policy to be applied at that time, *dynamically*. Extensions to the basic security model in JDK 1.4 allow this to occur, by permitting dynamic policy setting on class loaders.

To allow dynamic policy granting, the Java runtime must have the appropriate classes installed and trusted. This is the purpose of the jsk-policy.jar file from the Jini library. As part of the installation process for Jini, it is recommended that you install this file into the jre/lib/ext directory of your Java distribution to allow the Java runtime to pick these up as trusted classes when it starts.

The runtime needs to be told about these classes, which you can do by using the runtime define:

```
-Djava.security.properties=security.properties
```

where `security.properties` is a file containing the single line saying which Jini class to use for dynamic policies.

```
policy.provider=net.jini.security.policy.DynamicPolicyProvider
```

For the client, an array of permissions specifies the permissions the client will grant to a proxy. This array is set in the `BasicProxyPreparer`.

The server can set a permission in the `BasicILFactory`. This permission is used to perform server-side access control on incoming remote calls.

Summary

Ensuring security on the network is a complex task, and the Jini possibilities of mobile code increase the security risks. This chapter presented an end-programmer's view of the new Jini 2.0 security. The architecture behind the Jini security model is highly configurable, and we've looked at one set of "plug-ins" to make it (relatively) easy for you as a programmer. However, if you want more control over any part of this process, be aware that you can dig further into this architecture and roll your own for almost all parts of it.

CHAPTER 23

■ ■ ■

Transactions

Transactions are a necessary part of many distributed operations. Frequently, two or more objects will need to synchronize changes of state so that they all occur or none occur. This happens in situations such as control of ownership, where one party has to give up ownership at the "same" time as another asserts ownership. What has to be avoided is only one party performing the action, which could result in either no owners or two owners.

In this chapter, we'll examine the Jini transaction manager and show how this can be used to give transaction processing in Jini.

Two-Phase Commit Protocol

The theory of transactions often refers to the *ACID* properties:

- *Atomicity*. All the operations of a transaction must take place, or none of them do.

- *Consistency*. The completion of a transaction must leave the participants in a "consistent" state (whatever that means). For example, the number of owners of a resource must remain at one.

- *Isolation*: The activities of one transaction must not affect any other transactions.

- *Durability*. The results of a transaction must be persistent.

The practice of transactions, however, is that they use the *two-phase commit protocol*. This requires that participants in a transaction be asked to *vote* on a transaction. If all agree to go ahead, then the transaction *commits*, which is binding on all the participants. If any participants *abort* the transaction during this voting stage, then it forces abortion of the transaction on all participants.

Jini has adopted the syntax of the two-phase commit method. It is up to the clients and services within a transaction to observe the ACID properties if they desire. Jini essentially supplies the mechanism of two-phase commit and leaves the policy of meaning to the participants in a transaction.

Transactions Overview

Restricting Jini transactions to a two-phase commit model without associating particular semantics to this means that a transaction can be represented in a simple way: just as a long identifier. This identifier is obtained from a transaction manager, and it will uniquely label the transaction to that manager. (It is not guaranteed to be unique between managers, though, unlike service IDs.) All participants in the transaction communicate with the transaction manager, using this identifier to label which transaction they belong to.

The participants in a transaction may disappear, and the transaction manager may disappear. So transactions are managed by a lease, which will expire unless it is renewed. When a transaction manager is asked for a new transaction, it returns a `TransactionManager.Created` object, containing the transaction identifier and lease:

```
public interface TransactionManager {
    public static class Created {
        public final long id;
        public final Lease lease;
    }
    ...
}
```

A Created object may be passed around between participants in the lease. One of them will need to look after lease renewals. All the participants will use the transaction identifier in communication with the transaction manager.

Transaction Manager

A transaction manager looks after the two-phase commit protocol for all the participants in a transaction. It is responsible for creating a new transaction through its create() method. Any of the participants may force the transaction to abort with abort(), or they can force the transaction to the two-phase commit stage by calling commit().

```
public interface TransactionManager {
    Created create(long leaseFor) throws ...;
    void join(long id, TransactionParticipant part,
              long crashCount) throws ...;
    void commit(long id) throws ...;
    void abort(long id) throws ...;
    ...
}
```

When a participant joins a transaction, it registers a listener of type TransactionParticipant. If any participant calls commit(), the transaction manager starts the voting process using all of these listeners. If all of these are prepared to commit, then the manager moves all of these listeners to the commit stage. Alternatively, any of the participants may call abort(), which forces all of the listeners to abort.

Transaction Participant

When an object becomes a participant listener in a transaction, it allows the transaction manager to call various methods:

```
public interface TransactionParticipant ... {
    int prepare(TransactionManager mgr, long id) throws ...;
    void commit(TransactionManager mgr, long id) throws ...;
    void abort(TransactionManager mgr, long id) throws ...;
    int prepareAndCommit(TransactionManager mgr, long id) throws ...;
}
```

These methods are triggered by calls made upon the transaction manager. For example, if one client calls the transaction manager to abort, then it calls all the listeners to abort.

The "normal" mode of operation (i.e., when nothing goes wrong with the transaction) is for a call to be made on the transaction manager to commit. The manager then enters the two-phase commit stage where it asks each participant listener to first prepare() and then to either commit() or abort().

mahalo Transaction Manager

mahalo is a transaction manager supplied by Sun as part of the Jini distribution. It can be used as is, and it runs as a Jini service, like reggie. If LaunchAll has been used to start reggie, then it will also have started mahalo.

mahalo implements the service TransactionManager.

Transactions Example

The classic use of transactions is to handle money transfers between accounts. In this case, there are two accounts, one of which is debited and the other credited. This is not too exciting as an example, so we will try a more complex situation. A service may decide to charge for its use. If a client decides this cost is reasonable, it will first credit the service and then request that the service be performed. The actual accounts will be managed by an accounts service, which will need to be informed of the credits and debits that occur. A simple accounts model is that the service gets, say, a customer ID from the client, and passes its own ID and the customer ID to the accounts service, which manages both accounts. Simple, prone to all sorts of e-commerce issues that I have no intention of going into, and similar to the way credit cards work!

Figure 23-1 shows the messages in a normal sequence diagram. The client makes a call, getCost(), to the service, and receives the cost in return. It then makes another call, credit(), on the service, which makes a call creditDebit() on the accounts before returning. The client then makes a final call, requestService(), on the service and receives a result.

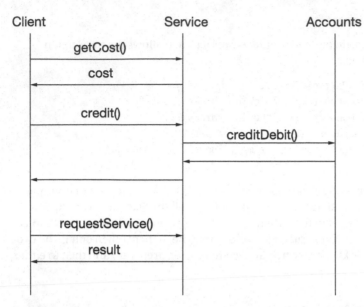

Figure 23-1. *Sequence diagram for credit/debit*

There are a number of problems with this sequence of actions that can benefit from the use of a transaction model. The steps of credit() and creditDebit() should certainly be performed either together or not at all. But in addition there is the issue of the quality of the service. For example, suppose the client is not happy with the results from the service, and it would like to reclaim its money or, better yet, not spend it in the first place. If we include the delivery of the service in the transaction, then there is the opportunity for the client to abort the transaction before it is committed.

Figure 23-2 shows the larger set of messages in the sequence diagram for "normal" execution. As before, the client requests the cost from the service. After getting this cost, the client asks the transaction manager to create a transaction and receives the transaction ID. It then joins the transaction itself. When it asks the service to credit an amount, the service also joins the transaction. The service then asks the account to creditDebit() the amount, and as part of this the account also joins the transaction. The client then requests the service and gets the result. If all is fine, it then asks the transaction manager to commit(), which triggers the prepare and commit phase. The transaction manager asks each participant to prepare(), and if it gets satisfactory replies from each, it then asks each one to commit().

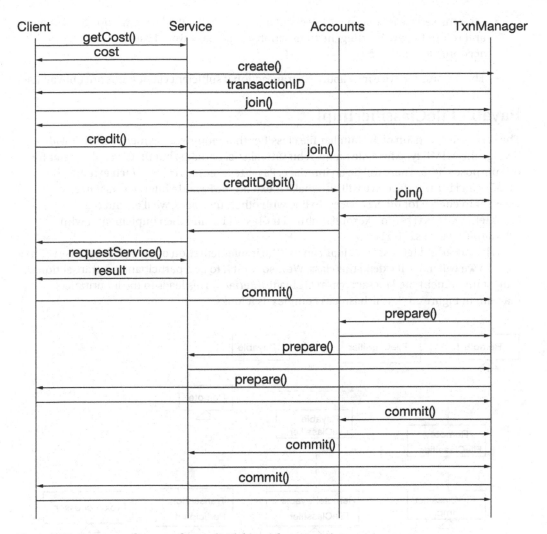

Figure 23-2. *Sequence diagram for credit/debit with transactions*

The points of failure in this transaction include the following:

- The cost may be too high for the client. However, at this stage, the client has not created or joined a transaction, so it's not an issue.

- The client may offer too little in the way of payment to the service. The service can signal this by joining the transaction and then aborting it, which ensures that the client has to roll back the transaction. (Of course, the service could instead throw a NotEnoughPayment exception; joining and aborting is used for illustrating transaction possibilities.)

- There may be a time delay between finding the price and asking for the service, and the price may have gone up in the meantime. The service would then abort the transaction, forcing the client and the accounts to roll back.

- After the service is performed, the client may decide that the result was not good enough and refuse to pay. Aborting the transaction at this stage would cause the service and accounts to roll back.

- The accounts service may abort the transaction if sufficient client funds are unavailable.

PayableFileClassifierImpl

The service is a version of the familiar file classifier that requires a payment before it will divulge the MIME type for a file name. A bit unrealistic, perhaps, but that doesn't matter for our purposes here. There will be an interface, `PayableFileClassifier`, which extends the `FileClassifier` interface. We will also make it extend the `Payable` interface, just in case we want to charge for other services. In line with other interfaces, we'll extend the `PayableFileClassifier` to a `RemotePayableFileClassifier` and then implement it with a `PayableFileClassifierImpl`.

The `PayableFileClassifierImpl` can use the implementation of the `rmi.FileClassifier`➡ `Impl`, so we will make it extend this class. We also want it to be a participant in a transaction, so it must implement the `TransactionParticipant` interface. This leads to the inheritance diagram of Figure 23-3, which isn't as complex as it looks.

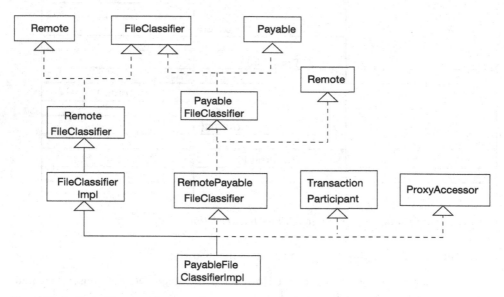

Figure 23-3. *Class diagram for a transaction participant*

A new element in this hierarchy is the interface `Payable`:

```
package common;
import java.io.Serializable;
import net.jini.core.transaction.server.TransactionManager;
/**
 * Payable.java
 */
```

```
public interface Payable extends Serializable {

    void credit(long amount, long accountID,
                TransactionManager mgr,
                long transactionID)
        throws java.rmi.RemoteException;
    long getCost() throws java.rmi.RemoteException;
} // Payable
```

Extending this interface is the PayableFileClassifier interface, which will be used by the client to search for the service:

```
package common;
/**
 * PayableFileClassifier.java
 */
public interface PayableFileClassifier extends FileClassifier, Payable {

} // PayableFileClassifier
```

with a simple extension to the remote form:

```
package txn;
import common.PayableFileClassifier;
import java.rmi.Remote;
/**
 * RemotePayableFileClassifier.java
 */
public interface RemotePayableFileClassifier extends PayableFileClassifier, Remote {

} // RemotePayableFileClasssifier
```

The implementation of the RemotePayableFileClassifier joins the transaction when credit() is called. The implementation object is passed the transaction manager as one parameter to this call. It then finds an Accounts service from a known location (e.g., using unicast lookup), registers the money transfer, and then performs the service. There is no real state information kept by this implementation that is altered by the transaction. When asked to prepare() by the transaction manager, it can just return NOTCHANGED. If there was state, the prepare() and commit() methods would have more content. The prepareAndCommit() method may be called by a transaction manager as an optimization, and the version given in this example follows the specification given in the Jini transaction document.

When the implementation object joins the transaction, it must pass an object that the transaction can make calls on. Since the transaction manager is running remotely, this means that the object passed to it must be a *proxy*, which in turn means that the implementation must prepare a proxy and pass it to the transaction manager. On the other hand, the server that contains the service object needs to have a proxy to register the service. You have seen this a few times before: the service implements ProxyAccessor, which allows the server to get the proxy from the service.

The service implementation is as follows:

```java
package txn;
import common.MIMEType;
import common.Accounts;
import rmi.FileClassifierImpl;
import net.jini.core.transaction.server.TransactionManager;
import net.jini.core.transaction.server.TransactionParticipant;
import net.jini.core.transaction.server.TransactionConstants;
import net.jini.core.transaction.UnknownTransactionException;
import net.jini.core.transaction.CannotJoinException;
import net.jini.core.transaction.CannotAbortException;
import net.jini.core.transaction.server.CrashCountException;
import net.jini.core.lookup.ServiceTemplate;
import net.jini.core.lookup.ServiceRegistrar;
import net.jini.core.discovery.LookupLocator;
import java.rmi.RemoteException;
import java.rmi.RMISecurityManager;
import net.jini.export.ProxyAccessor;
import net.jini.export.*;
import net.jini.jeri.BasicJeriExporter;
import net.jini.jeri.BasicILFactory;
import net.jini.jeri.tcp.TcpServerEndpoint;
/**
 * PayableFileClassifierImpl.java
 */
public class PayableFileClassifierImpl extends FileClassifierImpl
    implements RemotePayableFileClassifier, TransactionParticipant, ProxyAccessor {
    protected TransactionManager mgr = null;
    protected Accounts accts = null;
    protected long crashCount = 0; // ???
    protected long cost = 10;
    protected final long myID = 54321;
    protected  TransactionParticipant proxy;
    public PayableFileClassifierImpl() throws java.rmi.RemoteException {
        super();
        System.setSecurityManager(new RMISecurityManager());
        try {
            Exporter exporter = new BasicJeriExporter
                                    (TcpServerEndpoint.getInstance(0),
                                     new BasicILFactory());
            proxy = (TransactionParticipant) exporter.export(this);
        } catch (Exception e) {

        }

    }
```

```java
    public void credit(long amount, long accountID,
                       TransactionManager mgr,
                       long transactionID) {
        System.out.println("crediting");
        this.mgr = mgr;
        // before findAccounts
        System.out.println("Joining txn");
        try {
            mgr.join(transactionID, proxy, crashCount);
        } catch(UnknownTransactionException e) {
            e.printStackTrace();
        } catch(CannotJoinException e) {
            e.printStackTrace();
        } catch(CrashCountException e) {
            e.printStackTrace();
        } catch(RemoteException e) {
            e.printStackTrace();
        }
        System.out.println("Joined txn");
        findAccounts();
        if (accts == null) {
            try {
                mgr.abort(transactionID);
            } catch(UnknownTransactionException e) {
                e.printStackTrace();
            } catch(CannotAbortException e) {
                e.printStackTrace();
            } catch(RemoteException e) {
                e.printStackTrace();
            }
        }
        try {
            accts.creditDebit(amount, accountID, myID,
                              transactionID, mgr);
        } catch(java.rmi.RemoteException e) {
            e.printStackTrace();
        }
    }
    public long getCost() {
        return cost;
    }
    protected void findAccounts() {
        // find a known account service
        LookupLocator lookup = null;
        ServiceRegistrar registrar = null;
        try {
            lookup = new LookupLocator("jini://localhost");
```

```
            } catch(java.net.MalformedURLException e) {
                System.err.println("Lookup failed: " + e.toString());
                System.exit(1);
            }
            try {
                registrar = lookup.getRegistrar();
            } catch (java.io.IOException e) {
                System.err.println("Registrar search failed: " + e.toString());
                System.exit(1);
            } catch (java.lang.ClassNotFoundException e) {
                System.err.println("Registrar search failed: " + e.toString());
                System.exit(1);
            }
            System.out.println("Registrar found");
            Class[] classes = new Class[] {Accounts.class};
            ServiceTemplate template = new ServiceTemplate(null, classes,
                                                    null);
            try {
                accts = (Accounts) registrar.lookup(template);
            } catch(java.rmi.RemoteException e) {
                System.exit(2);
            }
        }
        public MIMEType getMIMEType(String fileName) throws RemoteException {
            if (mgr == null) {
                // don't process the request
                return null;
            }
            return super.getMIMEType(fileName);
        }
        public int prepare(TransactionManager mgr, long id) {
            System.out.println("Preparing...");
            return TransactionConstants.PREPARED;
        }
        public void commit(TransactionManager mgr, long id) {
            System.out.println("committing");
        }
        public void abort(TransactionManager mgr, long id) {
            System.out.println("aborting");
        }
        public int prepareAndCommit(TransactionManager mgr, long id) {
            int result = prepare(mgr, id);
            if (result == TransactionConstants.PREPARED) {
                commit(mgr, id);
                result = TransactionConstants.COMMITTED;
            }
            return result;
```

```
    }
    public Object getProxy() {
        return proxy;
    }
} // PayableFileClassifierImpl
```

The server for this implementation uses the variation that it gets the service proxy from the service. Code to do this was illustrated in the server in Chapter 16 and is not repeated here.

AccountsImpl

Let's assume that all accounts in this example are managed by a single Accounts service that knows about all accounts via a long identifier. These accounts should be stored in a permanent form, there should be proper crash recovery mechanisms, and so on. For simplicity, we will just have a hash table of accounts, with uncommitted transactions kept in a "pending" list. When a commit occurs, the pending transaction takes place.

The Accounts service joins the transaction when creditDebit() is called. It is passed the transaction manager as a parameter in this call. Figure 23-4 shows the AccountsImpl class diagram.

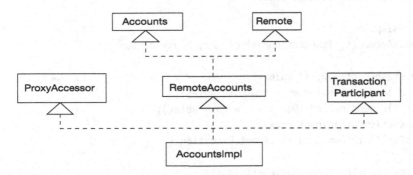

Figure 23-4. *Class diagram for Accounts*

The Accounts interface is

```
/**
 * Accounts.java
 */
package common;
import net.jini.core.transaction.server.TransactionManager;
public interface Accounts  {

    void creditDebit(long amount, long creditorID,
                     long debitorID, long transactionID,
                     TransactionManager tm)
        throws java.rmi.RemoteException;

} // Accounts
```

and the implementation is

```java
/**
 * AccountsImpl.java
 */
package txn;
// import common.Accounts;
import net.jini.core.transaction.server.TransactionManager;
import net.jini.core.transaction.server.TransactionParticipant;
import net.jini.core.transaction.server.TransactionConstants;
import java.util.Hashtable;
import net.jini.export.ProxyAccessor;
import net.jini.export.*;
import net.jini.jeri.BasicJeriExporter;
import net.jini.jeri.BasicILFactory;
import net.jini.jeri.tcp.TcpServerEndpoint;
// debug
import net.jini.core.lookup.ServiceTemplate;
import net.jini.core.lookup.ServiceRegistrar;
import net.jini.core.discovery.LookupLocator;
// end debug
public class AccountsImpl
    implements RemoteAccounts, TransactionParticipant, ProxyAccessor {

    protected long crashCount = 0; // value??
    protected Hashtable accountBalances = new Hashtable();
    protected Hashtable pendingCreditDebit = new Hashtable();
    protected  TransactionParticipant proxy;
    public AccountsImpl() throws java.rmi.RemoteException {
        try {
            Exporter exporter = new BasicJeriExporter
                                    (TcpServerEndpoint.getInstance(0),
                                     new BasicILFactory());
            proxy = (TransactionParticipant) exporter.export(this);
        } catch (Exception e) {

        }
    }
    public void creditDebit(long amount, long creditorID,
                            long debitorID, long transactionID,
                            TransactionManager mgr) {

        try {
            System.out.println("Trying to join");
            mgr.join(transactionID, proxy, crashCount);
        } catch(net.jini.core.transaction.UnknownTransactionException e) {
            e.printStackTrace();
```

```
        } catch(java.rmi.RemoteException e) {
            e.printStackTrace();
        } catch(net.jini.core.transaction.server.CrashCountException e) {
            e.printStackTrace();
        } catch(net.jini.core.transaction.CannotJoinException e) {
            e.printStackTrace();
        }
        System.out.println("joined");
        pendingCreditDebit.put(new TransactionPair(mgr,
                                                    transactionID),
                            new CreditDebit(amount, creditorID,
                                            debitorID));
    }
    public int prepare(TransactionManager mgr, long id) {
        System.out.println("Preparing...");
        return TransactionConstants.PREPARED;
    }
    public void commit(TransactionManager mgr, long id) {
        System.out.println("committing");
    }
    public void abort(TransactionManager mgr, long id) {
        System.out.println("aborting");
    }
    public int prepareAndCommit(TransactionManager mgr, long id) {
        int result = prepare(mgr, id);
        if (result == TransactionConstants.PREPARED) {
            commit(mgr, id);
            result = TransactionConstants.COMMITTED;
        }
        return result;
    }
    class CreditDebit {
        long amount;
        long creditorID;
        long debitorID;
        CreditDebit(long a, long c, long d) {
            amount = a;
            creditorID = c;
            debitorID = d;
        }
    }
    class TransactionPair {
        TransactionPair(TransactionManager mgr, long id) {
        }
    }
    public Object getProxy() {
```

```
        return proxy;
    }
} // AccountsImpl
```

The server for this implementation is standard and so its code is omitted.

Client

The final component in this example is the client that starts the transaction. The simplest code for the client would just use the blocking lookup() method of ClientLookupManager to find first the service and then the transaction manager. We use the longer way to show various other ways of doing things. This implementation uses a nested class that extends Thread. Because of this, it cannot extend UnicastRemoteObject, and so is not automatically exported. In order to export itself, it has to call UnicastRemoteObject.exportObject. This must be done before the call to join the transaction, which expects a remote object.

```
package client;
import common.PayableFileClassifier;
import common.MIMEType;
import java.rmi.RMISecurityManager;
import net.jini.discovery.LookupDiscovery;
import net.jini.discovery.DiscoveryListener;
import net.jini.discovery.DiscoveryEvent;
import net.jini.core.lookup.ServiceRegistrar;
import net.jini.core.lookup.ServiceTemplate;
import net.jini.core.transaction.server.TransactionManager;
import net.jini.core.transaction.server.TransactionConstants;
import net.jini.core.transaction.server.TransactionParticipant;
import net.jini.lease.LeaseRenewalManager;
import net.jini.core.lease.Lease;
import net.jini.lookup.entry.Name;
import net.jini.core.entry.Entry;
import java.rmi.RemoteException;
import java.rmi.server.UnicastRemoteObject;
import net.jini.core.lookup.ServiceTemplate;
import net.jini.discovery.LookupDiscoveryManager;
import net.jini.lookup.ServiceDiscoveryManager;
import net.jini.core.lookup.ServiceItem;
import net.jini.lease.LeaseRenewalManager;
import net.jini.export.*;
import net.jini.jeri.BasicJeriExporter;
import net.jini.jeri.BasicILFactory;
import net.jini.jeri.tcp.TcpServerEndpoint;
import java.rmi.server.ExportException;
/**
 * TestTxn.java
 */
public class TestTxn implements TransactionParticipant {
```

```
private static final long WAITFOR = 100000L;
long crashCount = 0;
PayableFileClassifier classifier = null;
TransactionManager mgr = null;
long myClientID; // my account ID
public static void main(String argv[]) {
    new TestTxn();
    // stay around long enough to receive replies
    try {
        Thread.currentThread().sleep(100000L);
    } catch(java.lang.InterruptedException e) {
        // do nothing
    }
}
public TestTxn() {
    System.setSecurityManager(new RMISecurityManager());
    classifier = findClassifier();
    long cost = 0;
    try {
        cost = classifier.getCost();
    } catch(java.rmi.RemoteException e) {
        e.printStackTrace();
    }
    if (cost > 20) {
        System.out.println("Costs too much: " + cost);
        classifier = null;
    }

    mgr = findTxnMgr();
    TransactionManager.Created tcs = null;

    System.out.println("Creating transaction");
    try {
        tcs = mgr.create(Lease.FOREVER);
    } catch(java.rmi.RemoteException e) {
        mgr = null;
        return;
    } catch(net.jini.core.lease.LeaseDeniedException e) {
        mgr = null;
        return;
    }

    long transactionID = tcs.id;

    // join in ourselves
    System.out.println("Joining transaction");
    // we need to give a proxy to the transaction mgr
```

```java
Exporter exporter = new BasicJeriExporter(TcpServerEndpoint.getInstance(0),
                                          new BasicILFactory());
// export an object of this class
TransactionParticipant proxy = null;
try {
    proxy = (TransactionParticipant) exporter.export(this);
} catch (ExportException e) {
    e.printStackTrace();
    System.exit(1);
}
try {
    mgr.join(transactionID, proxy, crashCount);
} catch(net.jini.core.transaction.UnknownTransactionException e) {
    e.printStackTrace();
} catch(java.rmi.RemoteException e) {
    e.printStackTrace();
} catch(net.jini.core.transaction.server.CrashCountException e) {
    e.printStackTrace();
} catch(net.jini.core.transaction.CannotJoinException e) {
    e.printStackTrace();
}

new LeaseRenewalManager().renewUntil(tcs.lease,
                                     Lease.FOREVER,
                                     null);
System.out.println("crediting...");
try {
    classifier.credit(cost, myClientID,
                      mgr, transactionID);
} catch(Exception e) {
    System.err.println(e.toString());
}

System.out.println("classifying...");
MIMEType type = null;
try {
    type = classifier.getMIMEType("file1.txt");
} catch(java.rmi.RemoteException e) {
    System.err.println(e.toString());
}

// if we get a good result, commit; else abort
if (type != null) {
    System.out.println("Type is " + type.toString());
    System.out.println("Calling commit");

    try {
```

```
                System.out.println("mgr state " + mgr.getState(transactionID));
                mgr.commit(transactionID);
            } catch(Exception e) {
                e.printStackTrace();
            }

        } else {
            try {
                mgr.abort(transactionID);
            } catch(java.rmi.RemoteException e) {
            } catch(net.jini.core.transaction.CannotAbortException e) {
            } catch( net.jini.core.transaction.UnknownTransactionException e) {
            }
        }
    }
}

public PayableFileClassifier findClassifier() {
    ServiceDiscoveryManager clientMgr = null;
    try {
        LookupDiscoveryManager mgr =
            new LookupDiscoveryManager(LookupDiscovery.ALL_GROUPS,
                                    null, // unicast locators
                                    null); // DiscoveryListener
        clientMgr = new ServiceDiscoveryManager(mgr,
                                    new LeaseRenewalManager());
    } catch(Exception e) {
        e.printStackTrace();
        System.exit(1);
    }

    Class [] classes = new Class[] {PayableFileClassifier.class};
    ServiceTemplate template = new ServiceTemplate(null, classes,
                                            null);
    ServiceItem item = null;
    // Try to find the service, blocking until timeout if necessary
    try {
        item = clientMgr.lookup(template,
                            null, // no filter
                            WAITFOR); // timeout
    } catch(Exception e) {
        e.printStackTrace();
        System.exit(1);
    }
    if (item == null) {
        // couldn't find a service in time
        System.out.println("no service");
        System.exit(1);
```

```
        }
        // Get the service
        PayableFileClassifier classifier = (PayableFileClassifier) item.service;
        if (classifier == null) {
            System.out.println("Classifier null");
            System.exit(1);
        }
        return classifier;
    }
    public TransactionManager findTxnMgr() {
        ServiceDiscoveryManager clientMgr = null;
        try {
            LookupDiscoveryManager mgr =
                new LookupDiscoveryManager(LookupDiscovery.ALL_GROUPS,
                                            null, // unicast locators
                                            null); // DiscoveryListener
            clientMgr = new ServiceDiscoveryManager(mgr,
                                        new LeaseRenewalManager());
        } catch(Exception e) {
            e.printStackTrace();
            System.exit(1);
        }

        Class [] classes = new Class[] {TransactionManager.class};
        ServiceTemplate template = new ServiceTemplate(null, classes,
                                            null);
        ServiceItem item = null;
        // Try to find the service, blocking until timeout if necessary
        try {
            item = clientMgr.lookup(template,
                                null, // no filter
                                WAITFOR); // timeout
        } catch(Exception e) {
            e.printStackTrace();
            System.exit(1);
        }
        if (item == null) {
            // couldn't find a service in time
            System.out.println("no service");
            System.exit(1);
        }
        // Get the service
        TransactionManager mgr = (TransactionManager) item.service;
        if (mgr == null) {
            System.out.println("Mgr null");
            System.exit(1);
        }
```

```java
        return mgr;
    }
    public int prepare(TransactionManager mgr, long id) {
        System.out.println("Preparing...");
        return TransactionConstants.PREPARED;
    }

    public void commit(TransactionManager mgr, long id) {
        System.out.println("committing");
    }


    public void abort(TransactionManager mgr, long id) {
        System.out.println("aborting");

    }

    public int prepareAndCommit(TransactionManager mgr, long id) {
        int result = prepare(mgr, id);
        if (result == TransactionConstants.PREPARED) {
            commit(mgr, id);
            result = TransactionConstants.COMMITTED;
        }
        return result;
    }
} // TestTxn
```

Summary

Transactions are needed to coordinate changes of state across multiple clients and services.
The Jini transaction model uses a simple model of transactions, with semantics details left to
the clients and services. The Jini distribution supplies a transaction manager that can be used
to assist the process.

■ ■ ■

CHAPTER 24

User Interfaces for Jini Services

Jini is designed to allow client programs to discover and interact with services. There is no user interface explicitly involved in this, although many clients will have a user interface to talk to a user. However, services may wish to offer a user interface for a client to show to a user. This could be for many reasons, such as extended functionality, or to give the service a particular look and feel.

In this chapter, we look at how a service can advertise user interfaces, how a client can choose an appropriate interface, and how the client can use a service's user interface.

User Interfaces As Entries

Interaction with a service is specified by its interface, and this is the same across all implementations of the interface. Just using the known interface doesn't allow any flexibility in using the service, because a client will only know about the methods defined in the interface. The interface is the defining level for using any service that implements the interface, but services can be implemented in many different ways, and service implementations do, in fact, differ. There is a need to allow for these differences, and the mechanism used in Jini is to put the differences in Entry objects. Typical objects supplied by vendors may include Name and ServiceInfo.

Clients can make use of the interface and these additional entry items, primarily in the selection of a service. But once clients have the service, are they constrained to use it via the type interface? The type interface is designed to allow a client application to use the service in a programmatic way by calling methods. However, many services could probably benefit from some sort of user interface. For example, a printer may supply a method to print a file, but it may have the capability to print multiple copies of the same file. Rather than relying on the client to be smart enough to figure this out, the printer vendor may want to call attention to the capability by supplying a user interface object with a special component for "number of copies."

The user interface for a service cannot expect to have all details supplied by the client—at best, a client could only manage a fairly generic user interface. The user interface should come from the vendor, or maybe even a third party (when your video player becomes Jini enabled, for example, it would be a godsend for *someone* to supply a decent user interface for it, since the video player vendors seem generally incapable of doing so!). The Entry objects are not just restricted to providing static data; as Java objects they are perfectly capable of running as user interface objects.

User Interfaces from Factory Objects

Chapter 15 discussed the location of code, using user interface components as examples. The chapter suggested that user interfaces should not be created on the server side but on the client side. So the user interface should be exported as a *factory* object that can create the user interface on the client side. More arguments can be given to support this:

- A service exported from a low-resource computer, such as an embedded Java engine, may not have the classes on the service side needed to create the user interface (e.g., it may not have the Swing or even the AWT libraries).

- There may be many potential user interfaces for any particular service. For example, the Palm Pilot, with its small grayscale screen, requires a different interface from a high-end workstation with huge screen and enormous number of colors. It is not reasonable to expect the service to create every possible interface, but it could export factories capable of doing so.

- Localization of internationalized services cannot be done on the service side, only on the client side.

The service should export zero or more user interface factories, with methods to create the interface, such as getJFrame(). The service and its user interface factory entry will both be retrieved by the client. The client will then create the user interface. Note that the factory will not know the service object beforehand—if it was given one during *its* construction (on the service side), it would end up with a service-side copy of the service instead of a client-side copy. So when it is asked for a user interface (on the client side), it should be passed the service as well in a parameter to user interface creation. In fact, it should probably be passed all of the information about the service, as retrieved in the ServiceItem obtained from a lookup service.

A typical factory is the one that returns a JFrame. This is defined as follows:

```
package net.jini.lookup.ui.factory;
import javax.swing.JFrame;
public interface JFrameFactory {
    String TOOLKIT = "javax.swing";
    String TYPE_NAME = "net.jini.lookup.ui.factory.JFrameFactory";
    JFrame getJFrame(Object roleObject);
}
```

The factory imports the minimum number of classes for the interface to compile and be exported. An implementation of this interface will probably use many more. The roleObject passes in any necessary information to the UI constructor. This is usually the ServiceItem, which contains all the information (including the service) that was retrieved from a lookup service. The factory can then create a UI that acts as an interface to the service, and it can use any additional information in the ServiceItem, such as entries for ServiceInfo or ServiceType, which could be shown, say, in an About box.

A factory that returns a visual component such as this should not make the component visible, in order to allow the component's size and placement to be set before showing it. Similarly, a "playable" UI, such as an audio file, should not be in a playing state.

Current Factories

A service may supply lots of factories, each capable of creating a different user interface object. This is to allow for the differing capabilities of viewing devices, or even for different user preferences. For instance, one user may prefer a web-style interface, another may be content with an AWT interface, a third may want the accessibility mechanisms possible with a Swing interface, and so on.

The set of factories currently includes the following:

- `DialogFactory` returns an instance of `java.awt.Dialog` (or one of its subclasses), which depends on AWT but not Swing.

- `FrameFactory` returns an instance of `java.awt.Frame` (or one of its subclasses), which depends on AWT but not Swing.

- `JComponentFactory` returns an instance of `javax.swing.JComponent` (or one of its subclasses, such as a `JList`).

- `JDialogFactory` returns an instance of `javax.swing.JDialog` (or one of its subclasses).

- `JFrameFactory` returns an instance of `javax.swing.JFrame` (or one of its subclasses).

- `JWindowFactory` returns an instance of `javax.swing.JWindow` (or one of its subclasses).

- `PanelFactory` returns an instance of `java.awt.Panel` (or one of its subclasses), which depends on AWT but not Swing.

- `WindowFactory` returns an instance of `java.awt.Window` (or one of its subclasses), which depends on AWT but not Swing.

These factories can be extended by any user, but to allow wide understanding, any new factories should be approved by the Jini community.

These factories are all defined as interfaces. An implementation will define a getXXX() method that will return a user interface object. The current set of factories returns objects that belong to the Swing or AWT classes. Factories added in later iterations of the specification may return objects belonging to other user interface styles, such as speech objects. Although an interface may specify that a method such as getJFrame() will return a JFrame, an implementation will in fact return a subclass of this, which also implements a *role* interface.

Marshalling Factories

There may be many factories for a service, and each of them will generate a different user interface. These factories and their user interfaces will be different for each service. The standard factory interfaces will probably be known to both clients and services, but the actual implementations of these interfaces will be known only to services (or maybe to third-party vendors who add a user interface to a service).

If a client receives a ServiceItem containing entries with many factory implementation objects, it will need to download the class files for all of these, as it instantiates the entry objects. There is a strong chance that each factory may be bundled into a .jar file that also contains the user interface objects themselves. So if the entries directly contain the factories, then the client will need to download a set of class files, before it even goes about the business of deciding which of the possible user interfaces it wants to select.

This downloading may take time on a slow connection, such as a wireless or home network link. It may also cost memory, which might be scarce in small devices such as PDAs. So it is advantageous to hide the actual factory classes until the client has decided that it does in fact want a particular class. Then, of course, it will have to download all of the class files needed by that factory.

Factories are wrapped in a MarshalledObject so they are hidden. The MarshalledObject keeps a representation of the factory, and also a reference to its codebase, so that when it is unwrapped the necessary classes can be located and downloaded. By putting the factory into entries in this form, no attempt is made to download its classes until it is unmarshalled.

The decision as to whether or not to unmarshall a class can be made based on a separate piece of information, such as a set of Strings that hold the names of the factory class (and all of its superclasses and interfaces). This level of indirection is a bit of a nuisance, but it's manageable:

```
if (typeNames.contains("net.jini.lookup.ui.factory.JFrameFactory") {
    factory = (JFrameFactory) marshalledObject.get();
    ....
}
```

A client that does not want to use a JFrameFactory will just not perform this test, unmarshalling, or attempted coercion. Using strings isn't really type-safe, and it does place a responsibility on service-side programmers to ensure this coercion will be correct. In effect, this maneuver circumvents the type-safe model of Java purely for optimization purposes.

There is one final wrinkle involved in loading the class files for a factory: a running JVM may have many class loaders. When loading the files for a factory, you will want to make sure that the class loader is one that will actually download the class files across the network as required. The class loader associated with the service itself will be the most appropriate for this.

UIDescriptor

An entry for a factory must contain the factory itself hidden in a MarshalledObject and some string representation of the factory's class(es). It may need other descriptive information about the factory. The UIDescriptor captures all this:

```
package net.jini.lookup.entry;
public class UIDescriptor extends AbstractEntry {
    public String role;
    public String toolkit;
    public Set attributes;
    public MarshalledObject factory;
    public UIDescriptor();
    public UIDescriptor(String role, String toolkit,
                        Set attributes, MarshalledObject factory);
    public final Object getUIFactory(ClassLoader parentLoader)
        throws IOException, ClassNotFoundException;
}
```

I haven't mentioned several features in the UIDescriptor yet, and the factory's type appears to be missing (it is one of the attributes). The second constructor has four parameters: role, toolkit, attributes, and factory. We have already discussed the factory. The following sections now discuss the other three.

Toolkit

A user interface will typically require a particular package to be present or it will just not function. For example, a factory that creates a JFrame will require the javax.swing package. This package can provide a quick filter on whether or not to accept a factory: if the factory is based on a package the client doesn't have, then the client can just reject this factory.

This isn't a bulletproof means of selection. For example, the Java Media Framework (JMF) is a fixed-size package designed to handle lots of different media types. So if your user interface is a QuickTime movie, then you might specify the JMF package. However, the media types the JMF handles are not fixed and can depend on native code libraries. For example, the current Solaris version of the JMF package has a native code library to handle MPEG movies, which is not present in the Linux version. So having the package specified by the toolkit does not *guarantee* that the class files for this user interface will be present. It is primarily intended for narrowing lookups based on the UIs offered.

Role

There are many possible roles for a user interface; the role is intended to cover this. The role is specified as an interface, with one field, role, that is the fully qualified path name of the interface. There are currently three interfaces:

- The net.jini.lookup.ui.MainUI role is for the standard user interface used by ordinary clients of the service:

```
package net.jini.lookup.ui;
public interface MainUI {
    String ROLE = "net.jini.lookup.ui.MainUI";
}
```

- The net.jini.lookup.ui.AdminUI role is for use by the service's administrator:

```
package net.jini.lookup.ui;
public interface AdminUI {
    String ROLE = "net.jini.lookup.ui.AdminUI";
}
```

- The net.jini.lookup.ui.AboutUI role is for information about the service, which is presentable by a user interface object:

```
package net.jini.lookup.ui;
public interface AboutUI {
    String ROLE = "net.jini.lookup.ui.AboutUI";
}
```

A service will specify a role for each user interface it supplies. This role is given in a number of ways for different objects:

- The role field in the UIDescriptor must be set to the string ROLE of the role interface.

- The user interface indicates that it acts a role by implementing the particular role specified.

- The factory does not explicitly know about the role, but the factory contained in a UIDescriptor must produce a user interface implementing the role.

The service must ensure that the UIDescriptors it produces follows these rules, but how it actually does so is not specified. There are several possibilities, including the following:

- When a factory is created, the role is passed in through a constructor. It can then use this role to cast the roleObject in the getXXX() method to the expected class (currently this is always a ServiceItem).

- There could be different factories for different roles, and the UIDescriptor should have the right factory for that role.

The factory could perform some sanity checking if desired. Since all roleObjects are (presently) the service items, it could search through these for the UIDescriptor, and then check that its role matches what the factory expects.

There has been much discussion about role "flavors," such as an "expert" role or a "learner" role. This discussion has been deferred, as it's too complicated, at least for the first version of the specification.

Attributes

The attributes section of a UIDescriptor can carry any other information about the user interface object that is deemed useful. Currently this includes the following:

- A UIFactoryTypes contains a set of Strings for the fully qualified class names of the factory this entry contains. The current factory hierarchy is very shallow, so this may be just a singleton set, such as {JFrameFactory.TYPE_NAME}.

There is an unfortunate wrinkle with Java sets and Jini entries: the lookup matching mechanism for entries tests byte equality of serialized forms, and most implementations of the Set interface are not constant across all JVMs. So instead of common set types such as HashSet, you should use special types such as com.artima.lookup.util. ConsistentSet. This type has a constructor that takes a Set in its constructor, which makes already messy code a bit more messy:

```
Set attribs = new HashSet();
Set typeNames = new HashSet();
typeNames.add(JFrameFactory.TYPE_NAME);
typeNames = new ConsistentSet(typeNames);
attribs.add(new UIFactoryTypes(typeNames));
attribs = new ConsistentSet(attribs);
```

Note that a client is not usually interested in the actual type of the factory, but rather of the interface it implements. This is just like Jini services themselves, where we only need to know the methods that can be called, and we are not concerned with the implementation details.

- Inclusion of an `AccessibleUI` object is a statement that the user interface implements `javax.accessibility.Accessible` and that the user interface works well with assistive technologies.

- A `Locales` object specifies the locales supported by the user interface.

- A `RequiredPackages` object contains information about all of the packages that the user interface needs to run. This is not a guarantee that the user interface will actually run, nor is it a guarantee that the interface will be usable! But it may help a client decide whether or not to use a particular user interface.

File Classifier Example

The file classifier has been used throughout this book as a simple example of a service, to illustrate various features of Jini. We can use the file classifier here, too, by supplying simple user interfaces into the service. Such a user interface consists of a text field to enter a file name and a display of the MIME type of the file name. There is only a "main" role for this service, as no administration needs to be performed.

Figure 24-1 shows what a user interface for a file classifier could look like.

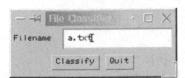

Figure 24-1. *File classifier user interface*

After the service has been invoked, it could pop up a dialog box as shown in Figure 24-2.

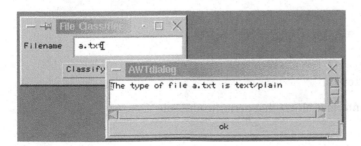

Figure 24-2. *File classifier return dialog box*

A factory for the "main" role that will produce an AWT Frame is as follows:

```java
/**
 * FileClassifierFrameFactory.java
 */
package ui;
import net.jini.lookup.ui.factory.FrameFactory;
import net.jini.lookup.entry.UIDescriptor;
import java.awt.Frame;
import net.jini.core.entry.Entry;
import net.jini.core.lookup.ServiceItem;
public class FileClassifierFrameFactory implements FrameFactory {
    /**
     * Return a new FileClassifierFrame that implements the
     * MainUI role
     */
    public Frame getFrame(Object roleObject) {
        // we should check to see what role we have to return
        if (! (roleObject instanceof ServiceItem)) {
            // unknown role type object
            // can we return null?
            return null;
        }
        ServiceItem item = (ServiceItem) roleObject;
        // Do sanity checking that the UIDescriptor has a MainUI role
        Entry[] entries = item.attributeSets;
        for (int n = 0; n < entries.length; n++) {
            if (entries[n] instanceof UIDescriptor) {
                UIDescriptor desc = (UIDescriptor) entries[n];
                if (desc.role.equals(net.jini.lookup.ui.MainUI.ROLE)) {
                    // OK, we are in the MainUI role, so return a UI for that
                    Frame frame = new FileClassifierFrame(item, "File Classifier");
                    return frame;
                }
            }
        }
        // couldn't find a role the factory can create
        return null;
    }
} // FileClassifierFrameFactory
```

The following is the user interface object that performs this role:

```java
/**
 * FileClassifierFrame.java
 */
package ui;
import java.awt.*;
```

```java
import java.awt.event.*;
import net.jini.lookup.ui.MainUI;
import net.jini.core.lookup.ServiceItem;
import common.MIMEType;
import common.FileClassifier;
import java.rmi.RemoteException;
/**
 * Object implementing MainUI for FileClassifier.
 */
public class FileClassifierFrame extends Frame implements MainUI {

    ServiceItem item;
    TextField text;
    public FileClassifierFrame(ServiceItem item, String name) {
        super(name);
        this.item = item;
        Panel top = new Panel();
        Panel bottom = new Panel();
        add(top, BorderLayout.CENTER);
        add(bottom, BorderLayout.SOUTH);

        top.setLayout(new BorderLayout());
        top.add(new Label("Filename"), BorderLayout.WEST);
        text = new TextField(20);
        top.add(text, BorderLayout.CENTER);
        bottom.setLayout(new FlowLayout());
        Button classify = new Button("Classify");
        Button quit = new Button("Quit");
        bottom.add(classify);
        bottom.add(quit);
        // listeners
        quit.addActionListener(new QuitListener());
        classify.addActionListener(new ClassifyListener());
        // We pack, but don't make it visible
        pack();
    }
    class QuitListener implements ActionListener {
        public void actionPerformed(ActionEvent evt) {
            System.exit(0);
        }
    }
    class ClassifyListener implements ActionListener {
        public void actionPerformed(ActionEvent evt) {
            String fileName = text.getText();
            final Dialog dlg = new Dialog((Frame) text.getParent().getParent());
            dlg.setLayout(new BorderLayout());
            TextArea response = new TextArea(3, 20);
```

```
                        // invoke service
                        FileClassifier classifier = (FileClassifier) item.service;
                        MIMEType type = null;
                        try {
                            type = classifier.getMIMEType(fileName);
                            if (type == null) {
                                response.setText("The type of file " + fileName +
                                                    " is unknown");
                            } else {
                                response.setText("The type of file " + fileName +
                                                    " is " + type.toString());
                            }
                        } catch(RemoteException e) {
                            response.setText(e.toString());
                        }
                        Button ok = new Button("ok");
                        ok.addActionListener(new ActionListener() {
                            public void actionPerformed(ActionEvent e) {
                                dlg.setVisible(false);
                            }
                        });
                        dlg.add(response, BorderLayout.CENTER);
                        dlg.add(ok, BorderLayout.SOUTH);
                        dlg.setSize(300, 100);
                        dlg.setVisible(true);
                    }
                }


} // FileClassifierFrame
```

The server that delivers both the service and the user interface has to prepare a
UIDescriptor. In this case, it creates only one such object for a single user interface, but
if the server exported more interfaces, then it would simply create more descriptors.

```
/**
 * FileClassifierServer.java
 */
package ui;
import complete.FileClassifierImpl;
import java.rmi.RMISecurityManager;
import net.jini.lookup.JoinManager;
import net.jini.core.lookup.ServiceID;
import net.jini.discovery.LookupDiscovery;
import net.jini.core.lookup.ServiceRegistrar;
import java.rmi.RemoteException;
import net.jini.lookup.ServiceIDListener;
import net.jini.lease.LeaseRenewalManager;
import net.jini.discovery.LookupDiscoveryManager;
```

```java
import net.jini.discovery.DiscoveryEvent;
import net.jini.discovery.DiscoveryListener;
import net.jini.core.entry.Entry;
import net.jini.lookup.ui.MainUI;
import net.jini.lookup.ui.factory.FrameFactory;
import net.jini.lookup.entry.UIDescriptor;
import net.jini.lookup.ui.attribute.UIFactoryTypes;
import java.rmi.MarshalledObject;
import java.io.IOException;
import java.util.Set;
import java.util.HashSet;
import com.artima.lookup.util.ConsistentSet;
public class FileClassifierServer
    implements ServiceIDListener {

    public static void main(String argv[]) {
        new FileClassifierServer();
        // stay around forever
        Object keepAlive = new Object();
        synchronized(keepAlive) {
            try {
                keepAlive.wait();
            } catch(InterruptedException e) {
                // do nothing
            }
        }
    }
    public FileClassifierServer() {
        System.setSecurityManager(new RMISecurityManager());
        JoinManager joinMgr = null;
        // The typenames for the factory
        Set typeNames = new HashSet();
        typeNames.add(FrameFactory.TYPE_NAME);
        typeNames = new ConsistentSet(typeNames);
        // The attributes set
        Set attribs = new HashSet();
        attribs.add(new UIFactoryTypes(typeNames));
        attribs = new ConsistentSet(attribs);
        // The factory
        MarshalledObject factory = null;
        try {
            factory = new MarshalledObject(new FileClassifierFrameFactory());
        } catch(Exception e) {
            e.printStackTrace();
            System.exit(2);
        }
```

```
                    UIDescriptor desc = new UIDescriptor(MainUI.ROLE,
                                              FileClassifierFrameFactory.TOOLKIT,
                                              attribs,
                                              factory);
            Entry[] entries = {desc};
            try {
                LookupDiscoveryManager mgr =
                    new LookupDiscoveryManager(LookupDiscovery.ALL_GROUPS,
                                          null,
                                          null);
                joinMgr = new JoinManager(new FileClassifierImpl(), /* service */
                                      entries /* attr sets */,
                                      this /* ServiceIDListener*/,
                                      mgr /* DiscoveryManagement */,
                                      new LeaseRenewalManager());
            } catch(Exception e) {
                e.printStackTrace();
                System.exit(1);
            }
        }
    public void serviceIDNotify(ServiceID serviceID) {
        // called as a ServiceIDListener
        // Should save the ID to permanent storage
        System.out.println("got service ID " + serviceID.toString());
    }

} // FileClassifierServer
```

Finally, a client needs to look for and use this user interface. The client finds a service as usual, and then it does a search through the Entry objects looking for a UIDescriptor. Once the client has a descriptor, it can check if that descriptor meets the requirements of the client. Here, we will check if it plays a MainUI role and can generate an AWT Frame:

```
package client;
import common.FileClassifier;
import common.MIMEType;
import java.rmi.RMISecurityManager;
import net.jini.discovery.LookupDiscovery;
import net.jini.core.lookup.ServiceTemplate;
import net.jini.discovery.LookupDiscoveryManager;
import net.jini.lookup.ServiceDiscoveryManager;
import net.jini.core.lookup.ServiceItem;
import net.jini.lease.LeaseRenewalManager;
import net.jini.core.entry.Entry;
import net.jini.lookup.ui.MainUI;
import net.jini.lookup.ui.factory.FrameFactory;
import net.jini.lookup.entry.UIDescriptor;
import net.jini.lookup.ui.attribute.UIFactoryTypes;
```

```java
import java.awt.*;
import javax.swing.*;
import java.util.Set;
import java.util.Iterator;
import java.net.URL;
/**
 * TestFrameUI.java
 */
public class TestFrameUI {
    private static final long WAITFOR = 100000L;
    public static void main(String argv[]) {
        new TestFrameUI();
        // stay around long enough to receive replies
        try {
            Thread.currentThread().sleep(2*WAITFOR);
        } catch(java.lang.InterruptedException e) {
            // do nothing
        }
    }

    public TestFrameUI() {
        ServiceDiscoveryManager clientMgr = null;
        System.setSecurityManager(new RMISecurityManager());
        try {
            LookupDiscoveryManager mgr =
                new LookupDiscoveryManager(LookupDiscovery.ALL_GROUPS,
                                           null /* unicast locators */,
                                           null /* DiscoveryListener */);
            clientMgr = new ServiceDiscoveryManager(mgr,
                                           new LeaseRenewalManager());
        } catch(Exception e) {
            e.printStackTrace();
            System.exit(1);
        }

        Class [] classes = new Class[] {FileClassifier.class};
        UIDescriptor desc = new UIDescriptor(MainUI.ROLE,
                                           FrameFactory.TOOLKIT,
                                           null, null);
        Entry [] entries = null; // {desc};
        ServiceTemplate template = new ServiceTemplate(null, classes,
                                                       entries);

        ServiceItem item = null;
        try {
            item = clientMgr.lookup(template,
                               null, /* no filter */
                               WAITFOR /* timeout */);
        } catch(Exception e) {
```

```
                    e.printStackTrace();
                    System.exit(1);
                }

            if (item == null) {
                // couldn't find a service in time
                System.out.println("no service");
                System.exit(1);
            }
            if (item.service == null) {
                // found a broken service
                System.out.println("service is null");
                System.exit(1);
            }
            // We now have a service that plays the MainUI role and
            // uses the FrameFactory toolkit of "java.awt".
            // We now have to find if there is a UIDescriptor
            // with a Factory generating an AWT Frame
            checkUI(item);
        }
        private void checkUI(ServiceItem item) {
            // Find and check the UIDescriptor's
            Entry[] attributes = item.attributeSets;
            for (int m = 0; m < attributes.length; m++) {
                Entry attr = attributes[m];
                if (attr instanceof UIDescriptor) {
                    // does it deliver an AWT Frame?
                    checkForAWTFrame(item, (UIDescriptor) attr);
                }
            }
        }


        private void checkForAWTFrame(ServiceItem item, UIDescriptor desc) {
            Set attributes = desc.attributes;
            Iterator iter = attributes.iterator();
            while (iter.hasNext()) {
                // search through the attributes, to find a UIFactoryTypes
                Object obj = iter.next();
                if (obj instanceof UIFactoryTypes) {
                    UIFactoryTypes types = (UIFactoryTypes) obj;
                    // see if it produces an AWT Frame Factory
                    if (types.isAssignableTo(FrameFactory.class)) {
                        FrameFactory factory = null;
                        try {
                            factory = (FrameFactory) desc.getUIFactory(this.getClass().
                                                        getClassLoader());
                        } catch(Exception e) {
```

```
                        e.printStackTrace();
                        continue;
                    }
                    System.out.println("calling frame with " + item);
                    Frame frame = factory.getFrame(item);
                    frame.setVisible(true);
                }
            }
        }
    }

} // TestFrameUI
```

■Note To use the service UI, additional classes are required that are not in the standard Jini distribution. These need to be downloaded from http://www.artima.com/jini/serviceui/index.html.

Images

User interfaces often contain images. They may be used as icons in toolbars, for general images on the screen, or for the application's desktop icon image. When a user interface is created on the client, these images will also need to be created and installed in the relevant part of the application. Images are not serializable, so they cannot be created on the server and exported as live objects in some manner. They need to be created from scratch on the client.

The Swing package contains the convenience class ImageIcon. This class can be instantiated from a byte array, a file name or, most interestingly, from a URL. So if an image is stored where an HTTP server can find it, then the ImageIcon constructor can use this image directly. There may be failures in this approach: the URL may be incorrect or malformed, or the image may fail to exist on the HTTP server. Suitable code is as follows:

```
ImageIcon icon = null;
try {
    icon = new ImageIcon(new URL("http://localhost/images/mindstorms.jpg"));
    switch (icon.getImageLoadStatus()) {
    case MediaTracker.ABORTED:
    case MediaTracker.ERRORED:
        System.out.println("Error");
        icon = null;
        break;
    case MediaTracker.COMPLETE:
        System.out.println("Complete");
        break;
    case MediaTracker.LOADING:
        System.out.println("Loading");
        break;
```

```
        }
    } catch(java.net.MalformedURLException e) {
        e.printStackTrace();
    }
    // icon is null or is a valid image
```

ServiceType

User interface code exported by the server may use the preceding code directly to include images. Alternatively, the service may supply useful images and other human-oriented information in a ServiceType entry object and leave it to the client to use it.

```
package net.jini.lookup.entry;
public class ServiceType {
    public String getDisplayName();        // Return the localized display
                                           // name of this service.
    public Image getIcon(int iconKind)     // Get an icon for this service.
    public String getShortDescription()    // Return a localized short
                                           // description of this service.
}
```

The class is supplied with empty implementations, returning null for each method. A service will need to supply a subclass of ServiceType with useful implementations of the methods. However, ServiceType is a useful class that could be used to supply images and information that may be common between a number of different user interfaces for a service, such as a minimized image.

Summary

The Jini specification from Sun did not include a specification for Jini user interfaces. The work described in this chapter was developed as a Jini Community standard. The key is that a user interface will be passed in an Entry. However, there are many considerations when taking this approach, such as not downloading classes that the client cannot handle. This chapter has examined these often subtle issues and shown how you can build user interfaces for services that can be used properly by clients.

CHAPTER 25

■■■

Activation

Many of the examples in earlier chapters use RMI/Jeri proxies for services. These services live within a server whose principal task is to keep the service alive and registered with lookup services. If the server fails to renew leases, then lookup services will eventually discard the proxy; if the server fails to keep itself and its service alive, then the service will not be available when a client wants to use it.

This results in a server and a service that most of the time will be idle, probably swapped out to disk, but still using virtual memory. Java memory requirements on the server side can be enormous. From JDK 1.2 onward, an extension to RMI called *activation* allows an idle object to be in a "dormant" state and brought to life when needed. In this way, the object does not occupy virtual memory while idle. Of course, another process needs to be alive to restore such objects, and RMI supplies the daemons rmid (in Jini 1.2) and phoenix (in Jini 2.0) to manage this. In effect, rmid/phoenix acts as another virtual memory manager as it stores information about dormant Java objects in its own files and restores them from there as needed.

There are serious limitations to rmid and phoenix: they are Java programs themselves, and when running they also use enormous amounts of memory. So it only makes sense to use them when you expect to be running a number of largely idle services on the same machine. When a service is brought to life, or *activated*, a new JVM may be started to run the object. This again increases memory use.

If memory use is the only concern, then a variety of other systems, such as echidna, which run multiple applications within a single JVM, may be adequate to solve memory issues. However, RMI activation is also designed to work with distributed objects, and it allows JVMs to hold remote references to objects that are no longer active. Instead of throwing a remote exception on trying to access these objects, the activation system tries to resurrect the object using rmid or phoenix to give a valid (and new) reference. Of course, if it fails to do this, it will throw an exception anyway.

The standard RMI activation system is supported by Jini 2.0, in the same way as it supports JRMP. But with the advent of Jeri, Jini 2.0 has a new version of activation with the phoenix activation server, which we'll cover in the next section. In the rest of the chapter, we'll look at how to build servers and services that use the activation system. We also look at more subtle issues such as nonlazy activation and how a system that is "reborn" each time can save state. If a service uses activation, then it will probably not be present to renew leases or to be discovered. We look at two additional Jini services, a LeaseRenewalService and a LookupDiscovertService, which can overcome these problems.

The phoenix Activation Server

phoenix replaces rmid in Jini 2.0. It comes in a variety of versions, depending on the protocol it supports. For example, if the services use Jeri, then phoenix should be configured to use Jeri also. Similarly, if the services use JRMP, then so should phoenix.

phoenix can be started by using the ServiceStarter or by shell scripts/batch files. Example scripts are given in the Jini distribution under the source/vob/jive/src/com/sun/jini/example/hello/scripts/ directory. For example, here is the shell script jeri-phoenix.sh, which starts the Jeri version of phoenix under Unix:

```
host=`hostname`
java -Djava.security.manager=                                    \
    -Djava.security.policy=config/phoenix.policy                 \
    -Djava.rmi.server.codebase=http://$host:8080/phoenix-dl.jar  \
    -DserverHost=$host                                           \
    -jar lib/phoenix.jar                                         \
    config/jeri-phoenix.config
```

And here is the batch file jrmp-phoenix.bat, which starts the Jeri version of phoenix under Windows:

```
java -Djava.security.manager= ^
    -Djava.security.policy=config\phoenix.policy ^
    -Djava.rmi.server.codebase=http://%computername%:8080/phoenix-dl.jar ^
    -DserverHost=%computername% ^
    -jar lib\phoenix.jar ^
    config\jrmp-phoenix.config
```

Each script file references a configuration script. A typical script such as config/jeri-phoenix.config contains the following:

```
com.sun.jini.phoenix {
    persistenceDirectory = "lib${/}phoenix-log";
    groupConfig = new String[] { "config${/}jeri-phoenix-group.config" };
}
```

which states the directory to store the activation log files and also a group configuration file, such as jeri-phoenix-group.config.

This file defines the protocol that will be used by phoenix (here, Jeri):

```
import com.sun.jini.phoenix.AccessILFactory;
import net.jini.jeri.BasicJeriExporter;
import net.jini.jeri.tcp.TcpServerEndpoint;
com.sun.jini.phoenix {
    instantiatorExporter =
        new BasicJeriExporter(TcpServerEndpoint.getInstance(0),
                              new AccessILFactory());
}
```

There is a little trap in running phoenix: it will create a new virtual machine for each different group. This new virtual machine will require several files, such as phoenix-init.jar, in its classpath. So it is not enough to specify phoenix.jar for phoenix—the phoenix-init.jar file must be in the classpath for any virtual machines created by phoenix, and this must be done for each activatable service. An alternative to explicitly setting the classpath is to copy the phoenix-init.jar file to the Java jre lib directory (as you probably did with jsk-policy.jar), but this approach is not really recommended. If the classpath is not set up, then when phoenix starts a new JVM, you will see errors such as the following:

```
Group-01: class not found ActivationInitGroup
```

The Sun documentation recommends including sharedvm.jar in the classpath, and the directory for this .jar file should also contain phoenix-init.jar and jsk-platform.jar.

A Service Using Activation

The major concepts in activation are the activatable object itself (which extends java.rmi.activation.Activatable) and the environment in which it runs, an ActivationGroup. A JVM may have an activation group associated with it. If an object needs to be activated and there is already a JVM running its group, then it is restarted within that JVM. Otherwise, a new JVM is started. An activation group may hold a number of cooperating objects.

In this section, we'll look in turn at building a service, building a server, and how to run these using the activation system.

Service

Making an object into an activatable object requires registering the object with the activation system by exporting it and using a special two-argument constructor that will be called when the object needs to be reconstructed. The constructor looks like this:

```
public ActivatableImpl(ActivationID id, MarshalledObject data)
    throws RemoteException {
    ...
}
```

Note The use of the marshalled data is discussed later in this chapter.

There is an important conceptual change from nonactivatable services. In a nonactivatable service, the server is able to create the service. In an activation system, the original server could have terminated and will not be available to start the service; instead, the activation server is responsible for starting the service. But the service still has to be exported, and it can't rely on the activation server to do that (e.g., it would have no knowledge of the protocol, such as Jeri, JRMP, or IIOP), so the service has to export itself. That is, within the constructor, the service must find an exporter and export itself. This is a change from "standard" activation as used in Jini 1.2, where many things were hidden from the programmer and it was not necessary to pay attention to the exporter.

That change in turn raises a problem: in a nonactivatable service, the server creates the service, gets a proxy by exporting the service, and then does things like register the proxy with lookup services. But if the export operation is buried within the service constructor, then a server cannot readily access it. This is the role of the ProxyAccessor interface: it supplies a method that a server can call on the service to give the proxy. Unless the service can do everything itself, it will usually need to implement this interface. (An exception to this occurs when the service is its own proxy; it just needs to be Serializable in that case.)

With these changes in place, the file classifier becomes

```java
package activation;
import net.jini.export.*;
import net.jini.jeri.BasicJeriExporter;
import net.jini.jeri.BasicILFactory;
import net.jini.jeri.tcp.TcpServerEndpoint;
import net.jini.activation.ActivationExporter;
import net.jini.jrmp.JrmpExporter;
import java.rmi.activation.ActivationID;
import java.rmi.MarshalledObject;
import net.jini.export.ProxyAccessor;
import common.MIMEType;
import common.FileClassifier;
import rmi.RemoteFileClassifier;
import java.rmi.Remote;
/**
 * FileClassifierImpl.java
 */
public class FileClassifierImpl implements RemoteFileClassifier,
                                           ProxyAccessor {
    private Remote proxy;
    public MIMEType getMIMEType(String fileName)
        throws java.rmi.RemoteException {
        if (fileName.endsWith(".gif")) {
            return new MIMEType("image", "gif");
        } else if (fileName.endsWith(".jpeg")) {
            return new MIMEType("image", "jpeg");
        } else if (fileName.endsWith(".mpg")) {
            return new MIMEType("video", "mpeg");
        } else if (fileName.endsWith(".txt")) {
            return new MIMEType("text", "plain");
        } else if (fileName.endsWith(".html")) {
            return new MIMEType("text", "html");
        } else
            // fill in lots of other types,
            // but eventually give up and
            return new MIMEType(null, null);
    }
```

```
    public FileClassifierImpl(ActivationID activationID, MarshalledObject data)
        throws java.rmi.RemoteException {
        Exporter exporter =
            new ActivationExporter(activationID,
                        new BasicJeriExporter(TcpServerEndpoint.getInstance(0),
                                            new BasicILFactory(),
                                            false, true));

        proxy = (Remote) exporter.export(this);
    }
    // Implementation for ProxyAccessor
    public Object getProxy() {
        return proxy;
    }
} // FileClassifierImpl
```

This listing makes explicit use of an exporter. Later we'll consider how managing the exporter could be done using a configuration.

Server

The server doesn't actually start the service—that is the task of a process such as phoenix. The server has to set up the parameters for the service so that phoenix will know how to handle it. These parameters may include the following:

- The activation group(s) the service will belong to.

- The security policy to run services in a particular activation group.

- The classpath for phoenix to run the service in a new JVM. Note that this classpath cannot be one that is relative to the server, since it will be used by phoenix.

- The codebase for the client to find the service (needed if the service registers itself with lookup services).

A service is run within an activation group. When a group is run in a new virtual machine, it may need explicit command-line options (such as setting the classpath or the stack size) and properties (such as a security policy). Of course, properties can be set as command-line arguments, too, but Java allows them to be set separately. For example, the command-line arguments can be set as follows:

```
String[] options = {"-classpath",
                    "activation.FileClassifierServer.jar"};
CommandEnvironment commEnv =
                    new CommandEnvironment(null, options);
```

The group parameters are set using an ActivationGroupDesc, which takes both a Properties list and a CommandEnvironment:

```
String[] options = {"-classpath",
                    "activation.FileClassifierServer.jar"};
ActivationGroupDesc.CommandEnvironment commEnv =
            new CommandEnvironment(null, options);
Properties props = new Properties();
props.put("java.security.policy",
          SECURITY_POLICY_FILE);
props.put("java.rmi.server.codebase",
          "http://192.168.1.13/classes/activation.FileClassifierServer-dl.jar");
ActivationGroupDesc group = new ActivationGroupDesc(props, commEnv);
```

Note Although the classpath shown references only the classes required for the server, in practice you may need to add more. For example, phoenix requires phoenix-init.jar, and other Jini class files may be required, too. The easiest way to work out what is required is to run the server and observe what phoenix complains about. Alternatively, include sharedvm.jar, which points to all likely .jar files that may be required by Sun's tools.

The next steps are to register the group and get a group ID from that. Then an activation description for the service is constructed that includes the group ID and the name of the service's class file. (Two other parameters are discussed later.) This service can then be registered with phoenix. At this point, the service is with phoenix, but it has not been initialized, so its constructor has not been called and there is no proxy for it. This means the service cannot yet be registered with a lookup service and cannot yet be found by any client. How, then, can you force it to be constructed? At this point, the server has an activation ID for the service from the registration. It uses this to ask phoenix to activate the service with the activate() method. The code looks like this:

```
ActivationGroupDesc group = new ActivationGroupDesc(props, commEnv);
ActivationGroupID groupID  = actSys.registerGroup(group);
ActivationGroup.createGroup(groupID, group, 0);
String codebase = "...";
MarshalledObject data = null;
ActivationDesc desc = null;
desc = new ActivationDesc(groupID,
                          "activation.FileClassifierImpl",
                          codebase, data, true);
ActivationID aid =  actSys.registerObject(desc);
Remote proxy = (Remote) aid.activate(true);
```

The server now has a proxy that it can register with lookup services. The server can terminate, since any calls on the service will be handled by phoenix, which will construct the service whenever a call to that service is made by a client. (I'll address later how the registration with lookup services is kept alive. If this server terminates, then it cannot do any lease renewals.)

The file classifier server that uses an activatable service is as follows:

```
package activation;
import java.rmi.Remote;
import net.jini.discovery.LookupDiscovery;
import net.jini.discovery.DiscoveryListener;
import net.jini.discovery.DiscoveryEvent;
import net.jini.core.lookup.ServiceRegistrar;
import net.jini.core.lookup.ServiceItem;
import net.jini.core.lookup.ServiceRegistration;
import net.jini.core.lease.Lease;
import java.rmi.RMISecurityManager;
import java.rmi.MarshalledObject;
import java.rmi.activation.ActivationDesc;
import java.rmi.activation.ActivationGroupDesc;
import java.rmi.activation.ActivationGroupDesc.CommandEnvironment;
import java.rmi.activation.Activatable;
import java.rmi.activation.ActivationGroup;
import java.rmi.activation.ActivationGroupID;
import java.rmi.activation.ActivationSystem;
import java.rmi.activation.ActivationID;
import java.util.Properties;
import java.rmi.activation.UnknownGroupException;
import java.rmi.activation.ActivationException;
import java.rmi.RemoteException;
/**
 * FileClassifierServer.java
 */
public class FileClassifierServer implements DiscoveryListener {
    static final protected String SECURITY_POLICY_FILE =
        "/home/httpd/html/java/jini/tutorial/policy.all";
    static final protected String CODEBASE =
        "http://192.168.1.13/classes/activation.FileClassifierServer-dl.jar";

    protected Remote proxy;

    public static void main(String argv[]) {
        new FileClassifierServer(argv);
        // stick around while lookup services are found
        try {
            Thread.sleep(100000L);
        } catch(InterruptedException e) {
            // do nothing
        }
        // the server doesn't need to exist anymore
        System.exit(0);
```

```
        }
        public FileClassifierServer(String[] argv) {
            // install suitable security manager
            System.setSecurityManager(new RMISecurityManager());
            ActivationSystem actSys = null;
            try {
                actSys = ActivationGroup.getSystem();
            } catch(ActivationException e) {
                e.printStackTrace();
                System.exit(1);
            }
            // Install an activation group
            String[] options = {"-classpath",
                "activation.FileClassifierServer-act.jar:phoenix-init.jar:jini-ext.jar"};
            CommandEnvironment commEnv =
                new CommandEnvironment(null, options);
            Properties props = new Properties();
            props.put("java.security.policy",
                SECURITY_POLICY_FILE);
            ActivationGroupDesc group = new ActivationGroupDesc(props, commEnv);
            ActivationGroupID groupID = null;
            try {
                groupID = actSys.registerGroup(group);
            } catch(RemoteException e) {
                e.printStackTrace();
                System.exit(1);
            } catch(ActivationException e) {
                e.printStackTrace();
                System.exit(1);
            }
            String codebase = CODEBASE;
            MarshalledObject data = null;
            ActivationDesc desc = null;
            desc = new ActivationDesc(groupID,
                                    "activation.FileClassifierImpl",
                                    codebase, data, true);

            ActivationID aid = null;
            try {
                aid = actSys.registerObject(desc);
            } catch(RemoteException e) {
                e.printStackTrace();
                System.exit(1);
            } catch(ActivationException e) {
                e.printStackTrace();
                System.exit(1);
            }
```

```
        try {
            proxy = (Remote) aid.activate(true);
        } catch(UnknownGroupException e) {
            e.printStackTrace();
            System.exit(1);
        } catch(ActivationException e) {
            e.printStackTrace();
            System.exit(1);
        } catch(RemoteException e) {
            e.printStackTrace();
            System.exit(1);
        }

    LookupDiscovery discover = null;
    try {
        discover = new LookupDiscovery(LookupDiscovery.ALL_GROUPS);
    } catch(Exception e) {
        System.err.println(e.toString());
        System.exit(1);
    }
    discover.addDiscoveryListener(this);
}

public void discovered(DiscoveryEvent evt) {
    ServiceRegistrar[] registrars = evt.getRegistrars();
    for (int n = 0; n < registrars.length; n++) {
        ServiceRegistrar registrar = registrars[n];
        // export the proxy service
        ServiceItem item = new ServiceItem(null,
                                           proxy,
                                           null);
        ServiceRegistration reg = null;
        try {
            reg = registrar.register(item, Lease.FOREVER);
        } catch(java.rmi.RemoteException e) {
            System.err.print("Register exception: ");
            e.printStackTrace();
            continue;
        }
        try {
            System.out.println("service registered at " +
                               registrar.getLocator().getHost());
        } catch(Exception e) {
        }
    }
}
```

```
    public void discarded(DiscoveryEvent evt) {
    }
} // FileClassifierServer
```

Running the Service

The service and the server must be compiled as usual. Nonactivatable services just require classes for the client and for the server. For activatable services, it is more complex: classes are required for the client, for the start-up server, and for phoenix.

The classes that are required by the client must be copied to an HTTP server. In this case, it is only the class file rmi/RemoteFileClassifier.class, if a protocol such as Jeri is used with proxy generation at runtime. If JRMP was used, the rmic compiler would need to be run on activation/FileClassifierImpl.class and the resultant proxy would also need to be copied to the HTTP server.

The classes needed by the start-up server are the file classifier server and the classes it needs. This gets a bit tricky. The server doesn't actually create the service at any time, so it doesn't need the class file for FileClassifierImpl. But when it activates the service, phoenix will create the service and return a proxy for it. This proxy will implement RemoteFileClassifier. So the server will need the class files to support a RemoteFileClassifier even though it doesn't explicitly create one. The files could be either in the server's classpath or in its codebase. This server uses the codebase as information in the proxy when it registers the service with a lookup service, so you don't want to put extra stuff in there for downloading to a client. Instead, the class files may be better off in the server's classpath.

- common/MIMEType.class

- common/FileClassifier.class

- rmi/RemoteFileClassifier.class

- activation/FileClassifierServer.class

Finally, the classes needed by phoenix are FileClassifierImpl and the classes it depends on, but not the start-up server:

- common/MIMEType.class

- common/FileClassifier.class

- rmi/RemoteFileClassifier.class

- activation/FileClassifierImpl.class

Before starting the service provider, a phoenix process must be set running on the same machine as the service provider. An HTTP server must be running on a machine as specified by the codebase property on the service. The service provider can then be started. This will register the service with phoenix and copy a proxy object to any lookup services found. The server can then terminate (as mentioned earlier, this causes the service's lease to expire, but techniques to handle this are described later).

In summary, typically three processes are involved in getting an activatable service running:

- The service provider, which specifies information about the service to phoenix.

- phoenix, which must be running on the same machine as the service provider and must be started before the service provider. It creates the service on demand.

- An HTTP server, which can be on a different machine and is pointed to by the codebase.

While the service remains registered with lookup services, clients can download its proxy. The service will be created on demand by phoenix. You need to run the server only once, since phoenix keeps information about the service in its own log files.

An Ant file to build, deploy, and run the service (but not phoenix) is activation. FileClassifierServer.xml:

```
<project name="activation.FileClassifierServer" default="usage">
    <!-- Inherits properties
        jini.home
        jini.jars
        src
        dist
        build
        httpd.classes
    -->
    <!-- files for this project -->
    <property name="src.files"
            value="common/MIMEType.java,
                common/FileClassifier.java,
                rmi/RemoteFileClassifier.java,
                activation/FileClassifierImpl.java
                activation/FileClassifierServer.java
                "/>
    <property name="class.files"
            value="
                common/MIMEType.class,
                common/FileClassifier.class,
                activation/FileClassifierServer.class
                "/>
    <property name="class.files.dl"
            value="
                rmi/RemoteFileClassifier.class
                "/>
    <property name="class.files.act"
            value="common/MIMEType.class,
                common/FileClassifier.class,
                rmi/RemoteFileClassifier.class,
                activation/FileClassifierImpl.class
                "/>
    <!-- <property name="no-dl" value="false"/> -->
    <!-- derived names - may be changed -->
```

```xml
        <property name="jar.file"
                value="${ant.project.name}.jar"/>
        <property name="jar.file.dl"
                value="${ant.project.name}-dl.jar"/>
        <property name="jar.file.act"
                value="${ant.project.name}-act.jar"/>
        <property name="main.class"
                value="${ant.project.name}"/>
    <property name="codebase"
                value="http://${localhost}/classes/${jar.file.dl}"/>
        <property name="jini.jars.start" value="${jini.jars}:${jini.home}/lib/
start.jar"/>
        <!-- targets -->
        <target name="all" depends="compile"/>
        <target name="compile">
            <javac destdir="${build}" srcdir="${src}"
                    classpath="${jini.jars.start}"
                    target="1.2"
                    includes="${src.files}">
            </javac>
        </target>
        <target name="dist" depends="compile"
                    description="generate the distribution">
            <jar jarfile="${dist}/${jar.file}"
                basedir="${build}"
                includes="${class.files}"/>
            <jar jarfile="${dist}/${jar.file.act}"
                    basedir="${build}"
                    includes="${class.files.act}"/>
            <antcall target="dist-jar-dl"/>
        </target>
        <target name="dist-jar-dl" unless="no-dl">
            <jar jarfile="${dist}/${jar.file.dl}"
                    basedir="${build}"
                    includes="${class.files.dl}"/>
        </target>
        <target name="build" depends="dist,compile"/>
        <target name="run" depends="build">
            <java classname="${main.class}"
                    fork="true"
                    classpath="${jini.jars}:${dist}/${jar.file}">
                <jvmarg value="-Djava.security.policy=${res}/policy.all"/>
                <jvmarg value="-Djava.rmi.server.codebase=${codebase}"/>
            </java>
        </target>
        <target name="deploy" depends="dist" unless="no-dl">
            <copy file="${dist}/${jar.file.dl}"
```

```
                todir="${httpd.classes}"/>
        <copy file="${dist}/${jar.file}"
                todir="${httpd.classes}"/>
    </target>
</project>
```

Nonlazy Services

The services just discussed are *lazy* services, meaning they are activated on demand when their methods are called. This reduces memory use at the expense of starting up a new JVM when required. Some services need to be continuously alive, but can still benefit from the log mechanism of phoenix. If phoenix crashes and is restarted, or the machine is rebooted and phoenix restarts, then it is able to use its log files to restart any "active" services registered with it, as well as restore lazy services on demand. Putting even active services under the activation system can help programmers avoid messing around with boot configuration files, by just ensuring that phoenix is started on reboot.

Maintaining State

An activatable object is created afresh each time a method is called on it, using its two-argument constructor. As a result, the object is created in the same state on each activation. However, method calls on objects (apart from get...() methods) usually result in a change of state of the object. Activatable objects will need some way of reflecting this change on each activation, and this is typically done by saving and restoring state using a disk file.

When an object is activated, one of the parameters passed to it is a MarshalledObject instance. This is the same object that was passed to the activation system in the ActivationDesc parameter to ActivationSystem.registerObject(). This object does not change between different activations, so it cannot hold changing state, but only data that is fixed for all activations. A simple use for MarshalledObject is to hold the name of a file that can be used for state. Then on each activation, the object can restore state by reading stored information, and on each subsequent method call that changes state, the information in the file can be overwritten.

The mutable file classifier, which was discussed in Chapter 16, can be sent addType() and removeType() messages. It begins with a given set of MIME type/file extension mappings. State here is very simple: it just stores all the file extensions and their corresponding MIME type in a Map. If you turn this service into an activatable object, you store the state by just storing the map. The state can be saved to disk using ObjectOutputStream.writeObject() and retrieved by ObjectInputStream.readObject(). More complex cases might require more complex storage methods.

The very first time a mutable file classifier starts on a particular host, it should build its initial state file. A variety of methods can be used to achieve this. For example, if the state file does not exist, then the first activation could detect this and construct the initial state at that time. Alternatively, a method such as init() could be defined, to be called once after the object has been registered with the activation system.

The "normal" way of instantiating an object—through a constructor—doesn't work too well with activatable objects. If a constructor for a class doesn't start by calling another constructor with this(...) or super(...), then the no-argument superclass constructor super() is called. But the class Activatable doesn't have a no-args constructor, so you can't subclass from Activatable *and* have a constructor such as FileClassifierMutable(String stateFile) that doesn't use the activation system. You can avoid this problem by not inheriting from Activatable, and register explicitly with the activation system with the following, for example:

```
public FileClassifierMutable(ActivationID id,
        MarshalledObject data) throws java.rmi.RemoteException {
    Activatable.exportObject(this, id, 0);
    // continue with instantiation
```

This is a bit clumsy in use, as you create an object solely to build up initial state, and then discard it because the activation system will re-create it on demand.

The technique adopted in this example is to create initial state if the attempt to restore state from the state file fails for any reason as the object is activated. This is done in the restoreMap() method, which is called from the constructor FileClassifierMutable (ActivationID id, MarshalledObject data). The name of the file is extracted from the marshalled object passed in as a parameter.

```
package activation;
import java.io.*;
import java.rmi.activation.Activatable;
import java.rmi.activation.ActivationID;
import java.rmi.MarshalledObject;
import java.rmi.Remote;
import java.rmi.activation.ActivationID;
import net.jini.core.event.RemoteEventListener;
import net.jini.core.event.RemoteEvent;
import net.jini.core.event.EventRegistration;
import java.rmi.RemoteException;
import net.jini.core.event.UnknownEventException ;
import net.jini.export.ProxyAccessor;
import net.jini.export.*;
import net.jini.jeri.BasicJeriExporter;
import net.jini.jeri.BasicILFactory;
import net.jini.jeri.tcp.TcpServerEndpoint;
import net.jini.activation.ActivationExporter;
import javax.swing.event.EventListenerList;
import common.MIMEType;
import common.MutableFileClassifier;
import mutable.RemoteFileClassifier;
import java.util.Map;
import java.util.HashMap;
/**
 * FileClassifierMutable.java
 */
public class FileClassifierMutable implements RemoteFileClassifier,
                                              ProxyAccessor {
    private Remote proxy;
```

```
/**
 * Map of String extensions to MIME types
 */
private Map map = new HashMap();
/**
 * Permanent storage for the map while inactive
 */
private String mapFile;
/**
 * Listeners for change events
 */
private EventListenerList listenerList = new EventListenerList();
public MIMEType getMIMEType(String fileName)
    throws java.rmi.RemoteException {
    System.out.println("Called with " + fileName);
    MIMEType type;
    String fileExtension;
    int dotIndex = fileName.lastIndexOf('.');
    if (dotIndex == -1 || dotIndex + 1 == fileName.length()) {
        // can't find suitable suffix
        return null;
    }
    fileExtension= fileName.substring(dotIndex + 1);
    type = (MIMEType) map.get(fileExtension);
    return type;
}
public void addType(String suffix, MIMEType type)
    throws java.rmi.RemoteException {
    map.put(suffix, type);
    fireNotify(MutableFileClassifier.ADD_TYPE);
    saveMap();
}
public void removeType(String suffix)
    throws java.rmi.RemoteException {
    if (map.remove(suffix) != null) {
        fireNotify(MutableFileClassifier.REMOVE_TYPE);
        saveMap();
    }
}
public EventRegistration addRemoteListener(RemoteEventListener listener)
    throws java.rmi.RemoteException {
    listenerList.add(RemoteEventListener.class, listener);
    return new EventRegistration(0, this, null, 0);
}
// Notify all listeners that have registered interest for
// notification on this event type.  The event instance
// is lazily created using the parameters passed into
// the fire method.
```

```
    protected void fireNotify(long eventID) {
        RemoteEvent remoteEvent = null;

        // Guaranteed to return a non-null array
        Object[] listeners = listenerList.getListenerList();

        // Process the listeners last to first, notifying
        // those that are interested in this event
        for (int i = listeners.length - 2; i >= 0; i -= 2) {
            if (listeners[i] == RemoteEventListener.class) {
                RemoteEventListener listener = (RemoteEventListener) listeners[i+1];
                if (remoteEvent == null) {
                    remoteEvent = new RemoteEvent(this, eventID,
                                                  0L, null);
                }
                try {
                    listener.notify(remoteEvent);
                } catch(UnknownEventException e) {
                    e.printStackTrace();
                } catch(RemoteException e) {
                    e.printStackTrace();
                }
            }
        }
    }
    /**
     * Restore map from file.
     * Install default map if any errors occur
     */
    public void restoreMap() {
        try {
            FileInputStream istream = new FileInputStream(mapFile);
            ObjectInputStream p = new ObjectInputStream(istream);
            map = (Map) p.readObject();

            istream.close();
        } catch(Exception e) {
            e.printStackTrace();
            // restoration of state failed, so
            // load a predefined set of MIME type mappings
            map.put("gif", new MIMEType("image", "gif"));
            map.put("jpeg", new MIMEType("image", "jpeg"));
            map.put("mpg", new MIMEType("video", "mpeg"));
            map.put("txt", new MIMEType("text", "plain"));
            map.put("html", new MIMEType("text", "html"));

            this.mapFile = mapFile;
```

```
            saveMap();
        }
    }
    /**
     * Save map to file.
     */
    public void saveMap() {
        try {
            FileOutputStream ostream = new FileOutputStream(mapFile);
            ObjectOutputStream p = new ObjectOutputStream(ostream);
            p.writeObject(map);
            p.flush();
            ostream.close();
        } catch(Exception e) {
            e.printStackTrace();
        }
    }
    public FileClassifierMutable(ActivationID activationID,
                                 MarshalledObject data)
        throws java.rmi.RemoteException {
        Exporter exporter =
            new ActivationExporter(activationID,
                        new BasicJeriExporter(TcpServerEndpoint.getInstance(0),
                                              new BasicILFactory(),
                                              false, true));

        proxy = (Remote) exporter.export(this);
        try {
            mapFile = (String) data.get();
        } catch(Exception e) {
            e.printStackTrace();
        }
        restoreMap();
    }
    // Implementation for ProxyAccessor
    public Object getProxy() {
        return proxy;
    }
} // FileClassifierMutable
```

The difference between the server for this service and the previous one is that you now have to prepare a marshalled object for the state file and register it with the activation system. Here the file name is hard-coded, but it could be given as a command-line argument (like services such as reggie do). I provide only the section of code relating to the marshalled object as that is all that changes from the previous server.

```
static final protected String CODEBASE =
        "http://192.168.1.13/classes/activation.FileClassifierServer-dl.jar";
    static final protected String LOG_FILE = "/tmp/file_classifier";
        String codebase = CODEBASE;
        MarshalledObject data = null;
        // set a log file for the service
        try {
            data = new MarshalledObject(LOG_FILE);
        } catch(java.io.IOException e) {
            e.printStackTrace();
        }
        ActivationDesc desc = null;
        desc = new ActivationDesc(groupID,
                                    "activation.FileClassifierImpl",
                                    codebase, data, true);
```

An Ant file for this server is `activation.FileClassifierServerMutable.xml`. It differs from the previous Ant file in the files used, so only these are given:

```
<!-- files for this project -->
<property name="src.files"
        value="common/MIMEType.java,
                common/FileClassifier.java,
                rmi/RemoteFileClassifier.java,
                mutable/RemoteFileClassifier.java,
                activation/FileClassifierMutable.java
                activation/FileClassifierServerMutable.java
                "/>
<property name="class.files"
        value="
                common/MIMEType.class,
                common/FileClassifier.class,
                activation/FileClassifierServerMutable.class
                "/>
<property name="class.files.dl"
        value="
                rmi/RemoteFileClassifier.class
                "/>
<property name="class.files.act"
        value="common/MIMEType.class,
                common/FileClassifier.class,
                rmi/RemoteFileClassifier.class,
                activation/FileClassifierMutable.class
                "/>
```

The example presented here uses a simple way to store state. Sun uses a far more complex system in many of its services, such as reggie: a *reliable log*, in package `com.sun.jini.reliableLog`. Note that this package is not a part of standard Jini, so it may change or even be removed in later versions of Jini, but there is nothing to stop you from using it if you need a robust storage mechanism.

Using a Configuration

The service implementations shown in the chapter so far have hard-coded the protocol Jeri. In general this is not a good idea, as a runtime configuration should specify this. The code to find an exporter should be handled by looking in a configuration, as shown in Chapter 19.

The start-up server will see the configuration file, typically a file name, as a command-line parameter. Previously for nonactivatable services, the server was able to extract the exporter directly from the configuration and use it to export the service. But as you have seen, it is now the responsibility of the service itself to define and use an exporter. The problem is how to get the command-line parameters from the start-up server into the service's constructor.

This problem can be solved by using the marshalled data discussed in the last section, but instead of using it for state, we can place the command-line arguments from the server into the marshalled data and so pass the configuration into the client.

The changes to the service are to add in configuration code to the constructor:

```java
package activation;
import net.jini.export.*;
import net.jini.jeri.BasicJeriExporter;
import net.jini.jeri.BasicILFactory;
import net.jini.jeri.tcp.TcpServerEndpoint;
import net.jini.activation.ActivationExporter;
import net.jini.jrmp.JrmpExporter;
import java.rmi.activation.ActivationID;
import java.rmi.MarshalledObject;
import net.jini.export.ProxyAccessor;
import net.jini.config.Configuration;
import net.jini.config.ConfigurationException;
import net.jini.config.ConfigurationProvider;
import common.MIMEType;
import common.FileClassifier;
import rmi.RemoteFileClassifier;
import java.rmi.Remote;
/**
 * FileClassifierConfig.java
 */
public class FileClassifierConfig implements RemoteFileClassifier,
                                             ProxyAccessor {
    private Remote proxy;
    public MIMEType getMIMEType(String fileName)
        throws java.rmi.RemoteException {
        if (fileName.endsWith(".gif")) {
            return new MIMEType("image", "gif");
        } else if (fileName.endsWith(".jpeg")) {
            return new MIMEType("image", "jpeg");
```

```
            } else if (fileName.endsWith(".mpg")) {
                return new MIMEType("video", "mpeg");
            } else if (fileName.endsWith(".txt")) {
                return new MIMEType("text", "plain");
            } else if (fileName.endsWith(".html")) {
                return new MIMEType("text", "html");
            } else
                // fill in lots of other types,
                // but eventually give up and
                return new MIMEType(null, null);
        }
    public FileClassifierConfig(ActivationID activationID, MarshalledObject data)
        throws java.rmi.RemoteException {
        // The marshalled object should be an array of strings
        // holding a configuration
        String[] args = null;
        try {
            args = (String[]) data.get();
        } catch(Exception e) {
            // empty
        }
        Exporter defaultExporter =
            new ActivationExporter(activationID,
                        new BasicJeriExporter(TcpServerEndpoint.getInstance(0),
                                        new BasicILFactory(),
                                        false, true));
        Exporter exporter = defaultExporter;
        try {
            Configuration config = ConfigurationProvider.getInstance(args);
            exporter = (Exporter) config.getEntry( "JeriExportDemo",
                                            "exporter",
                                            Exporter.class);
        } catch(ConfigurationException e) {
            // empty
        }
        proxy = (Remote) exporter.export(this);
    }
    // Implementation for ProxyAccessor
    public Object getProxy() {
        return proxy;
    }
} // FileClassifierConfig
```

The start-up server marshalls the command-line arguments and passes them into the activation description. I provide only the code showing the use of the marshalled object:

```
    static final protected String CODEBASE =
        "http://192.168.1.13/classes/activation.FileClassifierServer-dl.jar";
    String codebase = CODEBASE;
    MarshalledObject data = null;
    // marshall the command-line args for the service
    try {
        data = new MarshalledObject(argv);
    } catch(IOException e) {
        e.printStackTrace();
        System.exit(1);
    }
    ActivationDesc desc = null;
    desc = new ActivationDesc(groupID,
                         "activation.FileClassifierImpl",
                         codebase, data, true);
```

An Ant file for this server is activation.FileClassifierServerConfig.xml. It differs from the Ant file given earlier only in the files used.

```xml
<!-- files for this project -->
<property name="src.files"
        value="common/MIMEType.java,
                common/FileClassifier.java,
                rmi/RemoteFileClassifier.java,
                activation/FileClassifierConfig.java
                activation/FileClassifierServerConfig.java
                "/>
<property name="class.files"
        value="
                common/MIMEType.class,
                common/FileClassifier.class,
                activation/FileClassifierServerConfig.class
                "/>
<property name="class.files.dl"
        value="
                rmi/RemoteFileClassifier.class
                "/>
<property name="class.files.act"
        value="common/MIMEType.class,
                common/FileClassifier.class,
                rmi/RemoteFileClassifier.class,
                activation/FileClassifierConfig.class
                "/>
```

LeaseRenewalService

Activatable objects are one example of services that are not continuously alive. Mobile services, such as those that exist on mobile phones, are another. These services are brought to life on demand (as activatable objects), or join the network on occasion. These services raise a number of problems, one of which we skirted around in the last section: how do you renew leases when the object is not alive?

Activatable objects are brought back to life when methods are invoked on them. The expiration of a lease does not cause any methods to be invoked. There is no "lease-expiring event" generated that could cause a listener method to be invoked, either. It is true that a ServiceRegistrar such as reggie will generate an event when a lease changes status, but this is a "service removed" event rather than a "service about to be removed" event—it is too late.

If a server is alive, then it can use a LeaseRenewalManager to keep leases alive, but first, the renewal manager works by sleeping and waking up just in time to renew the leases, and second, if the server exits, then no LeaseRenewalManager will continue to run.

Jini supplies a lease renewal service that partly avoids these problems. Since it runs as a service, it has an independent existence; it does not depend on the server for any other service. It can act like a LeaseRenewalManager in keeping track of leases registered with it and renewing them as needed. In general, it can keep leases alive without waking the service itself, which can slumber until activated by clients calling methods.

But how long should the LeaseRenewalService keep renewing leases for a service? The LeaseRenewalManager utility has a simple solution: keep renewing while the server for that service is alive. If the server dies, taking down a service, then it will also take down the LeaseRenewalManager running in the same JVM, so leases will expire as expected after an interval.

This mechanism won't work for LeaseRenewalService, however, because the managed service can disappear without the LeaseRenewalService knowing about it. So the lease renewal must be done on a leased basis itself! The LeaseRenewalService will renew leases for a service only for a particular amount of time, specified by a lease. The service will still have to renew its lease, even though it is with a LeaseRenewalService instead of a bunch of lookup services. The lease granted by this service should be of a much longer duration than those granted by the lookup services for this to be of value.

Activatable services can only be woken by calling one of their methods. The LeaseRenewalService accomplishes this by generating renewal events *in advance* and calling a notify() method on a listener. If the listener is the activatable object, the LeaseRenewalService will wake it up so that it can perform the renewal. If the phoenix process managing the service has died or is unavailable, then the event will not be delivered and the LeaseRenewalService can remove this service from its renewal list.

This approach is not quite satisfactory for other types of "dormant" services such as might exist on mobile phones, since there is no equivalent of phoenix to handle activation. Instead, the mobile phone service might determine that it will connect once a day and renew the lease, as long as the LeaseRenewalService agrees to keep the lease for at least a day. This is still negotiable, in that the service asks for a duration and the LeaseRenewalService replies with a value that might not be so long. Still, it should be better than dealing with the lookup services, which may ask for renewals as often as every five minutes.

In the sections that follow, we'll discuss the norm service, Sun's implementation of a LeaseRenewalService.

Then we look at how a client can use this service to renew leases.

The norm Service

Jini 1.1 supplied an implementation of LeaseRenewalService called norm. This was a nonlazy activatable service that required rmid to be running. In Jini 2.0, it has been extended to be much more flexible and is controlled by various configurations:

- JRMP
  - Transient
  - Persistent
  - Activatable (requires an activation server such as phoenix)
- Jeri
  - Transient
  - Persistent
  - Activatable (requires an activation server such as phoenix)

Note These options are all documented in the Jini documentation doc/api/com/sun/jini/norm/ package-summary.html#examples.

For example, use this to run the transient Jeri version for suitable values of config_dir and install_dir:

```
java -Djava.security.policy=config_dir/jsk-all.policy \
    -jar install_dir/lib/start.jar \
    config_dir/start-transient-norm.config
```

The policy file could contain the following:

```
grant codebase "file:install_dir/lib/*" {
    permission java.security.AllPermission;
};
```

The start-transient-norm.config file should contain this:

```
import com.sun.jini.start.NonActivatableServiceDescriptor;
import com.sun.jini.start.ServiceDescriptor;
com.sun.jini.start {
    private static codebase = "http://your_host:http_port/norm-dl.jar";
    private static policy = "config_dir/jsk-all.policy";
```

```
    private static classpath = "install_dir/lib/norm.jar";
    private static config = "config_dir/transient-norm.config";
    static serviceDescriptors = new ServiceDescriptor[] {
        new NonActivatableServiceDescriptor(
            codebase, policy, classpath,
            "com.sun.jini.norm.TransientNormServerImpl",
            new String[] { config })
    };
}
```

This file points to the transient-norm.config file, which in turn contains the following:

```
com.sun.jini.norm {
    initialLookupGroups = new String[] { "your.group" };
}
```

Note that there is no mention of Jeri in any of these files—presumably it is a default (the JRMP version contains a definition of serverExporter as a JRMPExporter).

The norm service will maintain a set of leases for a period of up to two hours. The reggie lookup service grants leases for only five minutes, so that using this service increases the amount of time between renewing leases by a factor of over twenty.

Using the LeaseRenewalService

The norm service exports an object of type LeaseRenewalService that is defined by the interface:

```
package net.jini.lease;
public  interface LeaseRenewalService {
    LeaseRenewalSet createLeaseRenewalSet(long leaseDuration)
        throws java.rmi.RemoteException;
}
```

The leaseDuration is a requested value in milliseconds for the lease service to manage a set of leases. The lease service creates a lease for this request, and in order for it to continue to manage the set beyond the lease's expiration, the lease must be renewed before expiration. Because the service may be inactive around the time of expiration, the LeaseRenewalSet can be asked to register a listener object that will receive an event containing the lease, which will activate a dormant listener so that it can renew the lease in time. If the lease for the LeaseRenewalSet is allowed to lapse, then eventually all the leases for the services it was managing will also expire, making the services unavailable.

The LeaseRenewalSet returned from createLeaseRenewalSet has interfaces including the following:

```
package net.jini.lease;
public interface LeaseRenewalSet {
    public void renewFor(Lease leaseToRenew,
                          long membershipDuration)
              throws RemoteException;
    public EventRegistration setExpirationWarningListener(
                          RemoteEventListener listener,
```

```
                    long minWarning,
                    MarshalledObject handback)
        throws RemoteException;

    ....
}
```

The renewFor() method adds a new lease to the set being looked after. The LeaseRenewalSet will keep renewing the lease until either the requested membershipDuration expires or the lease on the whole LeaseRenewalSet expires (or an exception happens, such as a lease being refused).

Setting an expiration warning listener means that its notify() method will be called at least minWarning milliseconds before the lease for the set expires. The event argument to this will actually be an ExpirationWarningEvent:

```
package net.jini.lease;
public class ExpirationWarningEvent extends RemoteEvent {
    Lease getLease();
}
```

This allows the listener to get the lease for the LeaseRenewalSet and (probably) renew it. A simple activatable class that can renew the lease is as follows:

```
/**
 * RenewLease
 */
package activation;
import java.rmi.Remote;
import java.rmi.activation.ActivationID;
import java.rmi.MarshalledObject;
import net.jini.core.event.RemoteEvent;
import net.jini.core.event.RemoteEventListener;
import net.jini.core.lease.Lease;
import net.jini.lease.ExpirationWarningEvent;
import net.jini.export.*;
import net.jini.jeri.BasicJeriExporter;
import net.jini.jeri.BasicILFactory;
import net.jini.jeri.tcp.TcpServerEndpoint;
import net.jini.activation.ActivationExporter;
public class RenewLease implements RemoteEventListener,
                                   ProxyAccessor {

    private Remote proxy;
    public RenewLease(ActivationID activationID, MarshalledObject data)
        throws java.rmi.RemoteException {
        Exporter exporter =
            new ActivationExporter(activationID,
                        new BasicJeriExporter(TcpServerEndpoint.getInstance(0),
                                              new BasicILFactory(),
                                              false, true));
```

```
            proxy = (Remote) exporter.export(this);
        }

    public void notify(RemoteEvent evt) {
        System.out.println("expiring... " + evt.toString());
        ExpirationWarningEvent eevt = (ExpirationWarningEvent) evt;
        Lease lease = eevt.getRenewalSetLease();
        try {
            // This is short, for testing. Try 2+ hours
            lease.renew(20000L);
        } catch(Exception e) {
            e.printStackTrace();
        }
        System.out.println("Lease renewed for " +
                            (lease.getExpiration() -
                             System.currentTimeMillis()));
    }
    public Object getProxy() {
        return proxy;
    }
}
```

The server will need to register the service and export it as an activatable object. This is done in exactly the same way as in the first example of this chapter. In addition, it will need to

1. Register the lease listener (such as the previous RenewLease) with the activation system as an activatable object.

2. Find a LeaseRenewalService from a lookup service.

3. Register all leases from lookup services with the LeaseRenewalService. Since it may find lookup services before it finds the renewal service, it will need to keep a list of lookup services found before finding the service, in order to register them with it.

```
package activation;
import rmi.RemoteFileClassifier;
import net.jini.discovery.LookupDiscovery;
import net.jini.discovery.DiscoveryListener;
import net.jini.discovery.DiscoveryEvent;
import net.jini.core.lookup.ServiceRegistrar;
import net.jini.core.lookup.ServiceItem;
import net.jini.core.lookup.ServiceRegistration;
import net.jini.core.lookup.ServiceTemplate;
import net.jini.core.event.RemoteEvent;
import net.jini.core.event.RemoteEventListener;
import net.jini.core.lease.Lease;
import net.jini.lease.LeaseRenewalService;
import net.jini.lease.LeaseRenewalSet;
```

```java
import java.rmi.RMISecurityManager;
import java.rmi.MarshalledObject;
import java.rmi.activation.ActivationDesc;
import java.rmi.activation.ActivationGroupDesc;
import java.rmi.activation.ActivationGroupDesc.CommandEnvironment;
import java.rmi.activation.Activatable;
import java.rmi.activation.ActivationGroup;
import java.rmi.activation.ActivationGroupID;
import java.rmi.activation.ActivationID;
import java.rmi.MarshalledObject;
import java.util.Properties;
import java.util.Vector;
import java.rmi.activation.UnknownGroupException;
import java.rmi.activation.ActivationException;
import java.rmi.RemoteException;
/**
 * FileClassifierServer.java
 */
public class FileClassifierServerLease
    implements DiscoveryListener {
    static final protected String SECURITY_POLICY_FILE =
        "/home/jan/projects/jini/doc/policy.all";
    // Don't forget the trailing '/'!
    static final protected String CODEBASE = "http://localhost/classes/";

    protected RemoteFileClassifier proxy;
    protected RemoteEventListener leaseProxy;
    // Lease renewal management
    protected LeaseRenewalSet leaseRenewalSet = null;
    // List of leases not yet managed by a LeaseRenewalService
    protected Vector leases = new Vector();
    public static void main(String argv[]) {
        new FileClassifierServerLease(argv);
        // stick around while lookup services are found
        try {
            Thread.sleep(10000L);
        } catch(InterruptedException e) {
            // do nothing
        }
        // the server doesn't need to exist anymore
        System.exit(0);
    }
    public FileClassifierServerLease(String[] argv) {
        // install suitable security manager
        System.setSecurityManager(new RMISecurityManager());
        // Install an activation group
        Properties props = new Properties();
```

```
            props.put("java.security.policy",
                    SECURITY_POLICY_FILE);
            ActivationGroupDesc.CommandEnvironment ace = null;
            ActivationGroupDesc group = new ActivationGroupDesc(props, ace);
            ActivationGroupID groupID = null;
            try {
                groupID = ActivationGroup.getSystem().registerGroup(group);
            } catch(RemoteException e) {
                e.printStackTrace();
                System.exit(1);
            } catch(ActivationException e) {
                e.printStackTrace();
                System.exit(1);
            }

            try {
                ActivationGroup.createGroup(groupID, group, 0);
            } catch(ActivationException e) {
                e.printStackTrace();
                System.exit(1);
            }

            String codebase = CODEBASE;
            MarshalledObject data = null;
            ActivationDesc desc = null;
            ActivationDesc descLease = null;
            try {
                desc = new ActivationDesc("activation.FileClassifierImpl",
                                                codebase, data);
                descLease = new ActivationDesc("activation.RenewLease",
                                                codebase, data);
            } catch(ActivationException e) {
                e.printStackTrace();
                System.exit(1);
            }
            try {
                proxy = (RemoteFileClassifier) Activatable.register(desc);
                leaseProxy = (RemoteEventListener) Activatable.register(des-
cLease);
            } catch(UnknownGroupException e) {
                e.printStackTrace();
                System.exit(1);
            } catch(ActivationException e) {
                e.printStackTrace();
                System.exit(1);
            } catch(RemoteException e) {
                e.printStackTrace();
```

```java
                System.exit(1);
        }

        LookupDiscovery discover = null;
        try {
            discover = new LookupDiscovery(LookupDiscovery.ALL_GROUPS);
        } catch(Exception e) {
            System.err.println(e.toString());
            System.exit(1);
        }
        discover.addDiscoveryListener(this);
    }
    public void discovered(DiscoveryEvent evt) {
        ServiceRegistrar[] registrars = evt.getRegistrars();
        RemoteFileClassifier service;
        for (int n = 0; n < registrars.length; n++) {
            ServiceRegistrar registrar = registrars[n];
            // export the proxy service
            ServiceItem item = new ServiceItem(null,
                                                proxy,
                                                null);
            ServiceRegistration reg = null;
            try {
                reg = registrar.register(item, Lease.FOREVER);
            } catch(java.rmi.RemoteException e) {
                System.err.print("Register exception: ");
                e.printStackTrace();
                continue;
            }
            try {
                System.out.println("service registered at " +
                                    registrar.getLocator().getHost());
            } catch(Exception e) {
            }
            Lease lease = reg.getLease();
            // if we have a lease renewal manager, use it
            if (leaseRenewalSet != null) {
                try {
                    leaseRenewalSet.renewFor(lease, Lease.FOREVER);
                } catch(RemoteException e) {
                    e.printStackTrace();
                }
            } else {
                // add to the list of unmanaged leases
                leases.add(lease);
                // see if this lookup service has a lease renewal manager
```

```
                        findLeaseService(registrar);
                    }
                }
            }
            public void findLeaseService(ServiceRegistrar registrar) {
                System.out.println("Trying to find a lease service");
                Class[] classes = {LeaseRenewalService.class};
                ServiceTemplate template = new ServiceTemplate(null, classes,
                                                               null);
                LeaseRenewalService leaseService = null;
                try {
                    leaseService = (LeaseRenewalService) registrar.lookup(template);
                } catch(RemoteException e) {
                    e.printStackTrace();
                    return;
                }
                if (leaseService == null) {
                    System.out.println("No lease service found");
                    return;
                }
                try {
                    // This time is unrealistically small - try 10000000L
                    leaseRenewalSet = leaseService.createLeaseRenewalSet(20000);
                    System.out.println("Found a lease service");
                    // register a timeout listener
                    leaseRenewalSet.setExpirationWarningListener(leaseProxy, 5000,
                                                                 null);
                    // manage all the leases found so far
                    for (int n = 0; n < leases.size(); n++) {
                        Lease ll = (Lease) leases.elementAt(n);
                        leaseRenewalSet.renewFor(ll, Lease.FOREVER);
                    }
                    leases = null;
                } catch(RemoteException e) {
                    e.printStackTrace();
                }
                Lease renewalLease = leaseRenewalSet.getRenewalSetLease();
                System.out.println("Lease expires in " +
                                   (renewalLease.getExpiration() -
                                    System.currentTimeMillis()));
            }
            public void discarded(DiscoveryEvent evt) {
            }
        } // FileClassifierServerLease
```

An Ant file to build, deploy, and run the service is activation.
FileClassifierServerLease.xml. It only differs from the previous Ant files in the files used.

```
<property name="src.files"
        value="
                common/MIMEType.java,
                common/FileClassifier.java,
                rmi/RemoteFileClassifier.java,
                activation/FileClassifierImpl.java
                activation/RenewLease.java
                activation/FileClassifierServerLease.java
                "/>
<property name="class.files"
        value="
                common/MIMEType.class,
                common/FileClassifier.class,
                activation/FileClassifierServerLease.class
                "/>
<property name="class.files.dl"
        value="
                rmi/RemoteFileClassifier.class
                "/>
<property name="class.files.act"
        value="common/MIMEType.class,
                common/FileClassifier.class,
                rmi/RemoteFileClassifier.class,
                activation/RenewLease.class
                activation/FileClassifierImpl.class
                "/>
```

In order to run the server, the following need to be running:

- reggie to run as a lookup service.

- phoenix to act as an activation server for the FileClassifier service and also for the RenewLease service.

- norm as a lease renewal service. Each lease will be registered with this service, and it will have the RenewLease as listener for expiration events.

The server starts, finds lookup services, and registers the service with each of them. Each lease that it gets is also registered with the lease renewal service, and the listener is also registered. The server then terminates. The lease renewal service renews leases with the lookup service. When the lease renewal set is about to expire, it wakes up the lease renewal listener, which renews the set. Note that since the listener is activatable, this "wake-up" is performed by the activation server phoenix. Trace messages from the listener thus appear in whatever window the activation server is run from.

LookupDiscoveryService

It is easy enough for a server to discover all of the lookup services within reach at the time it is started, using LookupDiscovery. While the server continues to stay alive, any new lookup services that start will also be found by LookupDiscovery. But if the server terminates, which it will for activatable services, then these extra lookup services will probably never be found. This results in the service not being registered with them, which could mean in turn that clients may not find it. This is analogous to leases not being renewed if the server terminates.

In Jini 1.1, there is a LookupDiscoveryService that can be used to continuously monitor the state of lookup services. It will monitor these on behalf of a service that will most likely want to register with each new lookup service as it starts. If the service is an activatable one, the server that would have done this will have terminated, as its role would have just been to register the service with phoenix.

When there is a change to lookup services, the LookupDiscoveryService needs to notify an object about this by sending it a remote event (actually of type RemoteDiscoveryEvent). But again, we do not want to have a process sitting around waiting for such notification, so the listener object will probably also be an activatable object.

The LookupDiscoveryService interface has the following specification:

```
public interface LookupDiscoveryService {
    LookupDiscoveryRegistration register(String[] groups,
                                  LookupLocator[] locators,
                                  RemoteEventListener listener,
                                  MarshalledObject handback,
                                  long leaseDuration);
}
```

Calling the register() method will begin a multicast search for the groups and a unicast lookup for the locators. The registration is leased and will need to be renewed before expiration (a lease renewal service can be used for this). Note that the listener *cannot* be null—this is simple sanity checking, because if the listener were null, then the service could never do anything useful!

A lookup service in one of the groups can start or terminate, or it can change its group membership in such a way that it now does (or doesn't) meet the group criteria. A lookup service in the locators list can also start or stop. Any of these changes will generate RemoteDiscoveryEvent events and call the notify() method of the listener. The event interface includes the following:

```
package net.jini.discovery;
public interface RemoteDiscoveryEvent {
    ServiceRegistrar[] getRegistrars();
    boolean isDiscarded();
    ...
}
```

The list of registrars is the set that triggered the event. The isDiscarded() method is used to check if it is a "discovered" lookup service or a "discarded" lookup service. An initial event is not posted when the listener is registered; the set of lookup services that are initially found can be retrieved from the LookupDiscoveryRegistration object returned from the register() method, by its getRegistrars()method.

The fiddler Service

The Jini 1.1 release includes an implementation of the lookup discovery service called fiddler. This service has been modified in Jini 2.0 to be more flexible. It can be run in three modes, using either Jeri (the default) or JRMP:

- Transient

- Persistent

- Activatable (requires phoenix to be running)

Information about how to run fiddler in each mode is given in the Jini download, under doc/api/com/sun/jini/fiddler/package-summary.html.

To run fiddler in transient mode using Jeri over TCP, execute a command line such as the following:

```
java \
  -Djava.security.manager= \
  -Djava.security.policy=fiddler-start-transient.policy \
    -jar jini_install_dir/lib/start.jar \
        config/fiddler-start-transient.config
```

where fiddler-start-transient.policy could be the same as policy.all.

The contents of fiddler-start-transient.config could be as follows:

```
import com.sun.jini.start.NonActivatableServiceDescriptor;
import com.sun.jini.start.ServiceDescriptor;
com.sun.jini.start {
    private static serviceCodebase   =
            new String("http://myHost:8080/fiddler-dl.jar");
    private static servicePolicyFile =
            new String
                ("example_install_dir${/}policy${/}jeri-transient-fiddler.policy");
    private static serviceClasspath  =
            new String("jini_install_dir${/}lib${/}fiddler.jar");
    private static serviceImplName   =
            new String("com.sun.jini.fiddler.TransientFiddlerImpl");
    private static serviceConfig     =
            new String
                ("example_install_dir${/}config${/}jeri-transient-fiddler.config");
    private static serviceArgsArray  = new String[] { serviceConfig };
    private static nonActivatableServiceDescriptor =
                new NonActivatableServiceDescriptor(serviceCodebase,
                                                    servicePolicyFile,
                                                    serviceClasspath,
                                                    serviceImplName,
                                                    serviceArgsArray);
    static serviceDescriptors =
                new ServiceDescriptor[] { nonActivatableServiceDescriptor };
}//end com.sun.jini.start
```

The configuration file `jeri-transient-fiddler.config` would contain this:

```
import net.jini.jeri.BasicILFactory;
import net.jini.jeri.BasicJeriExporter;
import net.jini.jeri.tcp.TcpServerEndpoint;
com.sun.jini.fiddler {
    private invocationLayerFactory = new BasicILFactory();
    serverExporter = new BasicJeriExporter(TcpServerEndpoint.getInstance(0),
                                           invocationLayerFactory,
                                           false,
                                           true);
    initialLookupGroups = new String[] {"myGroup.myCompany.com"};
}//end com.sun.jini.fiddler
```

Using the LookupDiscoveryService

An activatable service can make use of a lease renewal service to look after the leases for lookup services discovered. It can find these lookup services by means of a lookup discovery service. The logic to manage these two services could be a little tricky, as we attempt to find two different services. We can simplify for this example by just doing a sequential search using a `ServiceDiscoveryManager`.

While lease management can be done by the lease renewal service, the lease renewal set will also be leased and will need to be renewed on occasion. The lease renewal service can call an activatable `RenewLease` object to do this, as in the last section.

The lookup discovery service is also a leased service—it will only report changes to lookup services while its *own* lease is current. So the lease from this service will have to be managed by the lease renewal service, in addition to the leases for any lookup services discovered.

The primary purpose of the lookup discovery service is to call the `notify()` method of some object when information about lookup services changes. This object should also be an activatable object. We define a `DiscoveryChange` object with the `notify()` method to handle changes in lookup services. If a lookup service has disappeared, we don't worry about it. If a lookup service has been discovered, we want to register the service with it, and then manage the resultant lease. This means that the `DiscoveryChange` object must know both the service to be registered and the lease renewal service. This is static data, so these two objects can be passed in an array of two objects as the `MarshalledObject` to the activation constructor. The class itself can be implemented as follows:

```
package activation;
import java.rmi.activation.Activatable;
import java.rmi.activation.ActivationID;
import java.rmi.MarshalledObject;
import net.jini.core.event.RemoteEvent;
import net.jini.core.event.RemoteEventListener;
import net.jini.core.lease.Lease;
import net.jini.lease.ExpirationWarningEvent;
import net.jini.core.lookup.ServiceItem;
```

```
import net.jini.core.lookup.ServiceRegistrar;
import net.jini.core.lookup.ServiceRegistration;
import net.jini.lease.LeaseRenewalSet;
import net.jini.discovery.RemoteDiscoveryEvent;
import java.rmi.RemoteException;
import  net.jini.discovery.LookupUnmarshalException;
import rmi.RemoteFileClassifier;
public class DiscoveryChange extends Activatable
    implements RemoteEventListener {
    protected LeaseRenewalSet leaseRenewalSet;
    protected RemoteFileClassifier service;

    public DiscoveryChange(ActivationID id, MarshalledObject data)
        throws java.rmi.RemoteException {
        super(id, 0);
        Object[] objs = null;
        try {
            objs = (Object []) data.get();
        } catch(ClassNotFoundException e) {
            e.printStackTrace();
        } catch(java.io.IOException e) {
            e.printStackTrace();
        }
        service = (RemoteFileClassifier) objs[0];
        leaseRenewalSet= (LeaseRenewalSet) objs[1];
    }

    public void notify(RemoteEvent evt) {
        System.out.println("lookups changing... " + evt.toString());
        RemoteDiscoveryEvent revt = (RemoteDiscoveryEvent) evt;
        if (! revt.isDiscarded()) {
            // The event is a discovery event
            ServiceItem item = new ServiceItem(null, service, null);
            ServiceRegistrar[] registrars = null;
            try {
                registrars = revt.getRegistrars();
            } catch(LookupUnmarshalException e) {
                e.printStackTrace();
                return;
            }
            for (int n = 0; n < registrars.length; n++) {
                ServiceRegistrar registrar = registrars[n];

                ServiceRegistration reg = null;
                try {
                    reg = registrar.register(item, Lease.FOREVER);
                    leaseRenewalSet.renewFor(reg.getLease(), Lease.FOREVER);
```

```
                    } catch(java.rmi.RemoteException e) {
                        System.err.println("Register exception: " + e.toString());
                    }
                }
            }
        }
    }
```

The server must install an activation group, and then find activation proxies for the service itself and also for our lease renewal object. After this, it can use a ClientLookupManager to find the lease service, and register our lease renewal object with it. Now that it has a proxy for the service object, and also a lease renewal service, it can create the marshalled data for the lookup discovery service and register this with phoenix. Now we can find the lookup discovery service and register our discovery change listener, DiscoveryChange, with it. At the same time, we have to register the service with all the lookup services the lookup discovery service finds on initialization. This all leads to the following code:

```
package activation;
import rmi.RemoteFileClassifier;
import net.jini.discovery.LookupDiscovery;
import net.jini.discovery.LookupDiscoveryService;
import net.jini.discovery.DiscoveryListener;
import net.jini.discovery.DiscoveryEvent;
import net.jini.discovery.LookupDiscoveryManager;
import net.jini.discovery.LookupDiscoveryRegistration;
import net.jini.discovery.LookupUnmarshalException;
import net.jini.core.lookup.ServiceRegistrar;
import net.jini.core.lookup.ServiceItem;
import net.jini.core.lookup.ServiceRegistration;
import net.jini.core.lookup.ServiceTemplate;
import net.jini.core.event.RemoteEvent;
import net.jini.core.event.RemoteEventListener;
import net.jini.core.lease.Lease;
import net.jini.lease.LeaseRenewalService;
import net.jini.lease.LeaseRenewalSet;
import net.jini.lease.LeaseRenewalManager;
import net.jini.lookup.ServiceDiscoveryManager;
import java.rmi.RMISecurityManager;
import java.rmi.activation.ActivationDesc;
import java.rmi.activation.ActivationGroupDesc;
import java.rmi.activation.ActivationGroupDesc.CommandEnvironment;
import java.rmi.activation.Activatable;
import java.rmi.activation.ActivationGroup;
import java.rmi.activation.ActivationGroupID;
import java.rmi.activation.ActivationID;
import java.rmi.MarshalledObject;
import java.rmi.activation.UnknownGroupException;
import java.rmi.activation.ActivationException;
```

```java
import java.rmi.RemoteException;
import java.util.Properties;
import java.util.Vector;
/**
 * FileClassifierServerDiscovery.java
 */
public class FileClassifierServerDiscovery
    /* implements DiscoveryListener */ {
    private static final long WAITFOR = 10000L;
    static final protected String SECURITY_POLICY_FILE =
        "/home/jan/projects/jini/doc/policy.all";
    // Don't forget the trailing '/'!
    static final protected String CODEBASE = "http://localhost/classes/";

    protected RemoteFileClassifier serviceProxy;
    protected RemoteEventListener leaseProxy,
                                  discoveryProxy;
    // Services
    protected LookupDiscoveryService discoveryService = null;
    protected LeaseRenewalService leaseService = null;
    // Lease renewal management
    protected LeaseRenewalSet leaseRenewalSet = null;
    // List of leases not yet managed by a LeaseRenewalService
    protected Vector leases = new Vector();
    protected ServiceDiscoveryManager clientMgr = null;
    public static void main(String argv[]) {
        new FileClassifierServerDiscovery();
        // stick around while lookup services are found
        try {
            Thread.sleep(20000L);
        } catch(InterruptedException e) {
            // do nothing
        }
        // the server doesn't need to exist anymore
        System.exit(0);
    }
    public FileClassifierServerDiscovery() {
        // install suitable security manager
        System.setSecurityManager(new RMISecurityManager());
        installActivationGroup();
        serviceProxy = (RemoteFileClassifier)
                    registerWithActivation("activation.FileClassifierImpl", null);

        leaseProxy = (RemoteEventListener)
                    registerWithActivation("activation.RenewLease", null);
        initClientLookupManager();
        findLeaseService();
```

```
            // the discovery change listener needs to know the service
            // and the lease service
            Object[] discoveryInfo = {serviceProxy, leaseRenewalSet};
            MarshalledObject discoveryData = null;
            try {
                discoveryData = new MarshalledObject(discoveryInfo);
            } catch(java.io.IOException e) {
                e.printStackTrace();
            }
            discoveryProxy = (RemoteEventListener)
                        registerWithActivation("activation.DiscoveryChange",
                                                    discoveryData);
            findDiscoveryService();
        }
        public void installActivationGroup() {
            Properties props = new Properties();
            props.put("java.security.policy",
                    SECURITY_POLICY_FILE);
            ActivationGroupDesc.CommandEnvironment ace = null;
            ActivationGroupDesc group = new ActivationGroupDesc(props, ace);
            ActivationGroupID groupID = null;
            try {
                groupID = ActivationGroup.getSystem().registerGroup(group);
            } catch(RemoteException e) {
                e.printStackTrace();
                System.exit(1);
            } catch(ActivationException e) {
                e.printStackTrace();
                System.exit(1);
            }

            try {
                ActivationGroup.createGroup(groupID, group, 0);
            } catch(ActivationException e) {
                e.printStackTrace();
                System.exit(1);
            }
        }
        public Object registerWithActivation(String className, MarshalledObject data) {
            String codebase = CODEBASE;
            ActivationDesc desc = null;
            Object proxy = null;
            try {
                desc = new ActivationDesc(className,
                                            codebase, data);
            } catch(ActivationException e) {
                e.printStackTrace();
```

```
                    System.exit(1);
                }
                try {
                    proxy = Activatable.register(desc);
                } catch(UnknownGroupException e) {
                    e.printStackTrace();
                    System.exit(1);
                } catch(ActivationException e) {
                    e.printStackTrace();
                    System.exit(1);
                } catch(RemoteException e) {
                    e.printStackTrace();
                    System.exit(1);
                }
                return proxy;
            }
        public void initClientLookupManager() {
            LookupDiscoveryManager lookupDiscoveryMgr = null;
            try {
                lookupDiscoveryMgr =
                    new LookupDiscoveryManager(LookupDiscovery.ALL_GROUPS,
                                               null /* unicast locators */,
                                               null /* DiscoveryListener */);
                clientMgr = new ServiceDiscoveryManager(lookupDiscoveryMgr,
                                                new LeaseRenewalManager());
            } catch(Exception e) {
                e.printStackTrace();
                System.exit(1);
            }
        }
        public void findLeaseService() {
            leaseService = (LeaseRenewalService) findService(LeaseRenewalService.class);
            if (leaseService == null) {
                System.out.println("Lease service null");
            }
            try {
                leaseRenewalSet = leaseService.createLeaseRenewalSet(20000);
                leaseRenewalSet.setExpirationWarningListener(leaseProxy, 5000,
                                                 null);
            } catch(RemoteException e) {
                e.printStackTrace();
            }
        }
        public void findDiscoveryService() {
            discoveryService = (LookupDiscoveryService)
                                        findService(LookupDiscoveryService.class);
            if (discoveryService == null) {
```

```
                System.out.println("Discovery service null");
            }
            LookupDiscoveryRegistration registration = null;
            try {
                registration =
                    discoveryService.register(LookupDiscovery.ALL_GROUPS,
                                              null,
                                              discoveryProxy,
                                              null,
                                              Lease.FOREVER);
            } catch(RemoteException e) {
                e.printStackTrace();
            }
            // manage the lease for the lookup discovery service
            try {
                leaseRenewalSet.renewFor(registration.getLease(), Lease.FOREVER);
            } catch(RemoteException e) {
                e.printStackTrace();
            }
            // register with the lookup services already found
            ServiceItem item = new ServiceItem(null, serviceProxy, null);
            ServiceRegistrar[] registrars = null;
            try {
                registrars = registration.getRegistrars();
            } catch(RemoteException e) {
                e.printStackTrace();
                return;
            } catch(LookupUnmarshalException e) {
                e.printStackTrace();
                return;
            }
            for (int n = 0; n < registrars.length; n++) {
                ServiceRegistrar registrar = registrars[n];
                ServiceRegistration reg = null;
                try {
                    reg = registrar.register(item, Lease.FOREVER);
                    leaseRenewalSet.renewFor(reg.getLease(), Lease.FOREVER);
                } catch(java.rmi.RemoteException e) {
                    System.err.println("Register exception: " + e.toString());
                }
            }
        }
        public Object findService(Class cls) {
            Class [] classes = new Class[] {cls};
            ServiceTemplate template = new ServiceTemplate(null, classes,
                                                           null);
            ServiceItem item = null;
```

```
        try {
            item = clientMgr.lookup(template,
                                    null, /* no filter */
                                    WAITFOR /* timeout */);
        } catch(Exception e) {
            e.printStackTrace();
            System.exit(1);
        }
        if (item == null) {
            // couldn't find a service in time
            System.out.println("No service found for " + cls.toString());
            return null;
        }
        return item.service;
    }
} // FileClassifierServerDiscovery
```

To run this example, you need to perform the following steps:

1. Run the lookup service reggie.

2. Run the activation server phoenix.

3. Run the lease renewal service norm.

4. Run the lookup discovery service fiddler.

5. Run the server. This will terminate, hopefully after finding the services and registering the DiscoveryChange with the lookup discovery service, and register the leases for the service and the discovery service.

An Ant file to build, deploy, and run the service is activation.FileClassifierServer➥ Discovery.xml. It only differs from the previous Ant files in the files used.

```
<!-- files for this project -->
<property name="src.files"
          value="common/MIMEType.java,
                 common/FileClassifier.java,
                 rmi/RemoteFileClassifier.java,
                 activation/FileClassifierImpl.java
                 activation/FileClassifierServer.java
                 "/>
<property name="class.files"
          value="
                 common/MIMEType.class,
                 common/FileClassifier.class,
                 activation/FileClassifierServer.class
                 "/>
<property name="class.files.dl"
```

```
            value="
                    rmi/RemoteFileClassifier.class
                    "/>
    <property name="class.files.act"
            value="common/MIMEType.class,
                    common/FileClassifier.class,
                    rmi/RemoteFileClassifier.class,
                    activation/FileClassifierImpl.class
                    "/>
```

Summary

Some objects may not always be available, either because of mobility issues or because they are activatable objects. This chapter has dealt with activatable objects, and also with some of the special services that are needed to properly support these transient objects.

■■■

CHAPTER 26

Introspection

Questions often asked in the Jini mailing lists are as follows: "How do I find all services?" and "How do I deal with a service if I don't know what it is?" The first question is answered by searching for Object. Introspection is the answer to the second question, but if you require your services to be introspected, then you have to pay extra attention to the deployment environment.

In this chapter, we look at how a client can deal with a service that it knows nothing about, and how services can cooperate up front by making enough information available to clients.

Basic Service Lister

The client of Chapter 9 looked for a particular class by specifying the class in the ServiceItem. How do we find all services? Well, all classes inherit from Object, so one way is to just look for all services that implement Object (this is one of the few cases where we might specify a class instead of an interface). We can adapt the client quite simply by looking for all services, and then doing something simple like printing its class:

```
package client;
import java.rmi.RMISecurityManager;
import java.rmi.RemoteException;
import net.jini.discovery.LookupDiscovery;
import net.jini.discovery.DiscoveryListener;
import net.jini.discovery.DiscoveryEvent;
import net.jini.core.lookup.ServiceRegistrar;
import net.jini.core.lookup.ServiceTemplate;
import net.jini.core.lookup.ServiceMatches;
import net.jini.core.lookup.ServiceItem;
/**
 * BasicServiceLister
 */
public class BasicServiceLister implements DiscoveryListener {
    public static void main(String argv[]) {
        new BasicServiceLister();
        // stay around long enough to receive replies
        try {
            Thread.currentThread().sleep(1000000L);
        } catch(java.lang.InterruptedException e) {
```

```java
            // do nothing
        }
    }
    public BasicServiceLister() {
        System.setSecurityManager(new RMISecurityManager());
        LookupDiscovery discover = null;
        try {
            discover = new LookupDiscovery(LookupDiscovery.ALL_GROUPS);
        } catch(Exception e) {
            System.err.println(e.toString());
            System.exit(1);
        }
        discover.addDiscoveryListener(this);
    }

    public void discovered(DiscoveryEvent evt) {
        ServiceRegistrar[] registrars = evt.getRegistrars();
        Class [] classes = new Class[] {Object.class};
        ServiceTemplate template = new ServiceTemplate(null, classes,
                                                          null);

        for (int n = 0; n < registrars.length; n++) {
            ServiceRegistrar registrar = registrars[n];
            System.out.print("Lookup service found at ");
            try {
                System.out.println(registrar.getLocator().getHost());
            } catch(RemoteException e) {
                continue;
            }
            ServiceMatches matches = null;
            try {
                matches = registrar.lookup(template, Integer.MAX_VALUE);
            } catch(RemoteException e) {
                System.err.println("Can't describe service: " + e.toString());
                continue;
            }
            ServiceItem[] items = matches.items;
            for (int m = 0; m < items.length; m++) {
                Object service = items[m].service;
                if (service != null) {
                    printObject(service);
                } else {
                    System.out.println("Got null service");
                }
            }
        }
    }
}
```

```java
    public void discarded(DiscoveryEvent evt) {
        // empty
    }
    /** Print the object's class information within its hierarchy
     */
    private void printObject(Object obj) {
        System.out.println("Discovered service belongs to class \n" +
                            obj.getClass().getName());
        printInterfaces(obj.getClass());
        /*
        Class[] interfaces = obj.getClass().getInterfaces();
        if (interfaces.length != 0) {
            System.out.println("  Implements interfaces");
            for (int n = 0; n < interfaces.length; n++) {
                System.out.println("    " + interfaces[n].getName());
            }
        }
        */
        printSuperClasses(obj.getClass());
    }
    /** Print information about superclasses
     */
    private void printSuperClasses(Class cls) {
        System.out.println("  With superclasses");
        while ((cls = cls.getSuperclass()) != null) {
            System.out.println("    " + cls.getName());
            printInterfaces(cls);
        }
    }
    private void printInterfaces(Class cls) {
        Class[] interfaces = cls.getInterfaces();
        if (interfaces.length != 0) {
            System.out.println("      which implements interfaces");
            for (int n = 0; n < interfaces.length; n++) {
                System.out.println("        " + interfaces[n]);
                printInterfaces(interfaces[n]);
            }
        }
    }
} // BasicServiceLister
```

Unknown Services

A common question from Jini programmers is "How do I deal with services that I know nothing about?" There are two answers:

- Are you sure you want to? If you don't know about the service beforehand, then what are you going to sensibly infer about its behavior just from discovering the interface? In most cases, if you don't already know the service interface and have some idea of what it is supposed to do, then getting this service isn't going to be of much use.

- On the other hand, service browsers may not have prior knowledge of the services they discover, but may still wish to use information about these services. For example, a service browser could present this information to a user and ask if the user wants to invoke the service. Or a client using artificial intelligence techniques may be able to guess at behavior from the interface and invoke the service based on this.

This (short) chapter is concerned with the second case.

Introspection

Java has a well-developed introspection library, which allows a Java program to take a class and find all of the methods (including constructors), and to find the parameters and return types of these methods. For noninterface classes, the fields can also be found. The classes that a class implements or extends can also be determined. The access methods (private, public, and protected) and the thrown exceptions can be found as well. In other words, all of the important information (except Javadoc comments) can be retrieved from the object's class.

The starting point for introspection is various `Class` methods, including the following:

```
Constructor[] getConstructors();
Class[]       getClasses();
Field[]       getFields();
Class[]       getInterfaces();
Method[]      getMethods();
int           getModifiers();
Package       getPackage();
```

Methods in the classes `Field`, `Method`, and so on allow you to gain extra details.

For example, you can use the following code to find information about interfaces of services on a lookup service:

```
ServiceRegistrar registrar = ...
ServiceTemplate templ = new ServiceTemplate(null, null, null);
ServiceMatches matches = registrar.lookup(templ, Integer.MAX_VALUE);
ServiceItem[] items = matches.items;
for (int n = 0; n < items.length; n++) {
    Object service = items[n].service;
    if (service != null) {
        Class cls = service.getClass();
        System.out.println("Class is " + cls.getName());
        Class[] ifaces = cls.getInterfaces();
        for (int m = 0; m < ifaces.length; m++) {
            System.out.println("  implements " + ifaces[m].getName());
        }
    }
}
```

Unknown Classes

In earlier chapters, we assumed that a client will know at least the interfaces of the services it is attempting to use. For a browser or a "smart" client, this may not be the case: the client will often come across services that it does not know much about. When a client discovers a service, it must be able to reconstitute it into an object that it can deal with, and for this it needs to be able to find the class files. If any one of the needed class files are missing, then the service comes back as null. That is why there is a check for null service in the previous example code: a service has been found, but cannot be rebuilt into an object due to missing class files.

Clients get the class files from two sources:

- Already known, and in their class path

- Accessed from a web server by the java.rmi.server.codebase property of the service

If you are a service provider, you may wish to make your service available to clients who have never heard of it before. In this case, you cannot rely on the client knowing anything except for the core Java classes. This may be in doubt if the client is using one of the "limited device" Java memory models—this is not a problem currently, since these models do not yet support Jini. You can make a pretty solid bet that the core Jini classes will have to be there, too, but nonessential classes in the package jini-ext.jar may not be present.

The example that we have been using so far is an implementation of FileClassifier. A typical implementation uses these noncore classes/interfaces:

- FileClassifier

- RemoteFileClassifier

- MIMEType

- FileClassifierImpl

The assumption in earlier chapters is that FileClassifier and MIMEType are well known and the others need to be accessible from a web server. For robust introspection, this assumption must be dropped: FileClassifier and MIMEType must also be available from the service's web server. This a *server* responsibility, not a *client* responsibility; the client can do nothing if the service does not make its class files available.

In summary, if a service wishes to be discovered by clients that have no prior knowledge of the service, then it must make *all* of its interface and specification classes publicly available from a web server. Any other classes that are nonstandard or potentially missing from the client should be on this public web server, too. There is a restriction: you cannot make some classes available to nonsignatories to various copyright agreements, meaning that licensing restrictions may not allow you to make some classes publicly available. For example, before the change to the Apache license you could make any of the Jini files publicly available "just in case the client doesn't have them."

Summary

This short chapter considered some of the issues for a client to deal with services about which it has no previous knowledge. Services that would like to be visible to all clients also have to take steps to make sure all required classes are available for download.

CHAPTER 27

■■■

Extended Example: Home Audio System

Traditional information systems concentrated on modeling information flows and quite explicitly avoided physical systems. The advent of object-oriented systems changed this focus, with increased emphasis on the behavior of real objects and how this could form the basis of an information system. In the meantime, there was a huge amount of work done in control systems, and a corresponding increase the computational power of everyday appliances, such as dishwashers, washing machines, and so on. One area in which the convergence of computer systems and devices has become a major commercial area is that of audio/visual (A/V) systems. The change from analog to digital systems has opened many opportunities that go far beyond copying MP3 files from one computer to another.

The home A/V market has become a battleground for ideologies and commercial interests. On one side are the set-top vendors who own the cable systems that pump entertainment into many homes. Their vision is to widen their pipe, while still maintaining control. The professional audio and hi-fi community, on the other hand, sees the hi-fi system as the control center. And, of course, the computer community sees the PC as the center of any home A/V system, because of its processing power, well-developed software systems, and capability to easily handle digital signals.

I belong to the PC-centric community to some extent—but even there are divergences of opinion. Most current A/V systems, such as the Java Media Framework (JMF) and the Microsoft Windows Media platform, treat the A/V sources and sinks as though they are on the same machine, so that all processing is done locally. It's true that JMF allows network access using HTTP or RTP, but it tries to hide the network layer and make all components appear to be local.

The mantra from Sun for many years has been "The Network Is the Computer." This idea could be applied to the A/V world: "The Network Is the A/V System." What makes it interesting for the A/V system is what a network can do: a wireless network can support friends visiting with their own A/V systems and joining in with yours to share music; it can support music following you around the house, switching from one set of speakers to another.

In this chapter I attempt to build a network wireless audio system using Jini. We'll consider an extended example, using Jini in a home audio situation. The chapter uses many of the concepts of earlier chapters and shows how Jini can be used to build nontrivial systems.

Distributed Audio

There have been many efforts to distribute A/V content. Many of these efforts are concerned with large servers, and these efforts have paid off with streaming media systems such as RealAudio. I want to look at a more local situation: my home is a medium-sized house, and now that I have a wireless network I can work in the living room, the family room, the study, or even in one of the bedrooms. I like to listen to music while I work—either CDs or the various community radio stations that I subscribe to, and possibly streaming audio from other stations from around the world later. I don't have any children or partner at the moment, but if I did, then they would have their own music sources and sinks, and would share the house network. Friends might come and visit with their own A/V sources and sinks, and just join the house network. In a little while, guitars and microphones will have Bluetooth cards, so we will be able to have a local network band.

The wireless network density in my neighborhood is low, but eventually I will be able to join a local community network, which should give me metropolitan access. I live in a city rich in music (Melbourne, Australia) and sometimes feel that I hardly need to go out to listen to live music because the local radio stations (RRR, PBS-FM, etc.) are so good, but soon I would also hope to tune into the folk concert on the other side of town through the community wireless network.

OK, so how do we build middleware for an A/V network that is network-centric, rather than proprieter-centric? There has been one attempt that I know of to build a network-based A/V system, by Marco Lohse and colleagues (as described in the article titled "An Open Middleware Architecture for Network-Integrated Multimedia"). Their system is CORBA-based, which gives it network objects. But a lot of their system has to be built on top of CORBA because it doesn't quite support what Lohse and his colleagues wanted. Much of this extra structure seems to fall out quite easily under Jini.

I approach the rest of this chapter from a software-engineering viewpoint, trying to make a system as simple as possible for consumers (clients). If you have any comments on this, please let me know—after all, this is the system I am using in my house right now, so if it can be made better, then I at least will be grateful!

Parameters for A/V Content

Many variables affect how A/V content is sourced, moved around a network, and delivered:

- *Transport*: The transport layer may be reliable (slow) TCP, unreliable (faster) UDP, or HTTP (even slower), with some quality of service (QoS), such as Real-Time Protocol (RTP), or another network technology protocol, such as Bluetooth or FireWire.

- *Format*: There are an enormous number of formats, from encumbered formats such as MP3 (for which you are supposed to pay license fees for encoders and decoders), unencumbered equivalents such as Ogg Vorbis, compressed (MP3 and Ogg Vorbis) or uncompressed (Sun AU or Microsoft WAV), and lossy or lossless. In addition, there are many wrinkles in each format: little- or big-endian; 8-, 16-, or 32-bit; mono, stereo, 5-1, . . . ; and sample rate, such as 44.1kHz, 8kHz, and so forth.

- *Content description*: Audio comes from many different sources—for example, tracks off a CD, streaming audio from an FM station, and speech off a telephone line. The MPEG-7 standard concentrates on technical aspects of an audio signal in an attempt to classify it, while the Compact Disc Database (CDDB) projects, such as freedb, classify CDs by artist and title, which breaks down with compilation CDs and most classical CDs (e.g., who is the artist—the composer, the conductor, or the orchestra?).

- *Push/pull*: An audio stream may be "pushed," such as an FM radio stream that is always playing, or it may be "pulled" by a client from a server, such as in fetching an MP3 file from an HTTP server.

Source/Sink Interfaces

Interfaces should contain all the information about how to access services. With audio, all the information about a service can be quite complex—for example, a service might offer a CD track encoded in 16-bit stereo, big-endian, 44.1kHz sampling in WAV format from an HTTP server. This information may be needed by a consumer who wants to play the file.

But in the type of A/V system I want to build, there are three players:

- Sources of A/V data

- Sinks for A/V data

- Controller clients to link sources and sinks

From the controller viewpoint, most of this information is irrelevant: it will just want to link sources to sinks, and leave it to them to decide how and if they can communicate, as shown in Figure 27-1.

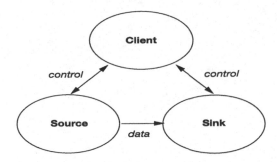

Figure 27-1. *Controller for an A/V source and sink*

For simplicity, we define two interfaces: Source and Sink. To avoid making implementation decisions about pull *versus* push, we have methods to tell a source about a sink, to tell a sink about a source, and to tell the source to play and the sink to record. Again, how they decide to do this is up to the source and sink. Sometimes this approach won't work: an HTTP source may not be able to deliver to an RTP sink, or a WAV file may not be managed by an MP3 player. If they don't succeed in negotiating transport and content, then an exception should be thrown. These interfaces violate the principle that a service should be usable based on its interface alone, but it considerably simplifies matters for controller clients.

Notice that neither a source nor a sink has a name or other descriptive information. We choose to consider all this information as "additional service information" that can be given by Entry objects.

A controller that wants to play a sequence of audio tracks to a sink will need to know when one track is finished in order to start the next. The play() and record() methods could block until finished, or return immediately and post an event on completion. The second method allows more flexibility, and so needs add/remove listener methods for the events.

Finally, there are the exceptions that can be thrown by the methods. Attempting to add a source that a sink cannot handle should throw an exception such as IncompatableSourceException. A sink that can handle only a small number of sources (e.g., only one) could throw an exception if too many sources are added. A source that is already playing may not be able to satisfy a new request to play.

These considerations lead to a pair of high-level interfaces that seem to be suitable for controllers to manage sources and sinks:

```java
/**
 * Source.java
 * A source for A/V data
 */
package audio.common;
import java.rmi.RemoteException;
import net.jini.core.event.EventRegistration;
import net.jini.core.event.RemoteEventListener;
import java.rmi.MarshalledObject;
public interface Source extends java.rmi.Remote {
    int STOP = 1;
    void play() throws
                RemoteException,
                AlreadyPlayingException;
    void stop() throws
                RemoteException,
                NotPlayingException;
    void addSink(Sink sink) throws
                RemoteException,
                TooManySinksException,
                IncompatableSinkException;
    void removeSink(Sink sink) throws
                RemoteException,
                NoSuchSinkException;
    EventRegistration addSourceListener(RemoteEventListener listener,
                                    MarshalledObject handback) throws
                                        RemoteException;
}// Source
```

and

```java
/**
 * Sink.java
 * A sink for audio
 */
package audio.common;
import java.rmi.RemoteException;
import net.jini.core.event.EventRegistration;
import net.jini.core.event.RemoteEventListener;
import java.rmi.MarshalledObject;
public interface Sink extends java.rmi.Remote {
    int STOP = 1;
    void record() throws
                RemoteException,
                AlreadyRecordingException;
    void stop() throws
                RemoteException,
                NotRecordingException;
    void addSource(Source src) throws
                RemoteException,
                TooManySourcesException,
                IncompatableSourceException;
    void removeSource(Source src) throws
                RemoteException,
                NoSuchSourceException;
    EventRegistration addSinkListener(RemoteEventListener listener,
                                    MarshalledObject handback) throws
                RemoteException;
    void removeSinkListener(RemoteEventListener listener) throws
                RemoteException,
                NoSuchListenerException;
}// Sink
```

Content Interfaces

The Java Media Framework (JMF) has methods such as getSupportedContentTypes(), which returns an array of strings. Other media toolkits have similar mechanisms. This type of mechanism isn't type-safe: it relies on all parties having the same strings and attaching the same meaning to each. In addition, if a new type comes along, there isn't a reliable means of specifying this information to others. A type-safe system can at least specify this by class files.

In this example system, I have chosen to use interfaces instead of strings: a WAV interface, an Ogg interface, and so on. This doesn't easily allow extension to the multiplicity of content type variations (bit size, sampling rate, etc.), but the current content handlers appear to be able to handle most of these variations anyway, so it seems feasible to ignore them at an application level.

The content interfaces are just placeholders:

```
package presentation;
public interface Ogg extends java.rmi.Remote {
}
```

A source that could make an audio stream available in Ogg Vorbis format would signal this by implementing the Ogg interface. A sink that can manage Ogg Vorbis streams would also implement this interface.

Transport Interfaces

In a similar way, I have chosen to represent the transport mechanisms by interfaces. A transport sink will get the information from a source using some unspecified network transport mechanism. The audio stream can be made available to any other object by exposing an InputStream. This is a standard Java stream, not the special one used by JMF. Similarly, a transport source would make an output stream available for source-side objects to write data into.

The transport interfaces are this:

```
/**
 * TransportSink.java
 */
package audio.transport;
import java.io.*;
public interface TransportSink {
    public InputStream getInputStream();
}// TransportSink
```

and this:

```
/**
 * TransportSource.java
 */
package audio.transport;
import java.io.*;
public interface TransportSource {
    public OutputStream getOutputStream();
}// TransportSource
```

Linkages

By separating the transport and content layers, we have a model that follows part of the ISO seven layer model: transport and presentation layers. The communication paths for a "pull" sink are shown in Figure 27-2.

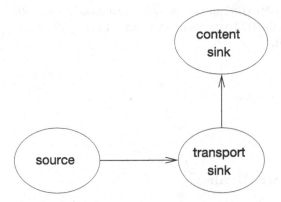

Figure 27-2. *Data flow from a source to a pull sink*

The classes involved in a pull sink could look like Figure 27-3.

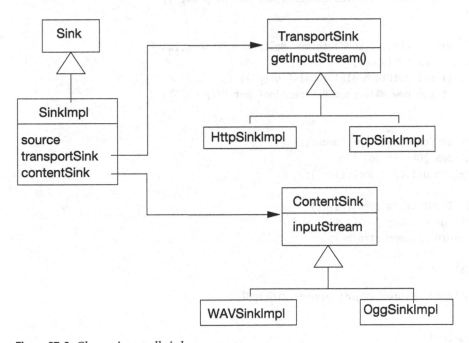

Figure 27-3. *Classes in a pull sink*

Here, the choice of transport and content implementation is based on the interfaces supported by the source and the preferences of the sink.

An HTTP Source

An HTTP source makes an audio stream available as a document from an HTTP server. It simply needs to tell a sink about the URL for the document. There is a small hiccup in this:

a Java URL can be an http URL, a file URL, an ftp URL, and so on. So I have defined an HttpURL class to enforce that it is a URL accessible by the HTTP protocol. The Java URL class is final, so we can't extend it and have to wrap around it.

```java
/**
 * HttpURL.java
 */
package audio.transport;
import java.net.MalformedURLException;
import java.net.*;
import java.io.*;
public class HttpURL implements java.io.Serializable {
    private URL url;
    public HttpURL(URL url) throws MalformedURLException {
        this.url = url;
        if (! url.getProtocol().equals("http")) {
            throw new MalformedURLException("Not http URL");
        }
    }
    public HttpURL(String spec) throws MalformedURLException {
        url = new URL(spec);
        if (! url.getProtocol().equals("http")) {
            throw new MalformedURLException("Not http URL");
        }
    }
    public URLConnection openConnection()
        throws IOException {
        return url.openConnection();
    }
    public InputStream openStream()
        throws IOException {
        return url.openStream();
    }
}// HttpURL
```

The HttpSource interface just exposes an HttpURL:

```java
/**
 * HttpSource.java
 */
package audio.transport;
import audio.common.*;
import java.net.URL;
import java.rmi.RemoteException;
public interface HttpSource extends Source {
    HttpURL getHttpURL() throws RemoteException;
}// HttpSource
```

The interface allows a sink to determine that the transport protocol it should use is the HTTP protocol and what URL it should use to fetch the document.

An HTTP source is a "pull" source—that is, a sink will fetch the data from it. A source of this type doesn't need to worry about listeners or playing the source data; all it needs to do is store the URL. An implementation of this could be as follows:

```java
/**
 * HttpSourceImpl.java
 */
package audio.http;
import audio.common.*;
import audio.transport.*;
import java.net.*;
import java.rmi.*;
import net.jini.core.event.EventRegistration;
import net.jini.core.event.RemoteEventListener;
import java.rmi.MarshalledObject;
/**
 * Stores an HTTP reference
 */
public class HttpSourceImpl implements HttpSource, Remote {
    private HttpURL url;
    private HttpSourceImpl() {
    }
    public HttpSourceImpl(HttpURL url) {
        this.url = url;
    }
    public HttpSourceImpl(URL url) throws MalformedURLException {
        this.url = new HttpURL(url);
    }
    public HttpURL getHttpURL() {
        return url;
    }
    public void play() {}
    public void stop() {}
    public void addSink(Sink sink) throws IncompatableSinkException { }
    public void removeSink(Sink sink) {}
    public EventRegistration addSourceListener(RemoteEventListener listener,
                                               MarshalledObject handback) {
        return null;
    }
}// HttpSourceImpl
```

An HTTP Ogg Vorbis Source

If the document is an Ogg Vorbis document, then the service signals this by implementing the Ogg interface:

```java
/**
 * HttpOggSourceImpl.java
 * Adds Ogg interface to HttpSourceImpl for Ogg files
 */
package audio.http;
import audio.presentation.Ogg;
import audio.transport.HttpURL;
import java.net.*;
public class HttpOggSourceImpl extends HttpSourceImpl
    implements Ogg{
    public HttpOggSourceImpl(HttpURL url) throws MalformedURLException {
        super(url);
    }
    public HttpOggSourceImpl(URL url) throws MalformedURLException {
        super(url);
    }
}// HttpOggSourceImpl
```

In an identical manner, a document can be a WAV or MP3C document by implementing the WAV or MP3C interface, respectively.

An HTTP Sink

An HTTP sink needs to find the URL from an HttpSource, open a connection to it, and get an InputStream. The Java URL class makes this quite straightforward:

```java
/**
 * HttpSinkImpl.java
 */
package audio.transport;
import java.io.*;
import java.net.*;
public class HttpSinkImpl implements TransportSink {
    protected HttpSource source;
    public HttpSinkImpl(HttpSource source) {
        this.source = source;
    }
    public InputStream getInputStream() {
        try {
            HttpURL url = source.getHttpURL();
            URLConnection connect = url.openConnection();
            connect.setDoInput(true);
            connect.setDoOutput(false);
            InputStream in = connect.getInputStream();
            return in;
        } catch (IOException e) {
            System.err.println("Getting in stream " + e.toString());
```

```
            return null;
        }
    }
}// HttpSinkImpl
```

Content Sinks

A ContentSink will get an InputStream from a TransportSink. Then it can read bytes from this stream and interpret the stream based on the content type it understands. There are some content handlers in the Java JMF, but many are missing: MP3 files are encumbered by patent rights, and encoders and decoders should cost (someone!) money to use, so currently there is no MP3 player in JMF (well, there is an MPEG movie player that can be called with no video stream). There is very little activity from Sun on new codecs, and there is no current Ogg Vorbis player. Attempts to fill the gaps are a pure Java Ogg Vorbis decoder called JOrbis and an MP3 decoder for JMF called JFFMPEG. But the situation has not settled down to any clarity yet.

In the meantime, it is easy enough to make operating-system calls into players such as mpg123 or sox (under Unix). I have generically labeled these as playmp3, and so on, and they are read from a pipeline. I am being lazy here: I should have a MP3ContentSink, and createSink() should act like a proper factory and return the right kind of content sink.

```java
/**
 * ContentSink.java
 */
package audio.pull;
import java.io.*;
import audio.presentation.*;
import audio.common.*;
public class ContentSink {
    private InputStream in;
    private OutputStream out;
    private String cmd;
    private boolean stopped = false;
    private SinkImpl sink;
    public static ContentSink createSink(SinkImpl sink,
                                         InputStream in, Source source) {
        String cmd = "";
        if (source instanceof WAV) {
            cmd = "playwav";
        } else if (source instanceof Ogg) {
            cmd = "playogg";
        } else if (source instanceof MP3) {
            cmd = "playmp3";
        } else {
            cmd = "true";
        }
        ContentSink csink = new ContentSink(sink, in, cmd);
        return csink;
```

```java
}
/**
 * There should really be a
 * WAVContentSink, OggContentSink, etc.
 * I cheated since they would be so simple
 */
private ContentSink(SinkImpl sink, InputStream in, String cmd) {
    this.sink = sink;
    this.in = in;
    this.cmd = cmd;
}
public void record() {

    Process proc = null;
    InputStream err = null;
    InputStream inn = null;
    try {
        proc = Runtime.getRuntime().exec(cmd);
        out = proc.getOutputStream();
        err = proc.getErrorStream();
        inn = proc.getInputStream();
    } catch(IOException e) {
        System.err.println("Playing " + e.toString());
        // ignore
        return;
    }

    int ch;
    try {
        while (((ch = in.read()) != -1) &&
                (! stopped)) {
            out.write(ch);
            // System.out.println("Wrote byte");
        }
    } catch(IOException e) {
        System.err.println("Exception writing: " + e.toString());
        int navail = 0;
        try {
            if ((navail = err.available()) > 0 ) {
                byte avail[] = new byte[navail];
                int nread = err.read(avail, 0, navail);
                System.out.println("Error channel: " +
                                    new String(avail));
            }
            if ((navail = inn.available()) > 0 ) {
                byte avail[] = new byte[navail];
                int nread = inn.read(avail, 0, navail);
```

```
                        System.out.println("Out channel: " +
                                        new String(avail));
                    }
                } catch(IOException ee) {
                    ee.printStackTrace();
                }
                return;
            } finally {
                if (stopped) {
                    System.out.println("Record stop called");
                } else {
                    System.out.println("Record finished naturally");
                    stopped = true;
                }
                try {
                    if (proc != null) {
                        proc.destroy();
                        try {
                            // wait for soundcard to be released
                            proc.waitFor();
                        } catch(InterruptedException ei) {
                            System.out.println("Int " + ei);
                        }
                    }
                    in.close();
                    out.close();
                } catch(IOException e) {
                    // ignore
                    System.out.println("Finally " + e);
                }
                sink.contentStopped();
            }
        }
    }
    public void stop() {
        if (stopped) {
            return;
        }
        stopped  = true;
    }
} // ContentSink
```

The playogg script for my Linux system is as follows:

```
#!/bin/sh
if [ $# -eq 0 ]
then
    infile="-"
else
```

```
    infile="$1"
fi
play -t ogg -c 2 $infile
wait            # ensure /dev/dsp is free
sleep 3         # and give it extra time to be really free :-(
```

While playmp3 is as follows:

```
#!/bin/sh
if [ $# -eq 0 ]
then
    infile="-"
else
    infile="$1"
fi
mpg123 -s $infile | sox -t raw -r 44100 -s -w -c 2 - - -t ossdsp -w -s /dev/dsp
wait            # ensure that /dev/dsp is given up
sleep 2         # and then give it more time, since "wait" isn't enough
```

Note that some of these programs won't work properly if the artsd daemon is running in the KDE environment. I typically kill it off, although there must be a better way.

Sink Implementation

A sink must create the appropriate transport and content handlers, and link the two together. It needs to look after listeners and post events to them when they occur. This sink will handle TCP and HTTP connections, and it will manage WAV, Ogg, and MP3 content.

```
/**
 * SinkImpl.java
 */
package audio.pull;
import audio.transport.*;
import java.io.*;
import java.net.*;
import java.rmi.*;
import net.jini.core.event.EventRegistration;
import net.jini.core.event.RemoteEvent;
import java.util.Vector;
import java.util.Enumeration;
import net.jini.core.event.RemoteEventListener;
import net.jini.core.event.UnknownEventException;
import java.util.Hashtable;
import audio.common.*;
public class SinkImpl implements Sink, Remote {
    private Source source;
    private boolean stopped;
    private CopyIO copyIO;
```

```java
private Hashtable listeners = new Hashtable();
private int seqNum = 0;
private Remote proxy;
private MimeType contentType = null;
private InputStream in = null;
public SinkImpl() {
}
public void setProxy(Remote proxy) {
    this.proxy = proxy;
}
public void record() throws RemoteException, AlreadyRecordingException {
    if ((copyIO != null) && ( ! stopped)) {
        throw new AlreadyRecordingException();
    }
    if (source == null) {
        return;
    }
    stopped = false;
    if (in  == null) {
        System.out.println("Couldn't get input stream");
        stopped = true;
        return;
    }
    // hand play over to a CopyIO object
    // This will run a ContentSink in its own thread
    copyIO = new CopyIO(this, in, source);
    copyIO.start();
    System.out.println("Play returning");
}
public void stop() throws RemoteException {
    stopped = true;
    if (copyIO != null) {
        copyIO.stopRecord();
    }
}
public void contentStopped() {
    copyIO = null;
    fireNotify(Sink.STOP);
    System.out.println("Stopped");
}
public void addSource(Source source) throws
    IncompatableSourceException,
    TooManySourcesException {
    TransportSink transportSink = null;
    this.source = source;
    // which transport sink to use?
    if (source instanceof HttpSource) {
```

```
                transportSink = new HttpSinkImpl((HttpSource) source);
                in = transportSink.getInputStream();
            } else if (source instanceof TcpSource) {
                System.out.println("Setting up Tcp sink");
                transportSink = new TcpSinkImpl((TcpSource) source);
                in = transportSink.getInputStream();
                System.out.println("Got tcp source input stream " + in);
            } else {
                throw new IncompatableSourceException();
            }
        }
        public void removeSource(Source source) throws
            RemoteException,
            NoSuchSourceException {
            if (this.source == source) {
                this.source = null;
            } else {
                throw new NoSuchSourceException();
            }
        }
        public EventRegistration addSinkListener(RemoteEventListener listener,
                                          MarshalledObject handback) {
            System.out.println("Adding listener: " + listener);
            listeners.put(listener, handback);
            System.out.println("  listeners size " + listeners.size());
            return new EventRegistration(OL, proxy, null, OL);
        }
        public void removeSinkListener(RemoteEventListener listener) {
            listeners.remove(listener);
        }
        public void fireNotify(int evtType) {
            Enumeration elmts = listeners.keys();
            seqNum++;
            System.out.println("Fire notify event seq id " + seqNum);
            while (elmts.hasMoreElements()) {
                RemoteEventListener listener =
                                        (RemoteEventListener) elmts.nextElement();
                MarshalledObject handback = (MarshalledObject) listeners.get(listener);
                RemoteEvent evt = new RemoteEvent(proxy, evtType, seqNum, handback);
                System.out.println("Notifying listener " + listener);
                try {
                    listener.notify(evt);
                } catch(UnknownEventException e) {
                    // ??
                } catch(RemoteException e) {
                    // ?
                }
```

```
        }
    }
    class CopyIO extends Thread {
        private SinkImpl sink;
        private ContentSink contentSink;
        CopyIO(SinkImpl sink, InputStream in, Source source) {
            contentSink = ContentSink.createSink(sink, in, source);
            this.sink = sink;
        }

        public void stopRecord() {
            if (contentSink != null) {
                contentSink.stop();
            }
        }
        public void run() {
            contentSink.record();
        }
    }
}// SinkImpl
```

Servers

Each source will need a server to create it, advertise it, and keep it alive, as will each sink. These servers are described in the sections that follow.

Sink Server

A sink server is audio.pull.SinkServer:

```
package audio.pull;
import net.jini.lookup.JoinManager;
import net.jini.core.lookup.ServiceID;
import net.jini.discovery.LookupDiscovery;
import net.jini.core.lookup.ServiceRegistrar;
import java.rmi.RemoteException;
import net.jini.lookup.ServiceIDListener;
import net.jini.lease.LeaseRenewalManager;
import net.jini.discovery.LookupDiscoveryManager;
import net.jini.discovery.DiscoveryEvent;
import net.jini.discovery.DiscoveryListener;
import java.rmi.RMISecurityManager;
import java.rmi.Remote;
import net.jini.config.*;
import net.jini.export.*;
import net.jini.id.UuidFactory;
import net.jini.id.Uuid;
import net.jini.core.entry.Entry;
```

```java
import net.jini.lookup.entry.*;
import java.io.*;
/**
 * PullSinkServer.java
 */
public class SinkServer {
    // explicit proxy for Jini 2.0
    protected Remote proxy;
    protected SinkImpl impl;
    private String sinkName = "No name";
    private ServiceID serviceID;
    public static void main(String argv[]) {
        new SinkServer(argv);
        // stay around forever
        Object keepAlive = new Object();
        synchronized(keepAlive) {
            try {
                keepAlive.wait();
            } catch(InterruptedException e) {
                // do nothing
            }
        }
    }
    public SinkServer(String[] argv) {
        File serviceIDFile = null;
        try {
            impl = new SinkImpl();
        } catch(Exception e) {
            System.err.println("New impl: " + e.toString());
            System.exit(1);
        }
        String[] configArgs = new String[] {argv[0]};
        try {
            // get the configuration (by default a FileConfiguration)
            Configuration config = ConfigurationProvider.getInstance(configArgs);

            // and use this to construct an exporter
            Exporter exporter = (Exporter) config.getEntry( "HttpSinkServer",
                                                            "exporter",
                                                            Exporter.class);
            // export an object of this class
            proxy = exporter.export(impl);
            impl.setProxy(proxy);
            sinkName = (String) config.getEntry( "HttpSinkServer",
                                                "sinkName",
                                                String.class);
            serviceIDFile = (File) config.getEntry("HttpSinkServer",
```

```
                                         "serviceIdFile",
                                         File.class);
            getOrMakeServiceID(serviceIDFile);
        } catch(Exception e) {
            System.err.println(e.toString());
            e.printStackTrace();
            System.exit(1);
        }
        // install suitable security manager
        System.setSecurityManager(new RMISecurityManager());
        JoinManager joinMgr = null;
        try {
            LookupDiscoveryManager mgr =
                new LookupDiscoveryManager(LookupDiscovery.ALL_GROUPS,
                            null, // unicast locators
                            null); // DiscoveryListener
            joinMgr = new JoinManager(proxy, // service proxy
                            new Entry[] {new Name(sinkName)},
                            serviceID,  // ServiceID
                            mgr,   // DiscoveryManager
                            new LeaseRenewalManager());
        } catch(Exception e) {
            e.printStackTrace();
            System.exit(1);
        }
    }
    private void getOrMakeServiceID(File serviceIDFile) {
        try {
            ObjectInputStream ois =
                new ObjectInputStream(new FileInputStream(serviceIDFile));
            serviceID = (ServiceID) ois.readObject();
        } catch(Exception e) {
            System.out.println("Couldn't get service IDs - generating new ones");
            try {
                ObjectOutputStream oos =
                    new ObjectOutputStream(new FileOutputStream(serviceIDFile));
                Uuid uuid = UuidFactory.generate();
                serviceID = new ServiceID(uuid.getMostSignificantBits(),
                                uuid.getLeastSignificantBits());
                oos.writeObject(serviceID);
            } catch(Exception e2) {
                System.out.println("Couldn't save ids");
                e2.printStackTrace();
            }
        }
    }
} // SinkServer
```

This server gets information from a configuration file, such as /http_sink_server.config:

```
import net.jini.jeri.BasicILFactory;
import net.jini.jeri.BasicJeriExporter;
import net.jini.jeri.tcp.TcpServerEndpoint;
import java.io.File;
HttpSinkServer {
    exporter = new BasicJeriExporter(TcpServerEndpoint.getInstance(0),
                                     new BasicILFactory());
    sinkName = new String("Jan's laptop");
    serviceIdFile = new File("sinkServiceId.id");
}
```

It exports a proxy for a SinkImpl, which will handle TCP and HTTP connections and manage WAV, Ogg, and MP3 content.

This sink server depends on the following classes:

- audio.pull.SinkServer

- audio.pull.SinkImpl

- audio.pull.SinkImpl$CopyIO (an inner class)

- audio.transport.HttpSinkImpl

- audio.transport.TcpSinkImpl

- audio.pull.ContentSink

- audio.transport.TransportSink

- All the classes in the audio.common package

These classes can be collected into a .jar file such as audio.pull.SinkServer.jar and run with a configuration such as the preceding one, as follows:

```
java -classpath audio.pull.SinkServer.jar audio.pull.SinkServer
http_sink_server.config
```

Source Server

An individual piece of music may be a song, a movement from a classical symphony, an instrumental piece, and so on. Individual pieces of music may be collected together in many ways: a symphony is formed of movements; a pop CD is made up of individual songs; a CD may be composed from a collection of CDs; a boxed set of CDs will be made up of CDs themselves; and the complete *oeuvres* of a composer is another classification. How do we want to represent all of these possibilities as services?

Databases of CDs such as CDDB have a simplistic solution: a CD is classified by an artist/title. So a CD is a collection of pieces, with no other structure. This breaks down with "best of" collections and almost all classical music—who is the artist? The composer? The conductor? The orchestra? The soloist? MPEG-7 is vast overkill from our point of view, and only a tiny part

("The Collection Structure DS") has anything to say about organizing music from our perspective. MPEG-7 Lite as used by the UPnP Audio/Visual framework (ContentDirectory1.0) has a simplified structure, but is quite good for representing the different possibilities just described.

But UPnP is a device-oriented system, where a device (such as a personal video recorder, or PVR) is responsible for all the individual items stored on it. Although the device may contain a complex directory structure, the individual components of this are not "first-class" objects, directly visible and addressable. This would make it hard to, say, set up a playlist across a set of devices such as a PVR, an iPod, and a home server storing copies of LPs.

The Representational State Transfer (REST) community criticizes Web Services (using SOAP) on the grounds that services have no "addressable endpoint" and that data returned from a service is an XML document that is not addressable at all. UPnP A/V directories are not addressable. In both cases, this leads to a loss of flexibility in that clients and services can only work within the bounds of the supplied services and are hence restricted in what they can do—in the case of UPnP, it is hard to build up cross-device playlists. So we adopt the extreme viewpoint: every piece of music is advertised as *its own* service. That allows any other service to build and structure service hierarchies in any way that it wants to. For example, a new service could link photos from an external web site to pieces of music, which would be hard to do with Web Services or UPnP.

File Source Server

In this book we present a single server that advertises a single piece of music available from an HTTP server. On the web site, we also show two more: one that advertises a group of pieces (such as a CD of many pieces) and one that advertises a collection of groups (such as all the CDs on a disk).

The file server will advertise one file as a service. Details of the file need to be stored in a configuration file, such as sting.cfg. The service itself will just be an HttpSource of some kind. *Descriptive* information (such as artist, name of song, etc.) is not given as part of the service, but as *service information* by Entry objects:

```
import net.jini.jeri.BasicILFactory;
import net.jini.jeri.BasicJeriExporter;
import net.jini.jeri.tcp.TcpServerEndpoint;
import java.net.URL;
import net.jini.core.entry.Entry;
import net.jini.lookup.entry.*;
import java.io.File;
HttpFile {
    exporter = new BasicJeriExporter(TcpServerEndpoint.getInstance(0),
                                     new BasicILFactory());
    url = new URL("http://localhost/soundfiles/sting/audio_01.wav");
    entries = new Entry[] {new Name("Sting / The Lazarus Heart")
                          };
    serviceIDFile = new File("sting01.id");
}
```

The server is quite straightforward: it gets information about exporter and service entries from a configuration file and advertises the source as a service using a JoinManager.

```java
package audio.httpsource;
import net.jini.lookup.JoinManager;
import net.jini.core.lookup.ServiceID;
import net.jini.discovery.LookupDiscovery;
import net.jini.core.lookup.ServiceRegistrar;
import java.rmi.RemoteException;
import net.jini.lookup.ServiceIDListener;
import net.jini.lease.LeaseRenewalManager;
import net.jini.discovery.LookupDiscoveryManager;
import net.jini.discovery.DiscoveryEvent;
import net.jini.discovery.DiscoveryListener;
import java.rmi.RMISecurityManager;
import java.rmi.Remote;
import java.net.URL;
import net.jini.lookup.entry.*;
import net.jini.core.entry.Entry;
import net.jini.core.discovery.LookupLocator;
import net.jini.config.*;
import net.jini.export.*;
import net.jini.id.UuidFactory;
import net.jini.id.Uuid;
import java.io.*;
import audio.http.*;
/**
 * FileServer.java
 */
public class FileServer {
    private Remote proxy;
    private HttpSourceImpl impl;
    private static String configFile;
    private Entry[] entries;
    private File serviceIDFile;
    private ServiceID serviceID;
    public static void main(String argv[]) {
        configFile = argv[0];
        FileServer serv = new FileServer(argv);
        // stay around forever
        Object keepAlive = new Object();
        synchronized(keepAlive) {
            try {
                keepAlive.wait();
            } catch(InterruptedException e) {
                // do nothing
            }
        }
    }
```

```java
public FileServer(String[] argv) {
    URL url = null;
    Exporter exporter = null;
    if (argv.length != 1) {
        System.err.println("Usage: FileServer config_file");
        System.exit(1);
    }
    try {
    } catch(Exception e) {
        System.err.println("New impl: " + e.toString());
        System.exit(1);
    }
    String[] configArgs = argv;
    try {
        // get the configuration (by default a FileConfiguration)
        Configuration config = ConfigurationProvider.getInstance(configArgs);
        // and use this to construct an exporter
        exporter = (Exporter) config.getEntry( "HttpFile",
                                               "exporter",
                                               Exporter.class);
        url = (URL) config.getEntry("HttpFile",
                                    "url",
                                    URL.class);
        serviceIDFile = (File) config.getEntry("HttpFile",
                                               "serviceIDFile",
                                               File.class);
        getOrMakeServiceID(serviceIDFile);

        Class cls = Class.forName("[Lnet.jini.core.entry.Entry;");
        System.out.println(cls.toString());
        entries = (Entry []) config.getEntry("HttpFile",
                                             "entries",
                                             cls);

    } catch(Exception e) {
        System.err.println(e.toString());
        e.printStackTrace();
        System.exit(1);
    }
    // Find the right implementation for the content type
    String urlStr = url.toString();
    try {
        if (urlStr.endsWith("wav")) {
            impl = new HttpWAVSourceImpl(url);
        } else if (urlStr.endsWith("mp3")) {
            impl = new HttpMP3SourceImpl(url);
        } else if (urlStr.endsWith("ogg")) {
            impl = new HttpOggSourceImpl(url);
```

```
                } else {
                    System.out.println("Can't handle presentation type: " +
                                        url);
                    return;
                }
            } catch(java.net.MalformedURLException e) {
                System.err.println(e.toString());
                System.exit(1);
            }
            try {
                // export an object of this class
                proxy = exporter.export(impl);
            } catch(java.rmi.server.ExportException e) {
                System.err.println(e.toString());
                System.exit(1);
            }
            // install suitable security manager
            System.setSecurityManager(new RMISecurityManager());
            JoinManager joinMgr = null;
            try {
                LookupDiscoveryManager mgr =
                    new LookupDiscoveryManager(LookupDiscovery.ALL_GROUPS,
                                        new LookupLocator[] {
                                            new LookupLocator
                                                ("jini://jannote.jan.home/")},
                                        null); // DiscoveryListener
                joinMgr = new JoinManager(proxy,     // service proxy
                                        entries,    // attr sets
                                        serviceID, // ServiceID
                                        mgr,        // DiscoveryManager
                                        new LeaseRenewalManager());
            } catch(Exception e) {
                e.printStackTrace();
                System.exit(1);
            }
        }
        private void getOrMakeServiceID(File serviceIDFile) {
            // try to read the service ID as
            // object from the file
            serviceID = null;
            try {
                ObjectInputStream ois =
                    new ObjectInputStream(new FileInputStream(serviceIDFile));
                serviceID = (ServiceID) ois.readObject();
                System.out.println("Got dir service id " + serviceID);
            } catch(Exception e) {
```

```
        System.out.println("Couldn't get service IDs - generating new one");
        try {
            ObjectOutputStream oos =
                new ObjectOutputStream(new FileOutputStream(serviceIDFile));
            Uuid uuid = UuidFactory.generate();
            serviceID = new ServiceID(uuid.getMostSignificantBits(),
                                  uuid.getLeastSignificantBits());
            oos.writeObject(serviceID);
            oos.close();
        } catch(Exception e2) {
            System.out.println("Couldn't save ids");
            e2.printStackTrace();
        }
    }
}
} // FileServer
```

The file source server requires the following classes:

- audio.httpsource.FileServer

- audio.httpsource.FileServer

- audio.http.HttpSourceImpl

- audio.http.HttpOggSourceImpl

- audio.http.HttpMP3SourceImpl

- audio.http.HttpWAVSourceImpl

- audio.presentation.MP3

- audio.presentation.WAV

- audio.presentation.Ogg

- audio.transport.HttpURL

- audio.transport.HttpSource

- All the classes in the audio.common package

These classes can be collected into a .jar file such as audio.httpsource.FileServer.jar and run with a configuration such as the preceding one, as follows:

```
java -classpath audio.httpsource.FileServer.jar audio.httpsource.FileServer
sting.cfg
```

Playlists

Much music comes on CDs, LPs, tapes, and cassettes, or in some similarly structured format (even a radio show has a structure). This structure often mirrors that of a directory, so a CD might contain a directory of tracks, and so on. A directory can be a service in its own right, so there is an interface to define it.

```
/**
 * Directory.java
 * A one-level directory of services. If the directory is also
 * a service then it allows a directory tree hierarchy to be built
 */
package audio.common;
import java.rmi.Remote;
import java.rmi.RemoteException;
import net.jini.core.lookup.ServiceID;
public interface Directory extends Remote {
    ServiceID[] getServiceIDs() throws RemoteException;
}// Directory
```

The directory defines the minimum about each of its services: their ServiceIDs. This allows a directory to contain any type of service: individual songs, other directories, and even image services or other services. For a directory like this to work, each service must have a persistent service ID, but this is expected of a Jini service, anyway.

There isn't room in this book to fully explore how directories like this can be used. They can be used to build playlists and lists of playlists. The services are not restricted to a single computer, and the playlists can be dynamically created. The web site for this book goes into much more detail on this topic.

Basic Client

A client will locate sources and sinks and allow a user to make selections from them. Each sink will be told about the selected sources, and each source will be told about the selected sinks. The client may register itself as a listener for events (such as STOP) from the services. Then the client will ask the sources to play() and the sinks to record(). I do not have space in this book to provide an all-singing, all-dancing client with a graphical user interface that can handle playlists; such a client is discussed on the web site for this book. Instead, I just discuss a minimal client that just connects a single source to a single sink (the first one found of each).

The basic client will just find a sink and a source (any source, any sink), tell each about the other, and then play/record to an audio stream. This can be done as follows:

```
package audio.client;
import java.rmi.RMISecurityManager;
import java.rmi.RemoteException;
import net.jini.discovery.LookupDiscovery;
import net.jini.core.lookup.ServiceTemplate;
import net.jini.discovery.LookupDiscoveryManager;
import net.jini.lookup.ServiceDiscoveryManager;
import net.jini.core.lookup.ServiceItem;
import net.jini.lease.LeaseRenewalManager;
import audio.common.Sink;
import audio.common.Source;
```

```java
/**
 * BasicClient.java
 */
public class BasicClient {
    private static final long WAITFOR = 100000L;
    private ServiceDiscoveryManager clientMgr = null;
    public static void main(String argv[]) {
        new BasicClient();
        // stay around long enough to receive replies
        try {
            Thread.currentThread().sleep(2*WAITFOR);
        } catch(java.lang.InterruptedException e) {
            // do nothing
        }
    }

    public BasicClient() {
        System.setSecurityManager(new RMISecurityManager());
        try {
            LookupDiscoveryManager mgr =
                new LookupDiscoveryManager(LookupDiscovery.ALL_GROUPS,
                                    null, // unicast locators
                                    null); // DiscoveryListener
            clientMgr = new ServiceDiscoveryManager(mgr,
                                    new LeaseRenewalManager());
        } catch(Exception e) {
            e.printStackTrace();
            System.exit(1);
        }
        // find a source and sink
        Sink sink = (Sink) getService(Sink.class);
        Source source = (Source) getService(Source.class);
        // tell them about each other
        try {
            source.addSink(sink);
            sink.addSource(source);
        } catch(Exception e) {
            System.err.println("Error setting source or sink " + e);
            e.printStackTrace();
            System.exit(1);
        }
        // play the audio
        try {
            System.out.println("Playing...");
            source.play();
            sink.record();
        } catch(Exception e) {
            System.out.println("Error in playing " + e);
```

```
                System.exit(1);
            }
        }
        private Object getService(Class cls) {

            Class [] classes = new Class[] {cls};
            ServiceTemplate template = new ServiceTemplate(null, classes,
                                                            null);
            ServiceItem item = null;
            // Try to find the service, blocking till timeout if necessary
            try {
                item = clientMgr.lookup(template,
                                        null, // no filter
                                        WAITFOR); // timeout
            } catch(Exception e) {
                e.printStackTrace();
                System.exit(1);
            }
            if (item == null) {
                // couldn't find a service in time
                System.out.println("no service for class " + cls);
                System.exit(1);
            }
            // Return the service
            return item.service;
        }
} // BasicClient
```

The basic client requires the following classes:

- audio.client.BasicClient

- All the classes in the audio.common package

These classes can be collected into a .jar file such as audio.client.BasicClient.jar and run with a configuration such as the previous one, as follows:

```
java -classpath audio.client.BasicClient.jar audio.client.BasicClient
```

Summary

This chapter discussed a framework for distributed audio. Jini makes it fairly straightforward to handle service advertisement and discovery, telling services about each other and generating and handling remote events. The architecture is extensible and just consists of adding in more interfaces and implementations. For example, although this chapter discussed only audio, the same framework could be applied to visual content, either still images or movies.

CHAPTER 28

■ ■ ■

Web Services and Jini

One of the middleware frameworks being heavily promoted at present is that of Web Services. Web Services are built upon the Simple Object Access Protocol (SOAP) invocation protocol, the Web Services Description Language (WSDL) specification language, and the Universal Description, Discovery, and Integration (UDDI) discovery system. In this chapter, we look at how clients and services from different frameworks can interoperate, with particular reference to Web Services and Jini.

Integrating Web Services and Jini

While this book has been about Jini, other middleware systems are in use, such as CORBA, Web Services, UPnP, and Salutation, among many others. While it would be very convenient for software developers if all but their favorite middleware were to disappear, this is unlikely to happen. There are technical and political reasons for many of these frameworks to survive, and so software developers will just have to live in a world of multiple middleware systems.

Users, on the other hand, just want their different pieces of software to work together, no matter what framework is used. It is up to software developers to figure out how to get a Web Services client to work with, for example, a mixture of Jini and UPnP services.

The most common way of getting such mixtures to work is through a *bridge*. That is, to get a Web Service *client* to talk to a Jini *service*, typically a bridge will be an application sitting between them and acting as a Web Service *service* and a Jini *client*. In the middle, the bridge translates from one framework to the other, in both directions, as shown in Figure 28-1.

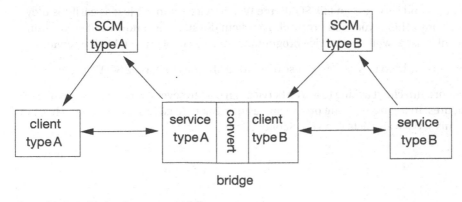

Figure 28-1. *Bridging between middleware systems*

There are two aspects to a bridge: one is concerned with discovery and the other with invocation.

- Discovery allows one middleware client to discover a different middleware service—for example, a CORBA client discovering a Jini service. Typically this is done by the client discovering the bridge and the bridge discovering the service. This may involve two service cache managers (lookup services, name services, etc.).

- The bridge allows one middleware client to make calls on another middleware service—for example, a CORBA client making calls on a Jini service. It will convert calls received under one protocol into calls in the other. This will often involve conversion of data from one format to another.

Web Services and Jini have special features that make this a simpler task than in general:

- Web Services are supposed to use the discovery system UDDI. However, UDDI was designed independently as a global white/yellow/green/blue pages directory, and it turns out to be poorly suited to Web Service discovery. In practice, it seems that most Web Service developers rely on the URLs hard-coded into WSDL files, and don't do any discovery at all.

- In Chapter 1, the section "The End of Protocols" discussed how Jini doesn't really care about invocation protocols, but only about discovery. Of course, a lot of this book has been about how to invoke a service, but much of that discussion is about the choices that a service developer has. The client doesn't care.

- The XML data types don't map directly to Java data types and vice versa. However, there are now standardized mappings with implementations from several vendors.

While building a bridge is in general a nontrivial process, the standardization of data mappings, the indifference of Jini to invocation protocols, and the hard-coded addresses of Web Services simplifies building a Web Services to Jini bridge in the following way:

- Web Services don't need to be discovered; they just need to be looked up. Web clients don't need to do discovery since they have the services' URLs hard-coded in the WSDL document.

- Jini clients and services can talk SOAP (the Web Service protocol) just as easily as they can talk any other invocation protocol. The client doesn't even know what invocation protocol is used, while the service programmer just has to SOAP-enable the services.

- Jini clients and services can make use of existing libraries to handle SOAP queries.

The case of a Jini client talking to a Web Service can lead to several models, as shown in the following figures. In Figure 28-2, the proxy can be an ordinary (e.g., Jeri) proxy talking back to its service. This service also acts as a Web Service client.

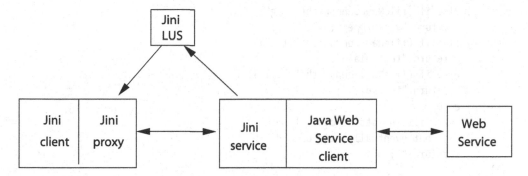

Figure 28-2. *Bridging between a Jini client and a Web Service*

Figure 28-3 shows a "smart" proxy that talks directly to the Web Service.

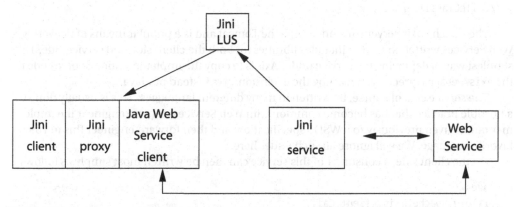

Figure 28-3. *Smart proxy bridging between a Jini client and a Web Service*

Simple Web Service

I'll illustrate this example with a simple Web Service, for file classification again. To avoid the complexities of Web Service types and with deployment of such services, let's simplify the service to one that takes a string as file name and returns the MIME type as a string major/minor. The class is not in a package, allowing simple deployment under Apache Axis. The implementation of this service is then straightforward:

```
/**
 * FileClassifierService.java
 */
public class FileClassifierService {
    public String getMIMEType(String fileName) {
        if (fileName.endsWith(".gif")) {
            return "image/gif";
        } else if (fileName.endsWith(".jpeg")) {
            return "image/jpeg";
```

```
        } else if (fileName.endsWith(".mpg")) {
            return "video/mpeg";
        } else if (fileName.endsWith(".txt")) {
            return "text/plain";
        } else if (fileName.endsWith(".html")) {
            return "text/html";
        } else
            // fill in lots of other types,
            // but eventually give up and
            return "";
    }
    public FileClassifierService() {
        // empty
    }


} // FileClassifierService
```

The Apache Axis server runs under Apache Tomcat and is a popular means of delivering Web Services written in Java. It includes libraries for both the client side and service side. The simplest way of deploying the service under Axis is to copy the implementation source code to the axis/webapps directory, renaming the extension .jws instead of .java.

The service can, of course, be written in many different languages. This is usually done by a horrible practice that has become common with Web Services: reverse engineer the implementation given previously to a WSDL specification, and then forward engineer this to your favorite language. We will ignore all such issues here.

On the client side, a consumer of this service can then be written most simply as follows:

```
package ws;
import org.apache.axis.client.Call;
import org.apache.axis.client.Service;
import javax.xml.namespace.QName;
import ws.MIMEType;
public class TestWSClient {
    public static void main(String [] args) {
        try {
            String endpoint =
                "http://localhost:8080/axis/FileClassifierService.jws";

            Service  service = new Service();
            Call     call    = (Call) service.createCall();

            call.setTargetEndpointAddress( new java.net.URL(endpoint) );
            call.setOperationName(new QName("http://soapinterop.org/",
                                       "getMIMEType"));

            String ret = (String) call.invoke( new Object[] { "file.txt" } );
```

```
            System.out.println("Type of file 'file.txt' is " + ret);
        } catch (Exception e) {
            System.err.println(e.toString());
        }
    }
}
```

There are other ways of achieving the same result, but this is good enough for the rest of this chapter, which is intended to show how Jini and Web Services can interoperate rather than delve into the arcanities of Web Services.

Bridging Between a Jini Client and Web Service, Example 1

A bridge that acts as a Jini service implementing the common.FileClassifier specification used throughout this book, and also as a client to the previous file classification Web Service, can be written by essentially including the Web Service client code from earlier into the implementation of the Jini service methods. The bridge is a normal Jini server advertising the following Jini service implementation:

```
package ws;
import common.MIMEType;
import common.FileClassifier;
import org.apache.axis.client.Call;
import org.apache.axis.client.Service;
import javax.xml.namespace.QName;
/**
 * FileClassifierImpl.java
 */
public class FileClassifierImpl implements RemoteFileClassifier {

    public MIMEType getMIMEType(String fileName)
        throws java.rmi.RemoteException {
        try {
            String endpoint =
                "http://localhost:8080/axis/FileClassifierService.jws";

            Service  service = new Service();
            Call     call    = (Call) service.createCall();

            call.setTargetEndpointAddress( new java.net.URL(endpoint) );
            call.setOperationName(new QName("http://soapinterop.org/",
                                      "getMIMEType"));

            String ret = (String) call.invoke( new Object[] { fileName } );
            return new MIMEType(ret);
        } catch (Exception e) {
```

```
                throw new RemoteException("SOAP failure", e);
        }
    }
    public FileClassifierImpl() throws java.rmi.RemoteException {
        // empty constructor required by RMI
    }

} // FileClassifierImpl
```

This service can export a Jeri or RMI proxy to a Jini client as we have seen before. Client calls on the proxy are sent to this service, which acts as a Web Service client using the model of Figure 28-2. When this implementation is built and run, it will need the Axis libraries on the Jini service side.

Bridging Between a Jini Client and Web Service, Example 2

A service can be written that follows the second pattern in Figure 28-3, simply by changing the inheritance from RemoteFileClassifier to FileClassifier and Serializable. A client then gets a copy of this service and all calls are made locally in the client.

```
package ws;
import common.MIMEType;
import common.FileClassifier;
import org.apache.axis.client.Call;
import org.apache.axis.client.Service;
import javax.xml.namespace.QName;
/**
 * FileClassifierImpl.java
 */
public class FileClassifierSerializableImpl implements FileClassifier,
                                            java.io.Serializable {

    public MIMEType getMIMEType(String fileName)
        throws java.rmi.RemoteException {
        try {
            String endpoint =
                "http://localhost:8080/axis/FileClassifierService.jws";

            Service  service = new Service();
            Call     call    = (Call) service.createCall();

            call.setTargetEndpointAddress( new java.net.URL(endpoint) );
            call.setOperationName(new QName("http://soapinterop.org/",
                                    "getMIMEType"));
```

```
            String ret = (String) call.invoke( new Object[] { fileName } );
            return new MIMEType(ret);
        } catch (Exception e) {
            throw new RemoteException(e);
        }
    }
    public FileClassifierImpl() throws java.rmi.RemoteException {
        // empty constructor required by RMI
    }

} // FileClassifierImpl
```

This has major implications for the classes downloaded to the client! In order to run this service on the client side, it needs access to the class files for the Axis classes Call, Service, and QName. The client cannot be expected to have these, since it doesn't need to know any details of the implementation. So the Axis libraries have to be placed on an HTTP server and listed in the Jini server's codebase. The libraries are over 1MB in size, so needing to send these across the network can result in a substantial download to the Jini client.

Bridging Between a Web Service Client and Jini Service

Forming a bridge between Web Service clients and Jini services follows the same general structure, as shown in Figure 28-4.

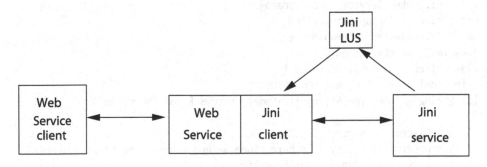

Figure 28-4. *Bridge between a Web Service client and a Jini service*

In this case, we put the Jini client code into the Web Service implementation.

There are a couple of wrinkles in getting this to work properly with Apache Axis and the Tomcat server:

- Jini class files

- Security policy

The Jini class files are not in the classpath for Tomcat. However, Tomcat and Apache allow any extra .jar files required by a Web Service to be placed in special lib directories under the service's WEB-INF directory. Copying the Jini files jsk-lib.jar and jsk-platform.jar to this directory will make them available to the Web Service. This will be part of the deployment mechanisms for the Web Service.

The issue of a security policy is potentially more difficult. A server such as Tomcat can be started either with or without a security manager. If it uses a security manager, then the default security policy does not allow a new security manager to be put in place. This blocks a Jini client from installing an RMISecurityManager, and so it cannot download a Jini registrar and find Jini services. Negotiation would then be required with the Tomcat administrator to add in sufficient permissions to the security policy to allow a Jini client to run.

If Tomcat is run without a security manager, then it is possible for the Web Service to install one. But it will then need to use a security policy. Up to now we have specified such a policy as a command-line argument, but the command line is not accessible to an Axis Web Service. The workaround is to use System.setProperty() to set the security policy file before installing a security manager.

All I/O to the console has to be cleaned up and put into remote exceptions. With these factors, the Web Service to bridge to a Jini service looks like this:

```
/**
 * FileClassifierJiniService.java
 */
import common.FileClassifier;
import common.MIMEType;
import java.rmi.RMISecurityManager;
import net.jini.discovery.LookupDiscovery;
import net.jini.core.lookup.ServiceTemplate;
import net.jini.discovery.LookupDiscoveryManager;
import net.jini.lookup.ServiceDiscoveryManager;
import net.jini.core.lookup.ServiceItem;
import net.jini.lease.LeaseRenewalManager;
import java.rmi.RemoteException;
public class FileClassifierJiniService {
    private final static long WAITFOR = 10000;
    public String getMIMEType(String fileName)  throws RemoteException {

        ServiceDiscoveryManager clientMgr = null;
        // set a security policy file here since we don't have command-line access
        System.setProperty("java.security.policy",
                           "/home/httpd/html/java/jini/tutorial/policy.all");
        System.setSecurityManager(new RMISecurityManager());
        try {
            LookupDiscoveryManager mgr =
                new LookupDiscoveryManager(LookupDiscovery.ALL_GROUPS,
                                           null, // unicast locators
                                           null); // DiscoveryListener
            clientMgr = new ServiceDiscoveryManager(mgr,
                                           new LeaseRenewalManager());
        } catch(Exception e) {
```

```
            throw new RemoteException("Lookup failed", e);
        }


        Class [] classes = new Class[] {FileClassifier.class};
        ServiceTemplate template = new ServiceTemplate(null, classes,
                                                       null);
        ServiceItem item = null;
        // Try to find the service, blocking until timeout if necessary
        try {
            item = clientMgr.lookup(template,
                                    null, // no filter
                                    WAITFOR); // timeout
        } catch(Exception e) {
            throw new RemoteException("Discovery failed", e);
        }
        if (item == null) {
            // couldn't find a service in time
            return "";
        }
        // Get the service
        FileClassifier classifier = (FileClassifier) item.service;
        if (classifier == null) {
            throw new RemoteException("Classifier null");
        }
        // Now we have a suitable service, use it
        MIMEType type;
        try {
            type = classifier.getMIMEType(fileName);
            return type.toString();
        } catch(java.rmi.RemoteException e) {
            throw e;
        }
    }
    public FileClassifierJiniService() {
        // empty
    }

} // FileClassifierJiniService
```

The steps to get all this running are as follows:

1. Download and install Apache Tomcat and Axis.

2. Edit the `FileClassifierJiniService.java` file to point to a valid security policy file on your system.

3. Copy the `FileClassifierJiniService.java` file to the Tomcat `webapps/axis` directory as `FileClassifierJiniService.jws`, changing the file extension.

4. Copy the Jini libraries `jsk-lib.jar` and `jsk-platform.jar` to the Tomcat `webapps/axis/WEB-INF/lib` directory.

5. Start Tomcat *without* a security manager (by default it starts without one).

6. Start a Jini lookup service and any Jini implementation of the `FileClassifier` interface that has been given in this book.

7. Run the Web Service client `ws.TestWS2JiniClient`.

This procedure should run the Web Service, which finds the Jini service, makes a call on it, and returns the result to the Web Service client.

Summary

Bridging between different types of services is not an easy matter, as there are many complex issues to be considered. Nevertheless, it is possible to build upon work performed to build Java Web Services and their Java clients, allowing you to use Jini services and clients in a relatively simple manner.

Index